A Communitarian Defense of Liberalism

EMILE DURKHEIM AND
CONTEMPORARY SOCIAL THEORY

A Communitarian Defense of Liberalism

EMILE DURKHEIM AND
CONTEMPORARY SOCIAL THEORY

Mark S. Cladis

Stanford University Press, Stanford, California

Stanford University Press, Stanford, California
© 1992 by the Board of Trustees of the
Leland Stanford Junior University
Printed in the United States of America

CIP data appear at the end of the book

TO SHEILA AND MY PARENTS

Acknowledgments

I WROTE THIS BOOK with the help of many. To three in particular, each whom I call friend and colleague, I am deeply indebted. Victor Preller, who has taught me a good deal about Durkheim, greatly influenced this study by his brilliant grasp of the philosophical and moral sensibilities of Wittgenstein. Jeffrey Stout, who gave astute and detailed comments on various drafts of this work, provided the inspiration for it when he highlighted the significance of Durkheim's description of "the individual" as a social ideal. His unstinting help and careful readings have saved me more than once from many errors. Henry Levinson, who read and commented on many of the following chapters, has graced the past five years of my life with his famous humor and keen mind.

My interpretation of Durkheim is not from scratch. I have profited greatly from the work of Jeffrey Alexander, Robert Bellah, Steve Fenton, Anthony Giddens, Steven Lukes, and Ernest Wallwork. My disagreements with them in no way belittle my respect for their accounts of Durkheim. Throughout this book I have placed Durkheim in conversation with Amy Gutmann, Alasdair MacIntyre, Michael Oakeshott, John Rawls, Richard Rorty, Michael Walzer, and Sheldon Wolin. From these authors I have learned much about moral pluralism and the practice of social criticism.

I have also benefited from helpful suggestions by Paul Courtright, Mary Douglas, Jean-Pierre Dupuy, John Ferejohn, Stuart

Hampshire, David Hull, Debra Satz, and two readers recruited by Stanford University Press. Portions of this work were presented at conferences and symposia, including "Conventions," hosted by CREA of the Ecole Polytechnique, Paris; the Stanford Philosophy Colloquium and Religious Studies Colloquium; the Stanford-Paris Symposium on Individualism and Social Justice; and various regional and annual meetings of the American Academy of Religion. I am grateful for these occasions of intellectual exchange.

At Stanford and Vassar I have taught some of this material, and in the process I was educated—by both colleagues and students. The Ethics in Society Program at Stanford provided opportunities for lively discussion and encouragement, as has the Department of Religion at Vassar. In that Department I am surrounded by congenial and bright colleagues. As I made the final revisions, Vassar proved to be a place of scholarship and goodwill.

Helen Tartar and Ellen Smith of Stanford Press have been expert and supportive editors. I also want to thank Bud Bynack for careful copyediting; indeed, he joined me in my project, and, as a skillful rhetorician, enhanced my arguments, making them more lovely and compelling. Jerzy Sokol perused the proofs, correcting typos and suggesting revisions for any future edition.

Earlier drafts of portions of this book appeared as the following essays: "A Communitarian Defense of Liberalism," *Soundings: An Interdisciplinary Journal* 72 (1989): 275–95; "Provinces of Ethics," *Interpretation: A Journal of Political Philosophy* 17 (1989–90): 255–73; "Pragmatism: French and American Styles," *Stanford French Review* 15.1–2 (1991): 139–63 (published by the Department of French and Italian, Stanford University and Anma Libri, Saratoga, Calif.); "Durkheim's Individual in Society: A Sacred Marriage?" *Journal of the History of Ideas* 53 (1992): 71–90.

I dedicate this book to my parents, John and Jenny, and to Sheila, my wife. My parents, each in their own way, are moral exemplars who have never been stingy with encouragement and affection. Sheila is my best friend (and also an able proofreader). The joy she has brought to my life sustained this project, making it a happy task.

Contents

A Communitarian Defense
of Liberalism

EMILE DURKHEIM AND
CONTEMPORARY SOCIAL THEORY

Introduction

IN AN ESSAY written six years before the publication of *The Division of Labor In Society*, Durkheim claimed that there are two extreme positions around which moral theories are grouped: liberalism and communitarianism.[1] The former views the individual as a radically autonomous, discrete self; the latter views the individual as socially determined. Durkheim's 1887 essay, "La Science positive de la morale en Allemagne," explored ways to express the normative relation between the private and the public that would avoid the tendency to reduce it to these two contrary positions. This endeavor continued throughout his career, as he sought to protect liberalism from egoism, and communitarianism from fatalism, the absorption of individuals into the social mass. The result was a social theory that articulated and promoted the dignity and rights of the individual within the moral idiom of social traditions and commitment to a common good. It remains a powerful piece of social criticism. Probing the features of collective life, it provides incisive commentary on and appraisal of various forms of liberalism and communitarianism, promising ways to maintain commitment to the nobler aspects of both social ideals.

This balanced commitment is news to those students of Durkheim who read him solely as a theorist of group solidarity and social order—as hostile to "the individual." It is also news to another group. Those who read Rawls and MacIntyre, Dworkin and Sandel, and who consider the liberal vocabulary of individual rights to be incompatible with, and antagonistic to, the communitarian vocabulary of virtue, tradition, and community, may be interested to find that Durkheim wrestled with many of the same issues a hundred years ago. In doing so, he found theoretical and practical ways to overcome what Amy Gutmann has aptly called "the tyranny of dualisms," the present impasse between liberals and communitarians.[2]

Today, there is renewed interest in the nature of the relation between individuals and their societies. "Community," "tradition," "the individual"—these big terms, conveying different meanings under different circumstances, once again are prominent features of debates in social and political theory between those called liberals and those called communitarians. The conversation between proponents of these positions, in short, stands to benefit from a new reading of Durkheim. Reciprocally, the nature of this debate has provided a novel perspective for surveying aspects of Durkheim's life and work. Durkheim has been portrayed with many faces: Durkheim the positivist, the sociologist, the moral philosopher, "the conservative" preoccupied with order, and so on. My portrait of him will be sketched against the background of the question that guided his 1887 essay: Can we capture the benefits associated with liberalism along with those of communitarianism, even in light of potential conflicts?

Durkheim met this question head-on, early on, because from the start of his career he attempted to do justice to the three ideals of the French Revolution—liberty, equality, and fraternity or community. He developed what I will call a communitarian defence of liberalism. That defense, in fact, is a set of different arguments addressing a host of issues: What is the normative relation between the private and public, the individual and the community? Are autonomy and authority irreconcilable? What is the social nature of knowledge, especially moral knowledge? Are moral discourse and the common good threatened by pluralism? Is public moral education coercive? What are the practices of social criticism? These issues are joined by a single thread: Durkheim's construction of a sophisticated sociohistorical account of modern social life that furthers the moral aims of both liberalism and communitarianism.

I

What characterizes the liberals, and what characterizes their opponents, the communitarians? The textbook account goes something like this. Utilitarian and Kantian vocabularies buttress, if not constitute, standard liberal outlooks, though not at all in the same way. Both Mill and Kant supposedly contributed to the formation of moral attitudes that express the priority of individuality and freedom over community and authority. For Kant, and often for Mill, individuals' rights precede the common good, and justice—the specification of rights and the procedures protecting them—is not to be determined by a particular community or personal authority. Otherwise, as Mill feared, a set of preferences could be imposed on an individual, obstructing the pursuit of utility; or, as Kant feared, irrationality in the form of superstition or political tyranny could enslave an individual, making it impossible to heed the voice of reason. In any case, the self must be free to pursue those goods that it deems worthy. Justice protects that freedom, restraining it only if it leads to an encroachment on others' rights. Many utilitarian positions, of course, while committed to individual rights, are willing to curtail some individual liberties for the sake of the greatest happiness of the greatest number. Still, they hold that maximizing the total welfare is often achieved by allowing individuals to pursue freely their own version of the good.

By contrast, in this textbook account, communitarians argue that liberal societies and their moral theories (Mill's utilitarianism and Kant's rights-based ethics) are built on the Enlightenment's illusory belief in utility or suprahistorical reason, and hence modern liberal societies, or at least their foundations, are bound to fail. Some suggest our situation is desperate. Having attempted to escape history in the quest for universality, we have neglected our moral traditions, and now we are without a moral compass. MacIntyre claims "we have—very largely, if not entirely—lost our comprehension, both theoretical and practical, of morality."[3] Recovery will not follow by simply acknowledging that there is no ahistorical moral truth. If that were the case, Nietzsche or Dewey could have helped us find our way. The liberals' politics of rights, rather, needs to be replaced by

Aristotle's or Hegel's or some one else's politics of the common good.

What, then, characterizes liberals and communitarians? The short answer is that they are characterized by mutual carica- tures. Liberals and communitarians are ideal types found in journals and books, each type defined by its adversary. Critics of communitarians describe them like this: people who, armed with the conviction that there is no such thing as a discoverable, essential human nature (or ahistorical reason) and a correspond- ing set of rights, wish to encumber all members of society with traditional, narrow forms of life, thus providing stable, endur- ing identities and social practices.[4] In their view, the common good of a people takes precedence over justice, that is, over in- dividual rights. Critics of liberals describe them something like this: people who, armed with the conviction that there is a dis- coverable, essential human nature (or ahistorical reason) and a corresponding set of rights, wish to free individuals from the shackles of tradition and enforced homogeneity, thus allowing individuals to fulfill their identities as reasonable humans. In their view, justice (individual rights) takes precedence over the common good.

Straw men abound, and they will continue to as long as we ascribe to others views that hardly anyone maintains. Describ- ing communitarians as collectivists who disdain individual rights, or liberals as anarchists who abhor any hint of commu- nity, serves little purpose.[5] Yet fair portraits of liberals or com- munitarians are scarce. In what follows, as I connect Durkheim to the contemporary debate I investigate not ideal types but spe- cific people: MacIntyre, Rawls, Rorty, Stout, Taylor, and Walzer. I try to avoid labeling individuals, though that convenient prac- tice is often difficult to dodge. Current labeling often points to a general confusion over what the labels stand for. Jean Hampton, for example, refers to "communitarians such as Rorty," while MacIntyre writes of "liberal writers such as . . . Rorty."[6] With the help of Durkheim, I hope to show that we need not see our- selves in the position of having to choose between "liberals" and "communitarians."

I have not dropped the labels "liberal" and "communitarian," however. They present genuine differences. Each stands for a cluster of (albeit general) values and dispositions. These, I will argue, are not necessarily incompatible. Often a communitarian stance is more appropriate for one set of issues, and a liberal one for another set. Although I have retained the terms, I do not as a matter of course oppose one to the other. I note which position is fitting for which issue, and when genuine conflicts arise I suggest ways to cope with them. This nuanced approach to the terms, I believe, can get us beyond the present impasse. If, however, you come to hold that the designations "liberal" and "communitarian" are of little use because you have been persuaded by the argument that rights and virtues, autonomy and authority, self-interest and common projects need not be contradictory, I will not be dismayed. Dropping the two terms while securing their varied connotations, or preserving while not opposing them, equally will assist us to construct useful theoretical accounts of modern democratic societies and to address pressing social problems.

II

The present caricatures of liberal and communitarian beliefs are not without precedent. Durkheim's peers occupied positions in a comparable debate. Some celebrated Hegel as champion of community, while others extolled Locke as defender of the individual. The liberals' blind spot was the reverse of the communitarians'. Whereas Hegel could not envision a stable pluralistic society, Locke could not envision a satisfying homogeneous one. Hegel's society required coercion to guarantee shared, rational beliefs for the sake of the flourishing community; Locke's required limited coercion, that of the minimal state, to guarantee private pursuits for the sake of individual happiness. I am not at all concerned with the accuracy of these portraits, but with the role they played in these debates. While one side was apt to complain about the coercion needed to create Hegel's homogeneous society, the other complained about the lack of concern to educate members in common practices and beliefs in Locke's pluralistic society.

Durkheim was unhappy with the way these lines were drawn. He did not do the interesting work of showing the liberal aspects of Hegel's work and the communitarian aspects of Locke's. He allowed the caricatures to remain unchallenged, yet he searched for ways to mediate them. This entailed showing how modern democratic societies can—indeed, must—possess attributes from both liberalism and communitarianism. For help he turned to Rousseau. Rousseau, in Durkheim's view, had attempted to join communitarian and liberal ideas: the individual is nurtured by a community but also protected by a social contract. It could be argued that Rousseau was the central figure of a French tradition—a tradition that would include Pascal, Malebranche, and Montesquieu—to which Durkheim belonged. Although I am not going to make that argument here, I want to highlight Rousseau's importance for Durkheim.[7]

The term *volonté générale* (the general will) belongs to a distinctively French tradition.[8] Rousseau referred to a generalized will that chooses not special interests but public legislation; not restrictive organizations but public membership; and not private goods but the general or common good. The public good, then, is qualitatively different from the private: "The public good," Rousseau wrote, "would not be merely the sum of private goods . . . as in a simple aggregation. . . . It would be greater than this sum, and public felicity, far from being based on the happiness of private individuals, would itself be the source of this happiness." What enables individuals to place the public before the private? Appealing to reason, according to Rousseau, is no answer. Rousseau's answer was education.[9] Individuals do not naturally pursue virtue or a common good. They must be taught to subdue their self-love and to attach themselves to a sphere larger than the self's. Once freed from "the passions of petty self-interest," the self is "carried into the common unity . . . receiving its life and being."

"The common good" and "general will" are not the only dominant themes in Rousseau's work. The dignity and liberty of the individual are also foremost in his thought. Citizens freely enter the social contract; obligations are met voluntarily. A tension, then, existed in Rousseau's writing: he championed both the liberal, autonomous individual and the authoritative, educative community. At times this strain was minimized, as when he described social freedom as an acquired disposition. One must learn how to become the autonomous individual who freely chooses the common good. Yet the strain did not go away so easily. In Rousseau's view, there is always something unnatural about society, and therefore individuals are constantly at war with the artificial constraints imposed by society. The "happy society" is something of an oxymoron. Durkheim took up the challenge of resolving this tension. He rejected the idea that the social is artificial, and set himself the task of exploring the normative social conditions of modern democratic societies. This involved defending the view that autonomy is a social product of liberal democratic traditions and institutions, including educational ones. Petty self-interest, constricted civic spirit, private willfulness—these were debilities that Rousseau decried and that Durkheim combated. The individual—free-spirited and civic-minded—was Rousseau's cherished ideal and it became Durkheim's as well.

Durkheim's late-nineteenth-century French social and intellectual environment has much to do with his attraction to Rousseau. There was a widespread sense that classical liberalism was failing, and that something needed to be done soon to stop alienation and the disintegration of society. This had not always been the case. Given their experience of devastating wars, civil and international, many framers of modern thought were deeply suspicious of traditional authorities and of crusades for a uniform citizenry. They sought after contracts and constitutions that established impersonal authorities, equipped with force, for the protection of individual rights. Political unity, if not community, could be expected. That unity was comprised of the harmony, or at least the coordination, of individual pursuits and interests. By the late eighteenth and early nineteenth centuries, many had accepted—even if they did so grudgingly—that modern societies are best arranged as aggregates of individuals who, protected by rights, may or may not be committed to a common good. Even Kant, who opposed the utilitarian focus on interests, justified a constitutional republic by noting that individuals' selfish pursuit of private interest might be organized such that "the one balances the other in its devastating effect, or even suspends it. . . . Thus a man, although not a morally good man, is compelled to be a good citizen."[10] Nonetheless, early liberalism was far from being thoroughly atomistic. It did not inveigh against every form of community and tradition, or place its sole hope in individuals' ability to reason their way to joy. Locke, as likely a candidate as any for the title of founder of classical liberalism, depicted humans neither as solitary creatures nor as basically rational beings who need only to be spared the opinions and superstitions of a backward education. He did not oppose voluntary communities, but he believed there could be no political community, for that would legitimate the permanent subjugation of a diverse citizenry.

Classical liberalism, however, received mixed reviews in nineteenth-century France. Social displacement wrought by the French revolutions and then by the Industrial Revolution led many there to be critical of laissez-faire economics and other individualistic aspects of classical liberalism. The time was right for those who proclaimed the need for *solidaire*. These prophets were of many political stripes: there were the reactionaries (such as Joseph de Maistre and Louis de Bonald) who wanted to bring back the traditional, hierarchical church-society; the Utopian Socialists (such as Saint-Simon and Charles Fourier) who called for rationalized, planned communities; and those who, like Auguste Comte, attempted to join aspects of both traditionalism and rationalism. Communal participation in society, specified social roles, shared expectations, and the counterpoise, if not the supremacy, of the general will to the particular—these were the features of the challenge to classical liberalism in France, regardless of political orientation.

There is some irony here. The liberal vision was initially inspired by the need to protect (usually religious) communities and individuals from oppressive, personal authorities such as popes and bishops, emperors and kings. Yet liberalism was now condemned by many as the new oppressor, crushing communities and individuals by a novel kind of power, the impersonal force of classical economics in the Industrial Revolution. There was perhaps more agreement on identifying the woes of the age than on prescribing the remedies. Marx, Weber, and Durkheim all accepted that modern Western societies and politics could not be adequately described in the categories of economics and narrow self-interest. They all believed that the Industrial Age was in need of shared beliefs and practices not securable by classical liberalism. Durkheim's famous "anomie" summarized a prevailing sentiment. Solidarity—a necessary condition for meaningful existence—was crumbling under the foot of the liberal, industrial Leviathan. Yet we find diverse answers to the question: What is to be done?

This is the background, the narrative, in which I want to place Durkheim. Within it we can make sense of his interest in Rousseau's attempt to capture the benefits of liberalism—individual rights and liberties—in a moral vocabulary featuring a good that is more than the aggregate of private goods, a distinctive common good. Durkheim's response to his generation can be viewed as his effort to advance, in theory and in practice, Rousseau's vision of a harmonious pluralistic society in the context of the industrial age. To this end, Durkheim developed sophisticated accounts of modern democratic societies, reflected on their traditions and ideals, and investigated their institutions and structural arrangements. In his effort to protect liberalism from egoism, and communitarianism from fatalism he joined sociohistorical skill to moral commitment and imagination.

III

Earlier I described this book as a reading of Durkheim in light of a set of questions. Think of "a reading" not as a positivistic report or summary, but as an active engagement with Durkheim's work in view of present debates between liberals and communitarians. Moreover, mine is not an exhaustive account of Durkheim's thought.[11] I can compare my selective interpretation— my strong reading—to Steven Lukes's excellent book on Durkheim.[12] Lukes provides a thorough, critical map of Durkheim's life and work. In contrast, I take my readers down a single stream of Durkheim's thought—"moral individualism," or what I am calling his communitarian defense of liberalism. This stream (actually it is more a network of tributaries) crisscrosses through much of the entire terrain. I have followed its bends and twists, but have not strayed far from them. Lukes's book opens with Durkheim's childhood; mine with Durkheim's involvement in the Dreyfus affair. Doing so provides me with a critical perspective—a partisan stance—from which to examine Durkheim's vision for the moral life of liberal democracies.

I have written with many audiences in mind. The theme of this book—the normative relation between the public and private in modern societies—is of interest not only to social theorists and political philosophers, but to many in the humanities and social sciences. I would like to think that I have made a contribution to a broad conversation taking place in various arenas concerning individuals in community. I often cross disciplinary boundaries. This is in part the result of my own pragmatic training, and also because Durkheim's work is, by today's standards, interdisciplinary. No doubt my nomadic roving has introduced some errors. Yet I am haunted by Victor Turner's plea that we "acquire the humanistic skills that would enable [us] to live more comfortably in those territories where the masters of human thought and art have long been dwelling." [13]

Durkheim's Communitarian Defense of Liberalism

INDIVIDUALISM IS the great sickness of the present age. . . . Each of us has confidence only in himself, sets himself up as the sovereign judge of everything. . . . The true intellectual is Nietzsche's "superman" or even "the enemy of laws" who was not in the least made for the laws, but for placing himself above them. . . . When individualism arrives at this degree of self-infatuation, there is or will become nothing but *anarchy;*—perhaps we are not as yet there, but we are approaching it at a great pace.[1]

This quotation is not from MacIntyre's *After Virtue* but from Ferdinand Brunetière's "After the Trial," which appeared in the *Revue des deux mondes* in March 1898. Brunetière, a Catholic literary historian and critic, denounced individualism and claimed that it was debilitating France's moral foundation. It is the "intellectuals" who carry this disease, and if they are not checked, he warned, traditional virtue and values will wither as anarchy and hedonism spread. In the same year Durkheim published a response entitled "Individualism and the Intellectuals." In it, Durkheim discussed "the argument, always refuted and always renewed," that "intellectual and moral anarchy would be the inevitable result of liberalism."[2] Some varieties of liberalism, Durkheim conceded, are egoistic and threaten the common good of societies by encouraging the individual to become excessively preoccupied with self-interest. But there is a strand of liberalism, Durkheim argued, that is moral and social. This form Durkheim called "moral individualism," and he claimed that "not only is [moral] individualism not anarchical, but it hence-forth is the only system of beliefs that can ensure the moral unity of the country." In industrial, democratic nations such as France, moral virtue and unity are promoted by the liberal practices and ideals of moral individualism.[3]

In this surprising and, I will argue, powerful defense of liberalism, Durkheim did not appeal to universal principles derived from natural reason or from any other tap into an "objective," ahistorical moral reality. He situated his defense in history—specifically, in France's history. France's modern moral traditions, Durkheim argued, are largely constituted by liberal institutions and values. To challenge those traditions is to court anarchy. What is more, to challenge those traditions is to commit blasphemy, for they have become sacred. Brunetière, it followed, was the true irreligious anarchist. "Individualism and the Intellectuals," like most of Durkheim's work, belongs to a distinctive French narrative, a narrative of struggle and accomplishment, of the Revolution and the Constitution. His arguments are not for all societies, even if they can be applied to many. His is an insider's argument, for the French, by a Frenchman.

I

The immediate historical setting for Brunetière's "After the Trial" and Durkheim's response was the Dreyfus affair.[4] A letter referring to secret French documents was found in the German embassy. The French Army claimed that the letter, addressed to the German military attaché in Paris, was written by Captain Dreyfus—a French officer who was also a Jew. In 1894 Dreyfus was convicted of treason by a military tribunal and was sentenced to life imprisonment on Devil's Island. Two years later, information surfaced that implicated Major Esterhazy as the author of the treasonous letter. The army, known at this time for its anti-Semitism, attempted to suppress the new evidence. Esterhazy was eventually tried, but was acquitted within minutes. Thereupon Emile Zola, in January 1898, published his famous letter "J'accuse" to the president of the Republic, charging various military officials, including judges and handwriting experts, with condemning an innocent man. By this time, the Dreyfus

case had become a popular cause célèbre, one of the most important episodes of political controversy in the history of France.

Many felt compelled to take a stand for or against Dreyfus.
Lines were drawn, sides chosen, alliances forged. The anti-
Dreyfusards were in the main from the army, the Roman Catholic Church, and the upper bureaucracy. They were monarchists,
and anti-Semites. Before the Dreyfus affair, the military and the
upper bureaucracy were largely composed of a variety of conservatives. These conservatives, however, were not united. The
conservative Catholic Right, for example, had been taken by
some to be anti-nationalist, "subordinating French national interests to those of the Church." However, as a result of the affair,
various politically conservative parties pulled together and
formed a lasting coalition. Anti-Semitism was now given "a particular ideological and political character which had been latent
but never explicit or organized [in France]."[5]

The Left forged its own alliances. Jaurès's socialists and Jacob-
ins, liberal and moderate Republicans, anti-clericals and Protestants, allied to defend Dreyfus and to combat the Right. Concerning the contest between the Right and the Left, historian
David Thomson writes:

The fact that Dreyfus was a Jew, and that his condemnation led to a
wider drive by the authoritarian militarists and clericals to exclude not
merely Jews but Protestants and Republicans from positions of military
and administrative power, raised the issue in dramatic form. It was a
clash of rival absolutisms. . . . Democracy had clearly to be a social and
political order based on common citizenship and civilian rights within
the Republic: or else it would be replaced by an authoritarian, hierarchic
order, dominated by Church and privileged ruling classes in the Army
and Civil Service. French logic interpreted the conflict in these clear
terms, and the battle began.[6]

Durkheim was a Dreyfusard activist. He strongly opposed
the Right; he persuaded his close friend Jaurès to enlist socialists
as Dreyfusards; and he was extremely active in what one has
called "the most effective and durable creation of all this Drey-
fusiste agitation," the Ligue pour la Défense des Droits de
l'Homme.[7] Durkheim was a Dreyfusard long before most. In
1896, at the grave of a colleague at Bordeaux, Durkheim gave a
Dreyfusite speech that "caused something of a sensation." In a
letter to Célestin Bouglé, dated March 1898, Durkheim stated, "I

was a member of the Ligue in advance; I was part of it before it existed."[8] In 1904, reflecting on the aftermath of the Dreyfus affair, Durkheim wrote:

Writers and scholars are citizens; it is thus evident that they have the strict duty to participate in public life. . . . We must be above all advisers, educators. It is our function to help our contemporaries to know themselves in their ideas and their feelings, far more than to govern them. . . . The moral agitation which these events [of the Dreyfus affair] have provoked has not yet been extinguished, and I am among those who think that it must not be extinguished. . . . The essential thing is not to let ourselves relapse into our previous state of prolonged moral stagnation.[9]

On June 6, 1900, Professor Stapfer, the Honorary Dean of the Faculty of Letters at Bordeaux, was "no less applauded when he spoke of M. Durkheim, professor at the Faculty of Letters at Bordeaux, whose fiery speeches bring supporters to the Ligue from far and wide."[10] Not everyone, however, applauded Durkheim's activism. In July 1899, the Rector of Bordeaux wrote of Durkheim to the Minister of Public Instruction, "I consider that whatever the position taken by teachers of the University of Bordeaux in their speechifying at militant meetings, they never do good: for they make their divisions more and more palpable to the entire population and above all to the students, to whom one should preach concord and unity, and who are led into demonstrating themselves, in the steps of, and in imitation of, several overexcited professors."[11]

II

In "Individualism and the Intellectuals" (1898), Durkheim noted that Brunetière wished to close debate on the details of the Dreyfus case in order to generalize from it, that is, to pass on, "in a single bound, to the level of principles." The heart of the issue, for Brunetière, was "the intellectuals'" advocacy of individualism and the anarchy that results from it. "The intellectuals" place "their reason above authority" and "the rights of the individual seem to them inalienable." The hubris of the intellectuals, in the words of Brunetière, was manifested by their refusal "to bend their logic before the word of an army general." Perhaps France appeared to Brunetière as England did to Hobbes, beset by wars, revolutions, and conflicting authorities. Order was to be preserved and anarchy checked by establishing one set of authorities as infallible. In any case, for Brunetière individualism was the public plight, the paramount issue of the Dreyfus affair. Brunetière's criticism of liberalism amounted to this: it is immoral and irreligious, and it threatens national solidarity by courting anarchy.

Durkheim accepted the debate posed in these terms. He began by addressing Brunetière's first criticism. Durkheim made a distinction between two types of individualism—egoistic individualism and moral individualism. The former is "strict utilitarianism and the utilitarian egoism of Spencer and the economists . . . a crass commercialism that reduces society to nothing more than a vast apparatus of production and exchange."[12] By "strict utilitarianism" I take Durkheim to have been referring to preference utilitarianism, which judges an act in terms of the satisfaction of individual preferences. The "utilitarian egoism of Spencer and the economists," on the other hand, refers to the belief that human happiness will increase as the economy is released from artificial social regulation and constraint. Both types of utilitarianism, in Durkheim's view, are atomistic, the one emphasizing the discrete individual's random wants, the other the individual's economic choices. Both types begin and, to a certain extent, end with self-interest. Utilitarianism is dedicated to the greatest happiness for the greatest number, but in Durkheim's account, these forms of utilitarianism describe society as no more than a group of disparate individuals pursuing external goods associated with wealth, status, and power. The end result is the maximizing of aggregate private interests.[13]

Durkheim asserted that "all communal life is impossible without the existence of interests superior to those of the individual." From the outset of his career, Durkheim insisted that in modern industrial societies happiness and freedom are achieved in the context of *Sittlichkeit* (to borrow Hegel's term)—moral beliefs and practices embedded in vital traditions and institutions. Individual desires require tutoring; economic transactions require regulation. As early as 1885, eight years before the publication of *The Division of Labor in Society*, Durkheim wrote that "the economists of the orthodox school have as their ideal a cult that is sometimes superstitious: liberty has become for them a kind of idol, to which they willingly sacrifice all else."[14] Such liberty, understood here as freedom from all constraint, is a prescription not for happiness but for despair, loneliness, and even suicide.

Durkheim failed to distinguish all stripes of utilitarians, and he never explored the good things to be said of various utilitarian positions. Perhaps, for the purposes of responding to Brunetière, Durkheim did not think he needed to linger on the subject. Brunetière, the anti-individualist, would have been only too willing to accept Durkheim's caricature and dismissal of utilitarians. The challenge for Durkheim was to persuade Brunetière to praise the other type of individualism—moral individualism. What, then, is moral individualism?

Moral individualism, wrote Durkheim, is "the individualism of Kant, Rousseau, of the *spiritualistes*—the one that the Declaration of the Rights of Man attempted, more or less happily, to formulate and that is currently taught in our schools and has become the basis of our moral character." This type of individualism is "profoundly different" from the egoistic type. "Far from making personal interest the object of conduct, this one sees in all personal motives the very source of evil. According to Kant, I am only certain of acting properly if the motives that influence me relate, not to the particular circumstance in which I am placed, but to my equality as a man *in abstracto*." Rousseau's concept of the general will, Durkheim noted, is an authentic expression of justice insofar as it is constituted not by personal interest, but by public goods and concerns. Durkheim concluded, "Thus, for both these men, the only moral ways of acting are those which can be applied to all men indiscriminately; that is, which are implied in the notion of man in general. . . . According to these moralists, duty consists in disregarding all that concerns us personally . . . in order to seek out only . . . that which we share with all our fellowmen."[15] By underscoring their suspicion of private interest, Durkheim linked Rousseau and Kant. He associated Kant's deontology ("man *in abstracto*") with Rousseau's general will.

Durkheim's reading of Rousseau and Kant was an attempt to locate them in a republican tradition that describes rights and duties as the result of a commitment to public, not only to private, concerns. To this tradition belongs Durkheim's concept of the moral individual as an active member of a political community whose duties and desires are directed toward that community and whose benefits (such as those in the Declaration of the Rights of Man) are protected by it.

It is perhaps more accurate to say that Durkheim's moral individualism invented this tradition as much as it belongs to it. Durkheim attempted to piece together his own "communitarian" account of his favorite varieties of liberalism. This was no invention from scratch. A set of liberal, democratic traditions already existed. But Durkheim was well aware of competing communitarian traditions, such as those of the Royalists and the conservative Roman Catholics, as well as of competing liberal traditions, such as those of the classical economists and utilitarians. Durkheim wanted to establish the sovereignty of moral individualism by arguing that it, in fact, represented France's most noble, legitimate traditions—and at a time when most liberals eschewed tradition, old or new.[16]

One might think, in light of the Dreyfus affair, that Durkheim would have proceeded to underscore the benefits of membership in the political community—in particular, the benefits derived from Dreyfus's rights as a French citizen. Instead, Durkheim emphasized an individual's obligations to the common good. Moral individualism, Durkheim claimed, was already a salient feature of France's political community, and hence any attack on moral individualism, such as the attempt to deprive Dreyfus of his rights, was an assault on the common good and contrary to a citizen's political obligations.

Durkheim attempted to show that in the vocabulary of moral individualism there is no fundamental opposition between individual rights and the common good. He first advanced what he considered to be the necessary communal, social interpretation of the Kantian autonomous individual. He said of Kant, "If he has sometimes been reproached for having exaggerated the autonomy of reason, one could equally well say, and not without foundation, that he placed at the base of his ethics an irrational act of faith and submission."[17] Kant would claim that our absolute obedience belongs to reason, but for Durkheim this is an "irrational . . . submission" because Kant could not answer the question, Whence comes reason? Durkheim would not accept Kant's derivation of reason from an impersonal source such as Nature. Years later, in *The Elementary Forms of the Religious Life,*

Durkheim would comment that "it is not an *explanation* to say
that [reason] is inherent in the nature of the human intellect."
He argued that what Kant called universal or pure reason is in
fact a set of contingent beliefs, produced by and entrenched in
social institutions and traditions.

In "Individualism and the Intellectuals," I take Durkheim to
have been suggesting that just this sort of connection pertains
between the absolutist nature of Kantian practical reason and an
absolute, irrational obedience to society. The "base of [Kantian]
ethics" is "an irrational act of faith" insofar as Kant could not
satisfactorily derive reason from any impersonal, atemporal
source, but also insofar as he was not willing to derive it from an
impersonal, social one. In Durkheim's account, we remain uncritical, and even irrational, as long as we do not recognize the
social base of moral reasoning, which could otherwise be subject
to scrutiny. Kant may not have understood as much, but according to Durkheim he did describe the rigorous demands of autonomous reason as binding the individual to a larger community—
the universal. In other words, Kant understood that there is no
conflict, in principle, between the moral individual and the common good of humanity. Durkheim provided an initial account of
why this is the case: the very notion of the moral individual is
an outcome of a set of modern moral and political European traditions.

Still attempting to establish the social, moral nature of this
type of individualism, Durkheim switched from a theoretical to
a genetic argument. He suggested that "doctrines are judged
above all by what they produce—that is, by the spirit of the doctrines to which they give birth." [18] Kantianism begat the ethics of
Fichte, the ethics of Fichte (already "impregnated with socialism") begat Hegel, and Hegel begat Marx. Durkheim hardly
provided an outline, much less a thick description, of a socialist
or communitarian family tree starting with Kant. But he didn't
need to. Durkheim was responding to Brunetière. He had only
to show that there is an individualism, emerging with Kant, that
contributes not to privatism but to a common good.

Rousseau, in Durkheim's reading, likewise balanced individualism with an "authoritarian conception of society." He thus
inspired the people of the French Revolution to make France
into an "indivisible and centralized entity," even while they

framed the Declaration of Rights. Durkheim interpreted Rousseau as one who attempted to locate liberal values and practices in the domain of a common good. Tension charges Rousseau's thought as he defends both the autonomy of the individual and the authority of the community, but Durkheim saw Rousseau's basic aim to be sustaining a community of independent, civic-minded individuals.

This irenic treatment of Rousseau and Kant is unusual for Durkheim. Durkheim always expressed a great debt to both, yet criticism usually accompanied his admiration. Perhaps Durkheim, wishing to present an accord—"an overlapping consensus," to use Rawls's phrase—among the various moral individualists, decided against developing arguments against Rousseau and Kant in "Individualism and the Intellectuals." He felt compelled, at least in a footnote, however, to raise his fundamental criticism of both:

This is how it is possible, without contradiction, to be an individualist, all the while saying that the individual is more a product of society than its cause. It is because individualism itself is a social product just like all moralities and religions. . . . This is what Kant and Rousseau failed to understand. They wanted to deduce their individualistic ethics not from society but from the notion of the isolated individual. This undertaking was impossible, and from it come the logical contradictions of their systems.[19]

Kant, failing to grasp the sociohistorical foundation of practical reason, could not describe the morally relevant ways in which individuals are socially constituted. He divided the self between individual desires and universal reason, making conflict between the private and the public a natural feature of the human soul. For Durkheim, this conflict is contingent. It is not necessary, even if it often cannot be avoided. The conflict has to do with particular and social narratives, not with universal structures. We can drop the very idea of a fundamental, natural antagonism between the private and the public, if we follow Durkheim in describing desires and reasons as socially spun dispositions, beliefs, and skills.

As I have said, Durkheim's debt to Rousseau was great. "Rousseau," Durkheim claimed in *Montesquieu and Rousseau*, "was keenly aware of the specificity of the social order. He conceived it clearly as an order of facts generically different from purely individual facts." Nonetheless, Rousseau severed the individual from the social. In his lectures on Rousseau, Durkheim argued that "Rousseau sees only two poles of human reality, the abstract, general individual who is the agent and object of social existence, and the concrete empirical individual who is the antagonist of all collective existence."[20] This led to two antithetical views in Rousseau's work: "on the one hand, society as a mere instrument for the use of the individual; on the other, the individual as dependent upon society, which far transcends the multitude of individuals."[21]

Rousseau correctly understood the specificity of the social order as an important, *sui generis* aspect of modern societies, yet he maintained, as did Kant, a radical dichotomy between the individual and the social. For Rousseau, society is an unnatural state for individuals. "Nature ends with the individual . . . everything that goes beyond the individual is bound to be artificial."[22] There will always be, in Rousseau's account, a fundamental conflict between the individual and the social, that of the natural versus the artificial.

III

By articulating the notion of moral individualism, Durkheim challenged Brunetière's claim that all individualism is immoral. Having its origin in France's liberal traditions, moral individualism is a set of social beliefs and practices that is characteristic of the modern common good and the ethical individual, he argued. Durkheim claimed that Kant and Rousseau had failed to understand that "individualism itself is a social product just like all moralities and religions." He consequently went on to damage Brunetière's claim that individualism is irreligious by articulating the religious nature of moral individualism.

[Moral individualism] so far surpasses the level of utilitarian goals that it appears to those who aspire to it to be completely stamped with religiosity. The human person (*personne humaine*) . . . is considered sacred in what can be called the ritual sense of the word. It partakes of the transcendent majesty that churches of all time have accorded to their gods; it is conceived as being invested with that mysterious property which creates a void about sacred things, which removes them from profane contacts and which separates them from ordinary life. And it is exactly this characteristic that confers the respect of which it is the object. Whoever makes an attempt on a man's life, on a man's liberty . . . inspires in us a feeling of horror analogous in every way to that which the believer experiences when he sees his idol profaned. Such an ethic is therefore not simply a hygienic discipline or a prudent economy of existence; it is a religion in which man is at once the believer and the god.[23]

Durkheim, in a way undoubtedly offensive to Brunetière, inverted the claim that individualism is anti-religious. Moral individualism is religious, and Brunetière is the blasphemer by denying it.

Religion, in Durkheim's view, is a body of shared beliefs and practices endowed with an impressive authority. "As soon as a goal is pursued by an entire people, it acquires . . . a sort of moral supremacy that raises it far above private aims and thus gives it a religious quality." By definition, then, religion is anti-utilitarian, for it presupposes common, not private, pursuits. As moral individualism has become a shared goal, with its attending beliefs and practices, it has acquired a sacred status. It has become a religious form of life; "moral supremacy" stains it with "a religious quality." If moral individualism were "a prudent economy of existence," composed of "private aims" alone, then it could not, by definition, be described as being genuinely religious. At best it would be magic, an association of disparate individuals who use the same cult. The beliefs and practices of magic, in Durkheim's words, do not "result in binding together those who adhere to it, nor in uniting them into a group leading a common life."[24]

Durkheim's utilitarian definition of magic is problematic, to be sure. But that does not take away from his argument that shared beliefs and practices promoting moral unity constitute the religious. Moral individualism includes such beliefs and practices; moral individualism is therefore anything but a form of "self-infatuation" or "moral anarchy." Liberalism is, in fact, a religious form of life. By Durkheim's lights, then, modern life is shot through with the sacred, and moral individualism is an umbrella term that covers many pivotal, liberal sacred beliefs and practices.[25]

Durkheim claimed that moral individualism, "this religion of humanity," "has everything it needs to speak to its faithful in a no less imperative tone than the religions it replaces." This imperative voice had become manifest during the Dreyfus affair. Many who thought they had little in common joined in intellectual and moral communion as they felt the "horror" of the trespass against Dreyfus's rights. "Nowhere," Durkheim claimed, "are the rights of the individual affirmed with greater energy . . . nowhere is the individual more jealously protected from encroachments from the outside, whatever their source." Not even the state or any of its branches, such as the army, can legitimately suspend individual rights and liberties. The imperatives of moral individualism, unlike many forms of utilitarianism, permit no compromises.[26] "The doctrine of utility," quipped Durkheim, "can easily accept all sorts of compromises without belying its fundamental axiom; it can admit of individual liberties being suspended whenever the interest of the greater number requires that sacrifice." Moral individualism, too, can require great sacrifice (that is, exacting commitments), but it does so for the sake of moral liberties, not in opposition to them.

Durkheim noted that although the sacredness of moral individualism "dominates us," it is not "alien to us." It is above all *"consciences particulières,"* addressing us in an authoritative voice. This voice, however, is none other than our own, that is, the voice of our moral traditions. "It is society that fixes for us this ideal as the sole common goal that can rally our wills." I take Durkheim here to be challenging some Marxist interpretations of religion by suggesting that there is a modern religion that does not fix our attention on the clouds, but rather on problems and benefits found in modern societies here and now. The religion is external to us in that we—you and I—did not create it. But we are not alien to it because it springs from our traditions, and because its focus is on our social life.[27]

Toward the end of "Individualism and the Intellectuals" Durkheim again attempted to invert Brunetière's religious argument against "individualism," this time by suggesting that individualism developed out of nothing less than Christianity itself. Durkheim noted that "the merits of Christian morality are praised and we are discreetly invited [by Brunetière] to embrace them. But are we to ignore the fact that the originality of Christianity consisted precisely in a remarkable development of the individualistic spirit?"[28] Durkheim went on to present a portrait of Christianity that is more Protestant than Roman Catholic.

Christianity, according to Durkheim, understands "the personal conviction of the individual" as the "essential condition of piety"; it teaches that "the moral value of acts" is to be measured not by "external judgments" but by the agent's intention, "a preeminently inward thing." In Durkheim's account, the individual becomes a sovereign judge, "accountable only to himself and to his God."

No doubt the author of *Suicide* knew that he was rendering a distinctively Protestant, liberal depiction of Christianity. In order to challenge Brunetière, he needed to give a reading of Christianity that supported his contention that "it is a singular error to present the individualistic ethic as the antagonist of Christian morality."[29] Protestant Christianity provided that reading. Yet anyone the least bit familiar with Durkheim's argument in *Suicide* may well be puzzled by this advocacy of individualism, written just three years after *Suicide*. In *Suicide* Durkheim argued that the individualistic ethos of Protestant Christianity is more likely to bring unhappiness and suicide than is Roman Catholicism, with all its traditional and communal practices. The puzzlement fades, however, when we recall that in "Individualism and the Intellectuals" Durkheim was not advocating every form or aspect of individualism. As I argue in Chapter 3, *Suicide* carried Durkheim's first mature communitarian defense of liberalism. He argued there that moral individualism, "something . . . very different from egoistic individualism," constitutes a modern common faith. From his first article "Social Property and Democracy" (1885) to his last book, *The Elementary Forms of the Religious Life* (1912), Durkheim consistently opposed those forms of individualism that he perceived as threatening the common good and spoiling human happiness.

IV

This brings us to Durkheim's treatment of Brunetière's third claim. Brunetière had asserted that individualism fosters anarchy. Durkheim responded, "Not only is [moral] individualism not anarchical, but it henceforth is the only system of beliefs that can ensure the moral unity of the country." The conservatives' attack on Dreyfus's constitutional rights was therefore a grave one, "for this eighteenth-century liberalism which is at bottom the whole object of the dispute is not simply a drawing-room theory, a philosophical construct; it has become a fact, it has penetrated our institutions and our mores, it has blended with our whole life, and if, truly, we had to give it up, we would have to recast our whole moral organization at the same stroke."[30] Brunetière feared anarchy; so did Durkheim. Yet Brunetière, by Durkheim's lights, was the despoiler challenging France's moral traditions and therefore the real anarchist.

Durkheim's defense of Dreyfus's rights was notably distinct from those of other Dreyfusards. Some argued that, out of sympathy to a fellow human, Dreyfus must be protected from the army. Others argued that if Dreyfus's rights are sacrificed today, yours may be tomorrow. Durkheim's defense of Dreyfus, in contrast, amounted to a far-reaching defense of the moral life of the Third Republic. If the abandonment of individual rights alarms us, "it is not only out of sympathy for the victim; nor is it from fear of having to suffer similar injustices. Rather, it is because such attempts cannot remain unpunished without compromising the national existence."[31]

"L'existence nationale"—what could Durkheim be referring to? Surely the anti-Dreyfusards were the faction most interested in the *"existence nationale."* They were willing to sacrifice Dreyfus for its sake. They were convinced that justice may be suspended for the sake of social order. In fact, social order, and not the guilt or innocence of Dreyfus, became the central issue in these debates. According to Thomson, "As the Dreyfus affair dragged on, the issue of the guilt or innocence of Dreyfus sank into the background, and the general defence of the military and nationalist leaders came to rest not on the thesis that Dreyfus was guilty, but that even if he were innocent, it was better that one man should suffer than that the whole prestige of the French Army should be undermined in the face of the enemy."[32] This path to national defense was alien to Durkheim. It is clear that by *"l'existence nationale"* Durkheim was referring to the nation's moral existence, not its racial identity or social stability.

We cannot disavow [moral individualism] today without disavowing ourselves . . . without committing a veritable moral suicide. Not long ago, people wondered whether it would not perhaps be convenient to consent to a temporary eclipse of these principles, in order not to disturb the functioning of a public administration that everyone recognized to be indispensable to the security of the state. We do not know if the antinomy really poses itself in this acute form; but, in any case, if a choice truly is necessary between these two evils, to thus sacrifice what has been to this day our historical raison d'être would be to choose the worst. An organ of public life, however important, is only an instrument, a means to an end. What purpose does it serve to maintain the means with such care if the end is dispensed with?[33]

Social goods and moral ends are to be served by public offices and departments, including the military; they are not to be sacrificed for the sake of such offices. The external goods of government institutions (in this case, bureaucratic stability and military prestige) are not to eclipse the relevant internal goods (in this case, Dreyfus's civil rights). In vitiating their social commitments, public officials and administrators destroy their raison d'être. "What a sad way of figuring, to renounce everything that makes life worthwhile and lends it dignity in order to live," Durkheim lamented. *"Et propter vitam vivendi perdere causes!"* — "On account of life you would cause the destruction of living!"[34]

Durkheim challenged those who would defend the social survival or stability of the nation at any cost. Implicitly, he also challenged those who would interpret him as a conservative social theorist, whose "problem" was "social order." He did not choose order over justice. Durkheim did claim that moral individualism promotes moral unity, and he did defend liberalism in the name of "the existence of the nation." But he was referring to the moral existence of the nation. Life—mere national survival—was not worth the renunciation of France's legitimate moral traditions.

If Brunetière was the anarchist, the Dreyfusards were the true patriots. Of the one who "defends the rights of the individual," Durkheim said, "He renders to his country the same service the aged Roman once rendered to his city in defending the traditional rites against foolhardy innovators."[35] The aged Roman is Cicero, who came out of retirement to defend the republic in opposition to the despotism of Mark Anthony and Octavian ("foolhardy innovators" who later crushed the republicans). The classical allusion likens Brunetière and his fellow anti-Dreyfusards to destroyers of the Third Republic, even as the Dreyfusards are likened to its defenders.

There can be little doubt that Durkheim placed justice over

order. It is true that he was not convinced that, in the case of the Dreyfus affair, there was a conflict between justice, the fair distribution of political and legal rights, and order, the maintenance of a reasonable level of social stability in light of unsettling events or revelations. He suggested, in fact, that the anti-Dreyfusards' disregard for justice was more likely to disrupt social order than was the Dreyfusards' "thirst for justice." But if there were a conflict, it is clear that Durkheim would unequivocally side with justice.

V

If we reflect a little on Durkheim's argument against Brunetière, we can see that it had two parts, and that the second, though not necessarily incompatible with the first, can eclipse it. (1) Anti-liberals are more likely to breed anarchy, disrupting our social order, because they challenge the moral, sacred traditions that bind us to one another; (2) in any case, it's wrong (that is, unjust as measured by France's prevailing moral traditions) to deprive Dreyfus of his constitutional rights. In doing so, we deprive ourselves of too much. We deprive ourselves of much of what makes our lives worthwhile—our virtue.[36]

If we take the first part of the argument along descriptive lines, and the second along normative, we may be tempted to think Durkheim has regrettably attempted to wear two hats simultaneously—the sociologist's and the moral philosopher's. The sociologist knows that solidarity requires some shared beliefs and practices, and if these are severely challenged social disruption follows—for better or for worse. The moral philosopher, in contrast, is the professional trained to adjudicate between the "better" and the "worse"; that is, her job is to help us both maintain and discover moral—and not necessarily stabilizing—beliefs and practices. Durkheim's argument combined both sociological and moral claims. Protecting rights prevails over ensuring social order and stability; yet Durkheim's defense of the priority of rights is largely based on an interpretation of and an appeal to France's authoritative liberal institutions and traditions. Durkheim, therefore, doubted that the Dreyfusards would contribute to social instability because France's social identity was, in fact (it was the "fact" of the sociologist), embedded in liberal traditions.

As my argument unfolds in the following chapters, I shall show that Durkheim increasingly came to hold the normative and descriptive in a creative tension. He joined sociological skill to moral imagination, and presented the practice of social criticism as the art of scrutinizing inherited moral material and present institutions in light of a host of steady yet contingent background beliefs. Additionally, Durkheim attempted to preserve the critical leverage that is expressed in the vocabulary of the moral philosophers by such terms as "moral truth" and "objectivity." This idiom, however, did not refer to ahistorical reality or infallible Reason, but to our best moral insights as they come to us from critical reflection on our social and moral circumstances and traditions.

In "Individualism and the Intellectuals" we find Durkheim awkwardly trying to wear both hats at once, or perhaps more accurately, exchanging the one for the other in rapid succession. Later—to continue the metaphor—he would fashion a new hat combining the style and substance of the other two. This novel construction, I believe, promises to be an elegant addition to contemporary debates in social, moral, and political philosophy once its features are brought into view, as they are in what follows. When I subsequently engage with such contemporary theorists as Rawls, Rorty, MacIntyre, Stout, Gutmann, Walzer, Taylor, and Bellah, the understanding of Durkheim's mature philosophy that I articulate in the following chapters enables me to cast new light on some fundamental issues concerning freedom, rights, authority, public moral education, the relation between the public and private, and the role of social criticism in democracies. It enables me to isolate the merits and liabilities of both liberal and communitarian theories, and show that we no longer need to see ourselves in the position of having to choose between them.

"Individualism and the Intellectuals" is the best example of Durkheim's way of thinking at the outset of his mature thought. It points to things to come. Without resorting to foundationalist or universalist arguments he attempted to hold his fellow citizens to those ideals and values that he identified as representing a common liberal faith. He provided us with both a theory and an example of social criticism. As he challenged Brunetière, he explored France's moral traditions, located liberalism within them, and placed the Dreyfusards in the light of a distinctively French moral beacon. Social theory, then, in Durkheim's view, is a normative discipline. Its task is to help us understand who we are by analyzing past and present institutions so that we can better understand where we are to go in the future. Its office is to show us with equal clarity what is to be preserved and what is to be reformed.

Tradition and Autonomy:
The Path to Moral Individualism

DIVERSITY MARKS Durkheim's work. He had no "System," no monolithic, definitive account that purported to provide an exhaustive description and explanation of human societies. His corpus is multifaceted, broaching countless subjects and intruding on many disciplines. This is not to say that characteristic themes and questions do not pervade the work. These include inquiries into the normative relationship between the individual and modern society and into the moral, material, and psychological well-being of individuals in that society. But Durkheim pursued these guiding concerns along many paths.

The path that led him to the concept of moral individualism provides one way to trace and to learn from that pursuit. "Moral individualism" is hardly a "Durkheimian" term, and may strike some Durkheimians as downright oxymoronic. In fact, the two words occur side by side only occasionally in Durkheim's writings. Yet the term captures much of Durkheim's thought on the social, historical foundations of moral liberalism. It therefore provides a useful way to focus on the outcome of Durkheim's efforts to reject, accept, and extend aspects of both liberalism and communitarianism. To focus on Durkheim in this way is no mere antiquarian exercise. It opens up present possibilities for the creative rethinking of these issues.

Moral individualism is a concept that was fully realized in Durkheim's writing only after his work had led him in a number of different directions. In the following two chapters I follow that varied trail. It offers us many valuable lessons, even when Durkheim went astray. In this chapter I show how the early Durkheim initially forged a notion of freedom that eventually would prove to be pivotal for his communitarian defense of liberalism. Rejecting both radical autonomy and social determinism as adequate accounts of human action, Durkheim described freedom as voluntary responses to one's own socially constituted beliefs and loves. He reached this conclusion via illuminating critical evaluations of the social theorists of his day, from the Spencerians and classical economists on the one hand to the Kantians on the other. But Durkheim temporarily moved away from this position in *The Division of Labor in Society*. In that work, as he battled against the radical voluntarism of Spencer and the classical economists, Durkheim drifted toward a mechanistic social determinism he earlier had sought to avoid. The idea of a common faith centered on "the individual" then appeared to him overly privatistic, even though the evidence he accumulated in that work invited a moral rendering of modern social pluralism and individual autonomy. Not until *Suicide* did Durkheim square the inconsistencies of *The Division of Labor* with his earlier work and produce his first sophisticated account of moral individualism.

I have divided the development of Durkheim's thought into four convenient periods: (1) his essays prior to *The Division of Labor in Society*, what I call the early Durkheim; (2) the *Division of Labor*; (3) *Suicide*; and (4) his work from "Individualism and the Intellectuals" (1898) to *The Elementary Forms of the Religious Life* and beyond. This chapter returns to the first two periods of Durkheim's thought.[1] His mature thought, the second two periods, is considered in the following chapters.

I

From the start, Durkheim was critical of both laissez-faire liberalism and socialism, and for largely the same reason.[2] Both, according to Durkheim, view the state as an economic, as opposed to a moral, entity. Classical liberals long for a minimalist state, powerful enough to enforce legal contracts and rights, yet wise enough not to interfere with that natural harmony of private interests guaranteed by laissez-faire economics. Socialists, on the other hand, prefer a strong state, powerful enough to enforce material equality, thereby insuring an economic communism. Both political visions, however, assume that if economic interests are appropriately addressed, a healthy society will emerge.

In "La Science positive de la morale en Allemagne," the article written in 1887 after his first visit to Germany, Durkheim applauded the work of the social economists Adolf Wagner and Gustav von Schmoller. Following their lead, Durkheim criticized "the school of Manchester" for whom "political economics consists in the satisfaction of individual needs and especially material needs." Durkheim quipped, and not entirely fairly, that isolated individuals "exchanging their products" is the greatest social bond the liberal economists could imagine. They "see in the social bond only a superficial union determined by private interests happening to coincide." [3]

Durkheim argued that the "orthodox economists" and the "moralists of the Kantian school" divorce the moral world from the economic one: "these two sciences appear to study two worlds without any connection between them." The two worlds, however, are deeply connected, and it is impossible, as Durkheim put it, to "abstract the one from the other."

One cannot comprehend the moral maxims pertaining to property, contracts, work, etc, if one doesn't know the economic causes from which they are derived; and, on the other hand, one would form a very false idea about economic development if one were to neglect the moral causes that influence it. For morality is not absorbed by the political economy; rather all social functions contribute to produce this form to which economic phenomena have had to submit while contributing to it. [4]

Without belittling the importance of economic categories, Durkheim insisted that these alone cannot adequately describe the "economic world," much less the social or moral one.

For example, he contended that self-interest, the favorite concept of orthodox economists, fails to provide an adequate account of human rationality. The economists and social theorists whose paradigm of rationality is the individual systematically pursuing economic self-interest are mistaken. They assume that modern Western institutions (at least the progressive ones) are solely the result of private minds and market forces. Durkheim, however, held that "the majority of moral and social institutions are due not to reasoning and calculation but to obscure causes." His hermeneutics of suspicion—his assumption that people cannot adequately account for their beliefs and actions because often they are unaware of the social forces that influence them— was aimed not so much at exposing the irrationality of social institutions as at exposing the reductive assumptions of economists and social theorists attending solely to private economic motives.[5] The social currents that sway institutions and individuals are many, and often difficult to sort out.

For Durkheim, then, individuals are not exclusively or even primarily motivated by self-interest. This claim poses a challenge to the guiding principle of many forms of utilitarianism and classical liberalism, which assume that, granted enough freedom, individuals can achieve happiness by pursuing self-interest. Not self-interest, but social habits and prejudices, according to Durkheim's early work, are the springs of human action and commitment. Glossing Schmoller, Durkheim wrote that "When we have repeated the same action a certain number of times, it tends to be reproduced in the same manner. Little by little, by the effect of habit, our conduct takes a form that imposes itself on our will with an obligatory force. We feel ourselves obliged to cast our action always in this same mold." Cultural norms and beliefs are instilled in individuals by habits, that is, by social customs and conventions passed on from one generation to the next by extensive training. "Morality and the law," Durkheim claimed, "are nothing but collective habits." Even economic life is made of established customs constituting "moral phenomena."[6]

Habits are the offspring of society. Like language, habits contribute to the individual's social existence. Often individuals cannot provide perspicuous accounts of, or philosophical justifications for, particular social habits. This is because such discourse requires the sort of special training we usually find in graduate schools and not in most other habit-forming situations. Children, for example, are taught not to lie, but are often spared the various (say, Kantian or utilitarian) arguments in support of truth-telling. Persons who habitually do not lie are not, in Durkheim's account, constantly deciding to tell the truth. Does this imply, then, that such truth-telling is irrational, since truthful individuals are not consciously acting on reasonable beliefs, in this case, the belief that lying is wrong? I think not. Durkheim would suggest that rationality includes virtuous habits. His early writings are filled with accounts of the complexity of social life and how it shapes the individual, but he never suggests that rationality requires total cognizance of one's social milieu. On the contrary, he asserts that such cognizance is impossible, and that if someone attempted to act only by self-conscious beliefs, she would be incapable of living.

Habits, according to Durkheim, account for the power and authority of social disciplines such as law, morality, and religion. In 1886, he published a review of Spencer's *Ecclesiastical Institutions* (Part VI of *The Principles of Sociology*). In this essay, he first considered the idea of a modern common faith, a set of beliefs and practices that promotes moral community. He rejected Spencer's view that religion is an exercise in metaphysical speculation about the unknowable. Religion, Durkheim claimed, ought to be seen as the product of habit, "an assembly of ways of acting fixed by custom." Like law or morality, it is "a form of custom." Spencer had predicted that religion in the future would become a "popular metaphysic . . . an assembly of personal judgments." If it were to do so, and lose its "irresistible authority of habit," Durkheim claimed, religion would become "a simple incident of the private life and the individual conscience." Spencer foretold the disappearance of religion as a public institution. This prediction, Durkheim claimed, followed from Spencer's erroneous belief that as civilization increases "the place and importance of custom will decline." Durkheim maintained that the reverse is true. Customs, habits, and, Durkheim added, prejudices will become more, not less, important as civilization increases its stores of knowledge and practices. Durkheim maintained that "In spite of the current meaning of the word, a prejudice [*préjugé*] is not a false judgment, but merely an acquired judgment or one regarded as such. It transmits to us, in an abbreviated form, the results of experiences that others have had and that we ourselves could not begin to have had. . . . A society without prejudices would resemble an organism without reflexes: it would be a monster incapable of living."[7]

Durkheim argued that some form of religion—some set of prejudices, some social discipline—will persist into the future.

"Sooner or later, custom and habit, then, will recover their rights, and this is what authorizes us to presume that religion will survive the attacks of which it is the object. As long as there are people who live together, there will be between them some common faith [*foi commune*]. What we cannot foresee and what only the future can decide is the particular form in which this faith will be symbolized." In this remarkable passage, Durkheim intimated a position that would become the hallmark of his later work: modern European civilizations, in order to remain civil, will require—and to some extent already possess—a common faith, that is, a common set of moral beliefs and practices embedded in traditions and institutions.[8] Durkheim's attempts to describe the strength and nature of those beliefs and practices that unite otherwise disparate modern individuals eventually compelled him to adopt a religious vocabulary—a development I discuss at some length in Chapter 5 below.

II

Social habits and prejudices were useful notions for the early Durkheim. With them he attempted to show that there is no fundamental abyss between the individual and society. We can, of course, describe all sorts of interesting differences between them. Durkheim wanted to foreclose the possibility of positing an unbridgeable gap between an essential natural self and artificial social convention, a gap that places the individual in a natural, ineluctable conflict with society. Classical liberalism has often assumed that the best society is one that sets its members free from social influence. Durkheim, however, wanted us to think of modern, moral individuals not as those who have escaped social "artificialities" in order to recover their natural selves, but as those who, via cultural training, embody social norms and ideals in the form of (often liberal) habits and prejudices. Much of this education takes place unconsciously, without critical reflection. This is not to say that critical thought is insignificant, only that it is one among many sorts of social activity, and that it relies on a provisionally unexamined assortment of background beliefs.

Durkheim's understanding of the social instruction of unwitting individuals may have resulted in part from the influence of Wilhelm Wundt's *Völkerpsychologie*.[9] The individual's mind, according to Wundt, is largely shaped by historical social influences of which the individual is unaware. *Völkerpsychologie* attempted to explicate the operations of individual minds by referring to their culture's collective life. Durkheim was attracted to this aspect of Wundt's work because he wanted to find ways to relate the individual to society. At the same time, however, he did not want to equate the individual *with* society. Durkheim was never interested in a perfect identification between the private and the public. In "La Science positive de la morale en Allemagne," Durkheim sought to find a way to express a normative relation between individuals and society that would avoid treating the individual as either a radically discrete social unit or nothing but a social product. He sought a way to mediate between the claims of individualists and communitarians. According to the individualists, Durkheim noted, "there is nothing real in the world except the individual, and everything is to be related to the individual. Family, country, and humanity are nothing but means to assure the free development of the individual. . . . Nothing exists beyond individual goals." This individualism, wrote Durkheim, "is based on a false metaphysical theory." The self is represented as a "transcendent being, an immutable substance," that is constantly being covered over by social artifice only to be rediscovered, time and again. Under this description, "the self is condemned to gravitate on itself, unable to be attached to anything but itself." Sacrifice and abnegation become nearly impossible because "this substantial entity is not capable of renouncing its nature."[10]

This metaphysical theory, Durkheim claimed, is based on a concept of substance. Some assume that beneath the appearance of various material things is an essential substance waiting to be discovered. This in turn leads them to posit an essential, discrete self that is independent of its environment. In this view, the self is a private, and often a mysterious entity. Durkheim had little use for this position. Someone may be complicated, may be difficult to understand, but insofar as she can be known (say, by her willingness to talk about herself, by our own social skills, or, I might add, by psychoanalysis), she is "directly known to us." We have no need, then, for a metaphysical theory. "The phenomenal reality is sufficient unto itself, and it is not necessary to search beyond it."[11]

This form of individualism, in short, "lacks a theoretical basis." Since the self is "nothing but the phenomenal," it cannot have "the hard-edged contours" that classically have "rendered impossible reciprocal relationships." The self is by and large informed by common ideas and sentiments. This shared cultural inheritance we hold "with our fellows, and above all with those whom we are near, our parents and compatriots." Far from seeing the individual as a disparate entity, the early Durkheim viewed the individual as a radically social being. "From this way of seeing things, then, we are melded together. In a word, we are a lump of impersonal elements and this explains our common nature."[12]

As soon as Durkheim offered this social description of the individual, he qualified it. He did not want to suggest that "the human personality disappears in the bosom of the collective being, able to make only superficial modifications." Durkheim avoided sociological determinism by articulating a description of individual creativity and freedom in an idiom that resembles, at least on its face, the Kantian individualist's notion of the will: "It is the will that prevents [the human personality] from dissolving into the milieu that surrounds it."[13] Still, Durkheim went on to write, "once the will emerges, it reacts in turn on all those phenomena that come to it from outside and that are the common inheritance of society; it makes them its own." Durkheim thus gave an interesting twist to the Kantian notion of the will—a Hegelian one that, again, may be attributable to the influence of Wundt. Kant needed a way to carve out a realm for human (and divine) freedom within a Newtonian, deterministic universe. The Kantian will therefore is situated apart from every form of influence—hence its autonomy. Durkheim, on the other hand, needed a way to make an arena for interaction between the individual and the social milieu, avoiding both radical autonomy and social determinism. The Durkheimian will therefore does not stand apart from every social influence. It is, in fact, initially created in and by the individual's social environment. Yet once "the will emerges," it reacts on the "common inheritance of society" and "makes [it] its own." Rousseau succinctly expressed the apparent paradox that voluntary acts require an initial educative authority when he had the pupil Emile say to his tutor, "I have decided to be what you made me."

Just as, in Durkheim's view, the classical account of the individual neglected the influence of the social environment on the human will, the classical communitarian account neglected the freedom of the individual. "Like Hegel," he wrote, communitarians make "the personality into a mere appearance, they cannot recognize its moral value. They do not see that if the individual receives much from society, he does not then stop reacting to it." Communitarians have difficulty accounting for those "great men" who have wielded tremendous influence on society. But Durkheim believed that communitarians were correct in arguing that the "powerful personalities" who transform society do not rise above their social milieu, escaping history. Geniuses, by Durkheim's lights, are firmly rooted in history. Gathering the "ideas and sentiments that remain tacit and dormant in society, focusing these," they are able to add something new to society. Geniuses thus become the "living conscience of society, which is transformed by their actions." Moreover, all of us, not just the geniuses, are not only made by but are makers of society. Even if we do not stir an entire population, we each in our own way jolt the spheres of our being, our "family, community, corporation, and so on."[14]

Durkheim's notion of the will and its social situation, as he articulated it in "La Science positive," most immediately resembled Wundt's voluntaristic account of people thinking up new "syntheses" from discrete social elements. The individual, according to Wundt, stands somewhat apart from its *Volksseele* (group mind) by private volition. The elements of the mind, its beliefs, thinking patterns, hopes, and so on, spring from the *Volksseele,* and the mind in turn creates new syntheses—all kinds of inventions and novelties. There can be little doubt that Wundt's notion of *Volksseele* and its relation to the will was inspired by Hegel.[15] In this essay, however, Durkheim was not concerned with acknowledging the debts his thought owed to others in the tradition within which he worked. Rather, he was trying to work creatively within that tradition, which stretched from Kant through Hegel to more contemporary thinkers. Consequently he could be critical of both the classical Kantian notion of the autonomous will and the Hegelian tendency to absorb the individual will into the community. For us, the chief interest lies not in adjudicating Durkheim's place in that tradition, but in bringing forward what is most valuable in what he made of it.

The chief accomplishment of the early Durkheim, I think, is his description of what the most distinguished current critic of Hegel has called "the situated freedom" of the individual who is both at home in society and able to transform it. Charles Taylor contrasts situated freedom, free activity grounded in and emerging from "our life as embodied social beings," to modern notions of freedom that "see it as something men win through to by setting aside obstacles or breaking loose from external impediments, ties or entanglements." In this account, freedom is understood as "self-dependence," to be "untrammelled, to depend in one's action only on oneself." [16] Hegel, Taylor notes, rejected this radical freedom. Absolute freedom is empty. It would require that we be free from all situations, because a situation entails predicaments and dilemmas that demand of us a limited range of responses.

Freedom from situations, therefore, sounds a lot like freedom from life. A person who loves and hates things is trammelled. Consequently, anyone who could experience complete freedom would be missing loves and hates that we normally associate with actual human beings. I do not mean particular loves and hates, but any and all such relations. If someone loves, say, Dickens and hates Milton, then she is not free to prefer *Paradise Lost* to *David Copperfield*. Any love, any hate, excludes certain beliefs and actions. Complete freedom requires that we lose our loves and hates, and this is a good description of how to lose our selves. Complete freedom seems to require something not larger than life but closer to death. The more conditions we satisfy for radical self-dependence, the less we find of ourselves to depend on.

Hegel understood as much, and Durkheim, I want to suggest, made the Hegelian turn to situated freedom. To be free, by Durkheim's lights, is to respond to our cultural inheritance. [17] Our language, institutions, beliefs and practices—these are the given. We all begin here. We go on to react to the given, to put our stamp on it, and to revise it, however slightly or significantly, so that those after us receive a somewhat changed world. Durkheim, then, like Hegel, situated human action and freedom in specific narratives and histories. Both Hegel and Durkheim historicized Kant, but Hegel transformed Kant's Universal Reason into an historical epic with the Perfect Ending, until

Nietzsche and company came along to interrupt Hegel's story, cutting off its climax, Absolute Knowledge. Durkheim, like Nietzsche, would have nothing to do with Hegel's ontology, his fanciful Geist. Nietzsche sought to free individuals from all prearranged plans—whether those of Geist or God or liberal humanism—so that individuals might radically recreate themselves in their own images. Durkheim, in contrast, wanted to locate individuals more securely in their particular culture's narratives and institutions. In this he went further than Hegel in historicizing Kant. Hegel's history of consciousness preserved, in Geist, an absolute origin and destination; Durkheim claimed humans are contingent historical creatures from beginning to end.

In Durkheim's hands there remained neither Kant's Universal Reason nor Hegel's sweeping Geist, but just history—history without philosophical or theological foundations. Both Nietzsche and Durkheim took this historicism as their starting point to combat essentialist views of human nature, whether liberal or communitarian. For Nietzsche, something like absolute freedom was the goal. Durkheim had a different mission. He was not combating liberal humanists eager to impose their morality, including democracy, on the masses; he was combating classical liberal economists like Herbert Spencer, who wanted to release modern societies from the social conventions and practices that prevent rational individuals from effectively pursuing private interest. Their hope always has been in the ahistorical rational agent, free from social prejudices and government intervention, and guided by self-interest. Their prescription for a happy and spontaneously harmonious society Durkheim found troubling. He did not believe there ever could be ahistorical rational agents. History shapes humans, and to take them out of history is to deprive them of their humanity. While both Nietzsche and the classical economists, for different reasons, cursed the extent to which humans are trammelled by social beliefs and practices, Durkheim celebrated it, claiming that our moral ideals and much of our joy spring from our cultural *Sitz im Leben*. Still, Durkheim worried that narcissistic aestheticism and economic greed could become institutionalized should the aesthete and the consumer become the new social heroes.

When many wanted to "free" individuals from social beliefs

and practices, Durkheim sought to situate individuals in a common, liberal, cultural inheritance. Language and beliefs, traditions and social practices—Durkheim shows how these contribute to who we are, and how we contribute to what they are to become. This is far from social determinism. Durkheim shows that we make new webs of belief as often as we traverse old ones. Autonomy is not absent from Durkheim's description of humans in action, but autonomy, for Durkheim, no longer refers to being free from influences. It refers, rather, to the freedom to understand how one has been influenced, and then to go on to influence others, often in novel and critical ways. "Moral philosophy," as Durkheim concluded in "La Science positive," can "make room for both the whole and the part, the individual and society."

I take Durkheim as having said that moral philosophy should take into account the various ways the individual is normatively related to society, without either identifying or severing the private and the public. This strikes me as a sane policy, especially in the light of debate between present-day liberals and communitarians. Many in the liberal camp still think of something like radical self-dependence when they speak of individual autonomy and celebrate diversity. Rational-choice and game theorists often leave out of their formulae "contingencies" such as the individual's traditional beliefs and commitments. The communitarian rejoinder is to speak of constituted selves, and to highlight the woes of pluralism. Durkheim, in his day, faced similar alternatives, and chose to find a way around them. He did so by locating autonomy within situated freedom, and by celebrating diversity within social membership. As I will argue below, his position satisfies the liberals' love of self-expression, as well as the communitarians' longing for socially related individuals—even some communitarians' desire for a sociolinguistic epistemology.

III

The early Durkheim was not always consistent about the extent to which the shaped will can reshape its social inheritance. Sometimes he suggested that the individual can introduce significant changes by "free burst of will"; other times he asserted that "everything occurs mechanically." [18] These two extreme positions, however, are not indicative of the principal position that emerges out of his early writing about the relation between the individual and society. He searched for a way to preserve the relative autonomy of the individual, given his social descriptions of the individual. An emphasis on the role of social habits and prejudices in the spontaneous behavior of the individual represents one of Durkheim's tactics. The moral individual, via cultural training, spontaneously acts morally. Kant would have the individual act morally in society without being influenced by society. Durkheim claimed, however, that morality is socially construed. To ask the individual to elude social prejudice is to ask the individual to elude morality and ultimately the self. "The individual is an integral part of the society into which he is born; the latter penetrates him from every side; to isolate and separate oneself from it is to diminish oneself." [19]

The complementary tactic, in Durkheim's early accounts of individual will, was to emphasize the individual's natural, instinctual predisposition toward the social. From the start, Durkheim opposed classical Hobbesian thought. Society is not the result of individuals self-consciously sacrificing their natural freedoms and inclinations for the sake of security and rights. Society, in other words, inflicts no violence on human nature. It is the spontaneous product of human nature. To support this contention, the early Durkheim claimed that individuals are naturally endowed with social sentiments. "There exists," he wrote in agreement with Alfred Espinas's *Les Sociétés animales*, ". . . a need of sociability and of social instincts that are absolutely disinterested. In order to satisfy them people form larger and larger societies." [20]

This is not an isolated example. The early Durkheim frequently endorsed theories about natural sentiments. Often, however, while discussing natural sentiments, Durkheim would discount their importance in favor of customs and social beliefs. For instance, while arguing that moral sentiments are not derived solely from religious sentiments, Durkheim stated that "there have been, since the very beginning, social inclinations that have their source in human nature itself. Everyone has in effect a natural inclination for its fellow-creature that manifests itself when some individuals aim at living together, which is to

say, from the first days of humanity."[21] Then Durkheim immediately qualified this by saying "What brings one another together, then, is not, as it is sometimes said, blood relations, but
similar language, habits, and customs." Individuals, because
they are human, act naturally when they exhibit social behavior.
Society, then, does not require individuals to renounce their nature. Human nature is inherently social. Yet individuals, because they are also members of a particular community, are knit
together by common language, habits, and customs. In this interpretation, social sentiments account only for a rudimentary
human sociability. They do not account for the specific and more
profound forms of solidarity achieved by a shared history and
common beliefs and practices.

The vocabulary of social sentiments allowed Durkheim to
make two related claims: (1) the individual does not inordinately
sacrifice its autonomy in society, since (2) social participation is
a natural inclination. But the early Durkheim, to his credit,
never specified the nature of these sentiments. He may have
sensed that the very notion of built-in inclinations would cause
more problems than it would solve. Later, in *The Division of Labor*, Durkheim explicitly rejected Spencer's position that modern
societies are held together by natural social sentiments. Solidarity is more precarious than that. It requires more than our being
told it will occur naturally. Durkheim would later write of "the
infinite diversity of the aspects that human nature can take
on."[22] Still, for the early Durkheim, natural social sentiments
represented an attempt, however flawed, to conceive of a harmonious relation between the individual and society, between
the private and the public. This is not to say that all conflict
dropped out of Durkheim's theoretical description of individuals in society. Early on, Durkheim recognized edifying and destructive conflicts between the private and the public. He
wanted to show, however, that there is no natural, fatal antagonism between them. This, then, represents a step toward moral
individualism: individuals who are innately social. The mature
Durkheim persisted in describing individuals as naturally social.
Yet in later accounts this sociability is not due to built-in sentiments, but to the absence of such sentiments: human beings are
naturally in need of social education and relations, not naturally
equipped with the results of these. Without social involvement

Homo sapiens are not human, but something else—perhaps a monstrosity.

Durkheim modulated the themes and strategies I have identified in his early writing when he published his doctoral dissertation, *The Division of Labor in Society,* in 1893. Unlike Nietzsche, Durkheim wrote with an eye on public policy, and he had come to fear that the doctrines of the classical economists posed the greatest threat to social justice. He believed their prescriptions would lead modern industrial societies toward egoism and that their advocacy of a minimalist government would create unjust social conditions. Durkheim's effort to do battle with the economists' rational-choice model of ahistorical agents pursuing self-interest led him temporarily away from the many sensible things he had written earlier about situated freedom. He did not altogether abandon the notion of situated freedom, but he did at times write of mechanistic, social forces that determine individuals' paths. The concept of the situated will, so important to the early and late Durkheim, was temporarily obscured in *The Division of Labor.* This partial eclipse is not evidence of Durkheim's conversion to Adam Smith's and Herbert Spencer's faith in benevolent invisible hands. If Durkheim drifted toward social determinism, it was because he wanted to counter the radical voluntarism of Spencer and the classical economists. *The Division of Labor* was a result of Durkheim's opposition to laissez-faire liberalism, and should be read with this in mind.

We can think of moral individualism as having two components, the first one being the principal element. Moral individualism is characterized by (1) a set of social beliefs and practices that constitute a pervasive shared understanding or common faith that supports the rights and dignity of the individual; and (2) a plurality of social spheres that permits diversity and individual autonomy, and that furnishes beliefs and practices that morally associate individuals occupying a particular sphere. Although we can see in Durkheim's early work steps toward this conception in its complete form, moral individualism in this form is not found in the work of the early Durkheim or in *The Division of Labor in Society.* Instead, in this body of work we see Durkheim emphasizing first one component, then the other. The first and more significant component, briefly mentioned and then rejected in *The Division of Labor,* was developed in the

Dreyfusard article, "Individualism and the Intellectuals" (1898) after having been initially proposed in *Suicide* the preceding year. The second and ancillary component was explored in *The Division of Labor* and later enhanced in *Suicide* and especially in Durkheim's lectures on "Professional Ethics and Civic Morals"—lectures written around the same time as the Dreyfusard article.

A communitarian defense of liberalism requires both components. The first element ensures that a diverse citizenry cares for a common political community that is sustained by, among other things, beliefs pertaining to the sanctity of the individual. The second element ensures that as individuals pursue their rights, they reside within a multitude of relatively distinct social spheres that provide them with shared meanings and identities, not within an increasingly contracted private space, sharing less and less with one another.

The early Durkheim's concept of situated freedom and his emphasis on social customs and sentiments underscored the ways that individuals are intimately related by social strands, yet not radically determined by them. It contributed to the development of the first component of moral individualism. Although Durkheim went so far as to claim that all societies, including modern ones, possess a common (albeit variable) faith, at this point he was not prepared to specify the existence of a modern liberal faith centered on the rights and dignity of the individual. The path that led him to the point where he was ready to do so began with *The Division of Labor* and its concept of organic solidarity, a concept that, when correctly understood, can be seen as contributing the basis for the second component of moral individualism.

In *The Division of Labor* Durkheim found himself on the horns of a dilemma. He wanted to continue to open up space for individual autonomy, while at the same time he wanted to challenge Spencer's privatistic description of and prescription for modern society. His response to this dilemma occasionally led him into inconsistencies, especially when he moved toward social determinism as he combated Spencer's voluntarism. Still, I want to suggest that Durkheim was successful, if we take organic solidarity as the chief result of his efforts. Organic solidarity is commonly understood as an interdependence between discrete individuals produced by morphological elements such as population densities. I will argue that we ought to interpret organic solidarity as a moral, social environment that relates individuals to a plurality of morals obtaining in diverse social settings—as in fact Durkheim's first exploration of the second component of moral individualism.

IV

Spencer argued that societies have advanced from an "incoherent homogeneity" to a "coherent heterogeneity." In the former mode of organization, "militant" traditional societies are maintained by "compulsory cooperation." In the latter, modern, industrial societies are maintained by "voluntary cooperation."[23] Voluntary cooperation, such as citizens entering into contracts, requires no regulation except perhaps the enforcement of the contract. "The checks," Spencer asserted, "naturally arising to each man's actions when men become associated, are those only which result from mutual limitations; and there consequently can be no resulting check to the contracts they voluntarily make."[24] Regulation, in Spencer's view, would topple industrial nations, returning them to a state of oppressive, "militant" life. Moreover, government intervention in the form of social welfare would prevent the salutary effects of natural selection. Of the "paupers' friends," Spencer declared,

Blind to the fact, that under the natural order of things, society is constantly excreting its unhealthy, imbecile, slow, vacillating, faithless members, these unthinking, though well-meaning men advocate an interference which not only stops the purifying process, but even increases the vitiation—absolutely encourages the multiplication of the reckless and incompetent by offering them an unfailing provision, and *dis*courages the multiplication of the competent and provident by heightening the prospective difficulty of maintaining a family. And thus, in their eagerness to prevent the really salutary sufferings that surround us, these sigh-wise and groan-foolish people bequeath to posterity a continually increasing curse.[25]

The healthy society, according to Spencer, allows individuals freedom to pursue their self-interest. It is axiomatic that from such spontaneity "coherent heterogeneity" will emerge. Spencer took this to be, for the most part, an apt description of modern societies, especially of England. These are the truly happy societies.

Durkheim disagreed on two counts. The individual pursuit of

self-interest does not by itself automatically produce social harmony and human joy, but more likely leads to social chaos and
unhappiness. Second, modern societies are not the laissez-faire
liberal models Spencer claimed they are. There are numerous
constraints on the modern individual. Some of these constraints
are of an explicit, overt nature, such as state laws. Others are of
an implicit, covert nature, such as social obligations not written
into contracts. These constraints, Durkheim tells us, have a social origin. They are derived from that repository of a culture's
experience in history known as tradition.

An examination of Durkheim's critique of Spencer will help
us grasp the steps toward articulating the second component of
moral individualism that Durkheim took in *The Division of Labor*.
He accurately portrayed Spencer's description of modern industrial solidarity as spontaneous, and wrote that in this view
"there is no need for any coercive apparatus either to produce it
or to maintain it. Society has therefore no need to interfere in
order to effect a harmony that is established of its own accord."
Presumably, individuals are increasingly liberated from social
influence, except insofar as society protects their legal rights. Society "would no longer be a regulating mechanism save in a negative way." We can think of it like this: the social contract of
Rousseau, which stresses a common good distinct from self-
interest, is replaced by private contracts. "Social solidarity,"
Durkheim claimed, "'would be nothing more than the spontaneous agreement between individual interests." Social relations
would become economic in nature, and, in short, "society
would be no more than the establishment of relationships between individuals exchanging the products of their labor, and
without any social actions, properly so termed, intervening to
regulate that exchange."[26]

Durkheim questioned the accuracy of Spencer's description
of modern industrial societies. If Spencer was correct, then "one
might reasonably doubt their stability."

For if mutual interest draws men closer, it is never more than for a few
moments. It can only create between them an external link. In the fact
of exchange the various agents remain outside one another, and when
the operation is over, each one finds himself entirely alone. Consciences are only superficially in contact; they neither penetrate nor
strongly adhere to one another. Indeed, if we look to the heart of the

matter we shall see that every harmony of interest conceals a latent conflict, or one that is simply deferred. For where interest alone reigns . . .
each self finds itself in relation to the other in a state of war, and any
truce in this perpetual antagonism cannot be of long duration. Self-
interest is, in fact, the least constant thing in the world. Today it is useful for me to unite with you; tomorrow the same reason will make me
your enemy.[27]

Durkheim claimed that where private interest does have a free
reign, deleterious effects follow.

In Durkheim's view, lack of social regulation has given rise to
two pathological forms in the division of labor that characterizes
modern societies. The first, which Durkheim called the anomic
division of labor, refers to social discord precipitated by lack of
governance over new economic activities and relations spawned
by the Industrial Revolution. Durkheim cited as an example the
growing "hostility between labor and capital." As a result of lack
of regulation, contracts between employees and employers are
often unjust, and employees are treated like machines:

[Unlike present conditions, a humane] division of labor supposes that
the worker, far from remaining bent over his task, does not lose sight of
those cooperating with him, but that he and they interact together. He
is not therefore a machine who repeats movements the meaning of
which he does not perceive, but he knows that they are tending in a
certain direction, toward a goal that he can conceive of more or less
distinctly. He feels that he is offering something.

Wholesome working conditions could have been assured if
"they [the classical economists] had not reduced it [the division
of labor] to being only a way of increasing the efficiency of the
social forces, but had seen it above all as a source of solidarity."[28]

The second pathological form, the forced division of labor,
can be thought of as a subdivision of the anomic form. It refers
specifically to the extortion imposed on laborers by employers.
Workers, given their powerless position, are often coerced to
embrace oppressive jobs and conditions. Enforced contracts between employee and employer support unjust inequalities insofar as the social structures and contracts are themselves unjust. "It is not enough," wrote Durkheim, "for rules to exist, for
at times it is these very rules that are the cause of evil. This is
what happens in the class wars." As long as the employers,
those of the privileged class, determine "the rules," a forced di-

vision of labor will continue. "If one class in society is obliged, in order to live, to take any price for its services, while another class can pass over this situation, because of the resources already at its disposal, resources that, however, are not necessarily the result of some social superiority, the latter group has an unjust advantage over the former with respect to the law." Social regulations need to be established that promise "greater equality in our social relationships" and a just "distribution of social functions."[29]

It is safe to say, then, that Durkheim's disagreement with Spencer over the nature of modern societies did not amount to a celebration of the status quo. After all, Durkheim concluded *The Division of Labor* with three chapters on "Abnormal Forms" of the division of labor.[30] The social harmony of industrial nations (insofar as there is any) is not based, empirically speaking, exclusively on the pursuit of self-interest. Where self-interest does dominate, injustice and unhappiness prevail. Modern societies suffer when they institutionalize the beliefs and dispositions of Spencer and the classical economists. Whether Durkheim, at this stage, considered modern societies to be more or less abnormal I cannot say. What I can say is that at no point in his career was he satisfied with existing social conditions.

Citing a few examples where "the individual has effectively emancipated himself from collective influences," Spencer claimed to have established that social influence is waning. Durkheim noted, however, that "it is very possible that in one respect social action has regressed while in others it has been enlarged, so that in the end we mistake transformation for disappearance." A better way to judge the presence of collective influence, he believed, is to trace historically "the apparatus through which social action is essentially exerted," namely, through the law.[31]

Durkheim claimed that the law, a significant indicator of social authority, has become more important and pervasive in modern industrial societies, not less. "If repressive law is losing ground, restitutory law, which in the beginning did not exist at all, is continually growing."[32] Though Durkheim's evolutionary claim is controversial and even doubtful, his distinction between repressive and restitutory law is nevertheless provocative.

Repressive law, or penal law, "consists essentially in some injury, or at least some disadvantage imposed upon the perpetrator of a crime."[33] It is the prevalent juridical form found in societies marked by mechanical solidarity, that is, in societies whose solidarity is generated by similarity. Given a limited division of labor, any member of these societies can perform practically any social task. And the members' similarity is not limited to their labor. They all essentially share a common conscience, *la conscience commune*. Because they share the same beliefs, goals, sentiments, and tasks, any crime is considered an offense against all, against the common conscience. The offender, unable to make amends to a particular individual or subgroup because of the universal interpretation of the offense, is punished by repressive law.

Restitutory law, on the other hand, allows a perpetrator "to *restore things as they were*, re-establishing relationships that have been disturbed from their normal form."[34] Restitutory law, consisting of civil, commercial, procedural, administrative and constitutional law, is the prevalent juridical form found in societies marked by organic solidarity, that is, in societies whose solidarity is generated in part by difference. Given a complex division of labor, each member of these societies performs a specialized task. And the members' dissimilarity is not limited to labor alone. The common conscience, though not altogether absent, is weak and diffuse. This in itself, however, does not jeopardize social cohesion, because specialization produces a new form of solidarity, that of cooperation and interdependence. An offense committed in a society marked by organic solidarity is usually not understood as an offense against all, but against a particular individual or segment of society. The offender, able to make amends to an individual or organization subsisting within a particular social sphere, is required by restitutory law to "restore things as they were."

The nature of professional ethics is similar to that of restitutory law. "Where restitutory law is very developed, for each profession a professional morality exists. Within the same group of workers a public opinion exists, diffused throughout this limited body, which despite the lack of any legal sanctions, is nevertheless obeyed. There are customs and usages common to the same group of functionaries which none can infringe without incurring the reprimand of the corporation."[35] The specificity of restitutory law in no way implies that it governs an atomistic society. Professional ethics and civic laws are categorical, that is, "they force the individual to act in accordance with ends that are not his proper, to make concessions, to agree to compromises, to take into account interests superior to his own."[36] Social forces, then, even if particularized, are effectual in modern industrial nations. The individual, far from being "emancipated" from social influence, is closely governed by specific laws and customs that obtain in specific social spheres. This influence goes far beyond the explicit regulation spelled out in contracts. Modern society "does not resolve itself into a myriad of atoms juxtaposed together, between which only external and transitory contact can be established. The members are linked by ties that extend well beyond the very brief moment when the act of exchange is being accomplished."[37]

Durkheim did maintain that "it is the division of labor that is increasingly fulfilling the role that once fell to the common consciousness." Never, however, did he say that modern individuals live increasingly outside the social: "although these [restitutory] rules are more or less outside the collective consciousness, they do not merely concern private individuals. . . . The law is pre-eminently a social matter."[38] The perpetrator of a restitutive crime still offends, even if the offense is felt only in a particular social sphere. Moreover, the collective consciousness, the set of beliefs and sentiments shared by the average members of society, is not entirely absent in modern societies. A murderer, for example, offends the entire society—the collective consciousness—and hence is punished by repressive law.

In modern societies, then, individuals dwell in a plurality of spheres of social influence. Moreover, these spheres are relatively united by some common pursuits and beliefs. Government, for example, becomes an increasingly important vehicle in modern societies for promoting a common moral life, a common good: "There is above all one organ in regard to which our state of dependence continues to grow: this is the state. The points where we come into contact with it are multiplied, as well as the occasions when it is charged with reminding us of the sentiment of our common solidarity."[39]

By arguing that restitutory law is a significant social force in the modern individual's life, Durkheim challenged Spencer's claim that the unity of modern societies springs from private, free economic exchanges. This was the design of his first argument against Spencer. His second argument claimed that even if solidarity were based on private contracts, a contract severed from its social matrix would be confusing at best, unjust at worse, "for in a contract not everything is contractual."[40] Rules belong to contexts as much as they govern them. In fact, we can understand rules as an expression of a social context. They cannot subsist outside one, much less create one. To understand as much is to balk at Spencer's conception of contract making as an essentially private affair. Contracts, then, are rooted in their native social milieu. Durkheim underscored the sociohistorical nature of the contract when he pointed out that contractual law, for instance, is not the result of individual reflection. "Epitomizing numerous, varied experiences, it foresees what we could not do individually; what we could not regulate is regulated, and this regulation is mandatory upon us, although it is not our handiwork, but that of society and tradition."[41]

V

Some call the social, regulatory forces described in *The Division of Labor* nonrational, and claim that Durkheim advocated "instrumentalist reasoning" to insure collective order by means of mechanical adaptation.[42] This assessment, I suspect, is partly based on a liberal, Enlightenment view of rationality that considers nonrational any action or belief not explicitly generated by the autonomous individual's consciously held reasons. No doubt Durkheim did on occasion suggest in *The Division of Labor* that society is guided by mechanistic laws divorced from human desires, customs, or beliefs and based on material density or other "morphological" elements.[43] Yet there is another stream of thought running through *The Division of Labor*. It suggests that in addition to morphological or material conditions, cultural beliefs and prejudgments culled from human experiences and embedded in living traditions play an enormous role in shaping societies and their members. It is this stream of thought that prevailed in Durkheim's later writings, and that connects them with his earlier work.

Both Durkheim's positing of mechanistic laws and his insis-

tence on the determinative role of cultural traditions run in opposition to classical liberal thought. The two streams actually
present alternatives to two standard lines of liberal thought. The
first stream is an alternative to the position taken by classical
economists, who declare that if individuals rationally pursue
their own self-interest then a harmonious society will spontaneously occur. Moral and financial equilibrium, they contend, is
the automatic consequence of unfettered, individual economic
rationality. Durkheim argued, however, that social equilibria are
the result, not of enlightened self-interest, but of mechanistic
social forces that determine individual action. These social
forces spring from social morphological features and not from
individual choices. I am arguing here against those who think
Durkheim was oddly Spencerian when he talked of automatic
social self-adjustments. Spencer asserted that social harmony is
guaranteed by individuals freely entering into private contracts.
Durkheim inverted this argument, claiming that social harmony,
including making and keeping contracts, is the result of mechanistic social forces above and beyond spontaneous individual
choice.

Durkheim's second stream of thought is an alternative to the
position taken by those Kantian liberals who long for a society
based on transcendent first principles embraced by free rational
agents.[44] They contend that the harmonious, moral society will
arrive when the yoke of tradition and opinion—the curse of history—is cast off, freeing ahistorical moral reasoning. Opposing
this view, Durkheim argued that moral reasoning is a result of
moral social traditions. Humans are naturally social creatures.
The attempt to sever individuals from their social biographies is
probably futile. If it is successful, it appears demonic, as when a
torturer "reprograms" an individual. Moreover, individuals are
often unaware of many of their deep-seated moral prejudices. It
is simply impossible to unearth the entire social background of
our institutions, practices, and beliefs. We can appreciate the efforts of writers like Foucault who are experts in such archaeol-
ogy, and who dig up the past to understand better the present.
Portions of a culture's implicit thought can always be made explicit, but not all, and certainly not all at once. As we expose
some segments, we necessarily modify others. What I am calling
the second stream of Durkheim's thought, then, does not con-

tain the deterministic or mechanistic elements that run in the first stream. We can expose and scrutinize and revise our moral traditions and practices, but we cannot and should not want to cast them all off. Trying to do so cuts us off from the source of our individual and social being, and places us in a politically and morally dangerous condition.[45]

Both Durkheimian streams of thought introduce a hermeneutic of suspicion. The classical economists and the Kantians assume that individuals can be fully aware of their motivations for action. But Durkheim, along with Freud and others, suggests that these models of human action are naive. We often do not know why we do what we do. Both streams, then, challenge the liberal penchant to understand action as a result of private minds. Yet the first stream should not be confused with the second. The first one is optimistic, like many Enlightenment projects. Instead of Reason, however, natural social mechanisms set things straight. Nature becomes the new guarantor of social well-being. During times of social transition such as the Industrial Revolution there may be considerable disorder and misery. But do not attempt to improve society, the mechanistic argument counsels, it is inscrutable and too complex. Social tampering, including Spencer's agitation for a minimalist government, is likely to make a bad situation worse. Just wait, because equilibria will be restored naturally. That's the law of nature, the way of societies.

The second stream of thought, which prevails in Durkheim's work outside *The Division of Labor* and *The Rules of Sociological Method*, contains no such guarantee for social well-being. We find in it nothing analogous to the Enlightenment's universal reason. Instead we find radical contingency. Durkheim invited us to think of societies and individuals as strands of cultural institutions and beliefs. They surround us and provide us with the moral fabric for our ordinary lives and our extraordinary dilemmas, for our instruction to children and our arguments to graduate students. These strands of beliefs and practices clothe us, envelop us, inform us—not mysteriously or inscrutably or irrationally, but implicitly. Any portion of the implicit, however, can be made explicit, and is thereby subject to revision. It is this capacity for ad hoc reformation that Durkheim put in the place of ahistorical reason, especially in his later writings.

This line of thought seems to put Durkheim in the communitarian camp. They, too, reject Kantian optimism, often preferring to call rationality the contingent beliefs of a particular people at a particular time. And they, like Durkheim, understand moral reasoning as so many narratives shaping our moral vision. A stable society, then, requires something like the preventive maintenance of its narratives—telling "the story" again and again to citizens, especially to future citizens. But this is where the family resemblance between Durkheim and many communitarians begins to fade. For Durkheim, "the story"—actually a host of narratives—is mutable. Reformation, according to Durkheim's second stream of thought, is both inevitable and subject to human desire and aspirations. The emergent will can say something new, creating novelties while reforming aspects of "the story" that no longer serve our highest moral ideals. Moreover, Durkheim increasingly identified the reformist, Kantian, liberal ideals centered on the rights and dignity of the individual as the most compelling ideals toward which modern industrial societies could work. This involves societal self-examination, and the active pursuit of social justice. Here, then, is where Durkheim departs from conservative communitarianism, as well as from Spencerian, as opposed to Kantian, liberalism.

In summing up his arguments against Spencer, Durkheim insisted that "the contract is not sufficient" and that "the role of society cannot be reduced to a passive one of seeing that contracts are carried out." Society must take an active role to prevent social injustice, especially in cases of immoral "legal" contracts. For example, "a contract, states Spencer, has the purpose of ensuring for the workman expenditure on his behalf equivalent to what his labor has caused him."[46] Yet even if this were the main function of the contracts, more rigorous social regulation would be required, according to Durkheim. "For it would indeed be a miracle if it [the contract] could guarantee to produce such equivalence. . . . The disproportion is often glaring. But, replies a whole school, if the gains are too small, the functions will be abandoned for others. . . . It is forgotten that one whole part of the population cannot thus quit its task, because no other is accessible to it. Even those possessing more freedom of mobility cannot replace it in an instant."[47] Over and above so-called private contracts, then, there are "rules of justice that social justice must prevent being violated, even if a clause has been agreed by the parties concerned." Intervention, guided by traditions aiming at social justice, must prevail "to determine the manner in which we should co-operate together." Durkheim asks that we not simply wait for an equilibrium to be established automatically by economic laws. Too much human misery is at stake. Our task is to insure greater justice in our social relationships and arrangements. And that task requires much activity. This activity includes, but is by no means exhausted by, government intervention in the form of "the education of the young, protecting health generally, presiding over the functioning of the public assistance system or managing the transport and communications systems."[48] This notion of an expanding state is in stark contrast to Spencer's minimalist state.

Durkheim's arguments about modern societies were directed at Tönnies as well as Spencer. In *Community and Society [Gemeinschaft und Gesellschaft]*, Tönnies presented an opposing view to Spencer's belief that industrial societies have advanced from an "incoherent homogeneity" to a "coherent heterogeneity." Traditional societies, argued Tönnies, enjoy wholesome community marked by cooperation. Modern societies, in contrast, exhibit destructive individualism marked by competition. They have moved, then, from a coherent homogeneity to an incoherent heterogeneity. Both Tönnies and Spencer characterized modern societies as the result of the pursuit of private interest. Durkheim denied that the vocabulary of self-interest can adequately describe modern, industrial societies. It lacks reference to those pervasive, moral social forces that are distinctive of modern existence. Yet Tönnies lamented what Spencer celebrated. Durkheim wept with Tönnies. He agreed that insofar as the vocabulary of the classical economists is adequate, it describes social disorder that results in human misery, not a spontaneous harmony yielding human happiness.[49]

VI

In *The Division of Labor*, Durkheim continued to maintain that modern individuals dwell within cultural traditions, prejudices, and customs, even if at times the thrust of his argument against the classical economists propelled him toward explanations that featured the mechanistic operation of natural social forces. Yet in that work the notion of internalized social dispositions, customs, and habits no longer played a central role in mediating between society and the individual. He also jettisoned the more fanciful notion that built-in social sentiments could play that mediating role. Durkheim believed natural social sentiments were too precarious a base on which to rest the development of moral individuals in what he feared was an era of increasing social fragmentation. Like the mechanistic account of social equilibria, the theory of social sentiments implies that societies flourish naturally. Each member, according to the theory, instinctively seeks charity, justice, and so on. Such universal, natural sentiments are no more plausible than Hobbes's laws of nature or Kant's practical reason.

In *The Division of Labor*, I contend, Durkheim's own account of the way in which morality enters into the behavior of individuals in modern societies was that modern individuals are fashioned morally in that pluralistic social arrangement he called organic solidarity. It was this account, I will argue, that led him toward the second component of moral individualism, a plurality of morally sustaining social spheres. In order to make this case, I need to highlight three related aspects of organic solidarity. First, organic solidarity entailed for Durkheim moral and not merely economic interdependence among individuals. Durkheim tells us, in criticizing Tönnies, that "it is wrong to oppose a society that derives from a community of beliefs to one whose foundation is cooperation, by granting only the first a moral character and seeing in the latter only an economic grouping." The cooperation that organic solidarity establishes is intrinsically moral.[50] Organic solidarity, in other words, refers to a modern moral order, not to a strictly economic one.

Second, organic solidarity presupposes that the division of labor—a cardinal feature of organic solidarity—is embedded in a moral form of life that closely regulates it. Buying a dealership or making a vow, closing a factory or imposing a new tax—all the multifarious dimensions of life in societies marked by an advanced division of labor are morally governed by long-standing traditions as well as by imaginative developments within those traditions. Insofar as this moral governance is absent, modern societies suffer. This moral governance, however, is highly specialized in modern societies. Although it has been informed by wide-ranging traditions, it has adapted those traditions to an array of particularized situations. This leads to the third aspect of organic solidarity, an aspect that subsumes the other two.

It has to do with what Durkheim would later call "moral polymorphism." Within modern society there exist various social spheres and secondary groups. These spheres and groups provide local environments that envelop individuals, and that sustain them with intimate ties and specialized moral education. Organic solidarity, thus understood, joins Durkheim's early work to his later thought. With this concept he attempted, once again, to connect individuals closely to social beliefs, practices, and traditions, while safeguarding pluralism and individual autonomy. He preserved the moral significance of both social diversity and shared understandings when he identified a plurality of moral spheres that support the individual in a host of social settings. This was his first articulation of what I have called the second component of moral individualism. Durkheim would later develop this in *Suicide* and in his lectures on "Professional Ethics and Civic Morals."

Durkheim's account of the fashioning of moral individuals through organic solidarity in *The Division of Labor* had as its premise the assumption that the collective consciousness is waning in modern societies. The diverse pockets of modern moral life, the plurality of morals, supplant the strong collective consciousness of traditional societies. In lieu of a pervasive common morality, modern societies possess skeins of interdependence and specialized social practices and traditions. This would suggest, then, that the first component of moral individualism, a set of pervasive social beliefs and practices that are not limited to this sphere or that, is absent from Durkheim's account of morality in *The Division of Labor*. At one point, however, Durkheim intimated that the collective consciousness has in fact become stronger, at least in one area:

There is indeed one area in which the common consciousness has grown stronger, becoming more clearly delineated, viz., in its view of the individual. As all the other beliefs and practices assume less and less religious a character, the individual becomes the object of a sort of religion. We have a cult of the dignity of the human person, which, like all strong acts of worship, has already acquired its superstitions. If you like, therefore, it is thus a common faith.[51]

This would suggest that modern individuals are shaped by a set of widely shared beliefs and practices about the dignity and worth, the rights and liberties of the individual. These beliefs and practices belong to the common consciousness, and make up a pervasive, common faith, the cult of the individual.

According to Anthony Giddens, "the cult of the individual," as found in *The Division of Labor*, "is the counterpart to the individualization produced by the expansion of the division of labor, and is the main moral support upon which it rests." This estimate is congenial to Steven Fenton. He claims that the "cult of the individual" in *The Division of Labor* is in fact "a new and significant basis of solidarity itself."[52] On this point I do not share Giddens's or Fenton's judgment. Later, of course, Durkheim did understand the cult of the individual as a set of widely shared beliefs and practices that contribute to the foundation of modern democratic morality and that promote solidarity. But in *The Division of Labor* Durkheim stopped well short of that position. His claim that the cult of the individual is a common faith is hardly emphatic: "If you like [*si l'on veut*] . . . [the cult of the individual] is thus a common faith." But more telling than this rhetorical subtlety is what Durkheim says immediately after his tentative assertion.

If the faith [the cult of the individual] is common because it is shared among the community, it is individual in its object. If it impels every will towards the same end, that end is not a social one. . . . It is indeed from society that it draws all this strength, but it is not to society that it binds us: it is to ourselves [*nous-mêmes*]. Thus it does not constitute a truly social link. This is why theorists have been justly reproached with effecting the dissolution of society, because they have made this sentiment the exclusive basis for their moral doctrine. . . . It is the division of labor that is increasingly fulfilling the role that once fell to the common consciousness. This is mainly what holds together social entities in the higher types of society.[53]

Durkheim did not claim that the cult of the individual is the moral basis of social solidarity, and he explicitly criticized those theorists who did. He claimed that the cult of the individual is pervasive yet private. It is not necessarily egoistic, for it bespeaks the dignity of the individual—a genuine good. Yet at this point in Durkheim's career there was no mention of how crimes against the dignity of the individual offend society; there was no discussion of how beliefs about the sacredness of "the individual" unify a people. The cult of the individual was not, here, a "truly social link."

For Durkheim in 1893, the truly social link in modern industrial societies was the division of labor in the context of organic solidarity. That context, I have argued, is all-important. Durkheim opposed the idea that the division of labor in and of itself is moral. He interpreted it as a moral development only insofar as it is embedded in moral institutions. The division of labor, as an economic phenomenon, does not spawn social solidarity. Divorced from moral traditions and practices, and wed to a minimalist laissez-faire state, the division of labor would not yield human happiness. Happiness, as Durkheim understood it, springs from the social and moral fixtures of society. He held that a life informed by customary morality "is also generally more abundant."[54] The rich and diverse moral traditions and practices of organic solidarity, Durkheim maintained in *The Division of Labor*, provide the basic conditions for human joy.

They also provide for individual diversity, preference, and initiative. Organic solidarity, Durkheim wrote, "develops as the individual personality grows stronger."[55] Professional and domestic options, for example, multiply within organic solidarity. These choices, however, in no way take us outside the moral environment of organic solidarity. We choose which social spheres to live and work in, and thereby, "through a voluntary act," accept the concomitant obligations. Such acceptance by no means implies obedience to a Rousseauian social contract. That would require (at least according to a strong communitarian reading of Rousseau) that the individual always yield to a single, common good. In Durkheim's account, however, individuals submit to a host of social agreements—agreements neither as common as Rousseau's social contract nor as private as Spencer's legal contracts.

We can think of organic solidarity, then, as a moral climate that fosters many spheres of social life and shared practices, and that permits various degrees of individual movement between and within these spheres. With this notion Durkheim effectively articulated the second component of moral individualism. Yet the first and primary component, a set of widely shared beliefs and practices derived from tradition and pertaining to the individual, *la personne humaine*, is not found in *The Division of Labor*. A common faith capable of uniting a modern democratic society is not described there. "Justice" is perhaps the only candidate for that position. Yet of justice Durkheim wrote, "Just as ancient peoples had above all need of a common faith to live by, we have need of justice."[56] Here Durkheim, like John Rawls, seems to place justice above a common good or faith. Within a few years of *The Division of Labor*, however, Durkheim would no longer juxtapose justice to a common faith. He would declare justice as a salient feature of a common faith. This, as we will see, became an important strategy in Durkheim's communitarian defense of liberalism.

Liberalism as a Common Faith

FOUR YEARS AFTER *The Division of Labor*, Durkheim published *Suicide* (1897). There is perhaps as much continuity as there is discontinuity between this latter work and his earlier thought. Durkheim was still assailing aspects of classical economic liberalism, and he extended his arguments against it. Yet he no longer understood the cult of the individual as being essentially private. He now described it as a central feature of a public morality able to check excessive individual and corporate egoism in industrial nations. In *The Division of Labor*, Durkheim had claimed that specialized social traditions and practices provide some moral protection from the development of a pathological, Spencerian society. Now, however, he claimed that more is required, and he began to speak of the necessity of shared goals and beliefs, hopes and practices that cut across various social groups and spheres. The cult of the individual—the first and primary component of moral individualism—furnished Durkheim with what he was looking for. He saw it as a hub for a variety of symbols, rites, and beliefs, all of which he was coming to see as spokes converging on a modern common faith. Durkheim did not abandon what I have called the second component of moral individualism, the notion of a plurality of moral spheres, each with its characteristic way of seeing and doing things. In fact, in *Suicide* we find his first extensive treatment of it. He explicitly stated, moreover, that the "political society," especially in the "great modern states," is "too far removed from the individual" to generate sufficient moral interaction.[1] Secondary groups, groups larger than the individual or the family yet smaller than the political society, are needed to create solidarity between individuals and to deliver them from egoism and anomie. It was not until his lectures on professional ethics and civic morals, delivered a year or so after *Suicide*, that Durkheim grasped the integral relation between a strong political community and moral individualism.[2] Still, *Suicide* marks a change in Durkheim's thought. He now believed that in addition to diverse spheres of participation, a widely shared public morality is needed to unite members of disparate groups. Having battled classical liberalism, Durkheim was starting to recognize the indispensability of a vital political community in modern democratic societies. For this, he began to acknowledge, a common faith is required.

I

The principal argument of *Suicide* is well known. Economic prosperity and individual autonomy were supposed to have graced modern industrial nations with private and social happiness. But in the late nineteenth century, suicide rates were rising, which suggests that human happiness was in fact waning. Durkheim gave this account of the phenomenon: in industrial, democratic societies, individuals are unhappy insofar as they lack meaningful participation in collective life, and are imprisoned in their own private space. A chief culprit, but by no means the only one, is "the sphere of trade and industry" in its chronic state of anomie—lawlessness.[3] "For a whole century," Durkheim wrote, "economic progress mainly consisted in freeing industrial relations from all regulation." Government, for example, "instead of regulating economic life, has become its tool and servant." This practice has been encouraged not only by classical liberalism but by that other modern political theory, socialism.

The most opposite schools, orthodox economists and extreme socialists, unite to reduce government to the role of a more or less passive intermediary among the various social functions. The former wish to make it simply the guardian of individual contracts; the latter leave it the task of doing the collective bookkeeping, that is, of recording the demands of consumers, transmitting them to producers, inventorying the total revenue and distributing it according to a fixed formula. But both refuse it any power to subordinate other social organs to itself and to make them converge toward one dominant goal. On both sides, nations are declared to have the single or chief purpose of achieving industrial prosperity; such is the implication of the dogma of economic materialism, the basis of both apparently opposed systems. And because these theories merely express the state of opinion, industry, instead of being still regarded as a means to an end transcending itself, has become the supreme end of individuals and societies alike.[4]

Durkheim was not saying that modern anomie is the result of a purely economic cause. Economic materialism is an ethic of sorts, though an impoverished one. It is a form of life—an evolved set of social institutions and practices—marked by a dearth of shared norms and goals, restraints and relations, other than those of economic rationality. It is an ethic that replaces public virtues with private interests, community with isolated individuals, tutored desires with boundless ones. In a Spencerian liberal state, this ethic recommends a minimalist government that protects individual natural rights, yet it encourages some linkage between public and private to the extent that it sanctions the state's commitment to advance the goals of the business community. Here, and perhaps here alone, the minimalist government is involved with the private sector, and in this case it may be difficult to differentiate the two.

This unhappy, modern ethic (which, though prevalent, is not the only set of goals and practices in modern democratic societies) gives rise to two types of suicide: egoistic and anomic. According to Durkheim, these types are characteristic not only of the dire circumstances of suicide victims but of the general conditions under which most of us live. Egoism and anomie are features of modern industrial societies; they refer to what he called a "current of collective sadness." It is as if the inhabitants of modern societies were the victims and survivors of a storm at sea. We all have been sailing the same ocean, encountering the same heavy winds. Some, for purely accidental reasons, have survived. For reasons that are equally accidental, others have met a harsher fate.

Egoistic suicide, for Durkheim, was one of the moral consequences of atomistic individualism. In modern industrial societies, the cultural trends, patterns of dispositions, and practices of classical economic liberalism place individuals in a state of moral isolation. Separated from meaningful communities and associations, individuals understand themselves as essentially solitary beings. Those who do not participate in communally oriented institutions such as Roman Catholicism are an example. They suffer, because detachment wounds, and some seek to escape this suffering in death. But their death sums up their identity: they die as solitary beings, cut off from meaningful social life.

Anomic suicide sums up the suffering that results from a different mode of modern social existence. Classical liberal society places individuals in a state of deregulation, as well as of isolation. The result is a sense of social lawlessness and disorder, or to put it more accurately and just a little ironically, a sense that social chaos is the distinctive pattern of modern social life. Freed from the regulation of social ideals and constraints, public goals and commitments, individuals suffer from the feeling that life lacks purpose, and that all desire is ephemeral. Those involved in industrial and commercial occupations that are subject to little regulation, for example, are more likely to commit suicide than those in agriculture, "where the old regulative forces still make their appearance felt and where the fever of business has least penetrated." "Feverish impatience" brings disillusionment, for one "cannot in the end escape the futility of an endless pursuit." Some do not endure their suffering. Their death sums up their sense of their identity as well. Its purposelessness repeats their sense of modern social life.

Egoistic and anomic suicide also can be understood in terms of the binary opposites Durkheim contrasted to each. The opposite of egoistic suicide, altruistic suicide, occurs when individuals are not sufficiently differentiated from their community or society. Social integration is too strong, and individuals lose themselves entirely in the life of the group. While modern manifestations exist, this is less characteristically a modern phenomenon. An example is the practice of suttee, in which a Hindu widow "willingly" cremates herself on her husband's funeral pyre. Without her husband (that is, without her social role as wife) she loses her raison d'être. The opposite of anomic suicide, fatalistic suicide, occurs when individuals are crushed by excessive social control, by "excessive physical or moral despotism," as Durkheim put it, not set adrift from all social regulation.[5] Durkheim cited the suicide of slaves as an example. This too, Durkheim believed, is less characteristic of modern societies.

Egoistic and anomic suicide thus can be distinguished from each other, and the distinction is not merely analytic, since Durkheim gave examples of individuals who suffered from one form of suicidal pathology and not the other. But for Durkheim, the distinction between them was less important than their prevalence. He usually described egoism and anomie as "merely two different aspects of one social state." Modern industrial nations possess both egoistic and anomic social currents, and individuals in these societies experience both moral isolation and a lack of appropriate social goals. The prevalence of egoistic and anomic suicide was for Durkheim a symptom of the destructive effects these currents have had on modern industrial society at large.

The suicide rates of contemporary European societies, Durkheim claimed, are abnormally high: "in less than fifty years, they have tripled, quadrupled, and even quintupled, depending on the country." He concluded that "our social organization must have changed profoundly in the course of this century, to have been able to cause such a growth in the suicide-rate."[6] Though social change is inevitable, rapid change can cause a morbid disturbance. The abrupt social and industrial changes of the nineteenth century have "uprooted the institutions of the past" and have "put nothing in their place; for the work of centuries cannot be remade in a few years." As Durkheim would later put it, sounding a lot like Matthew Arnold, "the old gods are growing old or already dead, and others are not yet born." In any case, the severance of the individual from collective life (egoism) and the absence of moral training and restraints (anomie) have brought on "a state of crisis and perturbation not to be prolonged with impunity."[7]

This is not to say Durkheim was alarmed by suicide in general. Though every suicide is tragic, a suicide rate can nonetheless be normal. "What is morbid for individuals may be normal for society."[8] This may sound coldhearted, but I take Durkheim to be saying that modern nations cannot protect each member from every influence that contributes to suicide. Moreover, any attempt to do so would amount to heavy-handed paternalism, and would likely lead to fatalistic or altruistic suicides. Still, he maintained, in modern democracies suicide rates are abnormally high, and are therefore not acceptable.

The normative categories Durkheim borrowed from nineteenth-century biology, "normal" and "abnormal," are no doubt problematic. How could Durkheim, by using a sociohistorical comparative method, determine what is a normal suicide rate for a relatively novel social development like a modern democracy? What could Durkheim possibly compare it to? Still, by employing these pseudoscientific categories Durkheim was able to describe contemporary egoism and anomie as chapters of a specific history or narrative. To say something has become abnormal is to suggest that there was a time, under different circumstances, when it was normal. Diseases, we say, develop. They begin at a specific time, under particular conditions, and move through a series of stages. Diseases, we might want to say, are historical. They are rooted in temporal specificity—ask any patient suffering from MS or AIDS. Modern industrial society, Durkheim wanted to say, is like a patient whose history, both individual and genetic, has made it likely she will contract a number of related diseases.

The disease that is egoism, in Durkheim's account, really *is* a disease. It is not an inherent, natural feature of humankind, as Hobbes would have it. It is not a permanent characteristic. Egoism does not spring from human nature, nor, for that matter, does it spring from social life in general. It springs from particular forms of life, from particular social arrangements and other contingencies. These social forms of life have a history, they belong to a specific narrative. The narrative of egoism in modern democracies, according to Durkheim, is roughly the story of societies that, as the result of a multitude of social and economic developments, implicitly force individuals to be radically free from traditional religion, institutional ethics, and other longstanding social practices and beliefs. In modern societies, freedom from public commitments and social involvement has been made into a social ideal, indeed, a common practice. There are, of course, many social beliefs and practices from which we should want to be free, but absolute freedom is a desperate and perilous goal. The belief that we should pursue this goal is nevertheless a social product. A particular history has produced it. Likewise, the sadness that cleaves to egoism—the loneliness, isolation, and despair—is a social construction. "At the very moment that . . . [the egoist] frees himself from the social environment, he still submits to its influence. However individualized a man may be, there is always something collective remaining—the very depression and melancholy resulting from this same exaggerated individualism. He effects communion through sadness when he no longer has anything else with which to achieve it."[9]

Anomie, like egoism, is a disease, not a natural feeling. It is a social product. It, too, belongs to a particular narrative that includes the Industrial Revolution and the rise of modern politics. For example, the theories of both classical economics and socialism reduce the government to a servant of the economy. Industry, hence, has become the "supreme end of individuals and societies alike. Thereupon the appetites thus excited have become freed of any limiting authority. . . . Even the purely utilitarian regulation of them exercised by the industrial world itself through the medium of occupational groups has been unable to persist. Ultimately, this liberation of desire has been made worse by the very development of industry and the almost infinite extension of the market." Beginning in the industrial realm, *le mal de l'infini* "has thence extended to other parts" of society. As Michael Walzer might put it, seepage has occurred. The dominant "ethic" of one sphere has immigrated to surrounding ones. This has resulted in the anomic individual who, like Kierkegaard's aesthete, suffers from infinite desires, preferring the realm of possibility to the world of actuality. "Reality seems valueless," Durkheim wrote of anomie, "by comparison with the dreams of fevered imaginations; reality is therefore abandoned, but so too is possibility abandoned when it in turn becomes reality." Anomie has to be taught, to be acquired. Durkheim noted that "it is constantly repeated that it is man's nature to be eternally dissatisfied, constantly to advance, without relief or rest, toward an indefinite goal. The longing for infinity is daily represented as a mark of moral distinction."[10]

Rousseau, long before Durkheim, also located anomie in a narrative, albeit a universal one. He took *le mal de l'infini* to be the inevitable condition of civilized, as opposed to primitive, societies. In the state of nature, humans were content insofar as they recognized plain limits imposed impersonally by nature. In civilization, however, humans incessantly imagine new needs and resent all obstacles barring their satisfaction. The cure for this disease, in Rousseau's view, is to circumscribe individuals within the *volonté générale*, thereby checking unhappy egoism, the self enslaved by its *volonté particulière*. Force, however, is needed to detach individuals from their private wills so that they can be "free" in the general will. A personal force, such as that of a tyrant, will not do. It could not bring about genuine freedom because it could not enact the general will. Only an impersonal force will do, such as that of an established common good. But the individual in society, in Rousseau's account, will always experience some fundamental, natural conflict between its own private good and the common good.

There can be little doubt that Rousseau inspired Durkheim's conception of anomie's cause and cure. The cause is runaway desire; the cure is the impersonal limits and social practices of a just society. Yet unlike Rousseau, Durkheim did not take anomie to be an inescapable condition of modern life. Anomie belongs to a particular narrative of contingent events, and it is a reversible condition. Its form is distinctive of modern industrial societies, having been caused by the at least partial eclipse of various traditions and institutions.

The historical specificity of Durkheim's notion of anomie also separated him from Hobbes. For Rousseau, excessive desire is an inevitable product of civilization. For Hobbes, on the other hand, runaway desire is an intrinsic characteristic of humans, and most conspicuously of humans in the state of nature. Equipped with memory and imagination, humans are naturally restless and ever dissatisfied. A "general inclination of all mankind," wrote Hobbes, is "a perpetual and restless desire for power after power which ceaseth only in death."[11] Yet Durkheim's anomie does not refer to a "general inclination of mankind." It refers, rather, to a particular (and Durkheim would add, abnormal) European, historical development.

In Durkheim's view, for centuries European societies had been losing their secondary groups, while the newly centralized states had attempted to absorb all remaining forms of social activity. The result was twofold. "While the state becomes inflated and hypertrophied in order to obtain a firm enough grip upon individuals, but without succeeding, the latter, without mutual relationships, tumble over one another like so many liquid molecules."[12] This description of individuals "forced to be free" from all sorts of moral communities shows governments attempting to provide national organization and solidarity, yet failing in this because they are too far removed from individuals' needs, goals, and social circumstances. These new social developments—large centralized states, multi-regional industries, and individuals severed from traditional associations—gave rise to various attempts, some socialist, some liberal, to justify, to improve upon, or to overthrow existing social arrangements. This is Durkheim's historical account of how France became—to borrow a phrase from C. Wright Mills—"a bureaucratized society of privatized men." Into this narrative, Durkheim wove his account of excessive, that is, abnormal, contemporary egoism and anomie.

When Durkheim evoked the biological concept of abnormality, he was attempting to gain "scientific" credibility. He should have been confident that his perspicuous accounts of egoism and anomie would convince many readers (though surely not all) that these modern developments are not desirable. He wanted, however, to convince everyone, or at least every scientist, and that meant arguing in the prevailing languages of science. Still, this much is clear: to call egoism and anomie abnormal is to say, if nothing else, that because of particular turns in history, modern industrial societies are not as they should be. All is not well, in specific ways, for specific, sociohistorical reasons. The supposedly privileged biological vocabulary was a means for Durkheim, who never fully escaped positivism, to attempt to ground "objectively" his assessment of modern societies. It was a way for Durkheim to speak both normatively and prophetically. Today we can drop the very idea of privileged vocabularies, as I believe Durkheim eventually did, and still find his normative message convincing.

II

We can take egoism and fatalism as descriptions of societies we wouldn't want to live in, or features of societies that appall us.[13] Barring a happy medium or balance between egoism and fatalism, some will prefer the problems and blessings of an egoistic society over a fatalistic one, others will opt for the contrary position. This choice is a way to characterize many contemporary issues and disputes that pit assorted liberals and communitarians against one another. Think of egoism as what communitarians hate more than just about anything, and what they usually accuse liberals of: leading society down the mud-cracked, dead-end road of individualism. Fatalism, on the other hand, frightens liberals more than just about anything, and they claim communitarians are attempting to steer society back down the well-paved, well-traveled road of oppressive paternalism.

Durkheim thought modern societies are heading away from fatalism toward egoism. Most today agree with that description, but disagree about whether to applaud this movement. Communitarians tend to look at the present with aversion. They search the past for models of community and signs of virtue, hoping to find a way out of the present darkness for the sake of a brighter future. Liberals, in contrast, look at the past and are glad they don't live there—in the ancient polis, the early Benedictine abbeys, or sixteenth-century Geneva. They applaud the developments of the last three centuries and look forward to extending individual rights and liberties into the future. So while the one camp envies the past, with its settled communities and standards of virtue, and laments the present, the other camp celebrates its emancipation from the past, and hopes for present trends to continue. Liberals like to remind us of the human suffering and repression that flow from traditional, hierarchical societies. These societies, they say, encumber their members with narrow and often stifling social roles. They probably would argue, then, that even if Durkheim was right about all the deleterious aspects of egoism, we should see these as unfortunate side effects of a basically healthy social prescription, that is, as inevitable fallout from the individualistic pursuits of liberal democracies. They recall Durkheim explicitly saying that if we wish to maintain free inquiry and social criticism, we must put up with some anomie and egoism. Communitarians, however, are likely to join Durkheim in pointing out all the woes of the present age—rootlessness, alienation, suicide, loneliness, despair— and to claim that the benefits of tightly knit communities and a virtuous citizenry outweigh the liberal values of tolerance, self-expression, individualism, and the like.

These responses to Durkheim entail two opposing narratives. The liberal one is the heroic epic of how the politics of rights has defeated fatalism, or at least is close to victory. The protagonists include the Stoics, Christianity (with its emphasis on the inward Kingdom), Luther, Kant, Mill, Nietzsche, and Martin Luther King, Jr. (with his appeal to rights). The communitarian narrative is the tragedy of how the politics of the common good willingly gave birth to "the individual," only to be killed by its own offspring. The vanquished heroes include Aristotle, Christianity (with its emphasis on community), Thomas Aquinas, Calvin, Rousseau, Hegel, and Martin Luther King, Jr. (with his appeal to civic-mindedness).

Durkheim, as I argue throughout this book, wished to rescue us from narratives like these. We are indeed between worlds, or between gods, with future paths uncleared and uncertain. This predicament is not unique. Every age has been "between times." Our task is neither to venerate and mourn the old world, nor to romanticize and glorify the new. We would do better to specify the various goods being championed, debate them, then figure out how to accommodate the most worthy ones or to work creatively with the tensions between them. This is the work Durkheim set for himself. His narrative did not simply set the old in opposition to the new. Our recent history has brought us new benefits and new problems. The rights and dignity of the individual, democratic institutions, helpful technology, increased standards in living—these are some of the goods that we associate with liberal, industrial societies. But most of us, along with Durkheim, are nervous about the loss of community that has accompanied the gain in rights, and about how the gain in rights has not usually been distributed equally.[14] We worry about how the internal goods of democratic institutions are threatened by the external goods of the marketplace; about ever-growing bureaucracies, public and private, that are inflexible and insensitive to our individuality; and about the large number of people whose standard of living has not improved, and whose employment has become more limited and less meaningful.

Durkheim did not set liberalism, with its egoistic aspects, in radical opposition to communitarianism, with its fatalistic aspects, but rather remained open to the nuances that link what in society needs to be preserved with what needs to be reformed. Some might claim that in *Suicide* there is little evidence of Durkheim's fear of the return of a full-fledged fatalistic, communitarian society. It is true that he saw history moving in the other direction. He seemed to think, at least before 1897, that liberal values were becoming deeply entrenched and that therefore the various counterrevolutionary forces, conservatives of all stripes—monarchists, Roman Catholics, high-level military and bureaucrats—were not likely to bring down the Third Republic and resurrect a traditional, authoritarian, hierarchical society. But his attitude soon changed. During and after the Dreyfus affair, as various conservative groups consolidated, Durkheim increasingly recognized the fragility of liberal democratic institutions.

Even in *Suicide*, however, Durkheim gave reasons why most of us would not want to live in a fatalistic society. The military spirit, which Durkheim described as a contemporary manifestation of fatalism, involves "intellectual abnegation" and "a weak tie" to one's own individuality. This spirit, Durkheim claimed, "recalls the structure of lower societies. It, too, consists of a massive, compact group providing a rigid setting for the individual and preventing any independent movement." [15] We can forgive Durkheim for his assumptions about "lower societies" and take this as an account of the kind of society we would not want our daughters and sons to grow up in.

There is also evidence in *Suicide* of Durkheim's concern about fatalism in modern societies. Durkheim noted that, unlike men, married women commit suicide more than unmarried women in countries where divorce is difficult to obtain. He concluded that, *"From the standpoint of suicide, marriage is more favorable to the wife the more widely practiced divorce is; and vice versa."* [16] Durkheim accounted for this by claiming that women are not allowed to participate fully in social life, and hence marriage, which severs women all the more from greater society, frustrates their social goals and aspirations. Consequently, although men suffer from egoism, women suffer from fatalism. Durkheim suggested that "only when the difference between husband and wife becomes less, will marriage no longer be thought . . . necessarily to favor one to the detriment of the other." [17]

Egoism, of course, occupied most of Durkheim's attention in *Suicide*—not "individualism" in general, but that condition of the individual in modern society that Durkheim described as unhealthy and sad. Much of *Suicide* diagnoses this pathological condition, but it also offers remedies. Some may be tempted to say that neither we nor Durkheim can have it both ways. Either societies grant individuals autonomy and suffer the consequences of egoism, or they enforce some set of social practices and ideals, and jettison individual liberties. If this response assumes that individual autonomy requires something like self-dependence, as discussed earlier, the objection can be dismissed. Anyone who has entered into this reading of Durkheim could reply that, although she rejects excessive state coercion, she accepts other kinds of influence, including benign coercion, that produce individuals who are normatively autonomous. She accepts any influence that produces autonomous individuals in socially and morally acceptable ways.[18] To entertain this position, however, it is necessary to understand these "other kinds of influence," and to understand what "benign coercion" means.

Durkheim examined several forms of social influence in *Suicide*, and he rejected the state, education, religion, and the family as possible cures for the pathologies of egoism. He did, however, identify two types of social influence that he believed can curb egoism while respecting individual liberties and rights. Before we consider them, we need to see why Durkheim rejected these other possible cures.

The problem with education, according to Durkheim, is that it merely reproduces the society of which it forms a part. "Education is healthy when people themselves are in a healthy state; but it becomes corrupt with them, being unable to modify itself."[19] He concluded that education "can be reformed only if society itself is reformed." Education in a society pervaded by egoism will produce a society of egoists.

How can society itself be reformed? How can a population of individuals disconnected from vital moral relations and social goals be reconnected with one another to form a flourishing, happy nation? Some communitarians might suggest that the state should impose national goals and employ the powerful appeal of national identity in order to curb egoism. Durkheim, however, believed that the modern state is "too far removed from the individual to affect him uninterruptedly and with sufficient force."[20] Moreover, the state is likely to attempt to impose a uniformity on its citizens that is inconsistent with notions of pluralism and moral autonomy.

On pragmatic grounds, Durkheim rejected religious influences on the individual as well. They won't work. They can't prevent egoism, or the social causes that produce it. He conceded that, at one time, religion did exert a beneficial influence on society, properly socializing individuals and protecting them from egoism. Its success, however, came in part by suppressing individualism, especially in the form of free thinking. And times have changed. Religion's "seizure of human intelligence is difficult at present and will become more and more so. It offends our dearest sentiments."[21] As soon as we reject religion's behest "Thou shalt go no further," we spurn its authority and become immune to its once-deep sway over us. After we allow or encourage critical thought, religion can no longer socialize individuals effectively.

Behind this simple pragmatic argument, some may see the operation of a general sociological principle that would foreclose any effort to develop an account of genuine moral individualism. If religion won't work as a cure for egoism, it's because the social forces and institutions that unite individuals and combat egoism necessarily discourage individual thought, pluralism, and moral autonomy. Solidarity, a social condition relatively free of egoism, cannot permit free inquiry or critical thought. If this is a general principle that governs all social formations, then the objection that neither we nor Durkheim can have it both ways returns with a vengeance.

I am not convinced, however, that Durkheim's rejection of the religious remedy carries with it the belief that solidarity requires excessive social uniformity and the prohibition of critical thinking. This would go against too many statements found in *The Division of Labor* and his prior essays. No general sociological principle, in other words, was being suggested. Durkheim was rejecting a specific means to solidarity, traditional Western religion, for a particular social type, modern Western society. Traditional Western religion involves, among other things, beliefs about God in Heaven above and devils in Hell below. These supernatural beliefs once belonged to a pervasive worldview, but that worldview is no longer in place, according to Durkheim, and religion has lost its authority. When critical thought is directed at religion, religion's ability to capture our commitment and love diminishes.[22] Perhaps there is after all a sociological principle here, if we're willing to make it rather modest: beliefs and related practices that lack authority cannot produce solidarity. Notice that this rule of thumb makes no claim about the relation between solidarity and aspects of individualism.

New religions, of course, can develop. The "viable ones," Durkheim wrote, will permit "more freedom to the right of criticism, to individual initiative, than even the most liberal Protestant sects." But by calling them viable, Durkheim did not mean these religions would be able to prevent egoism, only that, of all religions, the progressive ones are most likely to gain wide acceptance. He predicted that these religions, like speculative philosophy, will be imaginative, personal, and abstract. And like most philosophies they will be, as Durkheim put it, "more or less a stranger to our daily occupations." We might be tempted to take Durkheim's characterization of the new, viable religions as a statement about the incompatibility of solidarity and "individual initiative." This reading, however, would once again put a sweeping claim where there is only a limited one. "Individual initiative" and "the right of criticism" here refer to features of speculative thought. Such abstract thought is not likely to promote widespread solidarity because it is "more or less a stranger to our daily occupations." It is too detached from our daily practices and interactions to unite us in profound ways. I am not sure I would accept this claim.[23] But I am sure it is not a claim about solidarity precluding "individual initiative" and "the right of criticism."

"The family" is still another institution that Durkheim examined and rejected as a possible remedy for modern egoism. He wrote that although the family once "kept most of its members within its orbit from birth to death and formed a compact mass, indivisible and endowed with a quality of permanence, its duration is now brief." Durkheim was not distressed about this development. Elsewhere he said positive things about what we now call the nuclear family, but he believed the family is not suited to combat egoism. When Durkheim rejected religion and the family as possible remedies, he implicitly challenged many conservatives of his day, who longed for a restored, traditional Roman Catholic France. I could say, then, without being overly anachronistic, that Durkheim was opposing a communitarian response to modern egoism. Durkheim understood that cures for egoism must spring from our current situation. Nostalgic pinings for the past will not help. The spirit of individualism, for example, is entrenched, and therefore any successful cure for egoism must not attempt to turn back history by uprooting all aspects of individualism. Times have changed, and we must work from within those changed conditions. Likewise, cures are not likely to arise from the political philosopher's abstract and ahistorical thought. Philosophers' "imaginative flights," as Durkheim called them, are too far from the concrete detail of contemporary social life to affect that life.[24]

What, then, did Durkheim identify as social influences that could cure egoism and produce moral individualism? What social forces escape the sort of criticisms he leveled at education, the state, religion, and the family? Durkheim offered two possible cures for modern egoism in *Suicide*. The first, which he explicitly stated, was the influence of the occupational groups whose development he advocated. The second, which is implicit in the first, is probably more accurately understood as the moral, social context necessary for the establishment of those groups. I call it the entrenchment of liberal collective representations.

The establishment of occupational groups is a recurrent theme in Durkheim's writings. Its first substantial treatment is in *Suicide*. Most of my discussion of occupational groups is in Chapter 6, where I address Durkheim's mature ideas on the subject. For now, it's enough to think of occupational groups as moral associations suited for the needs, concerns, and interests of workers and their families in a particular occupation. These associations are an instance of what in the last chapter I called "moral polymorphism," and what I identified as the second component of moral individualism, social environments that envelop individuals, sustaining them with intimate ties and specialized moral education. Durkheim wanted individuals situated in meaningful social relations as a means to check egoism. Education simply reproduces egoism; the modern family is too private and transitory; the state is too distant from individuals' lives; and religion no longer provides meaningful solidarity, because its dogmas require intellectual serfdom. Durkheim believed that occupational groups, groups larger than the family, but smaller than the political society, would be well suited for building centers of common life. By encouraging just social practices among their members, they would acquire moral authority and curb egoism. Yet they would be close enough to individuals to sympathize with their legitimate needs and to work on their behalf for obtaining fair wages, reasonable hours, health insurance and other forms of assistance.[25]

Durkheim described the development of occupational groups as a result of a division of moral labor. "As labor is divided, law and morality assume a different form in each special function, though still resting everywhere on the same general principles. Besides the rights and duties common to all men, there are others depending on qualities peculiar to each occupation, the number of which increases in importance as occupational activity increasingly develops and diversifies." As common moral traditions and practices are applied to special circumstances, various social spheres develop and provide moral community and training for their members. "The workers" themselves are best qualified to establish these groups, Durkheim believed.[26] There is nothing chaotic or anomic about this plurality of occupational spheres. The ethics of each is an offspring of our shared understandings. The division of moral labor is a product of what a society holds in common, applied to the special circumstances of groups of individuals. The group is sensitive to the spirit of individualism, recognizing the various needs and desires of individuals. Yet it also provides a moral home, a source of affection and discipline that rescues individuals from egoism. There is, then, something both liberal and communitarian about occupational groups.

How are these groups to avoid what Durkheim called "corporate egoism"? They need to be made aware of the "public welfare" and be subject to the "general influence of the state." By directing them toward the common good, we can arrest "bureaucratic despotism and occupational egoism." Durkheim was vague on exactly how this "directing" is to take place. He wanted to place these groups "outside the state, though subject to its action." They need to become "a definite and recognized organ of our public life," as opposed to a private group "legally permitted, but politically ignored." They are, then, to become public institutions and a central feature of political society, but without becoming an arm of the state. It falls to the democratic state, however, to oppose excessive corporate particularism by reminding the groups of the public welfare and "the need for organic equilibrium."[27]

At one point, Durkheim admitted that his proposal seems far-fetched. Given the sad condition of corporations, it is difficult to imagine "their ever being elevated to the dignity of moral powers." Today, corporations are composed of individuals who are related only superficially, and who are even "inclined to treat each other rather as rivals and enemies than as cooperators." I share Durkheim's assessment of the difficulty. Yet I want to make clear what this difficulty consists of. Durkheim was not saying that money and status are odious and are causing people to become egoists. If this were the case, Durkheim would not describe occupational groups as agencies of "distributive justice" with jurisdiction over material goods. The groups would be nothing but agencies of abstinence, inculcating in their members a contempt for money and status. Durkheim explicitly rejected religious asceticism as a solution to the problem of egoism. Denying the importance of external goods such as salaries and titles is futile because they are now perceived, and rightly so, as legitimate goods. Durkheim concluded that "while it is no remedy to give appetites free rein, neither is it enough to suppress them in order to control them. Though the last defenders of the old economic theories are mistaken in thinking that regulation is not necessary today as it was yesterday, the apologists of the institution of religion are wrong in believing that yesterday's regulation can be useful today."[28]

The difficulty, then, is not that people shouldn't seek external goods because they are not in fact genuine goods. The problem is that the dominant institutions producing external goods often exist, as Durkheim would later put it, in a "moral vacuum." In Chapter 6 I describe this vacuum as a condition in which the relation between internal and external goods is not sufficiently informed by professional ethics. Without such ethics, the goods internal to social practices, whether they concern the practice of law, medicine, business, teaching, or carpentry, are vitiated by external goods such as money and power.[29] This, Durkheim argued, results from the lack of moral associations and "newly" crafted traditions in the marketplace—a place that increasingly dominates our lives and shapes our loves.

If a liberal nation is but a group of disparate individuals who have little in common besides contributing taxes for a variety of government services, if its citizens uphold the laws only for the sake of social stability while they pursue their own private projects, then egoism is likely to take root and thrive. Moreover, as Durkheim would later argue, a society of socially unanchored individuals is susceptible to social crazes that can place power in the hands of those not worthy of it. An egoistic society, in other words, can quickly turn fatalistic. But what if a liberal nation is comprised of individuals who share long-standing traditions and social practices that, among other things, support individual rights and liberties? What if liberalism is construed as a set of social traditions that morally unite individuals in common pursuits? In addition to advocating the creation of occupational groups, in *Suicide* Durkheim envisioned another way in which social influences can protect modern societies from the disease of egoism and promote moral individualism. This involved what I want to call liberal collective representations. These are shared beliefs and ideals that embody a society's common understanding of the relation that pertains between the public and private spheres.

Durkheim dismissed modern speculative religion as a source of solidarity because that religion is abstract, private, and detached from daily life. Solidarity requires some set of shared, authoritative beliefs and practices. Liberal solidarity requires no less. Liberalism resists egoism insofar as it is entrenched in what I earlier called the "benign coercion" of normative traditions and institutions that sustain moral practices such as those pertaining to the rights and dignity of the individual. Collective life, in Durkheim's view, always entails some constraints. There is nothing illiberal about this. Not radical freedom, but a moral milieu that sustains a host of liberal values and practices—this was Durkheim's aim. And this is what separates Durkheim's vision of liberalism from Spencer's "free" society, a society that places spontaneity above just social constraints. Durkheim believed that moral liberalism had roots in the Third Republic, but that it needed to be extended to benefit more citizens, and strengthened to repel both laissez-faire liberal and counterrevolutionary conservative assaults. Indeed, the existence of liberal collective representations was necessary for the establishment of just occupational groups. These groups, as I have argued, depend on respect for the individual and commitment to public welfare. They depend, in other words, on liberal collective representations.

Although Durkheim introduced the term *représentations collectives* in 1887, his first full discussion of it is found in the pages of *Suicide*. The renewed emphasis on the term marks, I believe, some important changes in Durkheim's thought. For the first time since his pre–*Division of Labor* essays, he explored the significance of widely shared beliefs and ideals. He claimed that "essentially social life is made up of representations" and that they are "of quite another character from those of the individual."[30] In *The Division of Labor* and in *The Rules of Sociological Method*, Durkheim often described society in terms of morphological social facts. Under this description, social beliefs and ideals, usually called collective sentiments, not collective representations, appear as external constraints imposed on individuals. The social substratum, comprised of morphological facts, produces collective sentiments. These sentiments have no life of their own. They are but an expression of the social substratum. Never determining social structures, always determined by them, beliefs and ideals played a slender role in Durkheim's mid-career explanations of social change and solidarity.

In *Suicide* Durkheim revised this position. Beliefs and ideals were still understood as social, as opposed to private, constructions, but they no longer were said to be produced principally by morphological factors. Under Durkheim's new description, beliefs and ideals take on a somewhat autonomous nature, and they themselves become agents of social change. Durkheim called these "collective representations," and liberalism is, in part, a result of them. Shortly after Christian societies were formed, Durkheim noted, suicide was formally forbidden. The prohibition was not a mere "idealized" reflection of morphological facts. It was the result of a "new conception of the human personality" engendered by Christianity. This new conception gave rise to still others, until a system of beliefs about the moral worth of the individual gradually emerged. Consequently, the human person has become "sacred," "something which no one is to offend."[31] Certain Christian beliefs, then, set society in a particular direction, and these beliefs were not simply an expression of a predetermined path established by a morphological structure.

After *Suicide*, Durkheim never again depicted social beliefs and goals as hovering above the individual, constraining action without penetrating the heart. The position that social beliefs and goals shape our vision and fashion our loves no doubt can be found in his earlier writings. There, however, it stands in tension with another position. In *The Division of Labor* and *The Rules of Sociological Method* there is a strand of thought, closely related to the account of mechanical social forces summarized in the previous chapter, that suggests social ideals and moral imperatives are imposed on the individual as external, social constraints. Collective sentiments unite individuals in group emotions such as the fear of punishment for social deviance. This view disappeared entirely in *Suicide*. There, individuals recognize the intrinsic moral worth of social ideals and imperatives. The Rousseauian vocabulary of social sentiments is dropped altogether, and it is replaced with a (socialized) Kantian vocabulary of collective representations that are inherently meaningful, not just meaningful in terms of social threat and punishment.

Society, in Durkheim's most characteristic formulation, has produced cognitive representations by which we meaningfully experience the world. Later, he would occasionally go so far as to say that collective representations *make* the worlds in which we dwell. These representations—shared beliefs and ideals—contribute to moral solidarity. "Habits" largely disappeared from Durkheim's vocabulary. More and more Durkheim came to understand habits as noncognitive, socially trained reflexes.[32] Important as these may be, Durkheim probably omitted them because their noncognitive nature does not provide the moral meaning and purpose that he believed modern individuals desperately need. Shared beliefs and ideals, unlike habits, can animate people, challenge them, and remind them of collective goals and aims.

This, then, is Durkheim's nuanced approach to analyzing contemporary social life. He did not pose liberalism, with its egoistic tendencies, and communitarianism, with its fatalistic tendencies, as two mutually exclusive alternatives between which we must choose. Rather he attempted to bring the good things that come with community and associations together with the benefits that come with individual rights and liberties. Egoism is the result of excessive individualism, not of individualism per se. Fatalism springs from extreme communism, not from community per se. Tradition and community, in Durkheim's hands, are not relegated to an old and superstitious epoch and then contrasted to autonomy and "the individual" as features of a new and approved modernity. It is not a matter of the old or the new age, tradition or autonomy, community or the individual, communitarianism or liberalism. In *Suicide* Durkheim did not present us with these either/or's. Rather, equipped with the vocabulary of egoism and fatalism, he determined in what way many modern institutions are pathologically egoistic or fatalistic, and then proposed therapies and reforms.

It may not be clear that egoism, like fatalism, is both a social ailment and a social product. This isn't plain because of a pattern of ambiguities that arises from Durkheim's practice of using his central terms descriptively in some places, normatively in others. This in itself would pose no problem, except that Durkheim often failed to signal to his readers which usage he was employing. Hence, he sometimes depicted egoism as a condition marked by the absence of social forces, while on other occasions he described egoism as a result of social forces, notably those spawned by the Enlightenment and by the French and Industrial Revolutions, insufficiently allied with other social forces that could supply meaningful social goals and relations. Under this latter description, egoism is as much an unfortunate social product as is fatalism. The total isolation of the self from social forces is not egoism, but an unthinkable sociological experiment with a monstrous outcome. Likewise, the total submersion of a self in society is not fatalism, but an alien scenario such as we find in the pages or frames of science fiction.

When Durkheim depicted egoism as a lamentable social product, he was speaking both descriptively and normatively. Descriptively, it is a social phenomenon; normatively, it is pernicious—it makes us unhappy and perhaps cruel. When, on the other hand, he portrayed egoism as a lonesome asocial state, he was speaking normatively, not descriptively. He was saying that egoism is a miserable condition in which individuals are divorced from all sorts of life-enhancing social commitments and relations.

In much communitarian literature today, the term *community* is often used ambiguously because of a similar shuffling between normative and descriptive usage.[33] Communitarians describe community, descriptively, as a natural, inescapable condition for humans. Just as Wittgenstein argued against the very possibility of a radically private language, so communitarians argue against the possibility of a radically solitary existence. On this I agree with many communitarians (and with Wittgenstein). On other occasions, however, they assert—normatively—that ours is a narcissistic culture that is unable to sustain social practices because we are short on community and lack a shared public rationality. I take them not to be saying that contemporary North Atlantic societies lack social practices and communities, but that they are short on the right kind of communities, and are in need of a shared conception of the good to support their moral practices. The communitarians' descriptive claim requires less argument than the normative one. Humans are indeed social creatures. They live in societies and communities of one kind or another. But which kinds of community are normative? If we can determine these, are they normative for all cultures, or only for those similar to our own?

By the end of Chapter 8, I hope to have cast some light on these issues. For now I want to point out that our assent to the communitarian descriptive claims need not commit us to all their normative claims. It is not clear that the latter claims necessarily follow the former. This is not to detract from any particular communitarian moral judgment. In fact, I find many of them compelling. But their insights are more probing and useful when combined with a pragmatic approach that avoids blanket judgments, that is willing to count many liberal projects as worthwhile, and that generates thicker descriptions of what is and is not admirable in contemporary institutions.

This is the approach I am attributing to Durkheim. In *Suicide*, he attempted to articulate a normative social condition that, depending on which institutions he was addressing, fell more or less between egoism and fatalism. We should take his term "solidarity" to represent this in-between ideal. Descriptively, egoism and fatalism are social conditions. Normatively, solidarity in

modern democracies avoids both extremes. In *Suicide*, Durkheim described "well-integrated" institutions as those "without
excess in one direction or the other."[34] Between the extremes of
authoritarian regulation (fatalism) and systematic abstention
(egoism) Durkheim plotted a series of courses for contemporary
institutions. He avoided extreme communitarian and liberal positions while forging a powerful *via media* between them. This
strategy I want to recommend for social theorists today, especially to those who are held captive by the idea that we need to
embrace either liberalism or communitarianism. Durkheim replaced this forced choice with the possibility of putting together
a more complicated—and accurate—account of contemporary
institutions.

III

I have been trying to present *Suicide* as discontinuous with
Durkheim's earlier work, but not radically discontinuous.[35] In
his pre–*Division of Labor* essays, a concern for social beliefs and
ideals is far from absent, but Durkheim did not describe them as
relatively autonomous collective representations that play an essential part in the social production of meaning. He did not see
them as a necessary good for human joy. In *The Division of Labor*,
as I have said, Durkheim occasionally rendered society's shared
understanding as no more than a reflection of its morphological
arrangements. This "materialism" (for lack of a better term) is a
useful tactic, and Durkheim after *The Division of Labor* never
abandoned it, but never again did he apply it systematically.
From *Suicide* on, he treated material structures and social ideals
as two sides of a rapidly spinning coin.

To understand a people, Durkheim claimed, you have to investigate their collective representations, their patterned mazes
of social meanings. Even the study of morphological elements,
if divorced from a society's shared understanding, cannot yield
useful accounts. Indeed, it would be difficult to understand
modern democratic societies if these representations were ignored. Social commitments to "the individual," for example political rights such as equal opportunity or freedom of expression,
could be misunderstood as specimens of narcissism. In light of
a liberal shared understanding, however, a society's concern for

"the individual" will appear differently. It will appear less egoistic. Durkheim argued that the collective representations carried in liberal traditions can morally unite individuals because these shared understandings provide social projects and vocabularies that are morally edifying. The preservation and extension of rights and liberties is one such set of common commitments. This set is not the only one found in liberal societies.[36] Still, it is distinctive of them, and to interpret it as a sign of egoism would be to view it outside its natural context and native ground: normative, European social traditions.

I suggest we interpret what Durkheim called in *Suicide* "the cult of the human person" as a label that refers to those many modern, moral collective representations that articulate the ways we cherish and protect individual rights and liberties. This cult—the symbols, practices, and beliefs centered on the sacrosanct character of the individual—is but another name for what I earlier called the first and primary component of moral individualism. Upon it, Durkheim claimed, rests modern Western morality. "Suicide is rebuked for derogating from this cult of the human person on which all our morality rests."[37] The central object of this modern common faith is "the new conception of the human person. It has become sacred . . . something which no one is to offend. . . . [The individual's existence] has become tinged with religious value; man has become a god for men. Therefore, any attempt against his life suggests sacrilege. . . . No matter who strikes the blow, it causes scandal by violation of the sacrosanct quality within us which we must respect in ourselves as well as in others."[38] Durkheim was compelled to adopt a religious vocabulary in order to convey the normative, communal aspect of "the individual" as a social concept. Within a year of *Suicide*, Durkheim in his Dreyfusard essay would describe religion (as opposed to magic) as a social creation that serves society's highest moral ideals, not private utility. Durkheim wanted us to think of the cult of the human person (a synonym for the cult of the individual) as a moral development, not as an essentially private narcissism. Individuals are not free, morally, to violate it. In fact, they do not even have the "right to die."

In his *Omicidio-suicidio*, Ferri argued that all condemnation of suicide is without basis. Science has demonstrated that there is nothing "superhuman" about the individual. From a rationalist point of view, the individual has no "extra-personal aim." Without a God to grant life, there can be no divine commandment prohibiting suicide. According to this line of thought, Durkheim noted, "the right to live seems logically to imply the right to die." But this slights the social and moral features of our concept of the individual. Ferri failed to perceive that suicide offends "the religion of humanity," that is, the cult of the human person.[39] This human religion is a symbol of society's commitment to the life of the individual. To violate this religion is to weaken what binds together members of liberal society, and what sustains liberal values and institutions. Rights and obligations, then, are promoted by this liberal faith. Far from declaring the individual to be an autonomous god, as does the creed of "egoistic individualism," moral individualism couples individual privileges with social commitments, and thereby contributes to solidarity. According to Durkheim, "this cult of the human person is something . . . very different from egoistic individualism. . . . Far from detaching individuals from society and from every aim beyond themselves, it unites them in one thought, makes them ministers of one work. . . . Such an aim draws [the individual] beyond himself; impersonal and disinterested, it is above all individual personalities."[40]

This liberal common faith, then, is neither solipsistic nor narcissistic. It links individuals to society, inspiring them to be partners in common pursuits and goods. This position departs from Durkheim's discussion of "the cult of the individual" in *The Division of Labor*. As we have already seen, there Durkheim claimed that "if the faith [the cult of the individual] is common because it is shared among the community, it is individual in its object. If it impels every will towards the same end, that end is not a social one. . . . It is indeed from society that it draws all this strength, but it is not to society that it binds us: it is to our selves. Thus it does not constitute a truly social link."[41] Now, however, Durkheim described the cult as a normatively social one. It links individuals to goals and aims beyond those of self-interest. The cult is thoroughly anti-Spencerian: "impersonal and disinterested, it is above all individual personalities." No doubt the cult benefits individuals, instituting their rights and liberties, equality and dignity. Yet it also establishes social responsibilities and affections. These, too, are important benefits, for they contribute to social justice and human joy.

Like other moral or religious imperatives, moral individualism urges us "to act by an authority exceeding ourselves, namely society. . . . and the aims to which it attaches us thus enjoy real moral supremacy."[42] Its imperative nature, however, does not alienate individuals. They "gladly defer to its commands," because they respect it. It exhibits, after all, public goods and individual entitlements.

Social traditions, then, have fashioned moral individualism, and from a democratic society's shared understanding—its collective representations—moral individualism draws its authority. But moral individualism is not inordinately vulnerable to the whims of society. Moral individualism, Durkheim argued, "is above [the individual] as well as above society." Durkheim insisted that society can produce a moral order to which it is also bound. Social traditions produce the beliefs and practices associated with moral individualism, yet once born they take on a life of their own. Collective representations can acquire (to use Gadamer's term) an "effective-history."[43] When we ask the question, Who are we? or In what do we believe? we are not free to offer *any* answer. The answer will be limited by (or granted by) the social worlds we inhabit. Of course questions and answers arise out of specific circumstances that involve our various positions and moves in a variety of social landscapes. Hence, even if our responses to changing situations are limited, they are not rigidly fixed or predetermined. We could even say, relative to our social possibilities, that our responses are indeterminate. But some moves, some replies, are ruled out in advance. Durkheim claimed that, at least for the time being, liberal collective representations have closed off some destructive paths down which modern societies might stray. Society, then, is bound by its own liberal social ideals. "This ideal [moral individualism] even dominates societies, being the aim on which all social activity depends. This is why it is no longer the right of these societies to dispose of this ideal freely. . . . They have subjected themselves to the jurisdiction of this ideal and no longer have the right to ignore it; still less, to authorize men themselves to do so."[44]

I suspect this is an oblique reference to the Dreyfus affair. As

Martin Luther King, Jr., sought to bind his fellow citizens to an American tradition of liberty and justice for all, so Durkheim sought to bind the French to a similar liberal tradition. Society, with its present institutions and practices, is no more at liberty to forsake these normative beliefs and ideals than is the lone individual. This, however, may have been more of a wish than a prediction on Durkheim's part. Although he claimed that democratic societies are not morally free to depart from certain paths as long as they possess institutions and ideals such as just constitutions and laws, and the means and will to support them, these societies in fact have conflicting ideals and practices. The specters of tyranny haunt democracies, especially when the powerful or the majority attempt to deprive others of their rights and liberties for their own gain and satisfaction. There were no guarantees that the Dreyfusards would be successful, and the extent of their success is debatable, especially in light of the Vichy government. There were no guarantees of Martin Luther King's triumph, and his death and the recent history of civil rights and race relations in the U.S. suggest that his dream, to a large extent, has remained one.

Durkheim, no doubt, was aware of this. The narrative he provided in *Suicide*, and the arguments he advanced in his Dreyfusard essay and elsewhere, represented his attempt to give a particular reading of France's traditions and contemporary society that would foster the progress of moral individualism in the Third Republic. The return of a conservative, fatalistic society in France became a constant worry for Durkheim and other Republicans and socialists. Yet Durkheim also worried about the tendency to slide toward the other extreme—egoism. Egoism, he believed, threatens the moral fabric of democracies and even leads to conditions conducive to a fatalistic society.[45] To provide an alternative to both extremes, Durkheim developed a normative account of the health and sickness of contemporary institutions. Between these extremes he located his communitarian defense of liberalism.

IV

My claim that moral individualism is a central feature of *Suicide* is likely to surprise many who would object that Durkheim delivered his heaviest blows against individualism in that book. Are not the pages of *Suicide* filled with pessimism about the future of France and, indeed, the future of the modern industrial world? The source of that pessimism, however, was Durkheim's fear that atomistic individualism, in the moral vacuum created by modern industrial societies, may become the prevailing way of life. This way of life, Durkheim thought, is an unhappy one, and often tolerates unjust social practices. If my reading is correct, *Suicide* also contained a spring of hope. It is the prospect of a liberal common faith penetrating more deeply society's institutions and practices. Far from inveighing against *every* notion of individualism, Durkheim proposed moral individualism as an antidote to both atomistic individualism and oppressive fatalism.

Suicide, then, should not be read as an anti-liberal tract supporting social order over and against individual liberties and rights. Read it, rather, as Durkheim's first mature communitarian defense of liberalism. I call it a communitarian defense because Durkheim articulated moral individualism in the vocabulary of traditions, beliefs, and a common faith, and because he placed common pursuits and communities at the heart of moral individualism. I call it a defense of liberalism because Durkheim advanced the dignity and equality, the rights and liberties of the individual. For Durkheim, however, the aims of liberalism are life-enhancing only within the context of what he called "a coherent and animated society." In such a society, "there is from all to each and from each to all a continual exchange of ideas and sentiments, like a mutual moral support, which makes the individual, instead of being reduced to his own forces alone, participate in the collective energy and rejuvenate his life when it is exhausted."[46]

Durkheim did not share the optimism of many nineteenth-century liberals who placed great hope in the advancement of the natural and social sciences. Even if these sciences could bring some financial prosperity, it was not clear to Durkheim that they could tackle the moral problems facing modern industrial societies. It was not clear that they could bring happiness to societies suffering from egoism and economic anomie. Yet Durkheim's pessimism was not paralyzing. He was not a Jonah in an alien country prophesying doom. More akin to an Amos, he crit-

icized his own people by reminding them of their most legitimate traditions and ideals.[47] When he pointed out the discrepancy between these ideals and many contemporary social
practices, he did so with an eye toward reformation.

Perhaps it is misleading for me to imply that *Suicide* is a pes-
simistic work. It calls attention to adverse features of industrial
societies, but we find in it none of that "terminal wistfulness"
we have come to expect from the pen of many communitarians.[48] Durkheim did not suggest that the dark ages are upon us
and that we wait for the likes of a St. Benedict. Our social problems are indeed grave, he believed. We suffer, he noted, not
from "economic poverty" but from "an alarming poverty of morality."[49] Yet his perception of the enormity of the predicament
did not lead him to inactivity. It led him rather to advocate social
reform. He warned that our social ills cannot be cured by "magical words" or "repeated exhortations." "We are far from thinking to reduce [the moral social evil] to some superficial ill which
may be conjured away by soft words. On the contrary, the
change in moral temperament that we have thus discovered at-
tests to a profound change in our social structure. To cure one,
therefore, the other must be reformed."[50]

Toward this reformation, we have seen, he proposed the establishment of occupational groups and the extension and deep-
ening of liberal institutions and collective beliefs. This task is not
utopian because democratic societies already have something of
a liberal common faith, and justice is one of its central features.
Our moral individualism requires care and attention, however,
lest we take it for granted and perhaps lose it, or become complacent and cease to work for moral progress. Durkheim did not
claim to have provided an exhaustive account of what needs to
be done to protect liberalism from egoism. It is worth remember-
ing, though, his warning that the "imaginative flights" of "our
political philosophers" are "too far from the complexity of facts
to be of much practical value.[51] Social reality is not tidy. Durkheim brought *Suicide* to a close by advising that we bring ourselves in "direct contact with things" and "set resolutely to
work."

Durkheim, Goodman, Rorty, and Mild-Mannered Pragmatism

AT PRESENT, an energetic and often volatile debate can be heard in many academic circles. A churlish description of this debate might read something like this: there is an argument between those who maintain that truth and knowledge are independent of human thought, and that therefore our job is to strive to find them, and those who claim that truth and knowledge are made by human thought. The "realists" maintain the former view while the "relativists" hold the latter. The realists are out to save such long-standing notions as "truth," "objectivity," and "sure knowledge," alleging that the relativists are leading us toward emotivism in morality, pragmatism in science, and anarchy in politics. The relativists, in contrast, are out to deconstruct such illusory notions as "truth," "objectivity," and "sure knowledge," claiming that the realists are leading us back to foundationalism in morality, positivism in science, and conservatism in politics.

This description is churlish for several reasons. "The" debate takes on myriad shapes, and hence it is misleading to address it as a single dispute. In literary criticism, we hear disagreement over "the meaning" of a text. Is it found in the text, or in the intention of the author, or is it made by the interpretive community or the solitary reader? In ethics, there is disagreement about whether morality is a single set of universal values to be discovered in human nature, or whether morality is the particular and contingent set of values asserted, variously, by cultures or even individuals. There is no necessary principle of coherence governing these issues. One can imagine a physicist arguing that in literature meaning is produced differently by each reader, that in ethics there is a single morality for all humanity, and that, as for her own work, she isn't concerned with whether particle waves *really* exist so long as she can make new and improved models and predictions, given everything physicists know so far.

How, then, can it be said that there is a single debate between realists and relativists about whether we make or find our moral, literary, or physical world? Moreover, not only does "the" debate appear differently from discipline to discipline, it can vary within a discipline and produce varieties of relativists and realists. In philosophy, ontological relativists argue with conceptual relativists, while metaphysical realists disagree with scientific realists.

Still, there is in the academic guilds much discussion over issues called epistemological, interpretive, or hermeneutical. A useful, albeit crude, way of noting family resemblances among these interlocutors is to divide them into two parties: those who subscribe to worldmaking and those who subscribe to worldfinding. I am not claiming that making versus finding represents the essence of the current discussions. I am claiming that the vocabulary of finding and making allows me to highlight and address a common feature of many current epistemological debates.

In those debates, Durkheim and Nelson Goodman stand forth as what I want to call "mild-mannered pragmatists." Each, in different ways, shows us the relevant and irrelevant differences between making and finding a world. Pragmatism, like most labels designating schools of thought, means different things to different people. I take mild-mannered pragmatism to exclude styles of pragmatism that are sometimes called vulgar. Jeffrey Stout's "Lexicon" gives examples of these: "consequentialism applied to mental acts; the view that cost-benefit calculation is the ultimate language of rational commensuration, . . . the doctrine that the essence of knowledge is problem-solving capability."[1] This is not the place to justify calling these vulgar. I note only that I am not including them. By mild-mannered pragmatism, I refer to those approaches that (1) reject the Enlightenment's metaphysical distinctions between knowledge and opinion, facts and values, reason and emotion, science and morality or art; and that (2) embrace a plurality of ad hoc methods and descriptions in order to account for particular aspects of the world.

This second feature ensures that, for my purposes, pragmatism and antifoundationalism are not taken as synonyms. It excludes, for example, reductionists like some Nietzscheans who systematically reduce morality to emotivism. It also ensures that pragmatism be mild-mannered. At the end of the eighteenth century, the Romantics offered an aggressive response to the Enlightenment's metaphysical dichotomies. They accepted them, but loudly championed art and the emotions over science and reason. The poet, not the scientist, was put forward as the cultural hero. Mild-mannered pragmatism, by contrast, refuses to make such sweeping pronouncements. It tends to shun both metaphysics and reductionism, keeping its eyes on the ground, suggesting specific judgments for particular cases.

There is a third feature of mild-mannered pragmatism closely related to the other two. It opposes the idea that morality, art, and science are best understood as the products of discrete individuals. In other words, it opposes a host of atomistic theories that can be labeled methodological individualism. I am interested in Durkheim's contribution to the first two features— antifoundationalism and epistemological pluralism. I am more concerned, however, with Durkheim's contribution to our understanding of the alternatives to methodological individualism. Here, we see again how Durkheim intimately related individuals to their social and linguistic worlds. Thus he poses still another challenge to classical liberalism and its assumption that society is composed of radically independent individuals.

To call mild-mannered pragmatism a particular style or approach is not to deny its general, imprecise character. It excludes some thinkers, but it can be applied to many, even to those not customarily called pragmatists. Durkheim explicitly rejected "pragmatism," and Goodman never identifies himself with it. Still, I think my definition reasonable and that they both can be usefully described by it.

In Chapter 5 I discuss Durkheim's social epistemology as it relates to conflict between the individual and society. In this

chapter I outline Durkheim's and Goodman's pragmatic approach to epistemology in light of the present debate between
realism and relativism, or as I will describe it, between finding
and making truth, knowledge, and objectivity. My goal is irenic,
for I show, with the help of Goodman and Durkheim, in what
way we both make and find a world. While enabling us to appreciate this, Goodman and Durkheim clarify some good and sensible sentiments found in forms of realism and relativism. Once
again, we learn that we no longer have to be in that uncomfortable position of having to choose one side against the other. Toward the end of the chapter, I examine the work of Richard
Rorty against the background of Goodman's and Durkheim's
views on the reciprocal relationship between finding and making. I want to show how Rorty's failure to attend to that relationship weakens his own version of pragmatism and impedes
sound and charitable readings of his work.

The mediating manner of Goodman and Durkheim, their
willingness to mix philosophical vocabularies and approaches,
can be called pragmatic, at least by the lights of William James.
In *Pragmatism* he listed a series of opposing philosophical positions, for example "rationalistic/empiricist," "idealistic/materi-
alistic," "free-willist/fatalistic," and went on to note that "most
of us have a hankering for the good things on both sides of the
line."[2] We professional philosophers, however, "cannot preserve a good intellectual conscience so long as we keep mixing
incompatibles from opposite sides of the line." To save us from
bad faith, James offered pragmatism as a philosophy that can
satisfy our intuitions about the "good things on both sides of the
line." Of course pragmatism also rejects things from both sides.
"A pragmatist," James wrote, "turns his back resolutely and
once for all upon a lot of inveterate habits dear to professional
philosophers. He turns away from abstraction and insufficiency,
from verbal solutions, from bad *a priori* reasons, from fixed principles, closed systems, and pretended absolutes and origins. He
turns towards concreteness and adequacy, towards actions, and
towards power."[3] Pragmatism, then, "unstiffens all our theories," setting each to work, insofar as it can, on concrete problems, specific cares. Durkheim and Goodman, I argue, exhibit
this philosophical style, this mild-mannered pragmatism. In
particular, they liberate us from those "inveterate habits" that
insist that the world is either found or made, but not both.

Goodman is at his best when he limns the ways of worldmaking. Durkheim is at his best when he delineates the ways of worldfinding. Each man's virtue has occasionally been taken as his vice: Goodman the radical relativist, Durkheim the conservative realist and positivist. The appellations are misplaced insofar as both thinkers disrupt the standard contours of the realist/relativist debate, handling many old philosophical problems in important new ways. They do this by discussing knowledge, truth, and objectivity in terms of entrenchment, authority, and tradition. Their approach no more belittles the objectivity of the world found than it denies the creativity of worlds made. They show the interdependence of finding and making and, more important, the nature of that interdependence.

I

In the foreword to *Ways of Worldmaking*, Goodman says of that book, "What emerges can perhaps be described as a radical relativism under rigorous restraints." A radical relativism under rigorous restraints recognizes that "the world"—and all therein, from Shakespeare's Hamlet to Fermi's neutrinos—is not "fixed and found," but rather consists of worlds or versions of the world that are fluid and ever in the making. Although embracing indeterminacy, it accepts that there are constraints on worldmaking. Worldmaking, most of the time, is not a capricious or whimsical activity. Goodman warns, "While readiness to recognize alternative worlds may be liberating and suggestive of new avenues of exploration, a willingness to welcome all worlds builds none." And elsewhere he notes, "Recognition of multiple alternative world-versions betokens no policy of laissez-faire. Standards distinguishing right from wrong versions become, if anything, more rather than less important."[4] A pressing issue, then, for Goodman is, What constraints are imposed on worldmaking?

Worldmaking is not a matter of an individual arbitrarily deciding how she wants the world to be and then proceeding to describe it as such. This radical form of relativism or subjectivism Goodman rejects. His talk of a plurality of worlds or versions of worlds in no way commits him to the claim that each individual lives in a separate, discrete one. He maintains that worldmakers—and that includes all of us—are born into worlds already made. "The many stuffs—matter, energy, waves, phenomena—that worlds are made of are made along with the worlds. But made from what? Not from nothing, after all, but *from other worlds*. Worldmaking as we know it always starts from the worlds already on hand; the making is a remaking."[5] We no more choose our first language or the colors of the rainbow than we choose our parents. The various shared descriptions of the world about us are "the given." Hence, Goodman writes, "reality in a world, like realism in a picture, is largely a matter of habit." Described reality is handed down to us, and we refashion it, rejecting some portions, accepting or modifying others, according to beliefs, needs, and goals at hand. Goodman is interested, then, in those "processes involved in building a world out of others," in "how worlds are made, tested, and known." Offering us detailed and perspicuous accounts of everyday ways of worldmaking (composition and decomposition, weighing and emphasizing, ordering and arranging, deleting and supplementing, quoting and lying) Goodman provides rich descriptions of what otherwise would be another abstract, philosophical concept.

"Reality in a world . . . is largely a matter of habit." This is bound to offend some. They will ask, "Is the nature of a rock contingent on human habit?" or "Are we really to suppose that the falling tree in the desolate forest makes no sound?" Goodman resists giving standard realist or idealist responses to this line of questioning. For example, when asked, "Is the seen table the same as the mess of molecules?" Goodman replies, "To such questions, discussed at length in the philosophical literature, I suspect that the answer is a firm *yes* and *no*. The realist will resist the conclusion that there is no world; the idealist will resist the conclusion that all conflicting versions describe different worlds. As for me, I find these views equally delightful and equally deplorable—for after all, the difference between them is purely conventional!"[6] Are the apparent table and the molecular one the same table? Would those hard, granular things we call rocks be rocks if humans never showed up? These questions, some claim, make up much of the history of modern philosophy. Goodman has not dismissed the traditional problems of modern philosophy. Rather, he has handled traditional issues in novel ways. How much of the world is made of facts, and how much of theories? Goodman answers, "facts are small theories, and true theories are big facts." Refusing to endorse one of the standard philosophical theories, or to construct an all-too-tidy, full-blown system, Goodman reworks old questions in handy and refreshing new ways. He works like a mild-mannered pragmatist, mediating and reconciling, "unstiffening all our theories," as William James recommended.[7]

Take Goodman's discussion of worldmaking, then, not as a reductive theory about the way the world "really is." It is not an attempt to disclose the essence of "the world." It is not even a theory about worldmaking, if "a theory about worldmaking" refers to something we need to become successful worldmakers. View it, rather, as an acknowledgement and analysis of the transactional relation between language, belief, knowledge, and a world in the making. Goodman shows various ways—some more traveled than others—in which we describe and redescribe, organize and recognize the world.

One of those ways is induction. It is of special interest to Goodman because it illustrates some notable features of worldmaking. In an early essay, Goodman describes induction as "the projection of characteristics of the past into the future, or more generally of characteristics of one realm of objects into another."[8] Hume had investigated the nature of induction and concluded that it has to do with custom and habit, not with the way things "really" are. Goodman is nearly satisfied with the first part of Hume's conclusion but dismisses the second. Hume, of course, was well aware how controversial the second part of that conclusion would be. It left experience as the sole basis for knowledge of the physical world, and one of the principal tasks of philosophy had been to eliminate experience, the particular and contingent stuff from which opinion emerges, in order to get at universal and certain scientific truth. Yet Hume realized that the more one weeds experience out of rational thought, the less one can say about anything. Many philosophers found this a dismal discovery, since they did not trust experience. Nonetheless, Hume never recanted. Accustomed and habitual ways of living in and coping with the world are our sources of understanding. Hence, concerning induction (and, for that matter, deduction), Hume wrote, "'tis impossible to determine, otherwise than by experience, what will result from any phenomenon, or what has preceded it."[9]

From the start, many complained that Hume merely described how an induction takes place, without telling how to justify or validate one. They agreed that observation and induction are largely guided by experience. The problem is how to escape from previous observations and inductions based on custom, and arrive at valid ones based on the way things or minds really are. This problem, of course, has never been solved, and it has become known to some as "Hume's." Goodman protests the designation "Hume's problem." The so-called problem of justifying induction largely *is* one of describing induction, he claims. Hume understood and accepted this. His critics are the ones who have the problem. If Hume's account of induction is inadequate, it is not because of its descriptive nature but because of the imprecision of the description. "Regularities in experience, according to [Hume], give rise to habits of expectation; and thus it is predictions conforming to past regularities that are normal and valid. But Hume overlooks the fact that some regularities do and some do not establish such habits; that predictions based on some regularities are valid while predictions based on other regularities are not." [10]

Prior to this passage, Goodman discusses grue emeralds, his famous illustration of a non-habitual regularity and its invalid prediction. The example begins: "Suppose that all emeralds examined before a certain time *t* are green. At time *t*, then, our observations support the hypothesis that all emeralds are green." [11] Next Goodman introduces an unfamiliar predicate, "grue." Grue "applies to all things examined before *t* just in case they are green but to other things just in case they are blue. Now, at time *t* we have, for each evidence statement asserting that a given emerald is green, a parallel evidence statement asserting that the emerald is grue." If the evidence is the same, we have no way of deciding between the prediction that the next emerald examined will be green and the prediction that it will be grue. Let's establish *t* at midnight. Since all emeralds examined before midnight have been green, we should predict that after waking tomorrow the first emerald examined will be green. Yet according to the definition of the predicate grue, all emeralds hitherto examined have been grue (because they were green). Should we not, then, predict that tomorrow's emerald will be grue, and hence blue? The beauty and puzzlement of the example is that, though we know which predicate is projectable and well-behaved, and which is non-projectable and ill-behaved, the "evidence statement" for each appears to be the same.

How do we determine the difference between well-behaved predicates like green and ill-behaved ones like grue? What are the constraints involved in this particular process of worldmaking known as induction? If worldmaking were simply a matter of making a world as I please, then I should be able to decide that tomorrow's emeralds will be grue. But we seldom settle such issues by fiat. Even if some evidence appears to be equal, we all know the predicate green has more going for it than grue, but what? According to Goodman, "we must consult the record of past projections of the two predicates. Plainly 'green,' as a veteran of earlier and many more projections than 'grue,' has a more impressive biography. The predicate 'green,' we may say, is much better *entrenched* than the predicate 'grue.'"[12] Here, then, is a constraint on worldmaking: "a projection is to be ruled out if it conflicts with the projection of a much better entrenched predicate."

Yet what exactly, one may ask, is entrenched? A class of predicates, or the actual colors they stand for? A human term or a worldly feature? This question is reminiscent of those about apparent tables and silently falling trees. Goodman, in good pragmatist form, avoids the narrow either/or responses commonly found in such debates. He prefers to cut and paste from seemingly opposing theories: "Like Hume, we are appealing to past recurrences, but to recurrences in the explicit use of terms as well as to recurrent features of what is observed. Somewhat like Kant, we are saying that inductive validity depends not only upon what is presented but also upon how it is organized; but the organization we point to is effected by the use of language and is not attributed to anything inevitable or immutable in the nature of human cognition."[13] This brings us to the heart of induction, and to the heart of worldmaking. Earlier I said that a valid prediction agrees with past regularities, and that past regularities give rise to habitual ways of seeing and inferring. Those regularities are not only described by, but are conceptually organized and constituted by our linguistic practices. "Thus the line between valid and invalid predictions (or inductions or projections) is drawn upon the basis of how the world is and has

been described and anticipated in words."[14] Thanks to Goodman, we can now drop the metaphysical issue of whether induction and other forms of worldmaking are a matter of getting in
touch with the actual world or of fabricating worlds out of mere
human convention. The metaphysical question, Do we make or
find a world? no longer has the force of a question that we can
answer. Or, if some think they can answer it, perhaps by theological or some other metaphysical commitments, their answer
will have little to do with how we go about making inductions
or love or cabinets. The answer to the metaphysical issue will,
for the most part, leave the world as it is.

Some readers may feel cheated because I have fettered worldmaking to a found world, and worldfinding to worlds made.
This maneuver is perhaps too constraining for some, too permis-
sive for others. Yet this delicate stratagem is none other than
Goodman's "radical relativism under rigorous restraints." And
the position is as liberating as it is assuring. It is assuring because it commits people to the claim that worldmaking is not an
arbitrary activity. We are bound by a cultural-linguistic world. To
say or to see something new is possible only because we are intimate with that world, with those old entrenched things like
green emeralds.

Those who are interested in the liberating possibilities of
worldmaking might complain, "How can you speak of anything
new? You say all that is has been inherited. Are we not, then,
tied to the past?" Novelty is both common and rare. It is common because we are constantly remaking things found. We
often give veteran concepts new jobs, or leave them to die
quietly in retirement. Novelty is also rare. Seldom do we hear
something highly original. Yet there is a continuum between
everyday remaking and exceptional creativity. All novelty
springs from the familiar world as it is found and lands on a new
territory, thus contributing to worldmaking.

My linking of worlds made to worlds found will perhaps be
judged overly conservative. But if what I have said is not wide
of the mark, it may be agreed that, epistemologically speaking,
the relation between making and finding worlds has little to do
with political conservatism or radicalism.[15] My claiming that
there will be continuity in our descriptions of things and events
in no way proscribes significant modification and openness. It is

safe to say that if no upheaval is noticed in most of our descriptions most of the time, this is because change, however subtle, is constant. Moreover, even the most revolutionary statements, if intelligible, spring from familiar material. Otherwise, we would hear only gibberish. The crank specializes in gibberish, inventing radically new vocabularies or using old ones in unfamiliar ways. The unrecognized genius often does the same. Both use far too many rookie predicates for us to follow, and hence we tend to abuse both. What is the difference between the crank and the genius? One speaks nonsense, the other *makes* sense, even if it is not comprehended at the time.

What has been said of induction applies to judgments of resemblance as well. We learn to compare things in various ways as we acquire sophisticated linguistic practices. To judge similarity among carpet samples, or among wines, or among friends, is to judge different things with various purposes in mind. Newly found similarities are based on older ones. Again, the point is that as we inherit ways of worldmaking, such as comparing and contrasting, we become worldmakers. The constraint on worldmakers is also the material for worldmaking. The assurance of a found world grants the liberty to make one.

We can think of entrenchment as a form of authority. Its authority, however, is not unconditional. We cannot be sure the more entrenched predicate is to be preferred to the less entrenched one. Goodman doesn't hang worldmaking on certitude. He simply offers the observation that we tend to go with the better-entrenched predicate most of the time. If we decide not to, it will be because the particulars of a case lead us in a different direction. Perhaps a rookie term (like quark) fits better than a veteran term (like electron) with the other entrenched features of an experiment. Radical and creative individuals are likely to support rookies. Conservatives and the unimaginative shun them. In any case, entrenchment plays a leading role.[16]

Goodman tells us "the reason why only the right predicates happen so luckily to have become well entrenched is just that the well entrenched predicates have thereby become the right ones."[17] This sounds circular, and of course it is. We justify the rightness of predicates and categories with other predicates and categories. We should fault Hume's critics not for their desire to justify induction, but for the kind of justification they want, the kind that can escape the circularity of justifying rookie predicates with veterans.[18] Justification depends on the authority of successfully entrenched concepts, and on the established organization in which they are found. Of course, to say as much won't help us come up with a good justification. There are as many good ways to assemble authority as there are puzzles to be solved, questions to be answered, results to be explained. The best—the most justifiable—solutions, answers, and explanations will be those that are most persuasive, given all we know about the problem or puzzle at hand. There is no foundation for or essence to justification that, if known, could spare us the hard work of producing it. There is no stepping outside the circle. To try to do so is to attempt to step into God's point of view, an attempt that in many ways characterizes modern epistemology. Hume was one of the first modern voices insisting that human knowledge will always be human. It will entail experience, custom, habit, authority, and tradition. Goodman follows his lead.

II

Some might feel uneasy about where Goodman, in turn, has led us. Entrenchment and authority may seem capricious when compared to the confidence we have in those scientific and everyday procedures such as induction and judging resemblance. The authority involved in these procedures, some might want to say, is the authority of objectivity or of rationality or even of truth. Those who balk at Goodman's talk of entrenchment are likely to reject his notion of worldmaking. It is here, I believe, that Durkheim can help. He accounted for the objectivity we sense in the world found, while also recognizing the creative, human aspect of a world in the making. His work shows the ways in which those who are suspicious of Goodman speak from a valid position, and yet, in the end that work supports Goodman's mild-mannered pragmatism.

Nothing illustrates this better than Durkheim's account of the variety of coherent worlds. Having read the available ethnographic material of his day, Durkheim was struck by the multiplicity of ways of organizing and categorizing the world. It was as if distinct societies and cultures lived each in their own world.

Even the most seemingly simple human ability, such as seeing resemblances, could be manifested variously. In his and Mauss's neglected 1903 essay in *L'Année sociologique*, "De quelques formes primitives de classification," they wrote that "what is conceived in one [society] as perfectly homogeneous is represented elsewhere as essentially heterogeneous." As Durkheim put it in the introduction to *The Elementary Forms of the Religious Life*, "the categories of human thought are never fixed in any one definite form; they are made, unmade and remade incessantly; they change with places and times."[19]

The two leading epistemological doctrines of his day, empiricism and a priorism, could not account for the variety of worlds Durkheim had encountered in ethnographies and historical studies. The empiricists, according to Durkheim, satisfy our sense that the individual's perception of the world is direct and unmediated, yet they deprive reason of its "universality," "necessity," and "authority." The upshot of his criticism was that the implicit individualism of empiricism cannot account for the coherence found within a given cultural worldview. Tlingit Indians, for example, don't choose to see the similarity between a dog salmon and a dog (a similarity I have never been able to see). They just see it. Such vision carries a sense of necessity, authority, and—from a Tlingit's perspective—universality. If one doubts this, try protesting the similarity to a Tlingit.

The a priorists, on the other hand, recognize the universality, necessity, and authority of human thought. The mind, transcending experience, imposes on it the universal and binding categories of reason. But the a priorists cannot give a satisfactory account of this. As Durkheim wrote, "it is no explanation to say that [the powers of reason] are inherent in the nature of the human intellect."[20] Kantians have shown why experience alone cannot produce human cognition. They are to be applauded for this. But "the real question," Durkheim claimed, "is to know how it comes that experience is not sufficient unto itself, but presupposes certain conditions which are exterior and prior to it." Moreover, a priorism cannot account for the variety of worlds. If the powers of the mind are innate, why can't I detect the similarity between a dog salmon and a dog?

Durkheim maintained that progress toward a solution is possible by studying religion, for we are thereby "given a means of renewing the problems which, up to the present, have only been discussed among philosophers." Some might ask, What solution to an epistemological problem could possibly arise out of studying that messy cultural stuff, religion? Durkheim's response was that reason itself is shaped by unkempt sociohistorical institutions, and religion has been an especially formative one. What might seem to be basic, universal categories of human thought, such as time, space, class, number, cause, substance, and personality, are in fact culturally specific categories whose medium is language. Even the law of noncontradiction and the distinction between right and left, according to Durkheim, are sociolinguistic artifacts and are "far from being inherent in the nature of man in general."[21]

Durkheim's account of the variety of coherent worlds proceeded in the style of mild-mannered pragmatism. He sought to retain what is valuable in both the empiricist and the Kantian positions. He noted that "if this debate seems to be eternal, it is because the arguments given are really about equivalent." He managed to salvage the valuable intuitions of both sides and to minimize their opposition by bringing to this epistemological debate insight from his religious investigations. The chief insight was that if "the *social* origin of the categories is admitted, a new attitude becomes possible, which will enable us to escape both of the opposed difficulties." His solution, then, was to socialize the idealists and the empiricists. He agreed with the idealists that human reason operates with categories, but contended these categories are not inherent in humans and are created in the particular activities of various peoples. He agreed with the empiricists that the individual does "directly" perceive the world, but contended that the world is and always has been a social world. As Durkheim put it, "the world is inside of society."[22]

Lest Durkheim sound like a radical relativist, which he was not, I need to add that even while Durkheim unabashedly fleshed out the social nature of knowledge, he insisted that, as individuals, we do not make our world. "We speak a language that we did not make; we use instruments that we did not invent; we invoke rights that we did not found; a treasury of knowledge is transmitted to each generation that it did not gather itself, etc. It is to society that we owe these varied benefits, and if we do not ordinarily see the source from which we get them, we at least know that they are not our own work." [23] Durkheim, more than Goodman, shows that our world as we know it—our reason and practices, our knowledge and beliefs—is the product of historical, social institutions. He did not provide, as does Goodman, perspicuous, detailed descriptions of ways of worldmaking that are found in our own culture. Rather, investigating distant times and places, Durkheim described diverse worlds, wrestled with the epistemological problems posed by them, and declared that the world is not a result of "our own work" but of evolving traditions, categories, and institutions.

When Durkheim claimed that the world is not a result of our making, he wasn't denying human creativity or claiming that novelty is impossible. Durkheim, the historian, was quite aware of the vital role played by imagination and ingenuity. He saw fatalism as an inaccurate description of the social life of modern individuals, and rejected it as a normative prescription for them. Durkheim did, however, recognize and feature the fact that people work with inherited materials. This social inheritance was all-important for him, because it signified an intimate relation between individuals and their sociolinguistic communities.

Consider, for example, how Durkheim accounted for the objectivity we sense in the world. He began his lectures on pragmatism by citing "the pragmatists'"—primarily James's and Dewey's—criticism of rationalism and empiricism. According to these two philosophical theories, "reason is thought of as existing outside of us . . . and truth is a given, either in the sensory world (empiricism) or in an intelligible world, in absolute thought or Reason (rationalism)." In contrast, the pragmatists, according to Durkheim, insist that "*we* make reality": "1) truth is human; 2) it is varied and variable; and 3) it cannot be a copy of a given reality." Durkheim shared the pragmatists' belief that "truth is not a ready-made system: it is formed, de-formed and re-formed in a thousand ways; it varies and evolves like all things human." [24] He saw an affinity between the pragmatists' project and the sociologists':

Herein lies the interest of the pragmatist enterprise: we can see it as an effort to *understand* truth and reason themselves, to restore to them their

human interest, to make of them human things that derive from temporal causes and give rise to temporal consequences. . . . It is here that
we can establish a PARALLEL BETWEEN PRAGMATISM AND SOCIOLOGY. By
applying the *historical* point of view to the order of things human, sociology is led to set itself the same problem. Man is a product of history;
there is nothing in him that is either given or defined in advance. . . .
Consequently, if truth is human, it too is a human product. Sociology
applies the same conception to reason. All that constitutes reason, its
principles and categories, has been made in the course of history.[25]

Durkheim's reference to history at this point is revealing, and
it became the basis of his criticism of pragmatism. The pragmatists, Durkheim claimed, say that we make reality, and for them
"the 'we' means the individual." This individualism Durkheim
found disturbing, for it fails to address his problem of how coherent, shared worlds are established: "individuals are different
beings who cannot all make the world in the same way; and the
pragmatists have had great difficulty in solving the problem of
knowing how several different minds can know the same world
at once." We can temporarily ignore Durkheim's assessment of
the pragmatists and still appreciate his solution to the problem
of how to reconcile a social epistemology with some philosophical and everyday intuitions about coherence, truth, and objectivity. "If one admits that representation is a *collective* achievement, it recovers a unity which pragmatism denies to it. This is
what explains the impression of resistance, the sense of something greater than the individual, which we experience in the
presence of truth, and which provides the indispensable basis of
objectivity."[26]

Durkheim accounted for, and thereby attempted to safeguard, the impersonal character of reason, objectivity, and truth
by disclosing their settled, sociohistorical grounding. Collective
representations—patterned ways of viewing, describing, and
explaining the world—guarantee a significant amount of social
agreement that furnishes coherence and constitutes objectivity.
In notable ways, then, he maintained that we do find a world. It
is not made or chosen by the individual. The world is "the
given," that is, the stuff of history—institutions, language and
beliefs—into which individuals are "thrown," to use Heideg-
ger's metaphor. The given is not a set of determinate facts to be
interpreted in one absolute way. Our interpretations of the
world, whether they concern *A Tale of Two Cities*, the Thirty

Years' War, or T-cell lymphoma, are indeed guided by objectivity, but that objectivity, whether it pertains to literary theory, to history, or to science, is itself constituted by the nature of history, which could be—and has been—described as interpretations of interpretations.

Durkheim, if in one of his positivistic moods, would talk as if institutions, language and beliefs are determinate, albeit social, facts. But at his best, he recognized degrees of both indeterminacy and determinacy in a variety of social facts. The constraints of history, including our thinking and speaking equipment, carry with them the weight of objectivity, the guiding force of reason, and the sacrosanct character of truth. If these qualities or virtues are esteemed, one reason is we know that they are found in the world, and not arbitrarily made.

III

Richard Rorty has said "nothing deep turns on the choice between . . . the imagery of making and finding."[27] Rorty jettisons the metaphysical distinction between making and finding, and for that he deserves praise. But reasons remain, epistemological and ethical, for distinguishing between making and finding. Epistemologically, it is worthwhile to remember that worldmaking begins with a world already made, with a world found. As we are trained, formally and informally, to use language, including predicates such as "green" and occasionally even "grue," and to participate in institutions, including gestures such as a wink, we inherit a ready-made world. This inheritance is necessary for all worldmaking and worldmakers, scientists and philosophers included. Goodman is a case in point. His familiarity with the various debates between philosophical parties enables him to speak imaginatively within them. The philosophical debates are themselves examples of entrenched vocabularies. The vocabularies of realism and relativism, and their sundry quarrels, have accrued "impressive biographies" indeed. The persistence of these vocabularies, and their continual reformation, suggest the interdependence of finding and making.[28] Both realism and relativism have that much going for them.

Another reason for preserving some distinction between making and finding has to do with truth telling. The found world is unavoidable. You and I cannot simply make it as we please. We belong to and are confronted by that world, by its communities and beliefs, by its thoughts and its histories. This is not a metaphysical remark, but an ethical one. We encounter limits, we incur obligations. These restraints—or resources, depending on one's point of view—need to be recognized. They are inescapable aspects of human existence.

Durkheim, unlike Rorty, was quite concerned with the notion of truth and with saving its reputation because truth plays an important social role. It pertains to what I am calling the inescapable aspects of human existence, our sociohistorical inheritance. Durkheim noted that "it is one thing to cast doubt on the correspondence between symbols and reality; but it is quite another to reject the thing symbolized along with the symbol. This pressure that truth is seen as exercising on minds is itself a symbol that must be interpreted, even if we refuse to make of truth something absolute and extra-human." [29] It is the social, historical aspects of those things called true that account for truth's "pressure" on us.

Most of the time Rorty seems content to deconstruct the seldom helpful metaphysical distinction between making and finding. This involves, among other strategies, highlighting the circularity of philosophical efforts that attempt to find the world-in-itself while employing languages that are made. Sometimes, however, Rorty puts forward a case for worldmaking. In *Contingency, Irony, and Solidarity*, for example, he claims that the Romantic notion that "truth is made rather than found" is correct in that "*languages* are made rather than found, and that truth is a property of linguistic entities, of sentences." This strikes me as a sensible epistemological statement, even if it does not acknowledge the ways we find a world in ready-made languages. [30]

Yet Rorty's case for worldmaking often goes beyond epistemological interests. He also advances moral claims. He begins the first chapter of *Contingency, Irony, and Solidarity* by declaring that

About two hundred years ago, the idea that truth was made rather than found began to take hold of the imagination of Europe. The French Revolution had shown that the whole vocabulary of social relations, and the whole spectrum of social institutions, could be replaced almost overnight. This precedent made utopian politics the rule rather than the exception among intellectuals. Utopian politics sets aside questions about both the will of God and the nature of man and dreams of creating a hitherto unknown form of society.[31]

This passage captures the general ethos of Rorty's book. He applauds the Western trajectory that replaced love of God with love of scientific truth, and then love of truth with love of ourselves. This is the path of freedom. Formerly bound to truths beyond the visible world, we now are free to author our own truths. This conviction leads Rorty to claim that "freedom as the recognition of contingency" is "the chief virtue of the members of a liberal society." Human solidarity, then, is "not a matter of sharing a common truth or a common goal but of sharing a common selfish hope, the hope that one's world—the little things . . . which one has woven into one's final vocabulary—will not be destroyed."[32]

There are many good things to be said of this line of thought. Emphasizing the contingency of knowledge, beliefs, practices, and institutions may be a step toward releasing individuals from harmful superstitions and traditions. It may even encourage individuals to be more likely to criticize the status quo, since no present state of affairs can claim to be beyond scrutiny because supported by divine or natural reason. I take this to be one of the chief moral lessons of worldmaking. Recognizing the contingency of our history and institutions, we may be more willing to entertain novel approaches to public and personal problems that would otherwise remain intractable. This is the benefit I have associated with Durkheim's and Goodman's mild-mannered pragmatism. Moreover, awareness of the contingency of our problems could make us more aware of the contingency, and therefore the limits, of our solutions. We may learn that there are no final solutions. We may become practitioners of what Michael Walzer has called "exodus politics," a politics of continual reform ("a long series of decisions, backslidings, and reforms") while successfully avoiding "messianic politics," a politics of absolutized revolutions and once-and-for-all solutions.[33]

But there's reason to pause. Durkheim, I have said, shows the ways we make *and* find a world. He worried about the pragmatists when they said we make the world, because for them "the 'we' means the individual." This worry, for the most part, was misplaced. Pragmatism, I have argued, often highlights the interaction between individual creativity and social traditions. James, for example, wrote that "new truth . . . marries old opinion to new fact so as ever to show a minimum of jolt, a maximum of continuity."[34] As if responding to Durkheim, he continued, "the point I now urge you to observe particularly is the part played by the older truths. Failure to take account of it is the source of much of the unjust criticism leveled against pragmatism. Their influence is absolutely controlling."

Still, Durkheim's concern about pragmatism was not entirely unfounded. James occasionally sounded unduly like he endorsed subjectivism, as when he claimed that "a new opinion counts as 'true' just in proportion as it gratifies the individual's desire to assimilate the novel in his experience to his beliefs in stock. . . . When old truth grows, then, by new truth's addition, it is for subjective reasons."[35] And at times, pragmatists seemed overly infatuated with the individual's will-to-power, as if the only things hindering human happiness and progress were weak wills. Durkheim feared that the pragmatists had not attended sufficiently to the world found. This is my concern about Rorty.

Rorty, patron of pragmatism and campaigner against unhelpful dualisms, claims to dismiss the difference between worldmaking and worldfinding. In fact he often champions the ethics of making and neglects the ethics of finding. I am not arguing, as does the philosopher Jenny Teichman, that Rorty's infatuation with making represents "nothing more or less than the tribal mores of teenage human males."[36] I want to give Rorty a fair reading. He successfully articulates some of the ethical implications of making. But more attention to the ways of finding would have strengthened his case.

For example, note again the paragraph cited above. He states that "The French Revolution had shown that the whole vocabulary of social relations, and the whole spectrum of social institutions, could be replaced almost overnight." The Revolution made room for utopian politics and its "dreams of creating a hitherto unknown form of society." But was the Revolution the beginning of something new, or the continuation of something old? Was it the result of individual imaginations set free, or of social forces already in motion? And did the utopian politics set aside "questions about both the will of God and the nature of man," or were its dreams a result of some answers to these questions?

I'm not looking for one-liner responses to the questions I just posed. The questions remind me of James's "Does the man go round the squirrel or not?"[37] There are as many good answers to these questions as there are good points of view. Mild-mannered pragmatism is willing to entertain many points of view. Rorty usually is. But his statement on the French Revolution illustrates his failure to explore the ways that new things, like revolutions, are connected with old things, like social traditions. He has failed to tell us about the ways we find, as well as make, truth, objectivity, and knowledge.

This has made him a target for abuse. Teichman claims that, for Rorty, there is no objective difference "between cruelty and kindness, no such things as human nature and human solidarity, no such thing as objective reason and no such thing as truth."[38] Saying that Rorty doesn't think there is such a thing as human solidarity is the only thing unequivocally false in her claim. The rest is ambiguous. The ambiguity springs from the term "objective." If by "objective" Teichman means something known in and of itself, independent of socially produced concepts or entrenched vocabularies, then her claim is mostly correct. If, on the other hand, "objective" refers to the capacity to make sound judgments, given everything we know—for example, on what counts as a cruel or a kind act—then her claim is clearly false. Rorty thinks there is an objective difference between cruelty and kindness, and he thinks certain novelists can deepen our sensitivity to varieties of both. If Rorty had followed Durkheim's lead in describing the ways we find a world—a world outfitted with objectivity, truth, and knowledge—he might have averted misleading reviews such as Teichman's. More important, he might have helped us understand some important features of the ethics of finding a world.

Worldmaking, if not sufficiently wed to the ways we find a world, could lead to outcomes different from those Rorty wants. It could, for example, lead to moral nihilism or to a form of moral relativism that maintains that it is impossible to judge or to be judged by a member of a foreign culture. It could fail to make clear the ways we are confronted with circumstances not of our

own choosing; the ways we can learn something new about ourselves by being attentive to those historical traditions that have
shaped us; the ways the world found can make or remake us.
Those who shun the world found are likely to miss its lessons.
Rorty exalts authors who create self-made worlds. Yet, if there
really are such authors, I suspect they risk becoming immune to
transformation. Genuine worldmakers, like good listeners, have
open, socially tutored hearts. They are disciplined in allowing
the world found to talk back to them. Again, no metaphysical
work is being done here. I am only reworking Durkheim's message: we belong to and are confronted by a world not of our own
making.

That world is still a contingent world, a world that can be remade. Virtuous and creative individuals felicitously navigate the
junctures of the found and the made world. They struggle to
know where change is required. They attempt to figure out
which traditions are helpful, which are destructive. They find a
world stocked with moral customs, works of art, and green emeralds. Their moral vision, artistic insight, and scientific know-
how springs from the world found. Yet from this world they
make new constructions. How do they know their new crea-
tions are better than those received? How can they discern the
difference between moral progress and amoral (or immoral)
change? They do the best they can, given the best beliefs available. What more could we ask of them? They, of necessity, justify
rookie concepts, beliefs, practices, and institutions with veterans. This is a natural circularity. It's human. The attempt to escape it is unnatural. Rorty claims that "freedom as the recognition of contingency" is "the chief virtue of the members of a
liberal society," but "the recognition of contingency" is not a virtue, it is simply one more description of the human condition.
We need all the virtues, including freedom, practical wisdom,
and courage, in order to live a good life in the midst of contingency, that is, in the absence of eternal, transcendent solutions.

I take Rorty's definition of human solidarity as "not a matter
of sharing a common truth or a common goal but of sharing a
common selfish hope, the hope that one's world—the little
things . . . which one has woven into one's final vocabulary—
will not be destroyed" to mean that the protection of private
space is a shared, common goal, and that it is sufficient for estab-

lishing solidarity. Durkheim, however, thought solidarity requires more than this. In an age marked by increased individualism and the eclipse of many traditional communities and social practices, Durkheim reminds us that when we inhabit the modern world (or worlds), we still receive many shared truths and goals from the public world, a world not simply of our own, private making. Durkheim attempted to expose and strengthen the ties that join us to each other and to a common past and shared future. The rights and dignity of the individual are no doubt salient features of our solidarity. Yet these are accompanied by various social commitments and obligations, and in modern Western societies they need to be situated in the shared, moral context of democratic republicanism, lest they promote egoism—"a common selfish hope"—instead of moral individualism—a common set of liberal dispositions and virtues.

IV

The plurality of versions of the world led both Durkheim and Goodman to investigate the crucial role played by history and tradition, authority and entrenchment in various processes of finding and making a world. They both follow Hume in reminding us of the thoroughly human, situated nature of knowledge. And they reject any scheme that would fundamentally sever knowledge in half by carving an absolute line between Natur- and Geisteswissenschaften, between science on the one hand and morality and art on the other. In *Ways of Worldmaking*, Goodman says that "a major thesis of this book is that the arts must be taken no less seriously than the sciences as modes of discovery, creation, and enlargement of knowledge in the broad sense of advancement of the understanding." Likewise, Durkheim, inquiring whether there is an essential difference between "value judgments and judgments of reality" concluded that "there is no difference in nature." [39]

Durkheim and Goodman do not deny that there are differences between the various pursuits we call the sciences and those we call ethics or the arts. Dissimilar goals and problems, however, account for most of these differences, not dissimilar levels of objectivity or subjectivity. Objectivity and subjectivity have more to do with the degree of agreement or entrenchment than with what the Enlightenment understood as knowledge and opinion. Durkheim and Goodman scrap the notion that the sciences are distorted by social and historical elements. Durkheim, though it might as well have been Goodman, writes:

We now know what a multiplicity of elements make up the mechanism by virtue of which we construct, project, and localize. . . . The faculties of definition, deduction, and induction are generally considered as immediately given in the constitution of the individual understanding. . . . This conception of the matter was not at all surprising so long as the development of logical faculties was thought to belong simply to individual psychology, so long as no one had the idea of seeing in these methods of scientific thought veritable social institutions.[40]

Given the present, fierce polarization between worldmakers and worldfinders, relativists and realists, we should applaud Durkheim and Goodman for providing a middle way that champions human creativity while avowing the felt pressure of truth.[41] As mild-mannered pragmatists, they have held on to what is good and true in two opposing theories, and have enabled us to describe ourselves, epistemologically and morally, as both makers and finders.

The Individual in Society: A Sacred Marriage?

THE CHARACTERISTIC *sacredness* with which the human being is now invested . . . is not inherent. Analyze man as he appears to empirical analysis and nothing will be found that suggests this *sanctity*; man is a temporal being. But . . . the human being is becoming the pivot of social consciousness among European peoples and has acquired an incomparable value. It is society that has *consecrated* him. Man has no innate right to this aura that surrounds and protects him against *sacrilegious trespass*. It is merely the way in which society thinks of him, the high esteem that it has of him at the moment, projected and objectified. Thus very far from there being the *antagonism* between the individual and society which is often claimed, moral individualism, the *cult* of the individual, is in fact the product of society itself. It is society that instituted it and made of man the *god* whose servant it is.[1]

This passage, from "The Determination of Moral Facts," an essay written by Durkheim in 1906, is replete with religious rhetoric, yet Durkheim was an atheist. Another curiosity: Durkheim claimed that there is no antagonism between the individual and society, yet anyone familiar with Durkheim's thought knows that he often talked of conflict between the individual and society. Concerning our individual and social natures, for example, Durkheim wrote that "there is a true antagonism between them. They mutually contradict and deny each other. We cannot pursue moral ends without causing a split within ourselves, without offending the instincts and the penchants that are the most deeply rooted in our bodies."[2] How are we to account for the pervasive religious vocabulary marking Durkheim's later work, and what was his mature position on the individual's relation to society? These two questions, I argue, are closely related, and by addressing the first I hope to shed light on the second. Religion, for Durkheim, underscored the fundamentally social nature of knowledge and, therefore, of human existence.

I

"Religion," wrote Durkheim, "is the way of thinking characteristic of collective existence." This remarkable claim needs to be understood in the context of Durkheim's social epistemology. In the previous chapter I claimed that Durkheim's epistemology preserved a relation between the ways we find and make the world. I now want to discuss the implications of this for the relation between the public and the private. But first I need to say more about Durkheim's theory of knowledge, especially as it relates to social, moral ideals.

Durkheim articulated the social nature of knowledge in the categories of (1) collective representations, (2) concepts, and (3) ideals. Collective representations, socially produced, patterned ways of viewing, describing, and explaining the world, are the most generic of the three. In "Individual and Collective Representations," an essay written in 1898, Durkheim argued for the relative autonomy of collective representations. As individual representations are not determined by an individual's neurological substratum, so collective representations are "partially autonomous realities with their own way of life. They have the power to attract and repel each other and to form amongst themselves various syntheses, which are determined by their natural affinities and not by the condition of their matrix." Durkheim, who had occasionally described society as a reflection of morphological, structural facts, now claimed that collective representations, the stuff of social life, are "immediately caused by other collective representations and not by this or that characteristic of the social structure."[3]

Concepts, a type of collective representation, "correspond to the way in which this very special being, society, considers the things of its own proper existence." They "express the manner in which society represents things." I call concepts a type of collective representation because of a special public role Durkheim attributes to them—that of communication: "conversation and all intellectual communication between men is an exchange of concepts. The concept is an essentially impersonal representation; it is through it that human intelligences communicate." Sensual representations such as a sensation, perception, or image are fleeting and private, but concepts are relatively fixed and entirely public. "A concept is not my concept; I hold it in common with other men." Durkheim did not maintain an absolute distinction between the sensual and the conceptual, for he recognized that there are probably no representations "where the two elements are not found closely united," and occasionally he abandoned the Kantian distinction altogether. In any case, he insisted that concepts cannot be held privately. Not only can there be no private language, in this account, but Durkheim also suggested that many concepts cannot be entirely grasped by a single individual even in a public context. Concepts are stores of knowledge. The individual must assimilate concepts in order to become a social creature, but that assimilation is always partial. "Which of us," Durkheim asked, "knows all the words of the language he speaks and the entire signification of each?"[4] As we become skillful with a variety of concepts, we are initiated into a public world, a world found.

Concepts, then, are bits of social reality that transcend the individual. I cannot hold them privately. I cannot exhaustively hold them publicly. Without them, however, I am not human. Durkheim wrote, "A man who did not think with concepts would not be a man, for he would not be a social being . . . he would be indistinguishable from the beasts." Concepts are pools of life in which we felicitously swim but which we cannot entirely control. They have defined contours, sources, outlets, and yet they are constantly changing. They surround individuals with a common environment, an environment that individuals manipulate for different ends. As environments, concepts shape individuals at least as much as individuals fashion concepts.[5]

Ideals, the third category Durkheim used to articulate the social nature of knowledge, are sacred collective representations that promote moral unity and well-being. They are cherished social values, beliefs, and goals, the soul of a society. As such, they combat egoism, "forcing the individual to rise above himself." Modern industrial society, with its sophisticated division of labor, could not flourish without public ideals. More is required than bureaucratic efficiency and experts in public policy. Moreover, societies cannot be understood adequately without reference to their ideals. "To see a society only as an organized body of vital functions is to diminish it, for this body has a soul which is the composition of collective ideals." In short, "the principal social phenomena, religion, morality, law, economics and aesthetics, are nothing more than systems of values and hence of ideals." Sociology, then, studies not only morphological facts but also social ideals.[6]

Ideals, in Durkheim's account, are not static, universal principles discovered in scholars' studies. They are "essentially dynamic, for behind them are the powerful forces of the collective." Nor, for that matter, are ideals abstract goals or utopian scenarios. They are not, as Durkheim said, "cloud cuckoo land." When Martin Luther King, Jr., said, "I have a dream," he was appealing to concrete, operative ideals embedded in portions of North American society. When Durkheim said, "to love one's society is to love this ideal [moral individualism]," he, too, was appealing to concrete ideals.[7]

Had Durkheim changed from a materialist to an idealist? I think not. First, the question implies that at some point Durkheim actually was a materialist. However, he never attempted systematically to render a culture's values, beliefs, and goals as an expression of its material substratum. Idealism is not an apt description of his mature position, either. In fact, he disassociated himself from the reductive forms of both materialism and idealism. In *The Elementary Forms*, for example, he noted that he wanted to avoid "a simple restatement of historical materialism. . . . In showing that religion is something essentially social, [I] do not mean to say that it confines itself to translating into another language the material forms of society and its immediate vital necessities."[8] Yet on the same page he wrote, "we take it as self-evident that social life depends upon its material foundation and bears its mark." When he added to the declaration "the ideal is not 'cloud cuckoo land'" that "it is *of* and *in* nature," he was distinguishing ideals from both noumenal principles and academic conjecture. Ideals are not the result of private speculation. More likely, such speculation springs from historically situated ideals. Nor are ideals innate features of the mind or of nature. They are, as Durkheim put it, subject to time and space. They are natural, but only insofar as they are produced by social, historical forces, and these forces are basic to human existence.

In good pragmatist form, then, Durkheim challenged not only the materialist/idealist dualism, but also the nature/culture dualism. Social and cultural phenomena—language, texts, customs, beliefs, means of production, any and all social institutions—are, in principle, no more or less mysterious than gravity or gravy. Social ideals, Durkheim wrote, are "subject to examination like the rest of the . . . physical universe." They are real. They are tangible. Durkheim's social epistemology, which sought to do away with the empiricism/a priorism dichotomy, was a middle way, or put better, a different way. It portrayed an inextricable, transactional relation between the material world and the conceptual world. To speak of two worlds, in fact, is misleading. Durkheim materialized ideals and idealized matter—and he historicized both.[9] In the process, he attempted to overcome a set of tyrannous dualisms—empiricism and a priorism, materialism and idealism, nature and culture. The resulting position, I believe, appropriately describes the materiality of beliefs, values, and customs, as well as the sociality of knowledge, facts, and logic.

II

To appreciate Durkheim's thought on the relation between individuals and society, it helps to see how his social epistemology emerged from changes in his understanding of religion's social role. From the start, Durkheim was interested in religion, but he claimed that he did not recognize its singular importance, especially for modern societies, until the mid-1890's. Contrary to many of his commentators, I believe Durkheim's position on religion in modern society developed not so much out of a new conception of religion as from a fresh understanding of the nature of modern societies that allowed him to see its pervasive influence there.

As we have seen, Durkheim's earliest essay on religion defined it as a set of collective representations providing a socially
indispensable common faith. In *The Division of Labor* he dismissed the accepted definition of religion as beliefs about "a
being or beings whose nature [man] regards as superior to his
own."[10] The definition, he claimed, is inadequate, for religion
pertains not only to relationships with the supernatural but to a
variety of "legal, moral and economic relationships." Religion's
characteristic feature is not a unique set of beliefs, in this case
beliefs about the supernatural. Religion's peculiarity, rather,
arises from how its beliefs and practices are held, and how they
operate. Collective convictions pertaining to any number of beliefs and practices, if "shared by a single community of people
inevitably assume a religious character."[11] Religion, then, is a
community's central or guiding beliefs and practices. This early
account of religion basically corresponds to Durkheim's later
thought. However, according to the Durkheim of *The Division of
Labor*, religion's days are numbered.

If there is one truth that history has incontrovertibly settled, it is that
religion extends over an ever-diminishing area of social life. Originally,
it extended to everything; everything social was religious—the two
words were synonymous. Then gradually political, economic and
scientific functions broke free from the religious functions. . . . In short
. . . the sphere of religion . . . is continually diminishing. This regres-
sion . . . is bound up with the basic conditions for the development of
societies and thus demonstrates that there is a constantly decreasing
number of beliefs and collective sentiments that are both sufficiently
collective and strong enough to assume a religious character.[12]

Within a few years of writing this, however, Durkheim reversed
his position. He now claimed that religion permeates modern
societies. Although its beliefs and practices have changed, at
least in Europe, its basic form has not. Robust, collective beliefs
and practices are still prevalent, Durkheim claimed, though not
in domains usually associated with religion. The political, economic, and even scientific realms are infused with the religious.
Individual rights, notions of economic fair play, and the spirit of
free inquiry, for example, are fraught with the sacred.

Durkheim's reversal was not the result of a radically new
understanding of religion; it was the result of a new understand-

ing of modern society that emerged from his reading of anthropological and ethnographic material. He began to perceive continuities between modern and traditional societies. As a consequence, he not only became interested in accounting for the variety of coherent worlds found in both, he began to see that a common faith is not just an attribute of traditional societies. Modern societies, too, need and develop their own common faiths. The distinction between the two types of society appeared to Durkheim merely to consist in the contents of their respective faiths—collectivism as opposed to democracy, for example, or blind faith as opposed to free inquiry. We can appreciate what Durkheim made of this insight into the continuities between traditional and modern societies without having to accept his description of their differences.

Durkheim applied that insight to the status of religion in modern societies in an 1899 article, "De la définition des phénomènes religieux," in which he noted that "between science and religious faith there are intermediate beliefs; these are common beliefs of all kinds, which are relevant to objects that are secular in appearance, such as the flag, one's country, some form of political organization, some hero, or some historical event, etc." Many secular beliefs, he claimed, are "indistinguishable from religious beliefs proper." They are indistinguishable because modern France, like traditional societies, has a common, even if "secular," faith. "The mother country, the French Revolution, Joan of Arc, etc., are for us sacred things that we do not permit to be touched. Public opinion does not willingly permit one to contest the moral superiority of democracy, the reality of progress, and the idea of equality."[13]

I am not suggesting that Durkheim's thinking on religion remained entirely unchanged from 1899 until his death in 1917. In the 1899 article on religion, for example, Durkheim attempted to distinguish religion as it is traditionally understood from other social phenomena by placing rituals within the special domain of religion.[14] As he later broadened his notion of ritual to include more and more "secular" activities, he abandoned this attempt. I am suggesting, however, that it was Durkheim's notion of modern society, rather than his notion of religion, that underwent radical revision.

Durkheim's new position is perhaps not surprising, given all we know about his earlier work. What is surprising is that in *The Division of Labor* he seemed uncertain and unconcerned about whether modern societies have a common faith, and that he asserted "the sphere of religion . . . is continually diminishing." Be that as it may, Durkheim's involvement in the Dreyfus affair and his reading of Robertson Smith in 1895 surely inspired him to pursue a course different from that found in *The Division of Labor.* "It was not until 1895," Durkheim wrote, "that I achieved a clear view of the essential role played by religion in social life. . . . [This reorientation] was entirely due to the studies of religious history which I had just undertaken, and notably to the reading of the works of Robertson Smith and his school." [15] In the midst of the Dreyfus affair, Durkheim read the following in Smith's *Lectures on the Religion of the Semites*:

> The most important functions of ancient worship were reserved for public occasions, when the whole community was stirred by a common emotion. . . . In renewing by a solemn act of worship the bond that united him to his god, [a man] renewed the bonds of family, social, and national obligation. . . . The compact between the god and the community of his worshippers was not held to pledge the deity to make the private cares of each member of the community his own. . . . Every complete act of worship . . . had a public or quasi-public character. . . . Every act of worship expressed the idea that man does not live for himself only but for his fellows, and that this partnership of social interests is the sphere over which the gods preside. [16]

This passage and others similar to it enabled Durkheim to perceive his own work in a new light. For some time he had argued that religion pertains to the shared beliefs and practices of a traditional moral community. He also had been mounting a sustained critique of classical liberalism and its assumption that modern society is, or should be, a group of disparate individuals pursuing private projects. Then, during the Dreyfus affair, Durkheim believed he was witnessing a modern society stirred and social ideals renewed as a moral community was being forged. He discerned a common liberal faith being reaffirmed and extended by the Dreyfus affair. This faith—call it civic republicanism or moral individualism—supported the rights and dignity of the individual, and the idea that one does not live for oneself alone but for one's fellows. Durkheim now had a powerful vocabulary for articulating the relationship between the individual and modern democratic society, the vocabulary of religion.

III

Just as a new insight into the common features of traditional and modern societies changed Durkheim's understanding of religion in modern society, his mature understanding of religion exerted a reciprocal influence on his social epistemology. In *The Elementary Forms* Durkheim defined religion as "a unified system of beliefs and practices relative to sacred things, that is to say, things set apart and forbidden—beliefs and practices which unite into one single moral community."[17] Durkheim maintained that in traditional societies, many collective representations initially were religious because they pertained to the entire society. Imagine that the eastern side of a river is sacred, the home of a Dog Salmon totem, while the western side is profane. On the western side lies the village where profane activities such as hunting, eating, defecating, and sex take place. On the eastern side occur the sacred feasts and rituals. Representations beget representations. From the religious distinction between the sacred and profane, according to Durkheim, is derived the scientific notion of the law of noncontradiction. Together, sacred and profane collective representations constitute the sociolinguistic world. Knowledge, then, is a set of varied public institutions and representations, some sacred, some not.

Durkheim's genealogy of sacred and profane representations strikes one as mythical. His work is more interesting and helpful when it investigates the character, not the origin, of religion. He is at his best when he explores the ways religion can be described as collective representations that inform a community's moral vision. Then he clearly treats religion and the sacred as authoritative, socially entrenched concepts and ideals that shape a common perception of, and therefore life in, the moral universe.

In this account, religion is pervasive in modern, secular society. We find it wherever public, normative concepts are employed. The upshot of this, morally and epistemologically, is that human life is, in a significant sense, life together. There can be no radically private human existence. To exist in a world is to understand that world, and understanding is comprised of public representations. "I think, therefore I am" is satisfactory if we take the "I think" as a social involvement. "I partake, and therefore I am" is probably more descriptive of human existence than is Descartes's formula. It is more descriptive, and, in Durkheim's view, it is also a normative position insofar as it challenges some atomistic assumptions found in classical liberalism.

This depiction of religion as sacred, social institutions fashioning our lives provided Durkheim with a vocabulary that enabled him to articulate the public, fixed nature of moral knowledge and practices. A society's moral existence is embedded in its institutions and traditions. Yet moral representations are subject to alteration. Religion, as Durkheim understood it, emerges variously out of the play of countless factors, some morphological, some not.

The both fluid and fixed nature of religious representations is, of course, true of all representations, including the scientific and prudential. Religious collective representations differ from these because theirs is the domain of guiding ideals and values that promote moral unity. Every society, then, to the extent that it exhibits moral unity, can be said to possess a common faith, that is, to be religious. This common faith does not require fatalistic uniformity. It can permit conflict. It can permit pluralism. These considerations depend on the content of the faith. In liberal democratic societies, a salient feature of a common faith could be a set of dispositions and procedures for resolving or living with a variety of conflicts. And a pluralistic society could be said to have a common faith that obtains in some spheres, and a variety of faiths in others. I discuss this possible description in the next chapter. For now it is enough to note that a common faith, in Durkheim's account, is not incompatible with pluralism.

I see no reason to complain that, given Durkheim's new position, virtually any set of shared ideals and practices promoting moral unity could be labeled "religious." Many in the field of religious studies have grown wary of essentialistic definitions of religion. Some, as mild-mannered pragmatists, are willing to adopt a variety of definitions for a variety of occasions. I find Durkheim's definition useful for articulating the social nature of ideals and practices that sustain and extend democratic institutions. Moral individualism, I have argued, is an especially important set of social ideals and practices, for it preserves the benefits of liberalism and communitarianism, while safeguarding these from egoism and fatalism.

IV

Moral individualism is not found exclusively in "Individualism and the Intellectuals" (1898). The concept pervades his later work. In "The Determination of Moral Facts" (1906), for example, Durkheim wrote, "Moral life begins with membership of a group. . . . Insofar as [an individual] is a member of the collectivity . . . he tends to take on some of its dignity and he becomes an object of our affection and interest. To be a member of the society is . . . to be bound to the social ideal. . . . It is then natural that each individual participates to some extent in the religious aspect which this ideal inspires."[18]

Léon Brunschvicg, the French neo-Kantian philosopher, objected to Durkheim's insistence that individual liberties are social institutions. He suggested that the progress of civilization be seen as allowing "individual freedom more and more the exercise of its right of resumption against the material structure of society." Durkheim replied,

It is not a matter of resumption but of an accession made by the grace of society. These rights and liberties are not things inherent in man as such. If you analyze man's constitution you will find no trace of this sacredness with which he is invested and which confers upon him these rights. This character has been added to him by society. Society has consecrated the individual and made him pre-eminently worthy of respect. His progressive emancipation does not imply a weakening but a transformation of the social bonds.[19]

What counts as emancipation, in Durkheim's view, is a whole host of things. In the context of his conversation with Brunschvicg, Durkheim said, "freedom consists in deliverance from blind, unthinking physical forces; this [the individual] achieves by opposing against them the great and intelligent force that is society. By putting himself under the wing of society, he makes himself also, to a certain extent, dependent upon it. But this is a liberating dependence. There is no paradox here." Freedom is frequently taken to refer to the absence of constraints. Durkheim, however, never accepted this. As a social theorist, Durkheim knew that to be humanly alive is to move felicitously within the many contours of social constraints, that is, social beliefs, practices, and institutions. "Kant," Durkheim wrote, "declares that the human person should be autonomous. But an absolute autonomy is impossible. The person forms part of the physical and social milieu; the person is bound up with it and can be only relatively autonomous."[20]

Employing the vocabulary of religion to articulate the relationship between the individual and modern society allowed Durkheim, in his mature work, to refine and extend these mediating accounts reconciling individualism and communitarianism. The moral authority that "religious" ideals possess and the moral unity that "religious" practices secure enabled Durkheim to give a radically social description of the individual's existence. Sacred ideals draw the individual into the collective, facilitating a moral existence. Far from there being an essential cleft between society and the individual, Durkheim claimed in *The Elementary Forms* that "the individual gets from society the best part of himself, all that gives him a distinct character and a special place among other beings, his intellectual and moral culture."[21] This is not to say that the individual's social nature precludes all conflict between the individual and various social spheres. The point is, there is no basic, natural antagonism between society and the individual, as, for example, Rousseau or Freud might have us believe. In fact, the very notion of "the individual" is a social convention. Modern democracies that champion individual rights, then, incur no unique or unusual problem relating the individual to society. Difficulties exist, but these have to do with specific, concrete situations (some of which I address in the following chapter) and not with a fundamental friction.

I have shown how sacred collective representations associate the individual with society. Mediation occurs on still another level. Profane concepts, like sacred ones, constitute a common ground on which diverse members of a society stand. Profane, here, means pedestrian and ordinary, not blasphemous or impious. To speak of a door as hard or a berry as sweet involves shared, profane concepts.[22] Ordinary events and activities, then, indicate social affinity. Durkheim underscored the depth of public connectedness to counter the individualistic bent of many Cartesian, Spencerian, and even some Kantian models of human nature.

Yet Durkheim never suggested that the social nature of knowledge, in and of itself, can bring about a flourishing society. He did not hold, contrary to the claims of some of his commentators, that every collective representation is sacred, that is, promotes moral community. Agreement on the hardness of a door or the sweetness of a berry does not morally connect individuals. Such "profane" agreement, morally speaking, often guarantees little more than success in finding our way to a battlefield. This leads me to question moral philosophers who have become sanguine in the light of Donald Davidson's arguments that disagreement can't go all the way down. The kind of epistemological agreement Davidson is referring to, the level of agreement necessary to make sense of disagreement, does not resolve disputes, but merely insures that we can recognize them.

This is one reason Durkheim's discovery of the sacred in modern existence is of some importance. Profane agreement is not enough. An elemental, social, communitarian description of human activity can counter baneful atomistic epistemologies. But if personal and public virtue are to be established or sustained, it will be largely by way of the promising forces of normative, sacred ideals and practices. And modern democratic traditions, if we sufficiently attend to them, carry such promise, according to Durkheim.

V

The connection is clear, then, between Durkheim's frequent use of religious language and his claim that "very far from there being the *antagonism* between the individual and society which is often claimed, moral individualism, the cult of the individual, is in fact the product of society itself."[23] The presence of the sacred signals the absence of radical conflict between individuals and society, and in democratic societies, moral individualism represents a set of sacred ideals and practices uniquely centered on the individual. Yet there is room for doubt—doubt as to whether Durkheim's claim that there is no antagonism between the individual and society is true; and, consequently, doubt as to whether Durkheim actually meant that there is no conflict whatsoever.

To some extent I have already addressed the second doubt.

There are a thousand and one ways to talk about the individual's relation to society. Durkheim knew this. He also knew that a multitude of contingent conflicts occur between individuals and various social spheres, such as the domestic or civic. When he claimed there is no antagonism between the individual and society, he was in conversation with historical figures such as Hobbes and Rousseau on the one hand and with contemporaries such as Brunetière and Bergson on the other. All four held that there is a fundamental antagonism, even if each understood the consequences of that antagonism differently. Durkheim, however, rejected the very idea of a basic antagonism. He asserted that "while society transcends us it is immanent in us" and that in fact "it is ourselves." Consequently, "to love society is to love both something beyond us and something in ourselves. We could not wish to be free of society without wishing to finish our existence as men. Society . . . is bound up in the very fibers of our being." Durkheim's position, then, was that "the characteristic attributes of human nature come from society."[24] Human beings are naturally social; culture is a natural phenomenon. These statements I take to be axiomatic and normative, and I have already rehearsed Durkheim's arguments for them.

The first doubt is settled. Insofar as I have suitably limited the scope of Durkheim's claim, the claim is true. In light of that, the second doubt is also settled, though it requires more discussion. To say that Durkheim's claim does not refer to all antagonism is not to say enough. I need to make sense of Durkheim's comments that suggest there is antagonism, as when he says, "society has its own nature, and consequently, its requirements are quite different from those of our nature as individuals; the interests of the whole are not necessarily those of the part." This example comes from an essay in which Durkheim described the human as *homo duplex*. Humans possess two qualities, traditionally known as body and soul. The former is profane, and refers to private sensations and egoistic propensities; the latter is sacred, and refers to public concepts and morality. Insofar as these two qualities are at war with each other, "our joy can never be pure; there is always some pain mixed with them; for we cannot simultaneously satisfy the two beings that are within us."[25]

Before I give my interpretation of Durkheim's *homo duplex*, it is worth summarizing what I take to be the standard reading of it. This reading, I believe, is forcefully and articulately advanced by Sheldon Wolin and Jerrold Seigel. The reading takes Durkheim to have been pursuing an "uncompromising campaign against the subject" displaying a marked "hostility against the individual."[26] For the sake of social order, in this view, Durkheim placed the highest premium on public agreement. Even mundane concepts he saw as significant means to engender profound agreement, and not as mere tools to capture reality. In this account, the individual's nature is twofold: it is a receptacle to be filled by society, yet it is a rebellious self, fighting against the mandates imposed by society. The result is a picture of "human nature sharply divided against itself," an opposition "between what came from inside the individual and what came from society."[27] The war Durkheim waged, then, was against "the individual" as a formidable menace to social cohesion.

To this interpretation I have three objections. First, it ignores an outstanding feature of Durkheim's mature work, his emphasis on the desirability of pursuing social goals. Durkheim complained that "Kant's hypothesis, according to which the sentiment of obligation was due to the heterogeneity of reason and sensibility, is not easy to reconcile with the fact that moral ends are in one aspect objects of desire."[28] If Durkheim objected to positing an absolute antagonism between individual desire and social (or universal) obligation, it was because he did not conceive of human nature as fatally divided against itself. From *Suicide* until his death, Durkheim increasingly used the voluntaristic vocabulary of love, respect, and desire—as opposed to fear, obligation, and coercion—to describe the individual's relation to society. In his renewed interest in religion we see Durkheim disputing the supposed dichotomy between private inclination and public obligation. Doubting that "the imperative was, in fact, the religious element in morality," Durkheim argued that "the more sacred a moral rule becomes, the more the element of obligation tends to recede."[29]

My second objection closely follows the first and can be stated briefly. The standard reading ignores Durkheim's commitment to that social ethic, moral individualism. Moral individualism suggests, if nothing else, that far from displaying "hostility against the individual," Durkheim championed the worth, dignity, and rights of the individual. Moreover, Durkheim claimed that moral individualism is a salient feature of modern democratic traditions and societies. Moral individualism does not place the individual in opposition to democratic society.

My third objection is that the standard reading overstates Durkheim's concern for social order. I will deal with the issue of Durkheim's alleged conservatism later. Here I will limit my response to Seigel's contention that

The possibility of objective knowledge diminished in the later Durkheim, not because he came to assign individual subjects a positive role in acquiring it, but because the distinction between subjective and objective mental contents was dissolved by the necessity to declare whatever arose from society to be objective. What loosened Durkheim's grip on the objectivity he desired so strongly was precisely his uncompromising campaign against the subject. . . . The smallest chink in the armor of discipline and objectivity threatens to give entry to a whole host of destructive demons and enemies. Here the fear of social collapse and of scientific breakdown are one fear.[30]

It is curious that Durkheim's sophisticated epistemology is construed as a design against "destructive demons and enemies," that is, against subjects or individuals. It is curious because Durkheim's mature epistemology developed concomitantly with his moral individualism; curious because near the end of his life Durkheim called the principle of free examination, holding suspect a piece of the "objective," the sacred of the sacred. Seigel describes Durkheim's epistemological position negatively. It is "the impulse to define as objective whatever can be set against the subject."[31] Durkheim, however, had no need to set objective knowledge over and against the subject. This, in fact, is the virtue of Durkheim's epistemology: he provides a way between objectivism and subjectivism. Objectivity, in Durkheim's view, is made possible by variously established social beliefs. But this no more means that anything set against the subject is objective than it means that society can hold anything to be objective. As if he were addressing Seigel on this very issue, Durkheim, in *The Elementary Forms*, asserted that the concept's "unique role is not the assuring of a harmony among minds, but also, and to a greater extent, their harmony with the nature of things. . . . The concept which was first held as true because it was collective tends to be no longer collective except on the condition of being held as true: we demand its credentials of it before according it our confidence."[32] It is hard to know how to take this passage, especially the phrase, "harmony with the nature of things." Perhaps Durkheim was merely saying that what's really important about concepts is not that they are shared but that they are true. Sharing concepts—social agreement—is a condition of knowledge, but not the object of knowledge. Or perhaps Durkheim was attempting to sneak in a correspondence theory of truth. In either case, the passage casts doubt on the claim that Durkheim had an "impulse to define as objective whatever can be set against the subject."

Some might claim that earlier I describe Durkheim's view on objectivity in the same way as Seigel does: objectivity is socially produced by collective representations. There are, however, two important differences. First, I do not claim that Durkheim's social epistemology was the result of his opposition to the subject. I claim, in fact, that his epistemology respected subjects by locating knowledge within the social world, the world of subjects. As I have said, this does not mean that subjects or societies fabricate knowledge and objectivity—that anything could be held as true. Rather, it means that a condition of knowledge is that knowledge is always socially construed and historically situated. At his worst, Durkheim maintained the traditional subject/object dichotomy, and gave the subject an engaging and dynamic role in the pursuit of objective knowledge. At his best, Durkheim challenged the dichotomy itself, and saw the subject as a part of the world, the world as a part of the subject. In either case Durkheim was not opposing the subject.

The second difference is that I take Durkheim's epistemology to be a normative description of the interconnectedness of human existence, and not a means, or an ideology, for securing social order. To say that knowledge is constituted by public representations, and that therefore there can be no radically private, human existence, is not the same as to say that objectivity, the standard employment of public concepts, insures social stability or that subjectivity, a unique employment of public concepts, threatens it. Durkheim the Dreyfusard is a case in point. His conscientious dissent from an anti-Semitic consensus was articulated in the shared moral languages of his day. Initiation and participation in public representations are prerequisites of rationality and therefore of moral dissent. They in no way block social criticism.[33]

VI

The standard interpretation of Durkheim's *homo duplex*, I believe, places the notion in great tension with much of Durkheim's thought. I hope to make clear the continuities between *homo duplex* and Durkheim's lifework. This requires removing *homo duplex* from the anti-individualist framework constructed by the standard reading and placing it in the anti-Spencerian, anti-egoistic, anti-utilitarian framework of Durkheim's own thought. Durkheim did not oppose the individual for the sake of order, yet he did oppose the egoist for the sake of the individual and society.

The text often cited in support of the standard reading is Durkheim's essay "The Dualism of Human Nature and its Social Conditions." Hence, I will concentrate on that essay. Durkheim began this work, as well as many others, with a reference to history. "It is only by historical analysis that we can discover what makes up man, since it is only in the course of history that he is formed."[34] He stated that his historical studies had revealed a duality in human nature. Actually, it would have been more apt to say "dualities," since Durkheim went on to mention more than one, and suggested that some are more prominent than others, depending on whose history is being discussed. A generic dichotomy is described in the vernacular, "the body and the soul." The body/soul dichotomy symbolically represents a host of dualisms. Durkheim mentioned three. Dualism number one opposes private sensations (like seeing red) to public concepts (like *homo duplex*). Dualism number two opposes private activity (quenching my thirst) to moral activity (providing for the homeless). Later in the essay Durkheim introduced another generic dichotomy, the profane and the sacred, and with it dualism number three, which opposes mundane personal preoccupations (washing the dishes) to extraordinary public occasions (the assassination of Martin Luther King, Jr.).

Not one of these dualisms is absolute. The first one Durkheim often qualified. In *The Elementary Forms*, for example, arguing that the difference between collective and private representations is not categorical, Durkheim wrote, "We do not wish to say that there is nothing in the empirical representations which shows rational ones. . . . A complete analysis of the categories should seek these germs of rationality even in the individual consciousness."[35] Experience involves collective representations, even as collective representations entail experience. The second dualism Durkheim qualified in "The Dualism of Human Nature." He stated, "It is an error to believe that it is easy to live as egoists. Absolute egoism, like absolute altruism, is an ideal limit which can never be attained in reality." And in the same essay he tempered the third dualism by noting that between daily routines and singular public incidents there are a host of periodic "public festivals, ceremonies, and rites of all kinds."[36]

I take the three dualisms as ideal types in the Weberian sense of the term. In "The Dualism of Human Nature" and elsewhere, Durkheim crafted conceptually precise polarities in order to highlight historical events and trends. However, when he applied these polarities to concrete empirical realities, he softened the contrasts. To fail to note this, to fix one's attention on the ideal types alone, is to miss Durkheim's nuanced interpretations of history and modern society. It is also to consider as literal dualisms that were intended to be ideal in the Weberian sense.

Although the three dualisms are in that sense "ideal," they are not illusory. Durkheim dismissed those theories, such as empirical and idealistic monism, that attempt to remove what these dualisms represent by simply denying them. Durkheim sided, rather, with "the great religions of modern man" that insist on "the existence of the contradictions in the midst of which we struggle."[37] Yet amid his talk of the human struggle springing from *homo duplex*, Durkheim did not oppose the individual pole and champion the social pole of the dualisms.

I do not mean to deny that Durkheim articulated a variety of dualisms. I do, however, question any interpretation that takes the dualisms as a sign of hostility against the individual. What, after all, does the antagonism in each dualism amount to? The discord between sensations and concepts amounts to this: "our concepts never succeed in mastering our sensations and in translating them completely into intelligible terms"; and therefore "a science that would adequately express all of reality" is but "an ideal that we can only approach ceaselessly, not one that is possible for us to attain." Dualism number one, then, appears in no way to be hostile toward the individual. It is simply one example of Durkheim's residual empiricism. Dualism number three, mundane personal preoccupations as opposed to extraordinary public occasions, does not carry any significant conflict. In fact, when noting how social ideals arising from extraordinary public occasions are "themselves individualized," Durkheim wrote that "because they [the ideals] are in close relation with our other representations, they harmonize with them, with our temperaments, characters, habits, and so on."[38] This dualism, then, suggests the promise of harmony at least as much as the possibility of conflict.

If hostility toward the individual exists in any of the three dualisms, it must be in dualism number two, private activity versus moral activity. And, in fact, there is, in some cases, much hostility on Durkheim's part toward the private side of this dualism. This animosity, however, is not aimed at the private per se, but rather at forms of life characterized by it. Egoists, whose loves are centered excessively on themselves, and who are often captivated by external goods such as wealth, power, and status, lead lives that conflict with the obligations and loves we associate with moral activity. These persons, in Durkheim's view, are unhappy and are alienated from both self and society. Of course the tension borne by dualism number two is not reserved for egoists alone. We all experience it. I love the expensive whiskey Wild Turkey and I desire to make monthly payments to sponsor an impoverished child. If I forgo the Wild Turkey so I can afford to help a child, Durkheim would say I am making a sacrifice, even if I desire it: "We can accept this sacrifice without resistance and even with enthusiasm, but even when it is accomplished in a surge of joy, the sacrifice is no less real."[39] No doubt Durkheim was correct. In placing one love above the other, I have lost my whiskey. But I have not lost myself. In fact, Durkheim would want to argue that I have made a small step toward finding (or making) it. The point is this: insofar as there is tension between private activity and moral activity, and insofar as Durkheim showed "hostility" toward the private side, it should be understood as a censure against self-seeking egoistic or Spencerian dispositions. This, however, fails to qualify as "hostility against the individual."

I have no desire to erase the lines of tension that Durkheim intended *homo duplex* to convey. In the next chapter I explore some relevant cases of conflict between the public and private. My aim now is to locate *homo duplex* in the context of Durkheim's life work. In that context, the interesting antagonism of *homo duplex* becomes clear: it expresses, in the words of Santayana, in what ways "we identify ourselves not with ourselves." Durkheim did not fear or loathe "the individual." His campaign, rather, was against atomistic individualism and egoism, and the sorrow that accompanies these.

In short, Durkheim was a defender and critic of both liberalism and communitarianism. When Durkheim employed a religious vocabulary to describe the deep commitments that modern individuals share, he was battling against those epistemological and political theories that support weak or strong versions of methodological individualism. In that context, Durkheim's statements regarding the relation between the public and private sound communitarian. Indeed, they are communitarian. But Durkheim's communitarianism, I have argued, needs to be understood in light of his elegant defense of the dignity and rights of the individual. He captured the merits of liberalism that spring from its high regard for the individual and used these as a foil against authoritarian communitarianism and its rigid traditionalism and classism. At the same time, he respected the many communitarian values that spring from its care for community and the common good and used these to criticize classical liberalism, its extreme individualism, and its economic obsessions.

Much of the history of liberalism and communitarianism can be seen as a series of attempts, since the Reformation, to join or to keep separate two models of society: society as a community pervaded by shared loves and common pursuits; and society as a group of more or less disparate individuals, protected by rights, pursuing private interests. In this history I want to place Durkheim as one who, with great deliberation, attempted to join features of both models. It is in that spirit that we are to read sentences like this one: "The human personality is a sacred thing; one dare not violate it nor infringe its bounds, while at the same time the greatest good is in communion with others."[40]

Provinces of Ethics: Moral Pluralism and a Plurality of Morals

"IT HAS BEEN observed by Aristotle," Durkheim noted, "that, in some degree, morals vary according to the agents who practice them." The observation is "on the mark," Durkheim continued in the posthumously published *Leçons de sociologie*, and "nowadays has a far greater field of application than Aristotle could have imagined."[1] Durkheim described four spheres of social life—the domestic, civil, economic, and universal or international. Each sphere exhibits its own moral reasoning and vocabulary. The diversity of this "moral particularism" or "moral polymorphism," as Durkheim called it, is in no way surprising. Moral beliefs and practices develop historically under various circumstances, and there is no reason to hope or desire that one ethical system could accommodate them all. "History and ethnography," claimed Durkheim, are the appropriate tools for studying the nature of morals and rights (5;1). What some ethicists would deplore and label moral fragmentation, Durkheim called "provinces of ethics"—historically fashioned spheres of morality. His reasoning here fit well with a central argument in *The Division of Labor* and with much of his other work: the acceptance of diversity need not imply the rejection of morality. As a society spawns various social milieux, each milieu brings into play relatively distinct moral practices and beliefs.

The individual's relationship with society, in short, develops within the moral particularism of the diverse provinces of ethics.

Social goods, goals, values, levels of homogeneity, rules of membership, and a host of other considerations are peculiar to each province of ethics. This is not to deny overlapping goals or shared values. It is to point out that a similarity between the arrangements, activities, and pursuits of each sphere cannot be assumed. Conflict within and between these provinces of ethics is not unusual or even necessarily regrettable, although it is not systematically encouraged or praised. Usually inevitable, at times avoidable, sometimes fruitful, at other times destructive, conflict is a general concept that applies to a multitude of situations. In Durkheim's view, conflict is to be understood—evaluated, ignored or resolved, praised or blamed—in the context of the common good. The common good, in fact, is the proper context for interpreting Durkheim's discussion of social life's four spheres and the attending moral polymorphism. "Social life," he wrote, "is above all a harmonious community of endeavors, when minds and wills come together to work for the same end" (22;16).

There is, then, a good that supersedes all other social goods, the common good. That is not to say, however, that there is a clear hierarchy of social goods, culminating in the common good. The common good is contextual. It emerges time and time again out of the deliberation, reflection, and critical spirit of a democratic society. Moreover, the common good in modern democratic societies need not oppose "the individual." By preserving the merits of both positions, Durkheim once again showed us how to rescue ourselves from the present impasse between liberals and communitarians who insist that our allegiance must be with either "individual rights" or a "common good." He argued, for example, that the common good resists authoritarian regimes that threaten the autonomy of the individual, and that it blocks secondary groups (unions, families, professional organizations, and so on) from "swallowing up their members," placing them under their "immediate domination" (76;62). If the common good and what Durkheim called moral individualism are not opposed to each other, it is because the nature and force of moral individualism guides how we establish the common good.

This chapter groups moral diversity into two categories. The first, which Durkheim called "a plurality of morals," refers to the moral beliefs and practices peculiar to the four spheres of social life. In addressing this form of pluralism, I concentrate, as Durkheim did, on the economic sphere. Durkheim complained that in "this whole sphere of social life, no professional ethic exists." I argue that Durkheim's remedy for this debilitated sphere, the formation of occupational secondary groups, needs to be understood in relation to the civic sphere, that is, the democratic political community. I also highlight how Durkheim articulated a plurality of morals in the idiom of social traditions and commitment to common goods. He continued to fashion a mixed vocabulary, an assortment of liberal and communitarian values. This vocabulary, as I have said, enables us to maintain commitment to features of both liberal and communitarian ways of thinking.

The second kind of pluralism, which I am here calling moral pluralism, refers to the normative relation between the beliefs and practices of the common good of the political community and the beliefs and practices of secondary groups, such as churches and synagogues, clubs, and political organizations. I am especially interested in those groups and associations that can be said to have comprehensive religious, moral, or philosophical notions of the good, and in the relation between these groups and the political community. I argue that the communitarian yearning for an all-encompassing (and in some accounts, national) homogeneous community is undesirable, given our traditions of moral individualism. Yet equally unsatisfactory is the atomistic individualism encouraged by some forms of liberalism. I applaud the communitarian support of community, but only if a community's claim on its members is not pernicious with respect to either its members' welfare or the political community's common good. I show that the common good does not require broad agreement in every sphere of social life. On some issues, however, agreement is essential. This second form of pluralism, moral pluralism, then, refers to a plurality of communities which may or may not share the goals and values of the common good. It refers to a society whose communities, however diverse, promote, or at least do not threaten, the common good. My arguments both draw from and criticize the work of Bellah, Hauerwas, MacIntyre, Walzer, and Rawls.

I

The provinces of ethics are relatively autonomous. We should not expect, for example, the moral ethos governing the domestic sphere to be the same as that of the civic sphere. Children, for instance, are not granted the same rights in the domestic sphere as in the civic. Yet the spheres are interrelated, and hence their autonomy is relative. When the state requires an education for a child that the child's parents consider morally offensive, there is a conflict between the rights of parents and those of the state. There is conflict within each sphere as well. Take, for example, the sixteen-year-old who desired a risky medical operation to alleviate his grand mal seizures. His parents, fearing the dangers involved in the difficult operation, forbade it, and the issue was settled in court. Here, conflict within the domestic sphere was transformed, in part, into conflict between the domestic and civic spheres. The young man's operation was a success.

Conflict between and within moral milieux is not necessarily grievous, and ought not be taken as a sign of moral anarchy. The moral ethos of each sphere is a "special form of common morality" (50;39). The special forms of morality are not combined additively to constitute a common morality, Durkheim argued. Rather, a shared understanding, the collective consciousness, shaped by common languages, histories, and cultures, provides a store of moral practices and beliefs that are applied to special circumstances. No doubt via this application the collective consciousness itself changes, however subtly, and no doubt the collective consciousness does not always "speak" unambiguously. Various readings can emerge from a common text. Still, a plurality of morals springs from a common source, he contended, even as it amends that source. Insofar as the individual consciousness—"the seat of all morals"—is fashioned by the collective consciousness, the individual moves felicitously within and between "the different fields of collective life." The point, again, is not that the collective consciousness excludes the possibility of conflict, only that a plurality of morals and the attending conflict need not necessarily alarm us, for these, too, can belong to a common, shared understanding, or what Durkheim occasionally called a common faith.

Tutoring individuals in a common morality, as manifested in the various spheres of social life, is a condition for a harmonious plurality of morals.[2] This condition, however, is not entirely met in modern industrial societies for a variety of reasons. Durkheim concentrated on reasons pertaining to the economic sphere. That sphere has "only a faint impression of morality, the greater part of its existence is passed divorced from any moral influence" (18;12). To make matters worse, the ethos of this sphere, marked by individual and corporate egoism, is threatening to dominate other social spheres.

The market economy of liberal democratic societies is itself quite pluralistic. In fact, there is more heterogeneity in the economic sphere than in the domestic or civic spheres (10;5). Diversity, however, is not the source of woe in the market realm. The trouble has to do with a dearth of professional ethics.

No doubt individuals devoted to the same trade are relating to one another by the very fact of sharing a similar occupation. Their very competition brings them in touch. But there is nothing steady about these connections: they depend on random meetings and they are strictly individual in nature. . . . Moreover, there is no association above all the members of a profession to maintain some unity, and to serve as the repository of traditions, of common practices, and to make sure they are observed at need. . . . The group has no life in common. . . . In this whole sphere of social life, no professional ethic exists (14;9).

Durkheim explained this "moral vacuum" as a result of economic and social change. "For two centuries," asserted Durkheim, "economic life has taken on an expansion it never knew before" (16;11). While this sphere grew and began to dominate society, a new "ethic" emerged that sought to deliver society from the traditional regulation of popes, monarchs, and guilds. These old monitors of behavior were to be replaced by a new, impartial one: the guiding hand of the spontaneous market. Durkheim, however, considered this spontaneous regulation as essentially no regulation. In *Suicide*, for example, he stated that "for a whole century, economic progress has mainly consisted in freeing industrial relations from all regulation . . . and government, instead of regulating economic life, has become its tool and servant."[3]

In his lectures on professional ethics, Durkheim summarized an account of the economic world that seemed to place it "outside the sphere of morals." He asked, "Is this state of affairs a normal one? It has had the support of famous doctrines. To start with, there is the classical economic theory according to which the free play of economic agreements should adjust itself and reach stability automatically, without it being necessary or even possible to submit it to any restraining forces" (16;10). He insisted, in response, that stable and just social practice "cannot follow of itself from entirely material causes, from any blind mechanism, however scientific it may be. It is a moral task" (18;12). We should not expect economic and social justice to emerge spontaneously from private contracts, from supply and demand, or from any other liberal market device. The laws of social evolution occasionally found in the early Durkheim will not accomplish what needs to be done in ethics. We cannot count on any so-called natural or automatic mechanism to create a moral equilibrium. A moral task is at hand because people must do something to bring peace and justice to the economic sphere. Human effort and planning are required. And there is more at stake than just the condition of the economic realm: "this amoral character of economic life amounts to a public danger."

The classical economists studied economic functions "as if they were ends in themselves," and hence "productive output seemed to be the sole primary aim in all industrial activity" (22;15). But the perspective of the classical liberal economists was shortsighted, for "if industry can only bring its output to a pitch by keeping up a chronic state of warfare and endless dissatisfaction amongst the producers, there is nothing to balance the evil it does" (22;16). These economists failed to see that "economic functions are not an end in themselves but only a means to an end; that they are one of the organs of social life and that social life is above all a harmonious community of endeavors." If this pivotal social sphere is in disarray, all are. For instance, after noting that "output is not everything," Durkheim declared that "there should not be alternating periods of over- and underproduction." This haphazard vacillation in the economic sphere, which brings to its workers either slavishly long hours or sudden layoffs, disrupts life in the domestic sphere.

I take what Durkheim called the public danger posed by the economic sphere to be similar to what Walzer describes as the opposite of the regime of complex equality, that is, tyranny. Walzer, like Durkheim, recognizes in modern societies a division of moral labor that is the result of historical contingencies. There are a variety of principles of justice that govern a variety of social goods. Complex equality obtains when the relative autonomy of the various spheres of justice is preserved. The general rule here is "different goods to different companies of men and women for different reasons and in accordance with different procedures."[4] The relative autonomy of the spheres, however, breaks down when the goods of one sphere are converted into dominant goods in a sphere alien to them. Walzer's work, much like Durkheim's, provides nuanced social maps of the spheres of justice and the sundry forms of dominance found in and between them.

There is, however, a notable difference between Walzer's *Spheres of Justice* and Durkheim's lectures on civic morals and professional ethics. Walzer worries about dominant social goods such as wealth or status. Durkheim, too, was concerned about these. But he was mainly interested in a different, though related, form of dominance. He feared that the anomic ethos of the economic sphere is starting to dominate all other spheres. This is not merely to say, "money corrupts." It is to claim that the economic realm has been freed from social accountability, divorced from moral traditions, and that its anomic character is starting to dominate spheres that, until recently, were relatively independent of it.

The spontaneous mechanisms of the market, Durkheim argued, are not fit to regulate the economic sphere, much less most of society. Liberal theorists who believe that a flourishing society naturally results from disparate individuals freely pursuing economic self-interests are naive. But liberal theorists who make the means into an end, who sever the economic order from its proper social context, are worse than naive, for their economic theories lack reference to larger, social considerations. The Industrial Revolution had arrived, and Durkheim was neither a Romantic, lamenting its coming, nor, like Marx, a visionary, placing great hope in what might yet come in a socialized, modern industrial society. For better, for worse, the revolution had occurred, and it was therefore imperative, according to Durkheim, that modern economic life be closely regulated, that it be directed toward moral aims. Durkheim interpreted the law-lessness of the economic realm in moral terms. It is a threat to the moral health and happiness of society. Its "moral vacuum" needs to be filled by new, just economic and social practices.

II

As we have seen, one of Durkheim's solutions to this moral bankruptcy was a call for the formation of occupational groups. "There must be a group about us to recall [a moral influence] again and again, without ceasing. . . . If we live amorally for a good part of the day, how could the springs of morality keep from going slack in us? . . . The true remedy for the sickness [economic anomie] is to give the professional groups in the eco-nomic order a stability they do not possess" (18–19;12–13). Durkheim's proposal for occupational groups deserves some further comment here.

In the nineteenth century, because of the social displacement brought on by the Industrial Revolution and the failed liberal promises of widespread prosperity and happiness, many social theorists, especially in France, longed for stable communities of-fering their members security and a lively sense of involvement. Association, that is, active participation, could bring vital agree-ment on issues of importance to all. Theorists as diverse as Jo-seph de Maistre and Saint-Simon, Alexis de Tocqueville and An-tonio Libriola envisioned organic communities engaging an active citizenry. These associations were not only to provide a psychological sense of belonging, they were to knit members into a corporate body, thus curbing private interest and instilling public commitment.

This is the context, I want to suggest, for interpreting Durk-heim's notion of occupational groups, a notion that, after 1897, is found throughout his work. These groups represented an at-tempt to situate individuals in morally nurturing, delightful spheres of communion. Occupational groups, however, were not supposed to be discrete, self-sustaining communities de-manding an individual's complete allegiance. Nor were they to be a substitute for the larger political community. That commu-nity contains all secondary groups, including occupational groups. It was here that Durkheim departed from theorists such as de Maistre and Saint-Simon. Although he first articulated the notion in *Suicide* as a remedy for egoism, it is important to keep in mind that Durkheim developed his concept of occupational groups in lectures on a plurality of social spheres, from the domestic to the universal. If Durkheim paid considerable attention to the economic sphere, it was because he worried about it more than the others.

Community, of course, was to be an important attribute of occupational groups. I note this because it is the nature of communities to contribute to the character of their members. Education, in other words, occurs naturally in communal activities, and perhaps above all Durkheim viewed occupational groups as agencies of moral education. Within them, shared understandings pertaining to the specific circumstances of a specific occupation were to be focused, developed, and augmented. The groups were to draw into a common fellowship individuals sharing the same occupational interests, establishing a moral ethos conducive to peace and justice. "It is not good," wrote Durkheim, "for a man to live [with endless friction] on a war footing in the sphere of his closest companions" (32;24). According to Durkheim, it also is not inevitable.

I believe that in Durkheim's advocacy of occupational groups, his premise—that moral practices and beliefs naturally arise from community—is sound, for the most part. It is certainly no more naive than the classical liberal hope for a harmonious pluralism via a spontaneous market mechanism. Morality is a product of human association. Not all associations, of course, are equal. Some are more likely than others to promote shared ethical practices. Yet if associations are established with the view that they are to channel a shared understanding—a common morality—toward issues of common concern and pertaining to a particular economic group, then a moral ethos, in principle, would likely emerge. Morality is, after all, the result of such practical human involvement.

Practical human involvement is required because, as Durkheim insisted, the needed "moralization cannot be instituted by the scholar in his study nor by the statesman" (39;31). This is not to deny the role played by professional, critical reflection. It is rather to affirm that morality is more a product of common human activities than of private speculation, and, more specifically, to suggest that "it is the work of the groups concerned." By this Durkheim meant that the appropriate practices are to emerge from the very spheres they are to enhance—or as Michael Walzer might have put it, the principles that emerge are internal to each distributive sphere.[5] They are to arise not by fiat but by communal reasoning: "It is not simply to have new codes superimposed on those existing; it is above all so that economic activity be penetrated by ideas and needs other than individual ideas and needs; it is so that it be socialized. This is the aim: that the professions should become so many moral milieux, encompassing constantly the various agencies of industrial and commercial life, perpetually fostering their morality" (37;29).

How can these occupational groups be initially established, in the absence of the essential moral milieux? Durkheim claimed that a common morality always already exists that can provide social intuitions and sensibilities for the development of diverse professional ethics. We never start from scratch. We are surrounded by shared understandings that guide the very questions we ask and the answers we give. Moreover, Durkheim conceded that some professional ethics already exist as social practices governing specific economic activities. His complaint was that they are not adequate, especially in the wake of the Industrial Revolution (38;29–30).

Durkheim was not sanguine about the emergence of morally sustaining spheres of justice. He often wrote as if liberal society were taking on the character of a Hobbesian war of all against all. At such moments he seemed to doubt the strength of a shared understanding and its capacity to spawn a plurality of morals in the context of common goods. This pessimism, however, did not lead to moral paralysis but to increased commitment to the tasks at hand.

Durkheim considered these tasks to be nothing less than the transformation of the economic sphere and the filling of its "moral vacuum" with new moral life. In *Suicide* Durkheim wrote that it is hard to imagine corporations "ever being elevated to the dignity of moral powers."[6] Durkheim was not simply suggesting that money corrupts, and hence that the economic sphere is likely to remain morally bankrupt. External goods such as wealth and status are not contemptible, but they need to operate in ethical social settings if they are to be distributed justly and not vitiate goods internal to social practices. I want to elaborate on this reading of Durkheim by drawing on Jeffrey Stout's helpful account of goods internal and external to a social practice.[7]

Stout enlarges MacIntyre's notion of a social practice. MacIntyre defines a social practice as "any coherent and complex form of socially established cooperative human activity through which goods internal to that form of activity are realized in the course of trying to achieve those standards of excellence which are appropriate to, and partially definitive of, that form of activity, with the result that human powers to achieve excellence, and human conceptions of the ends and goods involved, are systematically extended."[8] Stout focuses on the relation of external to internal goods, and he illustrates this relation in his discussion of medical care as a social practice. "Doctors and nurses," Stout notes, "pursue goods internal to the practice of medical care, goods that cannot be achieved in any other practice or by any other means than by being a good doctor or nurse, acquiring and exhibiting the qualities, forms of excellence, or virtues peculiar to those roles."[9] These roles require both technical skills (such as administering injections) and moral virtues relevant to medical care (such as *"courage,* the strength of character required to risk danger, embarrassment, alienation from one's cohort, loss of income . . . in order to pursue goods internal to the practice").

But this is only half of Stout's account. Medical practices, like other social practices, are embedded in institutions that are often preoccupied with goods external to the very practices the institutions were intended to support. Stout is not engaging in institution bashing. He recognizes that institutions sustain valuable practices. Still, he worries that external "goods like money and power and status, which have no internal relation to a social practice like medical care, can compete with and even engulf goods internal to the practice."[10] His concern, then, is that social practices are increasingly "dominated by the modes of interaction and patterns of thought characteristic of the market and the bureaucracies."

I want to relate Stout's worry to Durkheim's. Durkheim claimed that the ethos of the economic sphere tends to dominate other spheres. Among other things, it puts an end to traditional practices pertaining to workers' dignity, treatment, and fair compensation. It also puts private interest in the place of public commitment. Rather than simply treat the symptoms of economic anomie, Durkheim confronted its principal cause. He realized that as long as the economic sphere is morally anomic it will continue to threaten all other spheres. His solution was to infuse the economic sphere with moral principles internal to the various activities of that sphere. The role of occupational groups, then, was to provide moral connections between social practices and the internal and external goods relevant to them, thus checking economic anomie. The just distribution of external goods would be only one function of occupational groups. An equally significant one would be the establishment of public authorities and standards of excellence to govern what classical liberals have labeled private economic practices that nevertheless impinge on the domestic, civic, and international spheres.

One way to put this is to say that Durkheim wanted to see internal and external goods related in view of the public good. MacIntyre claims, correctly I believe, that external goods are typically understood as "some individual's property and possession" and are "characteristically objects of competition in which there must be losers as well as winners."[11] Internal goods, on the other hand, though often "the outcome of competition to excel," contribute to the public good and do not require losers. In order that external goods support internal goods, various economic activities that a Spencerian would call private would need to be viewed in a more public light. First, the workers involved in a particular occupation would need more say concerning its just operations. Second, the economic sphere in general would no longer be seen as a radically private one but as a realm subject to the political community. Neither of these recommendations was a call for socialism. Durkheim was warning that the needed moral economic practices will not develop under the present conditions of a Spencerian free market. To transform those conditions, according to Durkheim, modern industrial society has to take up the moral task of establishing occupational groups in order to fill its moral vacuum with moral associations and newly developed practices in the marketplace. This, I am suggesting, can be understood as one way to thwart what Stout has called "the tyranny of external goods."

148   *Provinces of Ethics*

From one perspective, occupational groups can be thought of as centers of moral life that, although bound up together, are distinct and relatively autonomous. In order for moral principles internal to each group to emerge, the groups should, as Durkheim said, "develop original characteristics." Together, these groups form the economic sphere. From another perspective, however, these groups are tributaries fed by shared traditions and institutions, by common projects and interests. It would be misleading to stress this latter perspective unduly. The social practices engendered by occupational groups are not expected to be shared, even if approved of, by the population at large. These groups are an example of moral differentiation. As such, they serve another of Durkheim's arguments against Tönnies, for they implicitly deny that heterogeneity amounts to immorality. Still, the latter perspective needs mentioning lest we lose sight of Durkheim's conviction that the foundation for society's ethical life is, ultimately, a society's shared ideals, traditions, and practices. Moreover, this perspective highlights Durkheim's view that the economic sphere needs to be accountable to the political community.

Improved conditions of labor (including job security, safe and wholesome working environments, and just wages), reduced hostility among and between employees and employers, a moral nexus between internal and external goods, and the recaptured warmth and moral ethos of community life: these are the features of modern social life that occupational groups could help create, according to Durkheim's vision of the future in modern industrial states. That vision may seem to be nothing but fantasy, though it boasts the ancient and medieval guilds as its antecedent, and British guild socialism and aspects of many Japanese corporations as its closest contemporary approximations. Even if the age of occupational groups never arrives, however, the critique of laissez-faire liberalism that motivated Durkheim's vision is perspicacious and relevant.

I say Durkheim's critique of laissez-faire liberalism, and not simply his critique of liberalism, because clearly there is something "liberal" about Durkheim's portrait of occupational groups. It represents Durkheim's attempt to establish a harmonious pluralism, the second component of moral individualism, in modern France. This pluralism was to have embraced a va-

riety of moral vocabularies operative in a variety of social settings. Furthermore, it championed the relative autonomy of the
individual moving within and among the spheres of social life.
Hence Durkheim condemned those guilds that repressed the individual. Occupational groups typify one of Durkheim's strategies for saving liberalism from itself. There was nothing illiberal,
then, about Durkheim's vision, and it was certainly not nationalistic.[12] Durkheim, as I will soon show, carefully placed the
state, secondary groups, and the individual in a normative, creative tension that protected the integrity of each. Fearing what
today we call fascism, Durkheim insisted that in order "to prevent the state from tyrannizing over individuals," secondary
groups, including occupational groups, must not be absorbed
by the state.

III

There is a social sphere that is greater in scope than the others,
according to Durkheim. It is the political community. The moral
understanding that governs this sphere he called civic morals.
Inquiry into the nature of this sphere and its relation to the other
social spheres is necessary for an intelligent reading of Durkheim's notion of a plurality of morals. If, for example, the domestic or the economic spheres are entirely independent of the
political one, or even if they dominate it, the result might be a
precarious laissez-faire pluralism that could lead to a society's
domination by a single sphere. On the other hand, if the other
spheres are dominated by the political community, the result
might be nationalism or fascism. I now turn, then, to Durkheim's discussion of the political community and the democratic
state.

The political community encompasses a plurality of secondary groups without becoming one itself. It includes all without
being dominated by any. Moreover, an essential feature of this
political group "is the contrast between governing and governed, between authority and those subject to it" (52;42). The
political community is "the coming together of a rather large
number of secondary social groups, subject to the same one authority" (55;45). In Durkheim's idiom, the political community
and the state are not the same. The state refers to "the agents of

the sovereign authority," while the political community refers to "the complex group of which the state is the highest organ." Far from being in radical opposition to the various secondary groups contained within the political sphere, Durkheim contended that "the state presupposes their existence . . . No secondary groups, no political authority [*Point de groupes secondaires, point d'autorité politique*], at least no authority which can legitimately be called political" (45;56).

These definitions, though important, provide only a starting place. The relation between the state, secondary groups, and the individual is still not clear. Some light is shed by examining two models of the state that Durkheim explored and rejected. The first is individualistic in nature, the second nationalistic. Take these models, too, as Weberian ideal types.

The individualistic model, according to Durkheim, was defended by Spencer and the classical economists on the one hand, and by Kant and (occasionally) Rousseau on the other. This model assumes that "the purpose of society . . . is the individual and for the sole reason that he is all that there is that is real in society" (63;51). Individuals are happiest if allowed to be productive in the realms of science, the arts, and industry. The state "can add nothing to this wealth." That is to say, it can make no positive contribution to the life of the individual. Its role is "to ward off certain ill effects of the association." The premise here, which Durkheim exposed, is that "the individual in himself has from birth certain rights, by the sole fact that he exists." These "inborn rights" (*droits congénitaux*), whether construed in a Spencerian or Kantian fashion, are threatened in associations, and therefore some agency is required to protect them. That agency is the state. The state does not need to establish, evaluate, extend, or debate individual rights. Rights are a given. In this view, "the province of the state should be limited to administering a wholly negative justice. Its role would be reduced more and more to preventing unlawful trespass of one individual on another and to maintaining intact in behalf of each one the sphere to which he has a right, solely because he is what he is" (64;52). Durkheim claimed that the state also has "other aims and offices to fulfil" besides administering a negative justice. Before I discuss these other aims, I want to explore the second model of the state, lest Durkheim's position be mistaken for it.

This other model assumes that "every society has an aim superior to individual aims and unrelated to them" (66;54). The individual is an instrument to be used by the state for the sake of its superior social aims. The individual works for the glory, the greatness, and the riches of society, finding some recompense for his labor "in the sole fact that as a member of the society he has some sort of share in the benefits he has helped to win." Individual interests are either underdeveloped or, if developed, are viewed as opposing the welfare of the nation. This nationalist model, Durkheim claimed, is useful for describing many early societies, especially when public religion and civic morals were fused. In these societies there was an indifference toward the rights and concerns of the individual. Prized above all were beliefs and aims held in common. In recent history, however, the individual has ceased to be absorbed into an anonymous social mass, and has become an object of respect.

This second model, Durkheim warned, is not of mere speculative or antiquarian interest. He maintained that his own country was beginning to welcome it. Many who were dismayed with classical liberalism had "thrown themselves in despair back on the opposite faith," trying to "revive the cult of the City State in a new guise" (67;54). No doubt Durkheim was referring here to proto-fascist political groups such as Charles Maurras' Action Française. These groups were unabashedly anti-liberal and anti-Republican. Durkheim, writing about these models during the Dreyfus affair, was self-consciously trying to make sense of liberalism and its discontents. He wanted to develop a model of society that would be neither individualistic nor nationalistic, one that combined the social goods associated with individual rights with those associated with a common good.

An active state, if legitimately representing the ideals and goals of the democratic political community, is not antithetical to moral individualism. This is the premise of Durkheim's model for the modern democratic state. He provided historical evidence to support a "relation of cause and effect between the progress of moral individualism and the advance of the state" (71;57). The individualist claims that a minimalist state is natural for modern societies, yet in history "we see the functions of the state multiplying as they increase in importance." The nationalist claims that the state should become absolute in modern societies, but, again, "that would be to go against all the lessons of history: for as we read on, we find the human person tending to gain in dignity."

Durkheim anticipated an objection: Is there not a contradiction in maintaining that both the state and moral individualism increase in scope and importance? This apparent contradiction, according to Durkheim, rests on the assumption that the rights of the individual are natural and inherent and that as a result there is no need for the state to establish them. The contradiction vanishes, however, when that assumption is denied.

> The only way of getting over the difficulty is to dispute the postulate that the rights of the individual are inherent, and to admit that the institution of these rights is in fact precisely the task of the state. . . . We can [now] understand that the functions of the state may expand, without any diminishing of the individual. We can see too that the individual may develop without causing any decline of the state, since he would be in some respect the product himself of the state, and since the activity of the state would in its nature be liberating to him (71;57).

Durkheim asked us to reject the idea that individual rights are inscribed in each individual by nature, and that, given the self-evident status of these rights, the role of the state is merely to recognize and protect them. The state, rather, is to "create and organize and make a reality" of individual rights, and not merely administer "an entirely prohibitive justice, as the utilitarian or Kantian individualism would have it" (74,79;60,65). This is not to suggest that the state arbitrarily "creates" rights. As I later show, Durkheim believed the state establishes them in light of the moral traditions and sensibilities of the political community. And the state is not the only group involved with "making a reality" of rights. It is, however, the only agency equipped with the legitimate power to institute them.

Durkheim's model of the state encompassed the public and the private without identifying the two. His general argument was that individual rights and liberties require intelligent public supervision over various social forces. The state insures private space for the individual, though it is more than a mere protector of that space. The state actively institutes rights, and extends their scope. Durkheim suggested, for example, that employment is likely to become a basic individual right. Durkheim's model has both liberal and communitarian features. It defends liberal rights, yet without appealing to the standard liberal meta-physical arguments so often thought necessary for shoring up the language of rights. Durkheim, unlike Ronald Dworkin, for example, was not impressed with legal naturalism. Durkheim would agree with the substance of many of Dworkin's conclusions regarding rights and social justice, but Durkheim argued that rights are a social development and insisted that rights are not antecedent to positive law. What can be said of Dworkin, with respect to Durkheim's position, also could be said of David Little or even G. E. M. Anscombe, though Anscombe's ethical naturalism, under the influence of Wittgenstein, is thin, lacking a copious Aristotelian or Thomistic metaphysics. Durkheim's argument for rights was distinctively communitarian. Our moral traditions have made us into the kind of people who insist that there are some things, such as discrimination by race and, perhaps in the future, unemployment, that individuals should not have to worry about. This characteristic of our moral liberal traditions is part of the "common good" we share as members of late-nineteenth- and twentieth-century democracies. Rights are bits of tradition, pieces of convention. They are not *mere* convention, *mere* tradition. That would be to put it badly, to speak with the wrong gesture. Individual rights, in Durkheim's view, are bits of convention and tradition that we cannot do without. To lose them would be to lose ourselves. Durkheim thus brought together in an interesting way the liberal's love of individual rights with the communitarian's regard for a common identity and good.

In what ways, specifically, can the state support moral individualism and a harmonious pluralism? First, according to Durkheim, "individual diversities can more easily have play" when the state checks various forms of "collective tyranny." Collective tyranny includes vicious crazes and majoritarian furies, though Durkheim was especially concerned about secondary groups that threaten to bring individuals within their "exclusive domination." The state, particularly its judicial branch, needs to worry about "all those secondary groups of family, trade and professional association, Church, regional areas and so on . . . which tend to absorb the personality of their members" (79;65). The state's moral task, as informed by the political community, is to remind secondary groups that they are a part of a whole.

This includes, Durkheim noted, rescuing "the child from patriarchal domination and from family tyranny," and the worker from corporate tyranny.

The active state seeks to protect individuals from social injustice. It falls to the state, then, to combat classism and racism and economic injustice. How, some might ask, can a racist or class society assail its own ugly features? Durkheim distinguished the state from the political community and its secondary groups. The state, "more than any other collective body, is to take account of the general needs of life lived in common." Durkheim's answer, then, is that if a liberal democratic society should lose sight of its own ideals, the state is responsible for reminding society of its highest ideals and working toward them. I will soon examine the relation between the state and the collective consciousness of the political community. Here, it's enough to point out that if the state should unjustly champion the interests of one group over another (say, business over education, or the upper class over the lower, or vice versa) then its legitimacy becomes problematic.

The democratic state, then, far from assuming a negative or passive role, actively strives to foster the beliefs and practices of moral individualism. This active or extensive state stands in opposition to Spencer's minimal state. Spencer's (or for that matter Robert Nozick's) ideal state would not associate itself with the public commitments and virtues of moral individualism. Their state is to function independently of such so-called sectarian positions. Spencer and contemporary libertarians would have considered coercive all attempts of the state to bring about common goals such as eradicating racism or sexism, or making the economic sphere more accountable to the political community. These, they would have argued, are private, not public, issues. Or if they are public (for who would want to deny their public import?) they should be handled by private associations, not state channels or agencies. Nozick writes that a state more extensive than a minimal one ("limited to the narrow functions of protection against force, theft, fraud, [and of guaranteeing] enforcement of contracts") "will violate persons' rights not to be forced to do certain things, and is unjustified."[13] If a thick line is not drawn between "exclusive" moral issues and the state's limited functions, between private virtue and public citizenship, in this account, then we make ourselves vulnerable to the state wielding its power illegitimately.

Durkheim, we have seen, rejected the libertarian minimalist state, claiming that moral individualism depends on an active state. But what would Durkheim have to say to Nozick and others about state despotism? What, in Durkheim's model, is to prevent the state from tyrannizing the individual? Isn't the idea that the state is to "create and organize and make a reality" of individual rights a bit scary? There are at least two answers to this line of questioning. The first, which I discuss in detail in the next section, involves the moral constraints placed on a democratic state. Though a democratic state does not merely reflect or mirror the diffuse collective consciousness, the state's decisions are informed and constrained by it. The second answer involves secondary groups. "If that collective force, the state, is to be the liberator of the individual, it has itself need of some counterbalance; it must be restrained by other collective forces, that is, by secondary groups" (77–78;63). Durkheim, in a fashion reminiscent of Tocqueville, championed secondary groups to check state tyranny, even as he advocated a strong state to check oppressive secondary groups. The purpose of secondary groups, then, is not only to tend to "the interests they are meant to serve," but also to "form one of the conditions essential to the emancipation of the individual." Secondary groups, accordingly, facilitate moral individualism.

Between secondary groups and the state there will be contingent conflict. In fact, Durkheim made the provocative claim that "it is out of this conflict of social forces that individual liberties are born" (78;63). Yet it is clear that, in Durkheim's view, there is no fundamental antagonism between secondary groups and the liberal democratic state. The one, in fact, is a condition of the moral health of the other. Without secondary groups to mediate between the state and the individual, the state would either be too distant from the individual to be effective, or it would control too many aspects of the individual's life, and become autocratic. Secondary groups, in turn, require the moral authority of the state to bring them harmony, lest they wage civil war of varying kinds. Moreover, the state safeguards the individual from potential group despotism.

There is thus a dialectical relation between the state and its secondary groups, and between the individual and the common good. The state, as a servant of the common good, blocks secondary groups from dominating the individual, an important feature of the common good. Secondary groups reciprocally prevent the state from becoming a Leviathan, and hence they, too, contribute to the common good. Durkheim depicted both social forces, the state and secondary groups, as vehicles of moral discipline "calling the individual to a moral way of life." Both institutionalize moral individualism.

I say "institutionalize" moral individualism, because Durkheim worried that it "is far from having any deep roots in the country." He cited as evidence "the extreme ease with which we have accepted an authoritarian regime several times in the course of this century—regimes which in reality rest on principles that are a long way from individualism" (73;60). This is not to say that, in Durkheim's view, moral individualism is purely theoretical. It is not. It is an important aspect of the moral ethos of many modern democratic nations. But having argued that individual rights are neither self-evident nor inalienable in theory or in practice, Durkheim recognized the frailty of individual rights and the need to entrench moral individualism more deeply.

The fragility of moral individualism brings me to one last feature of the dialectic between the state and its secondary groups. I have discussed some conditions under which individuals are likely to be oppressed by the state and by secondary groups. I still need to discuss those circumstances in which individuals could threaten the state. Without secondary groups mediating between the state and individuals, state tyranny is only one possibility. The other is "individuals absorbing the state" (127;106). Without secondary groups, individuals lack secure moral homes: "nothing remains but the fluid mass of individuals." This situation may seem democratic. It may seem conducive to social change, but it is in fact dangerous. Individuals can be swept up by transient crazes and ideologies, and when individuals and the state succumb to vacillating rages, little beneficial social change is likely to occur. Instead, tumultuous, unanchored individuals can unwittingly place absolute power in the hands of those not worthy of it. A weak state and an absolute one often lie on the same short path.

Durkheim's model for the state, which is neither individualistic nor nationalistic, assigned to the democratic state many significant roles, or, if you like, active roles. The state's authority is
unique. At its best, it guards against countless forms of tyranny;
it works for social justice, eradicating social inequalities; it di-
rects various spheres of society toward the common good, promoting a political community informed by moral individualism.
The state reaches many social realms: protecting children, instituting educational requirements that forbid repression and discrimination, establishing occupational groups, regulating trade
and commerce, funding the courts, and so on. In its various
roles the democratic state does not attempt to frustrate a fluid
plurality of morals. It recognizes the legitimacy of a variety of
spheres, and it seeks to bring justice and harmony to them. It
does this for the sake of the common good, with moral individualism being a salient feature of that good. The democratic state,
then, is not opposed to the individual, rather it contributes to
the very existence of normative individualism.

IV

Durkheim's model of the state is not for all societies. Its appropriate setting is a democratic society, and this also is a germane
condition for moral individualism. The quickest way to enter
into an exploration of Durkheim's understanding of democracy
and its relation to moral individualism is to begin with what
Durkheim claimed democracy is not. It is not "the political form
of a society governing itself, in which the government is spread
throughout the milieu of the nation" (99;82). A democracy requires that the state be an agency relatively distinct from society,
for "if the state is everywhere, it is nowhere." On the other
hand, a democracy is not that political form in which the state is
isolated from society (101;84). Between these two extremes lies
the democratic state as Durkheim understood it. The latter extreme, the state removed from society, is clearly not democratic,
but what of the former? Why would Durkheim reject this view?

Durkheim opposed the familiar belief that in a democracy the
will and thought of the state, the governing agency, are identical
with those of the citizenry. Under these conditions, the role of
the state "would consist in expressing [the sentiments diffused

throughout the collectivity] as adequately as possible" (110;91). But this would reduce the state to "an instrument for canalizing." The state would not be distinct from society; it would be absorbed by it. Durkheim maintained that in a democracy, the state must stand relatively independent of society. It is in contact with society, and this contact affects the decisions of the state, but it does not in every case determine them. A democracy, then, is poised between two extremes. Neither a mirror nor a sieve, the state intelligently and ethically represents its citizenry.

When I say "represents its citizenry," I mean the state, comprised of elected citizens, acts as an advocate for the common good. The common good, however, cannot necessarily be equated with the good of "the majority." Durkheim was clear about this. While discussing Rousseau's *Social Contract*, Durkheim stated: "The individuals who collaborate in the formation of the general will must strive for the end without which it does not exist, namely, the general interest. Rousseau's principle differs from that which is sometimes invoked in an attempt to justify the despotism of majorities. If the community must be obeyed, it is not because it commands, but because it commands the common good." [14] Durkheim knew that there will occasionally be discord between the decisions of the state and the sentiments of the majority. He said, "decisions taken by the government or parliamentary vote may be valid for the whole community and yet do not square with the state of social opinion" (60;49). Such conflict occurs under various conditions. A majority, for example, if overly preoccupied with immediate results, could oppose an essential feature of a long-term plan. Or worse, a majority, if provoked by a crisis or tragedy, could seek to scapegoat innocents. Alternatively, public officials could put special interests, including those of state agencies, before the good of the political community. In cases like this the public must protest and take action against corrupt representatives of the state. Durkheim saw the Dreyfus affair as an example of this.

Durkheim also identified discord between various interest groups. In this case, the state attempts to insure that the relative power of the groups involved does not determine the outcome of the conflict. "The different currents working within society are brought face to face, (in opposition) with one another, and are submitted to a comparative evaluation; and then either a choice is made, if one emerges which should outweigh the others, or else some new solution surfaces from this confrontation. This is because the state is situated at the central point where everything will touch; also because it can better get a clear idea of the complexity of situations and all the elements."[15]

The state is not necessarily being despotic when it imposes its will on society. First, it should not be assumed that all constraint is coercive. Second, a democratic state's power is not arbitrary, but rather works within the internal, moral constraints of a democracy. With respect to the first reason, Durkheim boldly announced that there is always something coercive about collective life. There is, however, nothing necessarily intolerable about this. Durkheim contested the coarse (and, today, increasingly scarce) liberal premise that any constraint imposed on individuals deprives them of their freedom in some important sense. On this premise Spencer and other libertarians charged that activist states are illegitimate, for they fail to respect citizens' most basic right—the freedom to pursue their own projects without interference as long as private projects fall within the bounds of the law. But Durkheim claimed that even under the best circumstances individual autonomy is never absolute. "The person forms part of the physical and social milieu; the person is bound up with it and can be only relatively autonomous" (82;68). A society without constraints, if one could imagine such an entity, would be monstrous. Moreover, it is simply wrong to equate state power with vicious compulsion. Durkheim disputed the position that government intervention into economic and other social activities is necessarily despotic. More likely, the constraints imposed by a just democratic state are the very conditions of freedom. A "spontaneous" Spencerian society, for example, is more likely to spawn "free" contracts that enslave workers than is a society equipped with an active democratic state. We once allowed slavery, that is, "material servitude," Durkheim noted. We have now abolished it. He asked, "Can we say that a man who has nothing to live on governs himself, that he is master of his actions? Which kinds of subordination, then, are legitimate and which unlawful?" (82;68). Durkheim admitted that "there is no final answer to these problems." Society will continually debate and try to define the conditions of oppression and freedom. But this much is clear: to ensure freedom for its citizens, negative justice is not enough. A democratic state must do more than prohibit what is commonly understood as slavery. It must actively and endlessly work for social justice. Freedom requires various material and moral provisions such as public education, health care, food and housing, job opportunities, and taxation to support these provisions. The conditions that produce freedom entail a variety of measures actively imposed by the democratic state.

These measures are not arbitrarily imposed on society, however. Ultimately, they arise from a society's shared understandings, that is, from common traditions, ideals, and institutions. This brings me to the second reason state intervention is not necessarily despotic. A democratic state's authority is not capricious. Durkheim claimed that the more a state embodies a society's shared understandings, the more democratic it is. The democratic state, among other social groups, helps to articulate the moral traditions and goals of the political community. I say articulate, not fabricate. The state, in its deliberations concerning a host of issues and conflicts, no doubt adds new dimensions to a society's traditions. Durkheim asked rhetorically, "Is it not inevitable that something new must emerge from all this activity?" Traditions do not remain stagnant. Nonetheless, the democratic state must be faithful to society's shared understanding while seeking the common good. The state's legitimacy springs from its accountability to society's moral traditions and social practices. This in no way contradicts Durkheim's belief that a state should remain relatively distinct from the rest of society. This critical distance enables the state to resist destructive, ephemeral movements that threaten the common good, and it ensures that the majority or the powerful do not win every debate. It does not remove the state from society's shared understanding, and it allows society's most authentic "voices" to be heard. Insofar as the state distorts those voices, it lacks legitimacy.

It is essential, in Durkheim's view, that the political community be able to contribute to the moral reasoning and deliberations of the state: "it is necessary that there should be as complete a harmony as possible between both these parts of the social structure." The citizens' capacity to participate actively in the state's judgments is the hallmark of a democracy. "This is what gives democracy a moral superiority. Because it is a system based on reflection, it allows the citizen to accept the laws of the country with more intelligence and thus less passively. Because there is a constant flow of communication between themselves and the state, the state is for individuals no longer like an exterior force that imparts a wholly mechanical impetus to them. Owing to constant exchanges between them and the state, its life becomes linked with theirs, just as their life does with that of the state" (110;91).

Democracies, then, place a premium on "submitting a greater number of things to collective debate" than do other political structures. The democratic political community strives to achieve a critical "consciousness of itself." This involves citizens' scrutinizing their customs and traditions, debating current events, and participating actively in a variety of secondary groups. The more democratic a society, "the more that deliberation and reflection and a critical spirit play a considerable part in the course of public affairs" (107–8;89).

It is disappointing that Durkheim did not have more to say about how the political community can resist the will of the state, if that will is deemed unacceptable or illegitimate. He wrote that democracies allow citizens intelligently and actively to accept laws, but what of challenging them? What of civil disobedience? What if the will of the state is but the will of dominant minorities? What if the state's version of a harmonious pluralism and common good is actually an ideological mask concealing, as Marx puts it, the "committee for managing the common affairs of the whole bourgeoisie"? There are "unmaskers" of all stripes (Marxist, Freudian, Nietzschean) who, for good reason, may be suspicious of how little Durkheim addressed these issues.

Durkheim was no doubt concerned about state dominance and tyranny. He feared that the nationalist bent of groups like Charles Maurras' Action Française could destroy France's most impressive democratic state, the Third Republic. He knew from history that France could become despotic literally overnight— and in fact the Third Republic fell rapidly to the dictatorial Vichy government that was supported by the very group Durkheim feared, Maurras' Action Française. Perhaps because of Durkheim's preoccupation with securing the Third Republic, he failed to explore the more subtle ways that a democratic regime can foster social injustices.

We do, of course, have a record of Durkheim's practical activities—protesting and unmasking—during and well after the Dreyfus affair. Moreover, Durkheim identified and promoted a particular type of critical spirit embodied in democratic societies. This is the spirit of free and boundless critical debate and inquiry, and this, I believe, can engender radical social change. I say radical because the more a society can freely criticize and debate the multifarious content of its social traditions, the more it can probe, as Durkheim put it, "uncharted customs, the obscure sentiments and prejudices that evade investigation." A critical spirit roots out those long-standing practices and beliefs that are undesirable. This aspect of Durkheim's thought needs to be emphasized, lest his communitarian penchant for locating social beliefs and practices in traditions be misinterpreted as a form of political conservatism. Understanding that we move in historical webs, according to Durkheim, is the first step toward understanding and reconstructing them.[16]

This work of reformation has no limits. It is not a matter of working out "a definite ideal which, one day or another, has to be attained determinately. . . . Rather, moral activity is indeterminate" (83;68). This does not mean that no progress is made. Democracies, Durkheim claimed, more than other political forms are capable of shedding harmful beliefs and practices. Here Durkheim sounds like "a pragmatic liberal," to borrow Stout's term. Durkheim did not want to let go of the spirit of reform that is associated with democracies. But like Rorty, he would not link reformation to a set of determinate, unchanging ideals toward which we constantly strive. We have ideals, to be sure. But these themselves are subject to critical, situated scrutiny, and hence to change.

Debate and a critical spirit, then, are conducive to radical social change. There is, however, a limit. Too much debate, too much division, too much pluralism, bring not creative social change but stagnation. As a ship, after having been tossed this way and that by a raging storm, finds that it has made no headway, so too "societies which are so stormy on the surface are often bound to routine" (113;94). Perhaps it is not a matter of "too much" debate or pluralism, however, but not the right kind. Debate and pluralism severed from their moral context of shared traditions and commitment to an array of common goods lead not to edifying dispute and reformation but to babble and an unchanged status quo. The moral context is protected by flourishing secondary groups and an active democratic state. Societies lacking these, Durkheim said, are subject to a "disjointed, halting, and exhausting" existence. This is because secondary groups and the state serve to preserve and foster moral traditions and their concomitant social practices. Without these, there is "constant flux and instability." "If only this state of affairs led to any really profound changes. But those that do come about are often superficial. For great changes need time and reflection and call for sustained effort. It often happens that all these day-to-day modifications cancel each other out and that in the end the state remains utterly stationary" (113;94).

V

"Democracy," according to Durkheim, "is the political system that conforms best to our present-day notion of the individual" (109;90). Moral individualism requires a political setting that honors the individual's relative autonomy and that is informed by the individual's situated moral reasoning. Moral individualism also requires social spheres and secondary groups of varying kinds in which the individual is in association with others and is morally educated. These spheres and secondary groups, however, are in need of an active state to bring them into relative harmony. We have seen that this harmony allows for conflict. Durkheim claimed, in fact, that novel ideas and social practices often spring from conflict. But conflict and debate are most fruitful when they take place within the context of a society's shared understandings and its common good. This good is in no way antithetical to moral individualism. Moral individualism presupposes social goods held in common. Moral individualism is a social good held in common.

I want to underscore the important role of the political community in Durkheim's thought. While some communitarians and liberal pluralists elevate the corporation, the church, or the local community as the only social setting necessary for satisfying the individual's communal and social needs, Durkheim insisted that secondary groups cannot supplant the role of a vital political community. This is because the political community supports the common aims and moral traditions of a society. All secondary groups are too particular to usurp that role.

This is not to denigrate groups other than the political community. Ray Oldenburg, for example, in *The Great Good Place*, has made a good case for the need for the "third place"—the local coffee shop, community center, beauty parlor, bar, and so on.[17] These public places between home and work no doubt facilitate political debate, not to mention that other social good commonly called "shooting the breeze." And, as we have seen, larger secondary groups, such as occupational groups, are indispensable for a healthy political community.

Durkheim was not a civic humanist who held the essentialist, Aristotelian notion that humans can only flourish by participation in an all-encompassing, democratic political community. Durkheim did insist on the importance of communal life in general, and of the political community in particular. But he did not commit the error that Allen Buchanan has correctly associated with some communitarian thinking, "the unwarranted slide from the value of community to the value of community as the highest or most-inclusive form of political organization."[18] Durkheim is best characterized as a classical republican in the tradition of Tocqueville. Rawls has described this tradition as "the view that if the citizens of a democratic society are to preserve their basic rights and liberties, including the civil liberties which secure the freedom of private life, they must also have to a sufficient degree the political virtues . . . and be willing to take part in public life."[19]

This description does not assume that citizens must share what Rawls calls a comprehensive religious, philosophical, or moral doctrine. Instead, it allows for a plurality of morals within the notion of a shared, common good—for a variety of moral beliefs and practices appropriate to the domestic, civil, economic, and international spheres of social life. What remains to be examined, however, is the relationship between the common good in democratic societies and the second kind of pluralism I've identified—moral pluralism. In those societies, what exactly is the relation between groups that do hold comprehensive conceptions of the good and the common good of the political community that contains these groups? This discussion of moral pluralism concerns, among other things, the communitarian propensity to envision self-sustaining communities that exist outside the larger political community or, on the other hand, that attempt to absorb the larger political community.

VI

In discussing moral pluralism as it appears, for example, in the relation between the beliefs and practices of the political community and those of associations such as churches and synagogues, clubs, and organizations, I am especially interested in those associations that can be said to have comprehensive religious, moral, or philosophical doctrines. The common good of the political community, Durkheim claimed, does not require broad agreement from these associations on every issue. Political unity, in other words, does not require social homogeneity. On some issues, however, widespread agreement is desirable. Moral pluralism, then, refers to a plurality of communities and associations that promote distinctive practices and beliefs, and yet also support, or at least do not threaten, the common good.

Moral pluralism, as I have described it, stands in opposition to three models of society: society as (1) a group of disparate individuals; (2) a group of disparate, morally self-sustaining, homogeneous communities; and (3) a single, national, homogeneous community. Think of these models, too, as ideal types. They will become less precise as I associate them with actual positions. The first one is commonly referred to as liberal, the third as communitarian, and the second can be construed as either liberal or communitarian, though I want to describe it as a communitarian compromise.

The first model needs little discussion, except perhaps to note that Durkheim's rejection of it suggests what he would admire about the other two models. The other two implicitly deny the crude liberal premise that society is composed of fundamentally private selves who, unable to agree on what makes life good, are protected by rights so that each individual can freely cut his or her own path to fortune and happiness. While this model does support individual rights, I call it crude because it is excessively individualistic, and, in fact, it is difficult to find liberals who subscribe to it. This becomes apparent as soon as we attempt to attribute it to anyone. Nozick, Rorty, and Ackerman, to name three very different thinkers, may come to mind. Nozick's vision for liberal society rests on Lockean convictions about private property; Rorty's on "the common selfish hope" that my little world will not be shattered by yours; and Ackerman's on the initial premise that "I am at least as good as you are."[20] Though their visions of a liberal society and their arguments for it are individualistic, they are not opposed to community life, and they would not gleefully describe liberal society as a group of disparate individuals. Why, then, associate them with the first model? There are different reasons, but the one applicable to all three is their failure to acknowledge the level of agreement that relates diverse individuals of the liberal political community (this they share with many communitarians), and their seeing no need to cultivate such agreement.

Although he rejected the first model, Durkheim would have approved of the other two models' concern to situate individuals in morally sustaining communities. Nonetheless, Durkheim's moral pluralism is not compatible with these models. The social ethics of the theologian Stanley Hauerwas does, however, lend itself to the second model. This model, in which society is taken to be a group of disparate, self-sustaining, homogeneous communities, is liberal from one point of view and communitarian from another. It is communitarian from the local community's perspective. This community, perhaps fearful of losing its distinctive identity and traditions, attempts to isolate itself from the larger political community. It will not risk pollution. As a result, the community refuses to participate in the general life of society, insofar as that is possible. Though this probably should not be construed as apathy, it often amounts to political inactivity. In order for the Christian community to remain Christian, Hauerwas argues, it must nurture its members in distinctive Christian narratives. There is nothing wrong with this, in and of itself. Yet wedded to it is the belief that secular, liberal society (seen as a realm of runaway pluralism and moral fragmentation) is hostile to the beliefs and practices of Christianity. The assumption is that non-Christians, not having been shaped by Christian scriptures and traditions, cannot agree with, or perhaps even understand, the Christian point of view. Hence, fidelity to the Christian way of life is taken to be fundamentally incompatible with championing the liberal political community's common good.

I do not want to write off Hauerwas as a paranoid religious separatist. His claim that Christianity, and presumably other religious traditions, fare poorly in liberal, pluralistic societies merits our attention, for it bears on the issue of compatibility between particular comprehensive notions of the good and the common good of the liberal political community. Hauerwas has forcefully denied such compatibility in a recent article, "Freedom of Religion: A Subtle Temptation." Following Durkheim, I take freedom of expression, religion, and association as fundamental rights springing from the liberal political community's common good. But it is one of these very rights, the freedom of religion, that Hauerwas associates with the demise of the Christian church. Freedom of religion has tempted Christians "to think that democracy is fundamentally neutral and, perhaps, even friendly toward the church."[21] He argues that Christians have come to believe that their faith entails supporting the liberal democratic state, and that doing so requires relegating their religious convictions to a private realm. The privatization of religion, then, is the price of religious freedom. And such privatization, in Hauerwas's view, represents the corruption of Christianity.

The religion we have is one that has been domesticated on the presumption that only a domesticated religion is safe to be free in America. . . . What "free" means is the right to entertain personally meaningful beliefs that have only the most indirect relation to the state. . . . The inability of Protestant churches in America to maintain any sense of authority over the lives of their members is one of the most compelling signs that freedom of religion has resulted in the corruption of Christians who now believe they have the right religiously "to make up their own minds."[22]

When we learn that Hauerwas considers it a corruption that some Christians now think they have the right "to make up their own minds" about religion, we may be tempted to go along with his other belief that there is not much overlap between Christianity, or at least his understanding of it, and liberal society. But before we come to that conclusion, I want to explore Hauerwas's alarm over Christians' making up their minds. I take him to be saying that an emphasis on autonomy, on freedom of choice,

opposes the predominant biblical notion that believers are chosen—elected—by God. To elevate the believer to the level of the
chooser is to diminish God's sovereign position. The spirit of
Christianity involves submission to God's will, not exalting the
human will. The spirit of democratic liberalism, in contrast,
places a premium on individual choice, especially in matters
such as religion. The conflict, then, as I understand it, is between democratic liberalism, which allows, and perhaps therefore encourages, pluralism and autonomy, and Christianity,
which demands uniformity and submission.[23]

It would seem that as long as democratic liberalism persists,
the Christian church will remain an endangered institution.
This, I believe, is the proper way to understand Hauerwas's sectarian leanings. Rather than becoming members of and identifying with a pluralistic society whose central tenets implicitly
challenge the ethos of Christianity, Christians should retreat
into their own communities, preserving and pursuing their distinctive way of life. Perhaps from their home base they can
speak prophetically to the rest of the nation, though Hauerwas
is convinced that they will not be listened to.[24]

This second model carries with it the assumption that comprehensive conceptions of the good are incompatible with a liberal common good. Hauerwas's argument about the liberal con-
tamination of Christianity is an example of this. My response is
to question both the general assumption of incompatibility and
Hauerwas's particular claim that Christian forms of life are jeop-
ardized in liberal democracies. To begin with the particular, I am
persuaded that Christianity, as Hauerwas understands it, is not
a favored community within liberal democracies. I do not believe, however, that it is subjected to unusual or excessive political or social threats. Hauerwas assumes that Christianity is now
assaulted by an uncommon pluralism, but the assumption is
questionable. Christianity emerged in a highly pluralistic environment. Moreover, by joining an illegal Jewish sect, early
Christians had to "make up their minds" in the face of occasional state and social harassment. Perhaps Hauerwas would
prefer an explicitly hostile environment for the sake of strength-
ening Christian identities. But that cannot count here, for we are
interested in political, social arrangements that we can call just,
and not in intolerant regimes that inadvertently generate Chris-

tian commitment in their victims. For similar reasons, we cannot consider a state of Christians.

Given the "fact of pluralism," it's not clear to me what political environment Hauerwas would deem congenial to Christianity. He cannot consider even the second model ideal, because it does not protect Christians from living in a fragmented society. It affords them the opportunity to "be themselves," but at the cost of isolation from the rest of society. Pluralism will still abound, even in their local communities, if they receive newspapers and television and outsiders.

More generally, I think democratic liberalism is suitable not just for Christianity but for most contemporary associations with comprehensive religious, philosophical, or moral doctrines. What disturbs Hauerwas about democratic liberalism is its acceptance of autonomy and pluralism. But this does not mean that democratic states require individuals to abandon comprehensive views of the good, only that they respect the right of others to pursue different life commitments. If Christians cannot handle this kind of pluralism, then their faith is frail indeed. Moreover, under Durkheim's notion of moral pluralism, individuals with diverse comprehensive doctrines can hold much in common. Religious believers and nonbelievers, for example, can disagree on salvation but agree on taxation, glasnost, AIDS, global warming, and so on.[25] This is not a sanguine statement on the possibility of consensus on difficult issues; it is a recognition that on many pressing issues that confront the political community of liberal democracies, agreement or disagreement does not necessarily follow religious lines.

Durkheim's notion of moral pluralism suggests that individuals can participate in a variety of spheres of commitment. Fidelity to the common good need not compromise allegiance to communities with detailed positions on "ultimate concerns" such as the nature and destiny of humans. And this does not require that religion be relegated to the private realm. It is well known that Judaism and Christianity, for example, have influenced a variety of (sometimes conflicting) moral and political positions. I see no reason why people aligned with these various religious traditions should not be encouraged to articulate public positions that have been informed by their distinctive religious commitments. And I see no reason why members of religious groups cannot remain faithful to their religious beliefs while sharing obligations and concerns for the liberal political community's common good. Christian and Jewish traditions do not possess a monopoly on liberal society's moral and political languages and practices, but these traditions have significantly influenced them. Many of our best past and present social critics, as recognized by believers and non-believers, have emerged from these traditions. What a sad thing if the very traditions that have contributed richly to society's moral life should be encouraged to abandon it.

Hauerwas's misgivings about the liberal political community are inspired by Alasdair MacIntyre. MacIntyre believes that our moral world is fragmented and in a "grave state of disorder": "we have—very largely, if not entirely—lost our comprehension, both theoretical and practical, of morality." He contends that the solution is to establish nooks of virtue and pockets of community effectively sealed off from the barbarism and darkness of the larger society. The assumption here is that there is no political community. There is no significant shared moral understanding. The evidence, according to MacIntyre, is that we are surrounded by a plurality of moral languages and practices, the result of a moral catastrophe that is evident to only a few. As astronomers attempt to piece together evidence that tells of the cosmic Big Bang, so MacIntyre hunts for signs of a moral cataclysm that put into motion the drifting debris (various "should's" and "ought's") of a once monolithic moral whole. What Durkheim described as the plurality of morals, the natural and not necessarily grievous condition of a society having various historically fashioned spheres of morality pertaining to diverse activities and social goods, MacIntyre has described as a condition of moral fragmentation. In MacIntyre's view, ours are the new Dark Ages. Just as during the last Dark Ages, "when men and women of good will turned aside from the task of shoring up the Roman *imperium*," we, too, should turn aside from the new *imperium*, liberal democratic society, and concentrate on "the construction of local forms of community."[26]

There is something liberal about MacIntyre's and Hauerwas's communitarian positions. If everyone were to follow MacIntyre's advice, for instance, society would consist of countless "local forms of communities," Reformed Jews in one, Conservatives in another, the Eastern Orthodox in one, Presbyterians in another, secularists who read Nietzsche in one, secularists who read Marx in another. This, of course, is absurd. And that is my point. The North American liberal society, for example, contains people from diverse backgrounds. If a widespread, shared understanding is missing, as the communitarians claim, then their position compels them to advocate tacitly a form of liberal pluralism. This pluralism, however, refers to a multitude of communities, not of individuals. In the end, their model for modern societies amounts to a group of disparate communities, protected by rights, each pursuing its own understanding of the virtues.

I am not saying that this pluralistic model is considered ideal by communitarians like MacIntyre and Hauerwas. I am not even saying that they identify themselves with it. I am saying that they are, at least implicitly, committed to this model under present circumstances. After all, they claim that we are in dark times. MacIntyre would have us develop sheltered communities and wait for a time when the politics of the common good can once again flourish. Hauerwas would like us all to become members of his community. But that's not going to happen. These communitarians, therefore, settle for a form of liberalism that guarantees the existence of vigorous communities dedicated to shaping the character of their members. Seldom do communitarians acknowledge that their own communities benefit from liberal rights. Some of the earliest defenders of the freedom of expression and association, we might remember, were attempting to gain legal recognition of their community's right to worship in a manner that, while not threatening the public good, differed from the dominant or state-sponsored religion. No doubt there are, or could be, many good communitarian arguments for advancing liberal rights. To my knowledge, however, such arguments have recently been put forward only by "liberals" such as Allen Buchanan or Joel Feinberg.[27]

Durkheim did not oppose in principle a liberal society containing a multitude of communities, many equipped with distinctive comprehensive doctrines. He did, however, oppose the pluralism of the second model. This form of pluralism, the plurality of disparate communities, weakens the integrity of the political community by threatening the prospects of "overlapping memberships," to use Feinberg's phrase. The liberal political community requires some common faith. It relies on a variety of associations, formal and informal, that articulate its steady yet changing shared understanding, and that inculcate political virtues such as commitment to a common good, which entails commitment to the rights of individuals and communities. Moral pluralism describes a society whose members, while perhaps belonging to associations equipped with comprehensive conceptions of the good, nevertheless recognize and are committed to the (limited) common good of the political community. The second model, however, advocates defection from the political community. From the point of view of moral pluralism, then, it is ironic that it is often communitarians who, desiring to reinstate the vocabulary of the common good, have perhaps inadvertently contributed to its erosion.

They have not, of course, seriously harmed it. They can't. There is a political community, and it has goods held in common. This seems to me indisputable. Most members of society, even, for example, the most religious ones, participate in what Durkheim called the plurality of morals. They are not isolated from the various spheres of society. In them they work and play and debate, and sometimes even vote or protest or run for office. They also, therefore, participate in moral pluralism. They know something of a common good that includes all others and that is more multifarious than any discrete association. Their knowledge of this does not derive from courses in ethics, and it cannot be easily surveyed by questionnaires or interviews.[28] It manifests itself in peoples' daily social and political activities: buying groceries, partaking in gossipy conversations, voting for environmental referendums, joining a union, hosting a block party, drawing social security, protesting foreign policy, and so on. These activities involve or point to shared traditions and issues. This is not to say all is well, only that things are not as some communitarians have claimed.

VII

As I said, this second model is not what communitarians like MacIntyre are aiming for. It is something of a compromise. Their hope is set on the third model—a single, national, homogeneous community, in which "my good as a man is one and the same as the good of those others with whom I am bound up in human community."[29] I say a homogeneous community, and not a pluralistic one, because MacIntyre wants to identify my good "as a man" (not as a citizen) with everyone else's good. His claim, then, refers to a comprehensive doctrine of the good. I am not claiming that MacIntyre is aiming for a national community free of all conflict. In *Whose Justice? Which Rationality?* he makes it clear that conflict within and between traditions is a standard feature of traditions. But he does wish for what Durkheim did not: a single social good that overrides all others in every social sphere. In *Whose Justice?* MacIntyre complains that

The liberal is committed to there being no one overriding good. The recognition of a range of goods is accompanied by a recognition of a range of compartmentalized spheres within each of which some good is pursued: political, economic, familial, artistic, athletic, scientific. So it is within a variety of distinct groups that each individual pursues his or her good. . . . The liberal norm is characteristically, therefore, one according to which different kinds of evaluation, each independent of the other, are exercised in these different types of social environment.[30]

This passage could have been written by Durkheim, except that he would have cast it as an ideal, favorable description of liberal society. Here MacIntyre, in contrast, rejects both a plurality of morals and moral pluralism. A range of goods pertaining to a variety of spheres, each independent of the other and each having a distinctive kind of evaluation, indicates to MacIntyre a lack of moral unity. Would he prefer that the economic and athletic spheres, for example, be even less independent of each other than they are today? Probably not. Rather he would like all social spheres to be gathered under a single moral ordering. He has assumed that a society with a number of moral realms lacks unity and order. Under his description, individuals choose arbitrarily to enter and exit the disparate social spheres, and in their wanderings they fail to experience shared traditions. "The liberal self," he writes, "is one that moves from sphere to sphere, compartmentalizing its attitudes."[31]

Durkheim, we have seen, portrayed the same situation differently. Individuals move in and out of various social spheres, and this is what we should expect in modern and even some traditional societies. Did not even Aristotle, champion of the Supreme Good, understand as much? Moreover, these spheres are only relatively independent; "compartmentalized spheres" implies too much autonomy. The ethos of each sphere, Durkheim claimed, is a "special form of common morality"; each springs from a latent shared understanding. When individuals participate in the provinces of ethics, they are tacitly educated and united in common traditions. This is not to belittle potential conflict within or between each sphere. Durkheim himself wrote of the dire need to remind participants in the various spheres that "social life is above all a harmonious community of endeavors." Nor is this to deny that some spheres, notably the economic, are lacking appropriate moral traditions and practices. It is simply to point out that MacIntyre assumes too hastily that a plurality of morals is the mark of a society of disparate individuals pursuing arbitrary preferences.

MacIntyre also fails to distinguish between moral pluralism and a plurality of morals. He says that "to be educated into the culture of a liberal social order is . . . characteristically to become the kind of person to whom it appears normal that a variety of goods should be pursued, each appropriate to its own sphere, with no overall good supplying any overall unity to life." But the fact that individuals are involved in a variety of spheres need not preclude their having (diverse) comprehensive notions of the good that provide relative unity to their lives as they travel within and between the spheres.[32] This, however, would probably not impress MacIntyre, since he would claim that a host of comprehensive goods is endemic to the very liberal societies he deplores. But I am tempted to say, again, that a variety of comprehensive doctrines strikes me as a "natural fact" of many modern and some traditional societies. Liberal societies are those which, in the face of this fact, have developed traditions, constitutions, and bills of rights that protect individuals and groups from those who would impose on them an alien conception of the human good.

Moreover, in Durkheim's view of moral pluralism, individuals' pursuit of their own comprehensive conceptions of the good does not, in and of itself, block their commitment to the indispensable but limited common good of the liberal political community. Citizens can and do identify with secular political con-

cerns as well as with religious ones, for example. This constitutes fragmentation only if the goods of the different spheres
are in a serious opposition. Liberal societies are clearly not immune from such opposition, but they prefer to cope with this
conflict as it occurs, sometimes in a legal fashion, sometimes
more informally, rather than to eliminate it by imposing or prohibiting comprehensive beliefs and practices. In fact, this feature of liberal society—its shunning of fatalism—is what Durkheim claimed to be an aspect of its common faith. Diverse
individuals are morally bound together by the shared belief that
it is better to have comprehensive doctrines tolerated rather than
legislated.

MacIntyre, like Durkheim, worries about anomie. Like Durkheim, he wants to bolster shared traditions and commitment to
goods held in common. But whereas Durkheim attempted to articulate common goods and traditions found in and appropriate
to liberal societies, MacIntyre rejects any form of pluralism, and
looks back to (or invents) a nonliberal time and philosophy ("the
Aristotelianism and Augustinianism of the Thomistic dialectical
synthesis") that support his vision of a single, morally homogeneous community. In the face of changing circumstances and
moral and political failings, Durkheim attempted to develop, reform, and extend liberal traditions and social practices. Mac-
Intyre, in contrast, responds to our present social predicaments
by producing narratives that portray liberalism as bereft of any
virtue, and by advising that we establish "local communities of
virtue within which civility and the intellectual and moral life
can be sustained through the new dark ages which are already
upon us."[33] Yet, as I noted, the establishment of local communities is not MacIntyre's ideal. It is not the final end. We are to
hope for a time when the virtues can prevail, that is, when a
virtuous, homogeneous, national community emerges. And it is
this anticipation, I want to say, that Durkheim would find disturbing.

The third model does not fit well with our traditions of moral
individualism. If a single community were to gain national
membership, Durkheim would suspect that excessive coercion
was at work. In fact, this is his charge against those conservatives of his day who desired to legislate back into existence a

traditional Catholic France. Durkheim understood moral individualism as an instance of moral progress in which many legitimate individual preferences and expectations are no longer
subject to social or political oppression. But oppression is perhaps not far from this third model of society, or from the communitarian compromise of the second model. The high degree
of homogeneity required for a national, communitarian society
is likely to lead to the implicit or explicit persecution of "de-
viant" individuals and communities. As to the second model,
societies lacking a political community that split into disparate
communities are susceptible to varieties of tyranny. Durkheim
feared, for instance, that without the counterbalance of a vital
political community upholding individual rights, authoritarian
communities could subjugate their own members.

I take as one of the strengths of the communitarian manifesto
Habits of the Heart its recognition of moral individualism as a valuable tradition that safeguards individuals from intolerable discrimination and oppression. I have little doubt that the authors
of *Habits of the Heart* overstate the problems that they associate
with what they call America's first language, utilitarian and ex-
pressive individualism. Still, it is to their credit that, like Durkheim, they have identified various types of individualism and
have evaluated them separately. Unlike utilitarian and expres-
sive individualism (which, not entirely fairly, are portrayed as
varieties of methodological or ontological individualism), biblical and civic individualism are depicted as genuinely social traditions that relate individuals to communal existence. In a passage that could have been lifted out of Durkheim's Dreyfusard
essay, "Individualism and the Intellectuals," the authors write,

We believe in the dignity, indeed the sacredness, of the individual.
Anything that would violate our right to think for ourselves, judge for
ourselves, make our own decisions, live our lives as we see fit, is not
only morally wrong, it is sacrilegious. Our highest and noblest aspirations, not only for ourselves, but for those we care about, for our society
and for the world, are closely linked to our individualism. . . . We do
not argue that Americans should abandon individualism—that would
mean for us to abandon our deepest identity.[34]

Think of *Habits of the Heart* as the work of moderate as opposed to radical communitarians. Here I am employing a distinction made by Allen Buchanan.[35] Radical communitarians re-

ject individual rights, maintaining that rights pose a threat to community life. Moderate communitarians, in contrast, support individual rights as long as rights are not assigned a lexical priority that systematically challenges the viability of communal life. The authors of *Habits of the Heart* are interested only in checking "the destructive side of individualism," not individualism per se, and not the good things that have resulted from individual rights. Their hope is that the United States has the moral resources to sustain "genuine individuality" and to nurture "both public and private life." It is clear, then, that *Habits of the Heart*, even though it is heavily informed by the work of MacIntyre, appreciates aspects of individualism and would reject the third model of society. This is perhaps not surprising, given Bellah's esteem for Durkheim.[36]

The liberal democratic society Durkheim envisions, a society informed by moral pluralism, captures the merits of all three models. Moral pluralism sustains a multitude of diverse communities (model two), all sharing a common, even if limited set of values and goals (model three), including those of moral individualism (model one). Durkheim agreed with the communitarians that human association is a social good necessary for well-being. But Durkheim did not hold that any one community, including the political one, has a monopoly on virtue or the good life. Happiness and an ethical life are not contingent on participation in any single, privileged community, but are procurable in a variety of spheres and groups which may or may not include churches, synagogues, or secular groups that inculcate comprehensive notions of the good. Moral pluralism does not require of these communities broad agreement on most issues, or even on most aspects of important issues, such as how to raise children or the way to salvation.

Still, moral pluralism does support the political community, a community that encompasses all others.[37] This inclusive social realm aims for agreement across the board on some issues. At times the most salient thing that needs to be agreed on may be what needs to be discussed. The likelihood of sensible agreement rests on the fact that citizens do share in common traditions, do in many respects share a common fate, and do often care about the problems and promises that are germane, not only to this or that particular community, but to the community in which all participate. No secondary group should attempt to block its members from taking part in this wider life of common pursuits.

Moral pluralism assumes, then, that there is a political community that is bolstered by shared traditions and practices such as moral individualism. This broad society is not conceived primarily as an arrangement for individuals to pursue private interests (as in model one), or as a homogeneous nation demanding uniformity of its members (as in model three). It aims, rather, at a corporate pluralism that recognizes the reality and desirability of diverse and common projects.

VIII

Durkheim's moral pluralism was an attempt to relate harmoniously what Michael Oakeshott wants to keep apart—*societas* and *universitas*. Oakeshott's "On the Character of a Modern European State" defines these as two alternative interpretations of the state. In *societas*, we find citizens "each pursuing his own interests or even joined with some others in seeking common satisfactions, but related to one another in the continuous acknowledgment of the authority of rules of conduct indifferent to the pursuit or the achievement of any purpose." Citizens of this civil association are related, then, not by "a common substantive purpose" or "common interest," but by a shared recognition of common legal and perhaps linguistic conditions. In *universitas*, by contrast, we find "a Family composed of families." Members of this family state are "associated in respect of some identified common purpose, in the pursuit of some acknowledged substantive end, or in the promotion of some specified enduring interest." In the idiom of *universitas*, Oakeshott describes Calvin's Geneva as a city-state in which all activities were directed toward a single goal, the glorification of God, and in which, therefore, there was no recognition of the distinction between public and private. In this tradition Oakeshott places Nazi Germany and "contemporary Russia," modern European examples of states "whose 'end' is the achievement and maintenance of a religious and cultural homogeneity."[38]

Given these infamous cases of *universitas*, it is little wonder that Oakeshott, like Quentin Skinner, provides historical narratives that support the liberal understanding of the ideal modern state as a civic, legal association that is demarcated from its citizens' various cultural, moral, and religious beliefs.[39] "On the Character of a Modern European State" can be read as a tribute to *societas*. Still, and without slighting Oakeshott's historical subtleties, I want to suggest that liberal societies are better off having some features of *universitas*. Durkheim would argue that if *societas* is to sustain itself, for the sake of itself and its members it must have some of the common purposes and substantive ends pursued by the entire citizenry that are characteristic of *universitas*. Such ends and purposes are not, in Durkheim's view, opposed to moral individualism. They sustain it. I am not simply saying that individual rights represent a shared private interest, a Hobbesian modus vivendi for securing peace and order. I am saying that the development and support of liberal rights is largely the work of shared moral traditions and common aims, since even constitutions require interpretive contexts. As we pursue divergent or even conflicting comprehensive conceptions of the good, there are traditions and practices that morally bind us together as a people, over and beyond legal and bureaucratic relations.

This Durkheimian position, in fact, is similar to what Oakeshott supports in some of his earlier essays, especially "The Tower of Babel" and "Political Education."[40] In these, he not only exposes the inadequacies of Enlightenment rationalism, he promotes the view that moral and political activity is the result of initiation into shared traditions. It is this strand in Oakeshott's thought that I find most helpful. He distinguishes the Enlightenment quest for ahistorical ideals from a liberal set of political arrangements that has emerged from historical experience, that is, from customs and traditions. Oakeshott's account of liberalism, unlike MacIntyre's, is richer than simply calling liberalism the tradition that doesn't want to be one.

MacIntyre is content to describe liberalism as "the history of attempts to construct a morality for tradition-free individuals, whether by an appeal to one out of several conceptions of universalizability or to one out of equally multifarious conceptions of utility or to shared intuitions or to some combination of these." However, MacIntyre is now claiming that this liberal project of building a social order out of tradition-independent norms and principles of rationality was eventually "transformed into a tradition whose continuities are partly defined by the interminability of the debate over such principles." Moreover, MacIntyre announces that the liberal tradition has what he once denied it—an overriding theory of the good. It would seem, then, that liberalism, in spite of itself, has all the marks of a complete, though not a rich, tradition. MacIntyre can now write that

liberal theory is best understood, not at all as an attempt to find a rationality independent of tradition, but as itself the articulation of an historically developed and developing set of social institutions and forms of activity, that is, as the voice of a tradition. Like other traditions, liberalism has internal to it its own standards of rational justification. Like other traditions, liberalism has its set of authoritative texts and its disputes over their interpretation. Like other traditions, liberalism expresses itself socially through a particular kind of hierarchy.[41]

As it turns out, then, liberalism is more than a destructive virus that eats away at moral traditions, leaving in its path nothing but discrete individuals lacking ordered lives. Liberalism, as MacIntyre now understands it, is a coherent, or at least a patterned, tradition, equipped with a distinctive rationality, a set of social institutions, internal justifications, and canonical texts. MacIntyre still has nothing good to say about this tradition and social order. He and Durkheim both agree that because of liberalism's early complicity with Enlightenment efforts to escape tradition, members of liberal societies lack opportunities to evaluate their guiding beliefs and, with a clear sense of their own identity, to encounter rival traditions. Durkheim, however, advised us to become more self-consciously liberal, that is, more aware of our liberal traditions, because, unlike MacIntyre, he maintained that they possess powerful moral resources for modern societies.

In contrast to MacIntyre, both Durkheim and Oakeshott depict liberalism as a set of viable moral traditions. Of course their interpretations of these—what they suppress, what they highlight—differ. Specifically, Durkheim, unlike Oakeshott, supports a strong political community and state that actively promote the common good, including redistribution of wealth so that social and political goods can be acquired more justly. On this issue of communal provision there are important connections between Durkheim, Michael Walzer and John Rawls. For present purposes, I want to propose that Walzer and Rawls hold notions similar to what I am calling moral pluralism.

In *Spheres of Justice* Walzer states that "there is no single set of primary or basic goods conceivable across all moral and material worlds."[42] This is a guiding proposition for Walzer's "complex equality," and I have already shown the affinity between this notion and Durkheim's moral polymorphism in the several spheres of the plurality of morals. But the recognition of multiple spheres of justice is not the only type of pluralism found in Walzer's work. Within each sphere—for example, in "kinship and love," in "education," in "divine grace"—he finds individuals pursuing the relevant set of goods in divergent legitimate ways. This diversity is one cause of conflict not only between but also within the spheres. Walzer, then, recognizes both a plurality of spheres and a pluralism within them.

What interests me is the appropriate setting Walzer designates for this complex pluralism: "the political community." The political community, for Walzer, is a world of "common meanings" in which "language, history, and culture come together (come more closely together here than anywhere else) to produce a collective consciousness." This is not to be confused with a permanent, fixed "national character." It is, rather, "the sharing of sensibilities and intuitions among the members of a historical community." The political community is where we often settle, with debate and deliberation, conflict between and within the spheres. Discussing disputes over redistribution, Walzer argues that "the ultimate appeal in these conflicts is not to the particular interests, not even to a public interest conceived as their sum, but to collective values, shared understandings of membership, health, food and shelter, work and leisure."[43] This reference to a "shared understanding" is not an appeal to a simplistic cultural homogeneity. He considers, for instance, the value of cultural diversity and autonomy as features of a shared understanding. Still, he highlights, as did Durkheim, the necessity of some shared beliefs and practices if a liberal democratic society is to flourish and achieve a measure of justice. A society capable of sustaining complex equality possesses some marks of a *universitas* because diversity is ordered and adjudicated in the context of shared beliefs and common ventures. For both Walzer and Durkheim, then, there is a logical and normative relation between pluralism, the political community, and a democratic society's shared understandings.

A similar relation can be found in John Rawls's recent essays. Pluralism, for Rawls, is a given, a fact. This social and historical condition, which has its roots in the Wars of Religion and the Reformation, dictates that any conception of justice "must allow for a diversity of doctrines and the plurality of conflicting, and indeed incommensurable, conceptions of the good affirmed by the members of existing democratic societies." In spite of this pluralism, however, or perhaps because of it, there are "certain fundamental intuitive ideas viewed as latent in the public political culture of a democratic society." [44] Think of these "fundamental intuitive ideas" as a democratic common faith that has historically emerged in the political community while pluralism has continued to mark other social spheres. Rawls does not evaluate pluralism, except to say it is here to stay (unless it is defeated by oppressive state power). This simple acceptance of pluralism as a historical fact about modern democratic societies pits Rawls against communitarians like Hauerwas and MacIntyre. But lately, Rawls, in a manner reminiscent of many communitarians, has recognized the need for shared political goals, virtues, and traditions.

In doing so, Rawls has hardly defected from "the" liberal camp. Like Durkheim, he illustrates that there can be significant overlap between liberal and communitarian positions. Rawls is now interested in the ways a liberal democratic society requires common aims and shared understandings, but he has concluded, *pace* Hauerwas and MacIntyre, that members of a well-ordered, just society need not affirm the same comprehensive conception of the good, and that the mark of a well-ordered, just, liberal society is a shared political conception of justice held by citizens who are free to affirm different and even conflicting comprehensive doctrines. A political conception of justice (based on democratic beliefs and practices embedded in our liberal traditions) is not a mere convenient set of arrangements to check civil war in an otherwise volatile pluralistic society. As Rawls puts it, it is not Hobbesian. It represents, rather, a set of final ends affirmed on moral grounds. This is why I suggested we view it as a common faith not unlike Durkheim's moral individualism. It protects the individual, yet it is not individualistic.

The goods it realizes are social in the deepest sense: we work together to sustain a society ordered by a political conception of justice because this work constitutes a significant aspect of our identity. Our political virtue is at stake. Rawls puts it like this: the well-ordered, liberal society

> is not a private society; for in the well-ordered society of justice as fairness citizens do have final ends in common. While it is true that they do not affirm the same comprehensive doctrine, they do affirm the same political conception of justice, and this means that they share one very basic political end, and one that has high priority—namely, the end of supporting just institutions and of giving one another justice accordingly, not to mention many other ends they must also share and realize through their political arrangements. Moreover, the end of political justice may be among citizens' most basic aims by reference to which they express the kind of persons they want to be.[45]

I can now quickly draw the connection between my account of a Durkheimian moral pluralism and Rawls's recent essays. Given the fact of pluralism, our political conception of justice must allow for different comprehensive notions of the good. But as Rawls explicitly states, this does not call for the abandonment of the political community or suggest that we view society as "so many distinct individuals, or distinct associations, cooperating solely to pursue their own personal, or associational, advantage without having any final ends in common." The political community, then, plays a significant role in Rawls's new work. It is the one sphere in liberal democratic societies where shared beliefs, virtues, and common projects are essential. Pluralism itself requires this, lest it be overcome by unjust, coercive forces that take by surprise "so many distinct" individuals or groups. Rawls now claims, with Durkheim, that a well-ordered society that recognizes the legitimacy of competing conceptions of the good requires common moral traditions and political virtues.[46]

We might well wonder whether the basic intuitions Rawls sees as embedded in our democratic traditions are really all that basic or embedded. Perhaps there is an "overlapping consensus" on upholding constitutional liberties, but what about Rawls's difference principle, which works for the greatest benefit of the least advantaged? And what of Rawls's suggestion that citizens of a democratic society can appreciate the public good because "many if not most citizens come to affirm their common political conception without seeing any particular connection, one way or the other, between it and their other views." [47] Even if this were true, Hauerwas and MacIntyre would take it as a sign of cultural moral dissonance. My point is that some of Rawls's sociological claims, and the conclusions he draws from them, may seem overly sanguine. And what of Walzer's allusion to our "shared understandings"? Is this a description of our North American society, or something to hope for and work toward? Similarly, what of Durkheim's moral individualism and pluralism? Are there, in fact, common moral traditions and institutions pervasive and strong enough to sustain these forms of social life? These issues I will address in the next three chapters. For now I will simply say that these three authors sometimes write as if the appropriate shared traditions and political community were already sovereign and in place, and at other times as if they needed to be cultivated and strengthened.

I have been interested in the ways in which Durkheim, Walzer, and Rawls have attempted to relate pluralism to a common good. Each, in his own voice, rejects the view of society as a group of disparate individuals, and also as a homogenous community or set of such communities. Each wants to establish that liberalism is not fatal to a political community and to other forms of healthy communal life. They do this, of course, in different ways, and often for different reasons. I have minimized their differences, though I will explore some of these in the final chapter. I will conclude here by noting that Durkheim, more than Walzer and Rawls, underscored the necessity of common traditions and practices in liberal democracies. As we have seen, he was compelled to draw on a religious vocabulary when describing this common inheritance, this shared faith. This may be why Durkheim was more explicit than Walzer or Rawls about the need to attend to and foster our shared understandings. For Durkheim, this involved moral education.

SEVEN

Education, Virtue, and Democracy

"IT IS NECESSARY that we never lose sight of what is the aim of public education. It is not a matter of training workers for the factory or accountants for the warehouse, but citizens for society. The teaching should therefore be essentially edifying [*moralisateur*]; it should detach minds from egoistic views and material interests."[1] Durkheim penned this in 1885; it is from his first published work. He argued that material power is not the only social good to be distributed justly. "Political power constitutes a sort of social fund," and in democracies this "collective capital is to be distributed equally." Such equality, Durkheim claimed, "can be justified on good and solid reasons." Yet lest there be a "contradiction between the quantity and the quality" of political participation, political power must be wed to "that other collective good" to be distributed equally—"intellectual capital," that is, education.

Early on, then, Durkheim was aware of the important role education plays in the life of a democracy. In 1887 he encouraged philosophers to see themselves as moral educators. Later in that same year he received his first university appointment at the University of Bordeaux, where a special position was created for him entitled "chargé d'un cours de science sociale et de pédagogie." After fifteen years at Bordeaux, Durkheim accepted another educational post, "chargé d'un cours de science de l'éducation," at the Sorbonne. From his first year at Bordeaux until his last at the Sorbonne (1916), Durkheim regularly lectured on education, especially on moral education.[2] Educational theory and practice were not, as some have claimed, merely peripheral to his life and thought.

A condition for a moral, politically liberal culture, I believe, is a public education similar to what Durkheim advocated. Its heterogeneous character, embracing critical thought and shared traditions, autonomy and community, human diversity and social unity, provides a powerful support for and challenge to liberal, democratic institutions. Durkheim again mingled standard liberal and communitarian values.

Shortly before his death, Durkheim gathered his Paris lectures on Rousseau's educational theory and affixed to them the following note to his publisher: "Rousseau. *Social Contract*. For possible publication. . . . I have attached some notes on *Emile* which should complete the *Contract*. The two themes are closely linked though this is not generally realized."[3] Linking the two works is a problem for students of Rousseau. Most of Durkheim's contemporaries had adopted the standard interpretation of Rousseau's educational work: education, as described in *Emile*, is to enable children to pursue their own natural goodness by protecting them from that cardinal source of corruption, society. This prescription is radically individualistic and, as many declared, would lead to anti-social behavior. There is, however, a difficulty with this anarchist interpretation of *Emile*. It contradicts the social features of *The Social Contract*. How can the two works, published in the same year, be reconciled? Durkheim harmoniously related the two works by providing a strong social reading of *Emile*. He underscored Rousseau's statement that, since the state of nature has been lost, "under existing conditions a man left to himself from birth would be more of a monster than the rest." Indeed, Durkheim continued, selectively quoting from *Emile*, "We are born weak, we need strength; helpless, we need aid; foolish, we need reason. All that we lack at birth, all that we need when we come to man's estate, is *the gift of education*." Education, then, is necessary if humans are to flourish as citizens of a community. The "natural man," said Rousseau, "lives only for himself." He is "the whole, dependent only on himself and on his like." The citizen, on the other hand, via education, "depends upon the whole, that is, on the community. . . . Good social institutions are those best fitted to make a man unnatural . . . so that he no longer regards himself as one, but as a part of the whole, and is only conscious of the common life."[4]

The link between *The Social Contract* and *Emile*, in Durkheim's reading, then, is education. Education is the indispensable means for transforming the individual from a (natural) private being to an (unnatural) social being. Rousseau's contract theory, unlike Hobbes's, is genuinely social; it pertains not to the exchanges between discrete individuals but to the social agreements arising from the general will. Knowledge and acceptance of that will, however, requires a social transformation of society's members. It requires education.

Rousseau's hope was that good social institutions can produce happy, virtuous individuals. Yet he believed happiness is usually the first thing we lose when we leave nature and enter the city. If only the joys of nature could be had within the restraints of the social. Yet this, in fact, is precisely where Rousseau located social joy. Just as natural joy is secured, in part, by natural limitations, so social joy is made possible by just social constraints. Genuine freedom, according to Rousseau as Durkheim read him, occurs when one's loves are directed at the general good and not merely at private pursuits. The objective of *The Social Contract* was to design a civic republic; the objective of *Emile* was to form virtuous citizens to dwell in it.

There was always, for Rousseau, something intrinsically unnatural and therefore unhappy about the social condition of the citizen, a manifestation of the tension between the individual and society that pervaded his thought.[5] Durkheim, however, saw nothing unnatural or unhappy about the socialized individual. He contended that social schooling is a precondition for both happiness and virtue. The tutored individual is the moral individual. Moral individualism was a central feature of Durkheim's theory of moral education.

Durkheim took to heart Rousseau's belief that education is necessary to transform individuals into citizens ready for moral participation in society. "Education," Durkheim said, "far from having as its unique or principal object the individual and his interests, is above all the means by which society perpetually recreates the conditions of its very existence." Socialization, then, not private self-expression, is the aim of education, and socializing individuals is a moral endeavor: "We are moral beings only to the extent that we are social beings." Education shapes social beings by instilling shared moral traditions, practices, and ideals. Despite all the assorted moral disputes, Durkheim claimed, "there exists a certain number of principles which, implicitly or explicitly, are common to all." These include "respect . . . for the ideas and sentiments which are at the base of democratic morality."[6] The civic basis of the modern faith, that is, of moral individualism as Durkheim understood it, is democratic morality. Through their moral education, youth become autonomous and develop the skills in reflective and critical thought that are so important to flourishing democracies, as they are nurtured in society's shared "ideas, sentiments, and practices." Durkheim resolved the dilemma that Rousseau's love for both the autonomous individual and the devoted citizen had posed by describing "the individual" as a cherished social ideal. Advancing this ideal, according to Durkheim, should be a prominent goal of modern education.

In what follows, I explore the various aims and methods specified in Durkheim's work on moral education. He advocated using the authority of society's shared understanding as a means of cultivating in students dispositions toward critical thinking. Consequently, toward the end of this chapter I address questions about educational authority and legitimacy. Durkheim described reflective thought as a social value that is cultivated by democratic traditions. The practice of scrutinizing social traditions and practices is an acquired skill, and it enriches the very traditions it criticizes. Tradition and critical thought, he argued, are not antithetical, but are complementary. Yet perplexing issues about authority and legitimacy arise from Durkheim's attempts to use the authority of social traditions to challenge those very traditions. I want to end this chapter by exploring those issues.

I

For Durkheim, education is a moral task. It is not self-evident that we should expect Durkheim, a professor of education, to hold this position. Many of today's educational theorists would not agree with him. Education, they would argue, is amoral. It imparts facts about the way the world is, and not values concerning the way it should be. Statements about how things should be or ought to be are normative and pertain to morality. Unlike education, whose domain is public facts for public consumption, morality is a matter of the individual's heart. It is private. The most that public education can do is clarify for students what they already believe.[7] Private education, say that of a Jewish or Catholic elementary school, can sneak in some morality, as long as their moral education does not tyrannize the children, or at least not too much. Adults, of course, can choose to join sects, but to force membership on children is to confine their ethical life to the group they happen to find themselves in, be it The Peninsula Temple Sholom, The First Presbyterian, The Astral Physics School–Church of Revelation, or The Humanist Community Fellowship. A child's public education must remain neutral on questions of morality so that he or she can, someday, freely choose a morally satisfying way of life. Proponents of this position argue that good parents, like good educators, respect this principle of neutrality.

Much of this chapter can be read as Durkheim's response to the very idea of a neutral or amoral general education. Let it suffice for now to say that, by Durkheim's lights, a society's moral ideals, those esteemed values that often are not as fully realized as they should be, are as real as the laws of thermodynamics or the jealousy of Othello. Ideals, like other cherished beliefs that occasionally bear the name "facts," are often taken for granted, but they are also, potentially, subject to critical debate and revision. They are public. They contribute to the creation and re-creation of the world about us. They are inescapable. If public education were to avoid them, its products would become as T. S. Eliot's Hollow Men,

> Shape without form, shade without colour,
> Paralysed force, gesture without motion.[8]

I do not want to suggest that Durkheim considered all education moral education, only that, contrary to many—perhaps most—educational theorists, Durkheim considered the moral aspect the most important aspect of education. He wrote that teaching is genuinely educational when "it has the capacity of exerting a moral influence on the way we are and the way we

think; in other words, in as far as it effects a transformation in
our ideas, our beliefs and our feelings. . . . An education whose
sole aim is to increase our mastery of the physical universe is
bound to fail in this central task." This is not to say that those
disciplines dealing with the "world of persons," to use Durkheim's vocabulary, are of greater moral worth than those dealing
with the "world of things."⁹ Durkheim the scientist was only too
willing to promote the moral merit of studying the natural sciences. He was not recommending one field or subject of study
over another. Rather, he was challenging any instrumental or
utilitarian position that would reduce the role of education to
the dispensing of information for the sake of manipulating the
world about us.

Moral education, in Durkheim's view, takes place in most
school subjects. It cannot be confined to a daily course. It is not
lessons in *Moralität*, to use Hegel's term—memorizing abstract
ethical codes and regulations. "Moral education cannot be so
rigidly confined to the classroom hour . . . it is implicated in
every moment. It must be mingled in the whole of school life, as
morality itself is involved in the whole web of collective life. . . .
There is no formula that can contain and express it adequately."¹⁰ The teaching of science, history, literature, and the
social sciences all contribute to the construction of the natural
and social worlds in which the child will ethically develop and
participate. Moral education occurs whenever palpable virtues,
concrete knowledge, and specific talents are communicated to
students, empowering them to live flourishing lives.

Education, Durkheim reminds us, takes place everywhere,
not only in the classroom. Educational influences are "always
present" and are usually implicit. "There is no period in social
life . . . not even a moment in the day when the young generations . . . are not receiving some educational influence."¹¹ Given
Durkheim's broad view of education as "a totality of practices,
of ways of doing things, of customs," it is not surprising that he
contended education cannot be limited to schoolroom instruction. Michael Oakeshott, about fifty years after Durkheim, articulates a position strikingly similar to his. "[Moral] education is
not compulsory; it is inevitable. . . . It is not a separable part of
education. One may set apart an hour in which to learn mathe-

matics and devote another to the Catechism, but it is impossible to engage in any activity whatever without contributing to this kind of moral education, and it is impossible to enjoy this kind of moral education in an hour set aside for this study."[12]

II

I have said that for Durkheim education is fundamentally a moral task. I still need to specify the nature of that task, that is, the nature of Durkheim's conception of moral education. A good way to begin is to note how Durkheim distinguished his position from Kant's and from the utilitarian positions of Bentham, James Mill, and Spencer.

Both Kant and the utilitarians, Durkheim claimed, advance the view that "morality resides entirely in the individual conscience, and that a simple glance inside ourselves will be enough to reveal [a universal moral formula]." Yet that introspection, Durkheim noted, has not produced the same result: "that of the Kantians is not that of the utilitarians, and each utilitarian moralist has his own." They all, however, agreed that morality consists in discovering the fundamental moral principle, and then applying it to specific situations. Durkheim pointed out that they carried this penchant for fundamental principles over to their educational theories. Kant declared that "the end of education is to develop, in each individual, all the perfection of which he is capable," while James Mill insisted the object of education is "to make the individual an instrument of happiness for himself and for his fellows."[13] Durkheim offered specific criticism of each. Of Mill he complained that, since Mill held that happiness is radically subjective, he left the end of education "undetermined" and subject to "individual fancy." Of Kant he argued, rather feebly, I believe, that his perfectionism invited students to try to cultivate all talents, and hence none.

For my purposes, however, these particular critiques are not as significant as Durkheim's general criticism of what these theorists had in common: "They assume that there is an ideal, perfect education, which applies to all men indiscriminately; and it is this education, universal and unique, that the theorist tries to define." History, however, provides no evidence of such an ideal. Moreover, these theorists failed to understand education as a "collection of practices and institutions that have been organized slowly in the course of time."[14] General rules do not constitute reality, but are abstractions of it. They are not starting points, but are, at their best, helpful abbreviations of an infinitely rich and various social reality. Durkheim claimed, then, that "there is no rule, no social prescription that is recognized or gains its sanction from Kant's moral imperative or from the law of utility as formulated by Bentham, Mill, or Spencer."[15] Their abstract principles do little work because they are divorced from concrete sociohistorical worlds.

Durkheim's approach to education, unlike Kant's and the various utilitarians', was that of the historicist. By historicists I am referring to those who, to use Richard Rorty's description,

have denied that there is such a thing as "human nature" or the "deepest level of the self." Their strategy has been to insist that socialization, and thus historical circumstance, goes all the way down—that there is nothing "beneath" socialization or prior to history which is definatory of the human. Such writers tell us that the question "What is it to be a human being?" should be replaced by questions like "What is it to inhabit a rich twentieth-century democratic society?" and "How can an inhabitant of such a society be more than the enactor of a role in a previously written script?"[16]

Durkheim, the historicist, complained that the Kantian or utilitarian educational theorist "asserts that human nature is universally and eternally the same: in its essence it does not vary from one age to another. . . . It is regarded as self-evident that to the questions of how to think about the world and how to behave in it there is a single right answer which holds true for the whole of the human race." Durkheim insisted that historical circumstance "goes all the way down" at a time when most of his colleagues in education contended that, as Durkheim put it, "humanity is not the product of history." When confronted with history's legacy of diverse human thought and behavior, the ahistorical theorists claimed that the "fundamental human nature" has been concealed from the naive observer by "the parasitic vegetation of diverse prejudice and superstitions which falsify and corrupt it." In this view, the barbaric, primitive peoples are those "whose humanity has been most completely buried beneath this layer of alien alluvial deposit"; the civilized, advanced cultures, in contrast, are those "in which man has been most successful in setting free and making manifest his essential nature."[17]

Durkheim offered a brief genealogy of this drive to uncover the essential yet hidden human nature. He noted that although "eighteenth-century *philosophes*" sought to discover *the* human nature—"for this was the unshakable rock upon which alone they could construct their political and moral systems"—they did not invent the quest. It goes at least as far back as the framers of Roman Law, who were inspired by the idea of creating a single legal system "which would be equally valid for the whole of humanity."[18] Christianity also contributed to the development of the notion of universal humanity. Its doctrine of original sin contrasts "a particular contingent event" that corrupted human nature to a universal act of Redemption that restores human nature to its pure form.

In any case, Durkheim thought it is wrongheaded for educational theorists to attempt to discover an essential human nature and then to use education as a means to elicit or instill it, thereby protecting it "from all the deceits and artificialities of different civilizations." This is not to say that Durkheim ruled out investigations into the identities we share. What is to be discovered in these investigations, however, is not a timeless touchstone, but those historically spawned collective institutions and practices that contribute to who we are. We discover what is best and worst about ourselves by investigating those legacies that have fashioned us, and it is these discoveries, not some timeless essence, that we need to teach.

Durkheim began his lectures on moral education by noting that "our aim is not to formulate moral education for man in general; but for men of our time in this country." The very idea of "man in general" had little application for Durkheim. All education, like all morality, is sectarian. It is for these people, at this time. But what we teach here and now cannot be developed from scratch. Durkheim noted that some imagine they can organize a system of education "voluntarily to realize a determined end; that, if this organization is not everywhere the same, it is because mistakes have been made concerning either the end that it is to pursue or the means of attaining it. From this point of view, educational systems of the past appear as so many errors, total or partial."[19] Yet Durkheim thought we suffer from self-deception when we believe that we can create, ex nihilo, the ways and means of education. Educational systems, he wrote, "are the product of a common life. . . . They are, moreover, in large part the work of preceding generations. . . . Historical investigation of the formation and development of systems of education reveals that they depend upon religion, political organization, the degree of development of science, the state of industry, etc. If they are considered apart from all these historic causes, they become incomprehensible."[20] The diverse folds and shapes of contemporary culture have emerged from history, and they need to be investigated historically so that we may discover what is to be preserved, abandoned, or reformed.[21] In sum, I take Durkheim's general complaint against the Kantian and utilitarian educational theorists to be twofold. Their quest for foundational moral and educational systems leads to abstract formulae that are of little help. Educational institutions, like most things social, are multifarious and resist investigations that do not attend to detail. Second, that quest is ahistorical. It fixes in place one abstract image of humanity, most likely one popular in some philosophical club, and accepts it without subjecting it to critical, historical inquiry. Another way of putting this twofold criticism is to say that in Durkheim's view the theorists were both too flexible and too stable. They were excessively flexible because each theorist invented an ideal, without taking into account "existing realities which he cannot create, or destroy, or transform, at will."[22] They were too stable because the theorist's ideal became fixed and immune to changing circumstances.

Durkheim's position was both flexible and stable, but in different ways. It recognized that educational systems are stable insofar as they are limited by and rooted in past and present institutions. Yet it also acknowledged that through critical inquiry institutions can be revised—perhaps not systematically, not by building anew from the bottom up, but substantially nevertheless. Such revision is boundless. Above I quoted Durkheim saying that no one can create or destroy existing realities "at will." He went on to say: "He can act on them only to the extent that he has learned to understand them, to know their nature and the conditions on which they depend." Detailed knowledge of a society's situatedness—its place in history, its history in place—is a condition of our ability to change it.

Educational institutions are contingent. They cannot be derived from God above or nature below. But they are not arbitrary. They belong to a vast though not shapeless narrative, or set of narratives, that a society tells itself about itself, even as they contribute to and teach this changing story. Durkheim wrote of the diverse educational aims of a variety of cultures. Of Roman culture, for example, he claimed that "education trained the individual to subordinate himself" to society. This is not the case for modern democratic societies. "Today," Durkheim noted approvingly, education "tries to make of the individual an autonomous personality."[23] A central aspect of Durkheim's principled understanding of moral education is that it should engender this social ideal, the autonomous individual, or as Durkheim might put it, moral individualism.

III

Moral individualism designates a cluster of values and goals, institutions and practices distinctive of liberal democratic traditions. This belief in the moral worth of the individual, Durkheim claimed, increasingly dominates "our whole present-day moral system."[24] However, he also insisted that it needs to permeate our institutions more deeply. This social ethos needs to be taught to our children, and to any others who would be active participants in society.

Education centered on moral individualism aims to foster a "sense of the dignity of man" and a "greater thirst for justice," Durkheim claimed. Moral individualism requires an education that shapes our vision to see "unjust social relations" as contrary to our understanding of human dignity. For example, Durkheim justified the prohibition of corporal punishment in schools because "one of the chief aims of moral education is to inspire in the child a feeling for the dignity of man. Corporal punishment is a continual offense to this sentiment."[25]

An education centered on moral individualism, moreover, is secular and rational. "We decided to give our children in our state-supported schools a purely secular moral education. It is essential to understand that this means an education that is not derived from revealed religion, but that rests exclusively on ideas, sentiments, and practices accountable to reason only—in short, a purely rationalistic education."[26] This line of thought is not as simple as it may appear. Durkheim was no Enlightenment rationalist. He was no more appealing to natural reason than to revealed religion. He was appealing, rather, to a broad range of "ideas, sentiments, and practices" that all sorts of people have deemed reasonable. What people call reasonable, in Durkheim's view, has to do with the ways their social, linguistic institutions enable them to describe the world, and not, as some would claim, with the ways ahistorical reason enables them to describe the world. Durkheim recommended an education that is informed by a plurality of society's members. A religious education is simply too sectarian, and it may not be committed to moral individualism. In a pluralistic society, a religious education is not likely to emerge from an overlapping consensus.

Secular education is not anti-religious. It does not, for example, attempt to subvert belief in God. Moreover, secular education, in Durkheim's account, is attentive to rational moral beliefs and practices that are embedded in religion, lest "we be left only with an impoverished and colorless morality."[27] Secular education, however, does combat what Durkheim called "intellectual servitude." Future citizens of democracies need to know about styles of belief and practices other than that of their family or local group. Otherwise a child, a future adult who had been held captive to a highly particular moral point of view, could find it difficult to respect those holding other worthy views. So when Durkheim wrote of secular education, he was referring to an inclusive education, an education that arises from the greater society, and that enables individuals to appreciate, if not to participate in, a variety of communities and associations.

An inclusive education does not bar what Durkheim called "pedagogical specialization." Social participation, a central aim of moral education, requires that education be both general and specialized. Rejecting the perfectionist position, Durkheim wanted education to encourage students to develop their particular interests and talents, not every conceivable one. He wrote, "each occupation . . . constitutes a milieu *sui generis* which requires particular aptitudes and specialized knowledge, in which certain ideas, certain practices, certain modes of viewing things, prevail."[28] Public education prepares students for making particular, meaningful contributions to a society marked by the division of labor.

Durkheim carefully qualified what he said about this aspect of education. A student's social position should not determine her education and vocation. Such discrimination is not, as Durkheim put it, "morally justified." He lamented that "even today, do we not see education vary with social class, or even with locality? That of the city is not that of the country, that of the middle class is not that of the worker." [29] He argued that access to education should not be socially arbitrary: "The education of our children should not depend upon the chance of their having been born here or there, of some parents rather than others." I say "socially" arbitrary because I take Durkheim's point to be that natural endowments are the only justifiable means to determine the nature of a student's specialized education. These natural skills and dispositions cannot be discerned until secondary education, he believed. Though this may seem too early to many of us, and for good reasons, it should be noted that in the late nineteenth and early twentieth centuries, only a small portion of students went on to receive a university education. It was still customary in most countries for students to move directly into careers upon graduation from secondary schools. Durkheim wanted students to be prepared for this transition.

Specialization, in any case, ought not be the chief aim of public education. Unlike many of his contemporaries, Durkheim rejected the view that secondary education should concern itself primarily with job training. He believed its more important task is to provide students with a general education, one that conveys, among other things, the shared beliefs and practices of moral individualism.

"The object of all secondary education," Durkheim wrote, "is to arouse and develop a capacity for thinking without trying to tie it down to any one particular vocation; it follows therefore that the whole concept of a secondary education system designed to give only a specialized training for particular jobs, say in commerce or industry, is radically incoherent." Education needs to develop certain "intellectual habits and attitudes" and to teach "towards what kinds of thing the public thinking should be directed." [30] This requires that students garner various dispositions, goals, and ideals embedded in a society's shared understanding. We can think of a society's shared understanding as the language in which the public thinks. More important than specialized education, then, are basic "ways of conceiving the world and life" that engender "public thinking."

Durkheim was saying that however important specialization may be, a more fundamental task of education is to train students to speak a common language and to view themselves as members of a common community.[31] A shared understanding is more fundamental than specialization, and is necessary if students, in the face of critical issues and debates, are to become full participants in shaping the society they are about to inherit. Public thinking, then, ranks higher than job training.

I find it perplexing that Amy Gutmann has written: "A rights theorist [one who gives priority to the equal right of all to civil and political freedom] cannot accept Durkheim's claim that, beyond teaching the basic principles upon which social unity depends, teaching specialized job-related skills is the most important role of schooling. Specialization may be necessary for the survival of industrial societies, but it does not follow that it is therefore a more important function of education in a liberal society than a broader, more general education."[32] This is perplexing because Durkheim never placed job training above "a broader, more general education." Gutmann concedes that the teaching of "basic principles upon which social unity depends" was Durkheim's first consideration, but she implies that these basic principles are paltry and somehow different from what she is advocating, "a broader, more general education." In fact, however, these "basic principles" amount to nothing less than a full-fledged "liberal education" that, as I show below, emphasizes critical thought and the study of alternative ways of life.

IV

I have been fleshing out the ways in which Durkheim's idea of a moral education embraced moral individualism. I want to continue this by turning to his lectures on moral education and inspecting the three concepts he considered central to this subject. If the term "moral education" sounds quaint, so will the terms Durkheim employed in these lectures to explicate it—the vocabulary of discipline, attachment, and autonomy. Durkheim was saying some novel things with these familiar terms, however.

In the lectures on discipline, Durkheim repeatedly referred to liberty, critical thought, innovation, and self-expression. These are not themes many would expect to find in a discussion of this topic. How did Durkheim connect them to discipline? In fact, what did Durkheim mean by discipline?

For Durkheim, discipline is an aspect of morality. One way to view morality is to regard it "like so many molds with limiting boundaries, into which we must pour our behavior." These molds are not derived "by deducing them from some general principles; they already exist, they are already made, they live and operate around us." Discipline is an acquired capacity for living in the various contours of a moral life. Durkheim was aware that all this talk of social constraint was bound to irritate Benthamites, classical economists, and Romantics. These considered constraints as "a pathology," "an abnormal thing," or as a necessary "evil." Many nineteenth-century writers, Durkheim noted, venerated that notion which is antithetical to discipline, "the infinite": "Here we have the lofty sentiment par excellence, since by means of it man elevates himself beyond all the limits imposed by nature and liberates himself, at least ideally, from restrictions that might diminish him." This view Durkheim rejected. Yet he also rejected what may be considered its opposite: the view that social constraints are necessary and good because they allow humans to overcome human nature, "the source of sin and evil."[33] In this view, human nature is not something to be unfettered, but, on the contrary, man "must triumph over it, he must vanquish it, silence its demands."

Both positions take social constraints as an unnatural distortion or reshaping of our native selves. In Durkheim's account, however, humans are naturally neither good nor bad. We are naturally social. "Physically, man is part of the universe; morally, he is part of society." This is only minimally an essentialist view of the human self or nature. When biologists tell us life requires H_2O, we take them to mean no species has been observed that could survive without it. This limit, however, still allows for a million or more forms of life. Durkheim's social definition of humanity, likewise, is essentialist only in a general and pragmatic way. Take it as claiming that Durkheim had never met or heard of a human who was radically severed from human association. He speculated that such a person would not resemble a human. Durkheim's social definition serves not to reduce humanity to an ideal type, but to highlight its indeterminacy. There are as many descriptions of human nature as there are cultures creating human natures.

In Durkheim's view, discipline, a capacity for being initiated into one's cultural tribe, neither distorts nor checks human nature. Rather, the shape of a human's nature is determined by, among other things, the kind of discipline received. The discipline found in moral education in liberal democracies, according to Durkheim, ought to be directed at furthering the values and goals of moral individualism; these give moral education its content.

Its form follows its content. Given the content of moral individualism, Durkheim insisted that the forms of discipline not be harsh or coercive. He wrote, for example, that "social life is not military life" and that "the child is not a man." Corporal punishment is strictly prohibited. A teacher's authority is not to be derived from physical power or threat of punishment, but from moral legitimacy. Moreover, "discipline must [not] involve blind and slavish submission," and it must not be removed "from the realm of discussion, converting it into icons to which man dare not, so to speak, lift his eyes."[34]

One of the results of discipline is something like Nietzsche's will-to-power, that is, the will to master one's life. From self-mastery a host of good things follows. "Self-mastery," Durkheim wrote, "is the first condition of all true power, of all liberty worthy of the name." Self-mastery protects freedom from "caprice" and emotional "gusts of wind." It produces the freedom to act from a defined character, checking the tyranny of being unduly subject to the influences that happen to surround us. Self-mastery enables us to focus our powers and talents to a precise point, thereby creating something splendid, something lovely, and something novel. Moral innovators such as Socrates and Jesus, Durkheim pointed out, dared "to shake off the yoke of traditional discipline." Such innovation does not entail spurning all received social "contours." It is a matter of knowing when some disciplines become yokes of slavery, or in Durkheim's words, knowing how to recognize "a legitimate need for change."[35]

Finally, out of self-mastery emerges the self. "The individual human being," Durkheim said, "is someone who can leave his imprint upon everything he does, a mark appropriate to himself, constant through time and by means of which he recognizes himself as distinct from all others." This is not an invitation to overcome what Harold Bloom has called "the anxiety of influence." On the contrary, the strong personality wields a distinctive influence only because it is enriched and stayed by the stable yet flexible intellectual and moral traditions of an age. The attempt to escape the influence of what has been achieved before is more likely to create vacuity, not originality. "Man possesses all the less of himself when he possesses only himself." [36]

This brings me to "attachment," the second concept Durkheim developed in his lectures on moral education. If discipline is the capacity to flourish within the various contours of social life, attachment is the disposition to love those contours—the beliefs, practices, and institutions of a culture. The person who allows the social world to permeate his life, Durkheim said, "certainly lives a richer and more vigorous life than the solitary egoist who bottles himself up and alienates himself from men and things." To understand this is to cherish the sources of our intellectual and moral life, that is, society's diverse traditions and practices. Like discipline, attachment is an aspect of morality. Discipline is central in those traditions that emphasize duty, self-control, and deference to authority. Attachment is central in those moral traditions that celebrate the desirability and loveliness of the good. Discipline characterizes Kant and *Moralität*, attachment Hegel and *Sittlichkeit*. [37] Durkheim was eager to keep these two aspects in a harmonious tension. Grace and law, love and duty—these are alternative descriptions of our moral life. Some personalities may tend more toward one than the other, as may some cultures. The point, however, is that both aspects spring from our twofold relation to society: we are both governed by it and attracted to it.

These two aspects need not be fundamentally opposed to each other. Durkheim often pointed out that there is nothing magical or mysterious about why, for example, one would be willing to sacrifice private interests for a public good. [38] Loving our duty is no mystery if we recognize ourselves as members of a society that issues legitimate obligations. This is not to say that there is never conflict between one's loves and duties. This conflict, however, arises case by case. It is not necessary, though it may be inevitable. It is contingent. It is not a natural feature of the human soul, as Kant would have it, or of the human psyche, as Freud would claim. Kant insisted that moral acts are a result of the goodwill overcoming desire, and that antagonism between will and desire is an inherent attribute of every self. Freud invented still another natural antagonism when he insisted that the superego (internalized social constraints) battles continually with the id (instinctual desire). Durkheim demurred, abandoning these portraits of a cleaved soul or self divided.[39] Durkheimians could, perhaps, take Kantian desire and the Freudian id to represent various culturally dependent forms of egoism. In Durkheim's account, however, desire is simply another word for the self's loves and goals; and these can be more or less egoistic, more or less altruistic, depending on a host of considerations. Moral education is one of these considerations.

The difference between egoism and altruism, according to Durkheim, is not that the one is pleasurable and the other is sacrificial. Rather, "it is the different direction that this activity follows in the two cases. When it is egoistical, it does not go beyond the acting subject; it is centripetal. When it is altruistic, it overflows from its subject. The centers around which it gravitates are outside of him; it is centrifugal."[40] The difference, then, has not to do with warring mental states or extinguished desires, but with how we describe a person's fidelity in light of observable activities. What is she faithful to? What loves and goals motivate her? What, in a phrase, is she attached to? The answers to these questions determine whether we call actions egoistic or altruistic.

One of the roles of moral education, then, is to cultivate virtuous attachments and establish moral goals. It is to direct the individual's loves toward common goods. Durkheim pointed out that "moral goals are those the object of which is *society*. To act morally is to act in terms of the collective interest."[41]

Durkheim recognized that "society" and "the common good" are general and abstract terms, and that people live in a plurality of social spheres and groups that contain a variety of public goods. In his lectures on moral education he mentioned a host of groups—for example, the family, the union, the business, the club, the political party, the nation or political group, and the international community, humanity. Durkheim was aware that social attachments can be various and can vie with one another. Durkheim was especially concerned that students be prepared for participation in the political community and in what he called the sphere of humanity. Assisting children to make the transition from the family to the political community is a central feature of moral education. This is not to champion a narrowly nationalistic education. We are to teach students to recognize all praiseworthy political communities. These are nations committed not to expansionist goals, or to gaining riches at the expense of other nations, but to furthering just domestic goals and the goals of humanity—justice, improved living and working conditions, and the alleviation of suffering.[42]

In the previous chapter I explored Durkheim's worry that modern industrial societies suffer from a dearth of secondary groups and a lack of commitment to the political community. "The spirit of association" has waned. In his lectures on moral education Durkheim discussed why this is difficult to remedy: "We can only reanimate collective life, revive it from this torpor, if we love it; we cannot learn to love it unless we live it, and in order to do so it must exist."[43] This vicious cycle can be avoided, in part, by public schools, "the means of training the child in a collective life different from home life."

Durkheim immediately noted, however, that education is no cure-all, and that "legislative action" for the sake of just institutions is necessary as well. But attachment to collective goals and associations is an important aspect of morality, and creating it is one aim of education. Justice, equality, and the dignity and rights of the individual—these are collective goals distinctive of modern democratic political communities, and these receive special attention in Durkheim's concept of moral education.

Autonomy, or self-determination, is the third concept Durkheim employed in his lectures. This concept represents still another aspect of morality. "To act morally, it is not enough—above all, it is no longer enough—to respect discipline and to be committed to a group. Beyond this, and whether out of deference to a rule or devotion to a collective ideal, we must have knowledge, as clear and complete an awareness as possible of the reasons for our conduct. . . . The third element of morality is the understanding of it." Autonomy does not spring from escaping collective influences or from a total immersion in collective influences such that society's justifications become the individual's. Neither account is satisfactory. Durkheim dissociated his position from these two extremes—the position of various Enlightenment liberals and Romantics who insisted that individuals be free from all social constraints in order to experience spontaneity in moral and aesthetic activities, and the position of those who claimed that individuals, by necessity, are "perpetually subject to restraints" and that the "personality can be nothing but a product of its environment." Kant, according to Durkheim, attempted to preserve the good and helpful aspects of both positions. Kant stressed the imperative quality of morality: "The relationship between the human will and [moral] law is one of dependence; we call it obligation which indicates a constraint." Yet, Durkheim noted, Kant also "refuses to acknowledge that the will can be completely moral when it is not autonomous, when it defers passively to a law of which it is not the maker." [44] Kant tried to resolve this by claiming that if the will were free from sensibility and conformed to reason alone, it would, as Durkheim put it, "move spontaneously toward duty through the impulse of its nature alone." The coercive and obligatory aspect of the moral law, in other words, would vanish for the purely rational individual.

Durkheim borrowed much from this Kantian line of thought. Morality commands us variously. The imperative quality of those values and practices that we call moral is plain. Yet as individuals become rational and understand the warrants for the moral life, they come to see themselves as freely choosing it. Autonomy, then, is the individual's ability to choose rationally the moral life without the need for external motivations such as threats or rewards. But Durkheim would not accept Kant's description of the autonomous will. "In order to conceive a pure autonomy of the will . . . Kant was obliged to admit that the will, at least the will insofar as it is purely rational, does not depend on the laws of nature. He was obliged to create a reality apart from the world, on which the world exerts no influence, and which, reacting on itself, remains independent of the action of external forces." The Kantian will purchases autonomy by violently separating itself from the world, and by aligning itself with unworldly reason. But the price is too high, for, as Durkheim noted, "our reason is not a transcendent faculty; it is implicated in society." [45]

As we have seen in previous chapters Durkheim socialized the Kantian faculty of reason. In doing so, he redefined it. Reason no longer was the faculty for producing universal and certain judgments to guide the autonomous will. Instead, it became the ability to recognize the best—the most helpful, or plausible, or beautiful, or profound—descriptions, explanations, and judgments that our historical communities have so far produced. Having said this, Durkheim could agree with Kant that as individuals become rational they become autonomous agents. It was understood now, however, that individuals become rational as they learn what a society or culture calls reasonable or unreasonable or problematic, and as they learn how it has arrived at these (often tentative) conclusions. Autonomous agents, then, are those who are aware of the social and historical warrants for moral beliefs and practices, and who are thereby free to embrace and criticize them. Autonomy is an important virtue in modern democracies, for these benefit from an active citizenry that explores present social practices, asks for reasons, and pursues just reforms.

V

Because the development of critical thought was a prominent feature of Durkheim's concept of moral education, he placed particular stress on encouraging critical skills. In order to prevent what Durkheim called "parrot-like morality," he insisted that a society's beliefs and practices should not be "internalized in such a way as to be beyond criticism or reflection, the agents par excellence of all change." Students need to be taught to expect change; they need "to understand that the morality of the future will probably not be that of today."[46] Continuity persists, to be sure, but social reality, while "relatively stable," is "perpetually in the process of becoming." It is this "process of becoming" that needs to be made "perceptible to the child." This may sound more like a sociological than a moral argument about education. Durkheim made it clear, however, that his concern was not simply that children be prepared for change per se, but that they be prepared for moral advances. Society is not to "content itself with a complacent possession of moral results that have been handed down to it." To that end, the teacher "must be on his guard against transmitting the moral gospel of our elders as a sort of closed book." Morality, then, is to be understood as an open canon. Understanding this, Durkheim felt, could enable students to see themselves as something more than performers reciting yesterday's lines. It could excite in them "a desire to add a few lines of their own, and give them the tools to satisfy this legitimate ambition." [47]

The study of history, literature, and science are especially helpful for developing skills in critical thought, according to Durkheim. The study of history promotes critical thinking because it both discloses to students their society's distinctive shared understanding and exposes them to alien ways of life. Accustoming students to the unfamiliar teaches students to appreciate otherness, to identify the stranger as a fellow human, and to acquire novel ways to cope with suffering and to celebrate life. It would be nothing less than a moral failure if students learned to judge all humanity by some textbook account of the ideal human. History, then, plays a critical role in moral education. "It is by learning to become familiar with other ideas, other customs, other manners, other political constitutions, other domestic organizations, other moralities and logics than those which he is used to that the student will gain a sense of the richness of life within the bounds of human nature. It is, therefore, only by history that we can give an account of the infinite diversity of the aspects which human nature can take on." [48] Durkheim was advocating a particular way of doing and understanding history, and he knew this. He explicitly rejected the evolutionary fancy that in history universal knowledge gradually reveals itself. "We must be wary of facile notions about continuity," warned Durkheim. "The teaching of history would be false to its goal if it did not leave the impression that . . . history neither begins nor ends anywhere." [49] This is not to say our moral ideals and accomplishments are to be presented as "a sort of unintelligible improvisation." Our rights and liberties, for example, are the result and gift of our social histories. We can delight in that without maintaining that history corresponds to the *philosophe*'s natural—or the theologian's heavenly—chart.

Durkheim rejected still another style of studying history, the one that identifies a few stellar individuals as the principal makers of history. This "trap of obsolete historical teachings" tells "the child that modern law was created by Napoleon, that the literature of the seventeenth century was caused by the personal influence of Louis XIV, and that Luther made Protestantism."[50] Durkheim did not discount individual innovation. He pointed out, however, that anyone interested in making historical sense of extraordinary individuals will need to locate them in particular social narratives, and that events and social structures such as the crusades, feudalism, or the Renaissance are usually best described as the result not of this or that individual but of an array of "collective forces"—some economic or political, some cultural or demographic, and so on.

Studying history, in Durkheim's view, enables students to have some sense of and appreciation for the rich complexity of social life, and to develop a critical understanding of their own society's place in history. How does contemporary society rate as compared to past or foreign cultures? What needs to be known to evaluate the merit of past events and institutions, individuals and decisions? How can the unfamiliar become lovable? What does the path leading up to the present tell of the one heading into the future? Questions and issues such as these are central in Durkheim's account of studying and teaching history. It's no wonder, then, that history played a profound role in his portrayal of moral education.

Literature and science also figured in, and for many of the same reasons. General and abstract talk about the practices and hopes of a people will not make a vivid impression on students. Thick descriptions are required, and literature can deliver these. The detail in literature allows the student "to touch [the manners, ideas, and institutions of a people] with his own hands," to "see them alive." Literature, then, like history, educates students in ways of life different from their own. As Durkheim put it, literature is "to arouse and exercise a feeling for things human . . . to show man as he is, with his almost limitless capacity for change, in the extreme complexity of his nature which is capable of manifesting itself in an immense diversity of forms."[51]

Science, too, provides a sense for the complexity of human nature, not just a knowledge of the material world. Studying science conveys to students the diverse and multifarious ways our knowledge is formed. Science is a general term applied to a variety of human institutions. The development of these institutions needs to be taught. "We must indicate the hypotheses that successively followed and displaced one another, the investment in thought and labor that they entailed. We must explain to [the student] that the knowledge we now have is itself provisional."[52] The approach of the Cartesian sciences is of little help here. They attempt to "reduce knowledge of the world to universal mathematics." This longing for physical simplicity is similar to the desire for human universality—the quest for the ideal human form. Durkheim noted that the philosophers of the eighteenth century were infected with these Cartesian aspirations. They imagined they could construct a new social science from scratch, "by way of definitions and deductions, with no need to resort to observation—in other words, to history."[53] Moreover, the attempt to study a science, social or natural, outside of history is misguided, for it implies that scientific institutions can do what no others can: shed their culturally specific descriptions of the world and equip themselves with neutral, transhistorical ones. Durkheim, however, wanted students to appreciate science as a thing human, even as it explores things nonhuman.

Durkheim summed up his position on the teaching of history, literature, and science in this passage from *The Evolution of Educational Thought*:

> We must remain Cartesians in the sense that we must fashion rationalists, that is to say men who are concerned with clarity of thought; but they must be rationalists of a new kind who know that things, whether human or physical, are irreducibly complex and who are yet able to look unfalteringly into the face of this complexity. . . . We must feel more vividly the infinite richness of reality. . . . This should be the goal of the triadic culture which is implied by an education concerned with the development of the whole man through the most effective methods: linguistic culture, scientific culture, and historical culture.[54]

Moral education takes place at the junctures of the familiar and the unfamiliar, the past and the present. Schools are charged with conveying to students a society's shared understanding—its fundamental beliefs, practices, and goals. Schools also are to cultivate in students dispositions for critical thinking, for evaluating contemporary practices in light of alternatives found in foreign or past cultures, in new developments taking place within contemporary society, or in long-standing ideals that need to be more fully realized in social practices. These two aims of moral education—teaching the ways of tradition and of criticism—go hand in hand, because social critics who are active participants in a democratic society consult the past as they look to the future. There is no immutable list of self-interpreting moral principles above scrutiny or behind variant readings. An overlapping consensus is not self-evident. Still, avoiding subjectivism, Durkheim maintained that we can offer interpretations of a shared, cultural inheritance, a common possession that is steady enough to be taught. Moral pluralism, as described in the previous chapter, is not threatened by this common inheritance; it is a part of it. Critical thought, a cardinal aspect of Durkheim's moral education and moral individualism, seeks to reform this inheritance even as it is sustained by it.

VI

In spite of my efforts to highlight the role of critical thought in Durkheim's account of moral education, the idea of transmitting a shared understanding will sound scary to many, and for good reasons. Some will ask, Is there such a thing as a shared understanding? What's in it? What's missing from it? Is there only one? If not, whose version of "it" are we to transmit? Is the shared understanding the same for African Americans and white Americans, Hispanics and American Indians, men and women, hetero- and homosexuals, lower class and middle, middle class and upper? Some, no doubt, will ask: Is not public, moral education a form of state dominance and coercion? Given "the fact of pluralism," to use Rawls's refrain, what shared moral understanding is to be imparted to our youth? There are no easy answers to these good questions. That, in fact, would have been one of Durkheim's responses. These are not problems to be "easily determined, once and for all." They are difficulties to be discussed through continual debate and argument in a democratic society. "It is not indeed up to the State to create this community of ideas and sentiments without which there is no society," Durkheim said.[55] That community is made and remade continuously by a host of social activities, from PTA meetings to national debates to marches on Washington.

Nonetheless, the state has an active role to play in education, Durkheim insisted, lest, for example, the majority should attempt systematically "to impose its ideas on the children of the minority."[56] Education should not be "completely abandoned to the arbitrariness of private individuals"; it is not an "essentially private and domestic affair." Since education is crucial to the common life of a nation, the state "cannot be indifferent to it." This is not to say that the state "must necessarily monopolize instruction," only that it must not remain aloof. It must insure the equal distribution of this crucial social good, education, and prevent it from falling under the domination of any particular group or class. There is no evidence to suggest that Durkheim viewed the state as an enforcer of state-sponsored ideologies. That would contradict everything he said about moral individualism and the life of democratic societies.

Still, questions having to do with legitimacy and authority remain. Durkheim assumed that a "community of ideas" exists, and this assumption raises questions about the relation between public education and the state, the family, the local community, and, of course, the individual. I begin addressing these questions by comparing Durkheim's model of public education to the three models Amy Gutmann identifies in *Democratic Education*: the family state, the state of families, and the state of individuals.[57]

The family state, which Gutmann attributes to Plato, is based on the belief that though there may be competing conceptions of the good, only one is correct, and social harmony requires that the true one be widely shared. What is good for the individual is good for society, and vice versa. In this view, the state, armed with authority over education, can secure individual virtue and social justice. Gutmann criticizes this model by claiming that "as long as we differ not just in our opinions but in our moral convictions about the good life, the state's educational role cannot be defined as realizing *the* good life, objectively defined, for each of its citizens."[58] Even if such a good life could be known by a few (perhaps by state officials or educational experts), it would not be consistent with democratic principles for the state to enjoin all citizens to adopt it.

The state of families model, associated with Locke, insists that educational authority rests with the family, not the state. Parents naturally have their children's best interests in mind, and have the right to teach them as they see fit. But this model, according to Gutmann, neglects to take into account that children, as future adults, belong not only to the domestic sphere but to the political sphere as well. Gutmann does not bar parents from all educational authority, only from an exclusive right to it.

The state of individuals model Gutmann derives from liberal statements like John Stuart Mill's that "all attempts by the State to bias the conclusions of its citizens on disputed subjects are evil."[59] In this view, schools are to educate in an unbiased, neutral fashion; they are to aim at maximizing students' future choice without prejudicing their preferences. As Gutmann points out, this view fails to appreciate our desire to rear children in specific ways likely to promote their well-being. Moreover, this model self-destructs insofar as it champions neutrality—a partisan, "liberal" value.

Durkheim's notions concerning moral education speak directly to each of these three models. The family state assumes (1) that there is such a thing as *the* good life, and (2) that one legitimate role of the state is to grasp and articulate it. Durkheim's historicism rules out the metaphysical devices needed to support the universalistic claims of the assumption. The family state requires that human nature be grounded on a single essence, and that at least some of us possess a mind agile enough to dodge our own cultural biases and apprehend it. This seems a decisive criticism. Yet what if we say, with Durkheim, that there are many languages and vocabularies that express different cultures' many differing conceptions of the good life? Can we then go on to claim that a state has the exclusive right to appropriate and articulate its own society's particular and contingent conception? In other words, if we socialize the first assumption, can we salvage the second? Durkheim would answer "No." He believed the state has no exclusive right to pronounce on and to perpetuate a society's conception of the good life, that is, those beliefs and practices that a society values. He showed how these conceptions are generated in a variety of ways, sometimes deliberately, sometimes tacitly. They are complicated social products, found in and transmitted through all the spheres of social life. The state, Durkheim warned, is not to "monopolize instruction."[60]

He did not mean the state has no role in moral education. Durkheim was equally critical of the second model, the state of families. He noted that, with respect to education, there is a tension between the rights and duties of the state and those of the family, and he opposed those who, in his words, claim that "education is . . . an essentially private and domestic affair."[61] Advocates of this position "forbid any positive action [by public education] designed to impress a given orientation on the mind of the youth." But education, Durkheim stated, "has a collective function," and hence it is "impossible that society should be uninterested" in it. It could have been Durkheim, but it was Aristotle who wrote that "the system of education in a state must . . . be one and the same for all, and the provision of this system must be a matter of public action. It cannot be left . . . to private enterprise, with each parent making provision privately for his own children, and having them privately instructed as he himself thinks fit. Training for an end which is common should also itself be common."[62] Durkheim argued that the state, given its structure and reach, should play a positive role in education for a variety of reasons. To begin with, the state facilitates reflection on and the communication of the shared understanding that education is charged with conveying, "the ideas and sentiments which are at the base of democratic morality." If it is shared, some may ask, why should the state concern itself? Will not a society's common languages and practices naturally persist? Durkheim maintained, along with Tocqueville, that as modern societies become increasingly pluralistic, older, more traditional forms of transmitting social ideals and practices wane. In modern, pluralist societies, it is essential that a common treasury of democratic principles be taught, lest education fall into the service of "private beliefs, and the whole nation [become] divided and break down into an incoherent multitude of little fragments in conflict with one another."[63] Unlike MacIntyre, Durkheim did not deplore pluralism, but he did insist that the more pluralistic a democratic nation, the greater the need for a common, democratic faith. Public education can contribute to this faith.

His argument for this had little in common with an earlier one found in *The Division of Labor in Society*. There he had maintained that specialization in labor engenders interdependence and hence social unity. Now he celebrated diversity, and not only in the occupational sphere, without assigning to it a social function such as promoting organic solidarity. Pluralism is an aspect of moral individualism, a relatively recent social morality. The difference between moral individualism and egoistic individualism is the difference between a public faith and a private cult. Pluralism, that is moral pluralism, is a principled assortment of social options that a democratic society has agreed to disagree on. It is a feature of, not a threat to, the common good. But it presupposes that there be, in Durkheim's words, "a sufficient community of ideas and of sentiments, without which any society is impossible." [64] Moral pluralism requires a shared context.

From this argument come other reasons for the state to take an active role in education. The state prevents the majority from imposing "its ideas on the children of the minority. The school should not be the thing of one party." Pluralism is lawful and needs to be ensured. The state also protects the individual child from some minorities. It blocks antisocial provincialism and prevents families from intellectually and emotionally tyrannizing a child. "There is no school which can claim the right to give, with full freedom, an antisocial education." [65] How are we to know the difference between the legitimate act of guarding a child from domestic tyranny and the unlawful interference of the majority imposing "its ideas on the children of the minority"? The answer is the same as the answer to the question, What acts and beliefs fall under moral pluralism? Our collective values and social institutions such as the Constitution provide steady yet fluid democratic guidelines. Citizens of modern democracies have agreed, for example, to disagree on religion. Hence any public school that attempts explicitly to sabotage a child's religious faith is likely to be charged with having coercively imposed its ideas on children. And if a public school (including state-approved home schools) teaches a child that whites are smarter than blacks, or that boys make better doctors than girls, or that the world is flat and NASA and others have fabricated pictures of earth as an oblate spheroid, then the state has the right to intervene.

Children are citizens. They have the right to an education that will enable them to become full participants in the various social spheres of a democracy. Democratic societies have a duty to uphold children's educational rights, and this includes providing an adequate moral education. Durkheim, then, unlike theorists supporting the state of families model, did not support parents' exclusive right to determine the moral education of their children.

The line between what counts as legitimate pluralism and its destructive excesses is by no means settled. It is drawn and redrawn continually and subtly by events and activities such as town council meetings, neighborhood block parties, worship services, teachers' meetings, academic lectures, popular movies, nomination hearings of Supreme Court justices, and so on. This is not to say that everything is subject to debate. Some liberties are fixed, though we often argue about how to interpret them. Whether there is much or little debate, the state should take an active role in public education, though without dominating it. It's clear to me that Durkheim would have agreed with Gutmann when she writes that children are "neither the mere creatures of their parents nor the mere creatures of a centralized state. Democratic education is best viewed as a shared trust, of parents, citizens, teachers, and public officials."[66]

The third model, the state of individuals, Durkheim unquestionably would have rejected. He wrote that education must "not be completely abandoned to the arbitrariness of private individuals."[67] Education, I have said, prepares children for active participation in the various spheres of society. It prepares them to participate in *their* society, not just in any society. There is nothing neutral or unbiased about this task. Even the educational decision not to encourage or discourage certain beliefs is a principled choice informed by a society's moral traditions—in our case, moral individualism and its democratic morality. Moral pluralism and the capacity to deliberate wisely when faced with decisions are features of our society that need to be inculcated. There is no getting around this kind of moral education, and there is no reason to want to. It's hard to imagine what an unbiased education would look like—what could be included in the curriculum, allowed in discussions, assigned in readings. Even if one could uphold the dubious distinction between fact and value, I doubt that most of us would want public education pared down to the "Dragnet" style: "just the facts, ma'am." Dickens showed us what that kind of education would look like in *Hard Times*. The life children need to prepare for is too complicated, too wonderful, too difficult for such a paltry education.

The former Secretary of Education, William Bennett, understands as much. He argues that there is a common culture, a set of values, that needs to be inculcated in our children. If we fail in this our society will become fragmented and will be in danger of losing its shared beliefs in democracy and other cherished American ways and institutions. He admits that the content of this common culture is not patent. But this in itself should not deter us: "The effort to achieve a consensus in what should be taught, particularly in the area of values, should not be undercut by allowing people to opt out of discussions of these things if they have disagreement with this or that." In a speech given at the University of Missouri Bennett called this common culture a "civil religion," and he criticized the Religious Right for their use of religion as "a kind of trump card to foreclose further debate."[68] Gutmann and Durkheim would agree with Bennett that there is a common culture that needs to be inculcated,[69] and that although there will be hard cases concerning the boundaries of this common culture, it is better to cope with that uncertainty than to be content with an amoral education.

But Gutmann and Durkheim would perhaps agree with few of Bennett's other educational views. For example, more than once Bennett sent to Congress a bill to finance educational vouchers with Chapter I funds. These vouchers would give parents annually a specified sum to buy their children the education of their choice. Most conservative neopluralists, those in favor of greater parental and local control over public education, regard Bennett as a champion of parents' rights. Considering Bennett's position on vouchers to enable these forms of local control and on the need to inculcate a more general, common culture, he seems to think parents and local communities can train children in those general democratic virtues better than can larger public associations and agencies. He recommends, for example, that it be up to the local communities to "agree (and they can agree) on what constitutes a minimum of historical knowledge that every high school graduate . . . must master."[70] He doesn't seem to worry that some schools in the deep South and the far West, for instance, will agree on different versions of what history should be taught. He wants to assure us that agreement is possible, yet I would have thought the issue of agreement was largely settled once he narrowed down the panel of discussants to the local community. Without depreciating the important educational value of parents and the local community, Gutmann argues that "voucher plans attempt to avoid rather than settle our disagreements over how to develop democratic character through schooling." Moreover, Congressman Augustus F. Hawkins, as chair of the House Education and Labor Committee, claimed that "choice will segregate on the basis of income, race and national origin."[71] This would perpetuate what Durkheim condemned, namely, educational opportunities based on class and locality.

If we agree with Gutmann and Durkheim that education is a public good directed toward collective aims, and if we agree that the state of families model is undesirable, then voucher plans will appear to "leave too little room for democratic deliberation," as Gutmann says.[72] Educational vouchers are likely to allow us to agree to disagree too quickly, and on too much. Durkheim warned that the path from political disintegration to political tyranny is often short. If a democratic morality is to be articulated, many parties must have their say, and in public arenas. The voice of parents and local communities certainly count here, but they should not be allowed to exclude other groups and individuals from contributing to the moral education of future citizens.

This inclusive public approach to education fits well with Durkheim's belief that, if we turn education over "to the service of private beliefs," we risk "the whole nation [becoming] divided," breaking down into "an incoherent multitude of little fragments in conflict with one another." During his day Durkheim often argued against powerful conservative Catholics who opposed public, secular education. He worried that a parochial education could not prepare students for the social and moral diversity of society, for it would fail to inculcate in students an important feature of our modern faith—moral pluralism.

VII

There is another and more profound disagreement between the educational positions of Durkheim and Gutmann and of Bennett. Bennett finds it "worrisome" that "Americans are no longer certain that their country and form of government are the best."

He agrees with Bernard Brown's observation that "all schools must transmit a cultural heritage and help legitimize the political system—otherwise the regime in the long run loses effectiveness and is replaced . . . by another regime that knows how to secure obedience."[73] Bennett's account of our common culture includes faith in American supremacy. Moreover, education, armed with the doctrine of American supremacy, is called on to legitimize the political system, securing political obedience. This account is not at all similar to Durkheim's or Gutmann's, and I want to explore the dissimilarities. Once again, questions of legitimacy and authority are at stake. The fact that Durkheim, Gutmann, and Bennett all believe in something like a shared understanding, but disagree on its nature, prompts concern about educational power and decision-making procedures. If there is disagreement about the nature of a common culture— and there is—then whose account of it is to be inculcated? Who will decide—the rich, the politically powerful, "the people," the experts?

Neither Durkheim's nor Gutmann's reading of a shared understanding includes notions of national supremacy. In their accounts, public education and the common inheritance it transmits do not serve to legitimate "the regime." A regime is valid insofar as it faithfully and justly fulfills its roles. We do not shape a shared understanding so as to legitimate the present regime. Rather, the regime is to be evaluated in light of the shared understanding. Skills in critical inquiry and deliberation are central to both Durkheim's and Gutmann's interpretation of a shared understanding that Durkheim sometimes called democratic morality and that Gutmann calls democratic, civil religion. These skills relegate notions like supremacy to the occasional pep rally, and ban them from serious daily discussion and debate on concrete, pressing problems. Critical inquiry will not accept legitimation as the aim or function of one's interpretation of a shared understanding. Critical thought does not set out to make a thing legitimate. Instead, it raises and answers a question: Is this thing (this nomination, that court ruling, this invasion, that embargo) legitimate?

Still, the very idea of educating students in a shared understanding is likely to give many pause. I suppose this is to say that many still find the very idea of public, moral education alarming. This may be especially true when they find it occurring in a discussion based on the work of Durkheim. Durkheim, some have said, had an inadequate conception of society. It was too homogeneous. He did not recognize that societies are fundamentally heterogeneous, comprised of conflicting groups with varying degrees of power. He did not fear that a society's public education can be determined by relations having more to do with power than with justice, that the standard reading of the shared understanding may be rendered for the benefit of powerful groups or social forces such as multinationals, PAC funds, or state ideologies. These criticisms have been voiced in one form or another by Lukes, Nisbet, Coser, Nizan, Levitas, and others.[74]

Durkheim's alleged conservatism will be addressed in the next chapter. For now I want to insist that, in spite of some truth in these criticisms, Durkheim's understanding of society and conflict was more nuanced than many of his commentators have realized. The more recent studies of Durkheim have recognized this. Jeffrey Alexander notes that moral education, in Durkheim's account, "will be accomplished through educators who are not servants of the state or of capital, but who represent the moral whole. . . . The state plays neither an ideological nor a coercive role."[75] Fenton claims that "there is little justification for the view that [Durkheim's] work on education provides evidence of his increasing attachment to the role of the state and its function of creating and sustaining a powerful collective conscience. As in his earlier recognition of the uncertain state of public opinion he acknowledges that where opinion is divided the state itself cannot simply create and impose a 'collective conscience.' "[76] And Mohammed Cherkaoui writes that "Durkheim regarded conflict as a fundamental trait of all educational systems. . . . *The Evolution of Educational Thought* reveals that Durkheim viewed the educational system principally as a powerful weapon in the hands of dominant political groups."

In *The Evolution of Educational Thought*, Durkheim pinpoints the ways groups have struggled to monopolize learning and to retain power. One of the merits of Durkheim's sociohistorical analysis of educational systems is that he does not neglect this factor in the field of forces shaping educational systems and that he shows how it sometimes plays an active role in the political sphere. . . . Readers of *The Evolution of*

Educational Thought can hardly fail to be astonished at the bold-ness with which Durkheim develops a theory of conflict in order to account for the sociohistorical development of educational systems.[77]

I should point out that in 1904 Durkheim composed the material published as *The Evolution of Educational Thought*, only a year after he wrote the lectures that appear as *Moral Education*, and before he wrote most of the articles found in his *Education and Sociology*. Early on, then, Durkheim was aware of and concerned about the role that dominant and conflicting social forces play in controlling education. Cherkaoui's remarks about Durkheim's *The Evolution of Educational Thought* should not come as a sur-prise. We have seen how Durkheim delineated the plurality of social spheres and worried about destructive "seepage" and conflict occurring between them. Harmful conflict distressed him, not all conflict. As we have also seen, Durkheim under-stood that institutions are creatively shaped by many sociohis-torical forces, sometimes by conflicting ones. Insofar as these conflicts can be settled, resolution is to emerge from democratic deliberation, not from the influence of money, power, or politi-cal fiat. Moreover, we have seen that Durkheim recognized that class and locality often determine the quality of a student's edu-cation. He called inequitable education an "organization" be-cause it had become institutionalized, and he insisted that this "organization" is not "morally justifiable."

Durkheim emphasized a common moral education because he was mindful of the abuses of power that emerge from conflict not governed by deliberation. Distressed by what he perceived to be a disintegrating collective moral consciousness and by the injustices that accompany it, Durkheim focused on the need for educating future citizens in their progressive moral traditions, in what he called moral individualism and democratic morality. This was no reactionary response. Durkheim was not attempt-ing to submerge the individual in the sea of society's institution-alized authority, nor was he trying to reductively equate society with a hierarchical organicism resistant to change. The moral traditions he promoted, and that he claimed are already embod-ied in many modern, liberal institutions, are those that cham-pion the dignity of the individual, including that individual whose beliefs and practices are foreign to us. They also champion the value of democratic institutions such as free speech and inquiry, due process, and other civil liberties, and they uphold the loveliness and necessity of human community, whether local, national, or international. His approach to education was perhaps lofty, but it was not dangerous. It may have been an attempt to offer a political solution to a problem larger than politics, but it was not nationalistic.

There was nothing neutral about Durkheim's approach to moral education. The value of individual rights, for example, is a substantive belief, one that Durkheim thought schools should teach. Public schools can no more afford to be neutral on this score than can other public institutions such as the courts. To abandon this value is to abandon the very virtue needed for practicing prudential neutrality or impartiality. Instilling a common morality, in this case, will not serve to silence diverse voices but will give them a greater hearing. No child should be ignorant of the democratic virtues, Durkheim said. These values open students' minds, and the collective debate they promote is an indispensable democratic practice. Durkheim, then, was interested in fostering liberal values, not radical neutrality. This is not to say that he abandoned the communitarian regard for community and fellowship. He contended that liberal values and practices can create in us a deep sense of moral unity. Moral individualism is not simply a means to secure private ends. It promotes shared public goods, and hence summons individuals to embrace some common projects and identities.

The account of this shared understanding that is to be taught to our children belongs to no single interest, according to Durkheim. It is not exclusively the state's, or a dominant class's, or parents', or professional educators' interpretation of shared values, and it is not simply the majority's account. Durkheim rejected a majoritarian approach. Majorities are subject to self-interest and transient fads that could work against the principles of moral individualism. Who or what, then, can legitimately shape public, moral education? Following Durkheim's lead, I want to suggest that the legitimate determinant of moral education is the social effort required to reconcile the variety of interpretations of a democratic society's moral principles. These interpretations are offered by state officials, educational authorities, parents, students, and all others who care. Democratic principles in general, Durkheim said, can bind a modern society to them. They will not be ignored. The interpretations of these principles, such as the right to free speech, are not self-evident, but their broad meanings are often clear enough to block those who work against them and to help those who work to extend them. Some of these principles or ideals may have been initially instituted by a majority, though this is not usually the case. They have taken on a life of their own, however, in the institutions and practices in which they have become embedded.[78] They contribute to our moral vision, and are reformed when we once again look hard at hard issues. Questions such as What are the limits to free speech in high schools? and How can schools legitimately combat sexism, racism, and economic injustice? get us thinking, usually implicitly, about our common, moral inheritance. This inheritance is neither fixed nor shapeless, neither determinate nor intangible. It is a part of who we are and is discovered and remade in our daily life and practices.

VIII

Durkheim himself worked at both discovering and remaking his society's moral inheritance in his own daily life. His work on educational theory needs to be understood in the way that he advocated understanding all moral endeavor—situated in its immediate and its broader social contexts. His life work, after all, was teaching, mostly teaching future educators about the nature of education at a time when debate about public education was dividing the French nation. Some have tried to give psychological explanations for Durkheim's work. He had a deeply conservative disposition, they say, and he sought to avoid conflict and controversy. This strikes me as an odd thing to attribute to a man whose career choice necessarily placed him amid turmoil. He advocated secular public education while much of France was clinging to traditional Roman Catholic private schooling. Moreover, Durkheim's lifelong commitment to advance the social sciences met overwhelming resistance from within the academic community. This so-called traditionalist seems to have chosen a nontraditional profession.

There are many good reasons why, in the France of his day, Durkheim was drawn to sociology and to education. He was aware that his country was undergoing complex and drastic changes as a result of the French and then the Industrial Revolutions. Sociology, he thought, could illuminate the nature of these changes and could provide some informed hunches for reforming society in light of the ever-moving horizon of past and future. France's educational system, Durkheim believed, required much reconstruction, for it had not yet developed an up-to-date, clear picture of its nature and tasks, given the changed and changing world around it.

We can think of Durkheim's educational goals as belonging to the tradition of the 1789 revolutionaries, and also to the Republicans and socialists of the Third Republic. French society before the Revolution could be described as what J. B. Schneewind calls "the Divine Corporation"—a cooperative endeavor, set up and directed by God, "in which agents join to produce a good that no one of them could produce alone."[79] Each agent performs a specific task and does not presume to understand or be responsible for the tasks of others. That rests with the Supervisor, that is, with God. The ancien régime functioned as a Divine Corporation in which every member received the proper education for his or her appointed task, and this meant a limited education for most. The French Revolution wanted to substitute for the Divine Corporation a human one. The revolutionaries believed—and demonstrated—that humans make societies, remake them, and are largely responsible for them. Each individual, in fact, was expected to make some contribution to the community and to progress. To this end, individuals would receive an equal, public education. The ideals of liberty, equality, and fraternity, and the skills to implement them, were to be taught to all, so that all could participate in the construction of the new society.

Institutions, however, often resist reform, and French education resisted very effectively. The Civil Constitution of the Clergy of 1790, the radical anticlerical legislation that required the clergy to swear oaths to civil authorities, had little effect, even under Napoleon, who encouraged the Roman Catholic Church to play an active educational role. The Roman Church, for the most part, identified with anti-democratic regimes, Napoleonic and Bourbon, and its control of education in France continued to grow until the Third Republic (1870–1940). The

Third Republic championed the ideals of 1789—a democratic, secular France. It is not an exaggeration to say that control over education became the symbol of conflict between rightists, monarchists, and Catholics on the one side and Republicans and socialists on the other. The Republicans, like the revolutionaries of 1789, saw the schoolroom as a way to promote liberty and equality. They were at least moderately successful in their efforts at reform. They established free secular education as well as scholarships for higher education. The public educational system became a "new 'establishment,' based not on titles, land, or industry, but on examinations."[80] This system was far from perfect. The middle classes no doubt were its primary beneficiaries. It provided, however, a more just educational system than had ever been known in France. Moreover, it was secular, and promoted democratic principles and critical thought. I do not mean it was anti-religious. Rather, as a democratic state institution, it was nonpartisan, at least concerning religion. I suppose it was partisan, politically speaking, insofar as it supported a democracy when many wished to restore the monarchy. In any case Durkheim was one of the chief contributors to reforming the Third Republic's educational system.

The innovators of the Third Republic, like those of the Revolution, saw themselves as initiating new projects, building new institutions created by human beings for human beings. Their vision was that each member of the new society should participate in its creation. Each member was called upon to experience freedom—"forced to be free," as Rousseau once said. Durkheim, however, realized that even new institutions steal much from their past. Unlike many contemporaries, he never lost sight of the value of traditions and communities. He worried, in fact, about their decay. He was convinced that the liberal values that motivated him were the gifts of noble moral traditions. Like Rousseau, he championed the rational, autonomous individual who is skilled in both self-mastery and self-expression. Again like Rousseau, he located the individual's heart and soul in the virtuous society whose common good is discovered in common deliberation. This deliberation, this active, intelligent participation in society, is not a gift of nature. It needs to be taught. Consequently, Durkheim devoted himself to promoting public moral education in modern, democratic societies.

Durkheim's mixed vocabulary, a mingling of standard liberal and communitarian values, has confused many. It has led, I believe, to various charges of conservatism. Durkheim's work on education, in particular, has been misinterpreted as a result of his heterogeneous moral vocabulary. It has been labeled authoritarian, an apologetic for the status quo, an enemy to the individual, to reason, and to liberalism. I have offered a different reading. Autonomy, critical thought, and a reforming spirit are some of the elements I have stressed. I believe Durkheim's educational work has been misread largely because education does involve, in some form or other, socialization, and socialization, for many, is something anti-liberal. But I think I can now sum up Durkheim's liberal educational position by using the phrase that the self-professed liberal Amy Gutmann uses repeatedly to describe her own position. "Conscious social reproduction" is the aim of a democratic education, according to Gutmann.[81] The phrase is dialectical. It suggests in good Hegelian fashion that an *Aufhebung* takes place as the old (that which is to be reproduced) is critically (consciously) preserved, thereby creating something new. Gutmann contrasts this process to unconscious social reproduction, the indiscriminate transmission of a society's values, beliefs, and practices. Conscious social reproduction is a shorthand prescription for citizens to participate in and intelligently shape their society, the human corporation. Unconscious social reproduction is a prescription for the generation in power to replicate its ways and beliefs in the younger generation, thus perpetuating yet another version of the Divine Corporation, with or without belief in a Supervisor.

Durkheim endorsed "conscious social reproduction." Members of democratic societies are to reflect on the past and the present to determine what is to be taught to its future citizens, and the value of and capacity for such reflection are to be cultivated by moral education. The chief aim of Durkheim's educational theory was not furnishing workers for the market but teaching citizens to be full members of pluralistic democracies. It is disheartening that Gutmann herself has implied that for Durkheim education serves "only to maintain the present state of social and political organization."[82] A necessary condition for moral liberalism, I argue in the next chapter, is something like

Durkheim's understanding of public education. Its heterogeneous character, embracing critical thought and tradition, autonomy and community, human diversity and social unity, promises to contribute toward a nuanced description and robust enhancement of liberal democratic institutions.

Wittgenstein and the Activity of a Durkheimian Social Critic

DURKHEIM'S PRESCRIPTION for education was that of a practical social reformer. He understood the limits of education. It is not a cure-all. In *Suicide* he wrote that education "can be reformed only if society itself is reformed." Education contributes to social revision, but more is required. The practices of social critics are also needed.

I read Durkheim as a nonconservative social theorist and critic. For some time now, Durkheim has been interpreted as a conservative sociologist preoccupied with understanding and maintaining social order. I believe, however, that Durkheim investigated the webs and patterns of social order for the sake of establishing social justice. No doubt many have attributed conservatism to Durkheim because of his commitment to viewing humans and their moral principles and practices as ineluctably rooted in their histories. The logic here goes something like this: social theorists who begin and end with human situatedness can never rise above present or past social ideals, customs, and institutions. These allegedly conservative theorists are bound to the stagnant status quo, unlike "rational" theorists who discover moral universal truths outside present or past social worlds.

I contend that it was Durkheim's commitment to the historical, social stuff of human existence that enabled him to be a radical critic. I call him radical because he went to the root of many problems of modern social life, exposing their historical origins as well as their present social circumstances.[1] We can't criticize what we can't see. "True sociology," said Durkheim, "is history." Uncovering our guiding prejudices requires the sensibilities of the historian. Durkheim was a social critic equipped with such sensibilities. He reformed inherited traditions by furnishing immanent critiques.

Moreover, Durkheim's sensitivity to the historical, far from tying him to a status quo, exposed him to social change and diversity. That exposure helped him to envision wholesome social change, and also to recognize the fragility of many cultural accomplishments. The dignity and rights of the individual, for Durkheim, are an important piece of moral, social progress. They are not, however, immutable. They are subject to immoral threats as well as to moral amelioration.

My argument that Durkheim was a social critic entails a general defense of what I will call internal social criticism: criticism that seeks to reform society by self-consciously working within its historically fashioned social inheritance, that is, its historically situated ideals, customs, beliefs, institutions, and practices.[2] This defense pertains not only to Durkheim, but also to figures as diverse as Alasdair MacIntyre, Richard Rorty, and John Rawls. Rawls, for example, increasingly looks like a philosopher satisfied with working in Plato's cave. This has inspired some to complain that he is no longer trying to get "outside the cave, in the blaze of Truth."[3] His new emphasis on "an overlapping consensus" and on shared intuitions have led some to claim that he is now more interested in social agreement than in truth. By studying Durkheim we can gain novel insight into this and other issues facing contemporary social philosophy. In this chapter, then, I explore the ways of Durkheim's internal social criticism; in the next chapter I relate this approach to Rawls, Walzer, MacIntyre, and Rorty.

My argument begins with Wittgenstein, a philosopher who is often charged with, or praised for, supporting conservatism. There are many parallels between Wittgenstein's and Durkheim's general philosophical stances, and predictably the complaints against them share a family resemblance. Ernest Gellner has claimed that Wittgenstein's thought "refuses to undermine any accepted habits, but, on the contrary concentrates on showing that the reasons underlying criticisms of accepted habits are in general mistaken."[4] In a similar fashion, Herbert Marcuse has argued that "the [Wittgensteinian] self-styled poverty of philosophy committed with all its concepts to the given state of affairs, distrusts the possibilities of a new experience. Subjection to the rule of the established facts is total."[5] Lewis Coser has written similarly of Durkheim: "He did not duly appreciate the import of social innovation and social change because he was preoccupied with social order and equilibrium." And again, "to Durkheim any type of nonconformity is criminal by definition, so critical periods, periods of social disequilibrium, are by definition aspects of social pathology. Such a definition prevents the study of these crises in terms of the opportunities they offer for the emergence of alternatives to the existing order."[6]

I intend to defend Durkheim from charges of conservatism by deflecting the same charges from Wittgenstein. Both, I believe, are labeled conservatives because they hold that knowledge and objectivity are products of relatively stable social forms of life. I bring in Wittgenstein because his work, more than Durkheim's, investigates the sociolinguistic bases of human emotion, pain, custom, belief, certainty, and knowledge. Wittgenstein's work will take us to the heart of the issue: Can internal social criticism, which assumes there is no foundation from which it springs besides human convention, profoundly challenge society?

I

There are many ways to discuss Wittgenstein's philosophy. I begin by describing an account of human knowledge that Wittgenstein came to believe has taken possession of us. We are possessed by the thought that propositions are true only insofar as they correspond to atomistic facts inherent in the natural (as opposed to the social) universe. Granted, we have different languages that seemingly describe different worlds, but that is merely the regrettable result of a host of social conventions that have yet to be replaced by a more accurate universal language, i.e., true propositions expressed in logic or in some form of Esperanto. Objective statements about the world or human nature are justified by appealing to ahistorical foundations, whether a priorist or, in the case of the early Wittgenstein, empiricist. This account entails all the standard Enlightenment distinctions: fact/value, Natur-/Geisteswissenschaften, knowledge/opinion, cognition/emotion. Some foundationalists have claimed that true statements about values and ethics correspond to natural facts. Others, like the early Wittgenstein, have denied the existence of moral facts and have subscribed to some form of Nietzschean emotivism or Schopenhauerian voluntarism.

This account, which the early Wittgenstein more or less accepted, the later Wittgenstein steadily undermined. He questioned and probed it, examined and cross-examined it and reexamined it still again. The various claims characteristic of this account have seemingly usurped control of our critical faculties ("'But *this* is how it is—' I say to myself over and over again"). Eventually, however, if Wittgenstein's therapeutic questioning is successful, their spell over us gradually departs. There is something unphilosophical, in the classic modern sense, about his later work. Rather than develop epistemological foundations leading toward a universal, uniform language that corresponds to the structure of the natural world, Wittgenstein offered "perspicuous remarks" about linguistic practices. These comments seem to be about everyday language, but Wittgenstein's aim was to exorcise (technical) philosophical language and practices of its bewitchment. In response to Frege's attempts to flatten out language to true assertions about the state of affairs, for example, Wittgenstein asked, "But how many kinds of sentence are there? Say assertion, question, and command?—There are *countless* kinds: countless different kinds of use of what we call 'symbols,' 'words,' 'sentences.' And this multiplicity is not something fixed, given once for all; but new types of language, new language-games, as we may say, come into existence, and others become obsolete and get forgotten."[7]

Wittgenstein replaced the idiom of a scientific, uniform philosophical language with that of a multiplicity of language-games, an indeterminate number of social practices that do not spring from a single, universal foundation. Moreover, though some of these language-games may have much in common, they cannot, as a whole, be subsumed under a single theory or ordering principle, such as utilitarianism, Kantianism, or behaviorism. These language-games spring from shared human activities, or forms of life.[8] This is tautological, and that is the point. Social practices are grounded in social forms of life. Outside them there is no touchstone to guide or shape them. It could be said, then, that the social practices of a community do rest on a foundation of sorts, if that foundation is understood as the shared forms of life of a sociolinguistic community.

This foundation will not uphold the standard epistemic distinctions that, for example, divide facts and values. The idiom of natural science, in Wittgenstein's view, is but one of the many languages that can participate in the objectivity and authority sustained by the (often implicit) agreement in the sociolinguistic community. Objectivity or knowledge or truth is no longer the unique possession of a particular field of human inquiry, such as physics. This is not to suggest that any statement from one idiom is necessarily as objective as a statement from another. Rather, statements from any idiom can be as objective as those from another. The claim that slavery is immoral is more objective than the claim that black holes swallow solar systems.[9] The latter claim may eventually share the former's certitude. The claim that the fetus is a person is more subjective than the claim that the earth is round and not flat. The objectivity of a statement has more to do with its level and extent of entrenchment than with the particular idiom it is spoken in.[10]

Why does this Wittgensteinian approach invite allegations of conservatism? Surely his approach shares little with that taken by naturalistic conservatives such as John Casey, who argue that traditional virtues are grounded in a fixed human nature, and that any deviance from them is unnatural. Wittgenstein's conservatism, supposedly, comes from the opposite direction. An account of it goes something like this: since there is no human nature to be discovered, in Wittgenstein's view it is made by the sociolinguistic conventions associated with a community. My identity is not uncovered by introspecting my nature as an example of Homo sapiens. My identity, rather, is acquired by training and participation in particular "forms of life." The conservatism, then, involves Wittgenstein's answer to the question, Who am I? His answer requires that we describe the forms of life about us, that is, describe the status quo. What are my loves, my goals, my ideals? Those of my community. Different individuals, of course, will have somewhat varied sets of loves, goals, and so on, but all sets stem from the same "bedrock," the same shared linguistic grounding.

The basis of my identity is my training in a sociolinguistic community—a society—but that society has no absolute origin or foundation. Like language, society grows and develops over the years, without any blueprint except its own internal, somewhat flexible grammar. Like any developing language (or organism), the general arrangements of a society form a coherent whole even though its formation is not planned. It is therefore hazardous to tamper with the social order. It is held together by tangled threads of traditions, institutions, and habits. Snipping this thread, or pulling that, could unravel the whole ball.

The conservatism here arises from the answer to the question, How can we bring about change in society? This answer requires that we describe the existing state of affairs, attempt to discern where it is heading, and cautiously help it get there. The best we can do, then, is practice social midwifery, assisting society to bring forth its preconceived offspring. Stepping outside society to ask how society should be arranged is not an option. First, there is no place outside. Your particular social nature is inescapable. Moreover, if you should isolate a single social ideal or set of ideals and attempt to pattern society after it, you risk heresy. Fixating on one part of the whole, you distort both the ideal and the larger society. You risk disrupting society's delicate equilibrium. Heretics, then, need to be resisted, for they threaten the stability of the social order.

Are these allegations fair? In part, yes. A Wittgensteinian approach, for example, can rightly be labeled conservative insofar as it opposes many assumptions associated with classical Marxism and with the classical liberalism of either Kant or Mill. It rejects Kantian universal moral reason, a pillar of liberal rights. It rejects utilitarian calculation that flattens out a plurality of activities to a single, quantitative scheme purportedly justified on grounds other than those embedded in particular moral traditions and forms of life. And it undermines the historical teleology and the reductive, deterministic features that we associate with Marx. In sum, Wittgenstein challenged varieties of liberalism and Marxism at least to the extent that they rest on assumptions common to Cartesians and empiricists.

Moreover, a Wittgensteinian approach is conservative in that it does in fact locate the ground of critical moral judgment and practice in existing traditions and communities. Ultimately, no justification or criticism can come from outside the historical moral community. Even the "outsider's" judgment, say, from a foreign culture, must be understood and evaluated in terms familiar to the "local" language and practices. This suggests that when new participants are initiated into what is to become their community, their training involves more imitation and trust than "rational" explanations. At least this is the case for children. As the child acquires a self, and therefore skills in reasoning, appealing to situated reason becomes appropriate.

Sabina Lovibond has aptly characterized this aspect of Wittgensteinian conservatism as "its emphasis upon *continuity*." She notes that "the shared practice which Wittgenstein sees as the material basis of communication has not only a synchronic, but a diachronic aspect." [11] Wittgenstein underscored the continuity, the agreement, found in the present activities and beliefs of a community. Yet his emphasis on training—a training characterized as "do the same"—seems to promise significant continuity between generations and hence between the past, present, and future.

I will soon address whether these traits inevitably lead to substantive conservative stances in ethics and politics. Here, I want to note quickly some ways a Wittgensteinian approach is erroneously construed as conservative. Morality is socially produced. This vague statement can correctly be inferred from Wittgenstein. But the statement, and the conclusions that flow from it, should not imply that society is a monolithic force that reproduces itself as a seamless moral whole. Wittgenstein, I have said, emphasized sociolinguistic diversity, not uniformity. Society, if we can put a Wittgensteinian face on this very un-Wittgensteinian term, is a pragmatic label referring to a multitude of heterogeneous social practices, institutions, and groups that from some perspectives have much in common but that from others share little. If I am right about this, then it would appear silly to claim that an implication of Wittgenstein's approach is the idea that modern states must actively promote and enforce a homogeneous, uniform culture. This identification of the state with public culture cannot legitimately be called a Wittgensteinian position. It is true that Wittgenstein would want to say that political institutions such as bills of rights and constitutions are interpreted in the context of a people's shared understanding. Yet this says nothing about the possibility or desirability of a state's attempt to shape that understanding.

Another misconception that erroneously leads some to judge Wittgenstein a conservative assumes that his statements about justifying rules ("This is simply what I do" or "I obey the rule *blindly*")[12] discredit autonomy and critical reason. Wittgenstein's remarks on rules need to be read in the context of the notions from which he was attempting to free us. One is the idea that a special mental process—call it interpretation—accompanies every correct application of a rule. Another is the idea that rules are supported by the irresistible force of logic. His statements on rules belittle autonomy only in that they controvert the autonomy of logic and the isolated individual's ability to follow a rule without prior social training. His comments, however, do not touch on practical human autonomy (for example, a senator courageously taking an ethical though unpopular stand on a public issue during election year) or on critical reasoning (the senator's ability to offer reasons in opposition to those who say, "this is simply what we do"). "Trust" and "blind acceptance," in Wittgenstein's work, are features of a particular kind of training, such as when learning the color red; they are not prescriptions for a comprehensive way of life or for grounding moral character. Moreover, to say there are no transcendent justifications for rules is not to say there are no good justifications. Wittgenstein opposed rationalism as a theory, not rationality as a practice. He opposed empiricism, not experiments.

Read out of context, Wittgenstein's work might seem blatantly conservative. And the format of most of his books (*Zetteln*, arranged by subject) is easy prey to prooftexting. His arguments, however, seldom address issues capable of being approached conservatively as opposed to, say, radically or liberally, except insofar as they challenge many epistemological defenses of Marxism and liberalism. Think of Wittgenstein's writings as professional conversations with interlocutors such as Frege, Russell, Dilthey, or Moore on a limited (even if important) set of philosophical issues. This is not to say that his work was not normative or that it was value-free,[13] it is only to say that Wittgenstein was occupied by problems that are of a different, more rudimentary nature than those appropriately labeled conservative or radical. For example, his case against private language or for public criteria of pain behavior does not bear on the distribution of wealth or the right to employment.

Implications of his work, however, can bolster conservative

positions in politics and ethics. This, as I said, is often the result of reading Wittgenstein's remarks out of context. But there is more to it than this. Conservatives who read Wittgenstein's work sensitively and in context could draw and have drawn support from his work. I contend that a nonconservative social critic could do so as well. The possibilities of a Wittgensteinian nonconservative internal social criticism are what I want to explore next. I don't want to argue that there are no conservative implications in Wittgenstein's work. Rather, I want to show that his philosophy, and Durkheim's social theory, did not inevitably lead to conservatism, and that they both in fact can support vigorous and rich social evaluation and protest.

II

Social evaluation and protest are two notable features of social criticism. Evaluation entails dialectical thought, an exploration of our best norms, standards, and thinking about social justice, ethics, and political theory, while simultaneously investigating specific institutions, customs, and social arrangements. Although this activity may encourage us to revise our norms, it inevitably leads to protest. Protest takes place when we determine that social institutions and arrangements contradict our social norms and ideals, and, in addition, when we have the courage to act on that knowledge. This activity usually involves challenging various authorities and entrenched customs, and it can lead to a revision of norms and ideals.

My definition of protest has, at least in a limited way, rescued internal social criticism from the standard objection: How can situated social criticism emerge from its social embedment? If our thought and practices are shaped by a shared form of life, how can we achieve a critical perspective on that form of life? My notion of protest, however, suggests what is intuitively understood and what Marx powerfully recounted—in modern industrial societies there exist contradictions and tensions between norms and institutions. Internal social criticism highlights these and strives to alleviate them by implementing social norms.

This response, however, does not spare internal social criticism from a forceful aspect of the standard objection, namely,

How can internal social criticism evaluate its own critical resources? Above I mention contradictions between norms and institutions. But what of contradictions within the norms themselves? How is the situated social critic to discriminate between conflicting moral and political norms and arguments? I will address this question shortly. For now, however, I want to note how this very question solves a problem for me. The question implies that social norms do not form a seamless whole. It intimates what Durkheim well understood: modern industrial societies are not marked by mechanical solidarity, a solidarity generated by widespread agreement on practically every issue and practice. I am saved, then, from explaining how internal social criticism can offer any protest if the critic's moral vision is shaped by the norms of the age. Having admitted the "fact of pluralism," to borrow Rawls's phrase again, the question itself posits some room for social criticism. The "norms of the age" are not uniform, and different social critics will favor different norms.

A conservative internal social critic like Michael Oakeshott excludes radical protest and change by definition. Radical, here, means an innovation with no antecedents: something from nothing. In his account, the most extreme protest can always be traced, at least in part, to some segment of social belief. It would be impossible, then, to give an example of a radical statement. Any example, that is, any comprehensible example, would not qualify, for if we understood it, it would necessarily entail some bit of previously known sociolinguistic convention. Not change per se, but only radical change is ruled out. I note this not to criticize Oakeshott, but to underscore how unreasonable it is to claim that protest, in a Wittgensteinian account, is impossible because the critics' resources are determined by the very society to be probed. This position would not only have to ascribe to Wittgenstein the belief that society is entirely homogeneous, but also that reformation is logically impossible. Neither belief, I am arguing, is tenable, and neither is Wittgenstein's.

Although I want to deny, with Oakeshott, the possibility of radical protest in the absolute sense, I also want to deny that internal criticism will necessarily maintain the present state of affairs. I want to show that there is a form of internal criticism that can offer radical protest. By radical here I mean (1) criticism that subjects society to a normative scrutiny that extends down to society's roots—to its "natural" beliefs, prejudices, and power structures; and (2) protest that, based on such scrutiny, advocates new, that is, relatively discontinuous social beliefs and practices.

By briefly looking at a model of self-criticism, I can garner some intuitive support for my claims. Self-criticism, we know, is common. Yet how do we account for it? How can I criticize myself? If my beliefs are the basis, the ground, of my understanding and perspectives, can I protest against myself? The form of these questions should sound familiar, as will, I hope, some of the replies. One response is that I can discover discrepancies between a portion of my stated beliefs and some of my actions. This discrepancy is often known as hypocrisy. To simplify things, however, and perhaps to describe the condition more accurately, I want to call this a discrepancy between beliefs, and not between actions and beliefs. I will assume that our actions spring from our beliefs, and that hypocrisy is one result of a person's holding conflicting beliefs pertaining to the same subject or issue. Self-criticism, then, involves determining which beliefs best describe my identity, at least ideally, and committing myself more fully to them. This will necessitate evaluating dialectically a portion of my beliefs while holding another portion in place. This process is as natural as it is intricate.

There are other aspects of self-criticism, and my account here is not meant to be exhaustive. Through introspection I can become aware of deep-seated prejudices—beliefs so much a part of me and seemingly so self-evident that I never imagined alternatives to them. Exposed prejudices enhance self-understanding, and, depending on the nature of the prejudice, can lead to significant transformation of the self. I can, then, learn something about myself by myself. But I am more likely to learn something with the help of someone, or some group or thing. Spouses, friends, colleagues, support groups, psychoanalysis, strangers (perhaps especially strangers), books, plays, newspapers, movies, a drive across the tracks—these are some of the avenues to self-awareness and to self-transformation. They entail confronting something new. A person's willingness to be challenged by the unfamiliar, and to undergo transformation, may be a matter of one's disposition. Yet Durkheim, in his work on moral education, argued that a society can either encourage or discourage our disposition for critical thought and action based on it.

If my account of self-criticism is convincing, I can extend its features to social criticism. The social critic evaluates conflicting social beliefs and practices in the same dialectical fashion as do individuals wishing to rid themselves of hypocrisy or other unseemly or immoral traits. Internal social critics, it is true, can no more subject all society to evaluation than individuals can doubt all their beliefs at one time. Global doubt is no more possible than complete self-doubt. Yet critics can weigh conflicting arguments, protest against some aspects of a society while sustaining that protest by appealing to other aspects, unearth social prejudices, and attempt to remain open to the judgments of the outsider, who may live down the street or across the sea.

"Outsider" is a term often signifying someone alien not to one's geographic locality but to one's beliefs and commitments, even if locality and held beliefs can often be correlated. Relative to some Anglo-American sensibilities, I probably have more in common with members of the Ku Klux Klan than with the Tlingit Indians (who, for example, place a higher premium on humor than on wealth—an admirable trait I would like to emulate). Relative to issues of racism, however, I share more with the Tlingit Indians. *Pace* Peter Winch, a Wittgensteinian view does not rule out my ability, as an "outsider," to judge an alien culture, as long as I have understood what I am judging, usually through hard, patient work. The flip side of this, of course, is that I and those similar to me can be judged by those standing outside our "form of life." If we can understand the stranger's message, we would do well to listen, whether that "stranger" be a nearby person or a distant culture, living or dead. My distinction between internal and external criticism, then, does not refer to judgments generated inside a group as opposed to those outside it. This inside/outside distinction is relative to what counts as being a member of the group in question. A person can be an outsider in her own family with respect to political issues, while being an insider among, say, a protest march of diverse individuals who are otherwise strangers. There are an infinite number of boundaries that unite and separate us. By internal and external criticism I refer to the distinction between those approaches that appreciate how critical rationality is variably produced under different sociohistorical circumstances and those that try to escape history in order to discover an ahistorical overarching structure to the moral universe.

There is the following relative difference between critics of self and critics of society. The former look inward, the latter outward. The activity of self-criticism is private in that one often does not attempt to publicize or get others to rally around the results of such activity. Social critics, on the other hand, often air their results broadly—outside City Hall or the Capital, within synagogues or churches or lecture halls, in journals or newspapers or on television. There is, then, an effort to gain support, and this frequently prompts counterpositions. Depending on the social critic and the opposition, this exchange can be enriching or demeaning.

Fundamentally, however, self-criticism and social criticism are two aspects of the same interpretive process. In a Wittgensteinian account this is not surprising, since an individual's capacity to inspect the self is essentially not unlike the capacity to interpret other public entities. Both activities entail imagination, the ability to move from the familiar to the novel.[14]

Social protest entails some form of quarrel or disagreement with a friend, fellow workers, a company, state officials or policies, and so on. It is this aspect of protest that many suspect Wittgenstein blocked with his emphasis on the necessity of public agreement to sustain everyday communication and activity. The suspicion arises, I believe, from misreading Wittgenstein. In the *Zettel* he explicitly discussed the roles of agreement in human judgments:

429. You say, *"That* is red," but how is it decided if you are right? Doesn't human agreement decide?—But do I appeal to this agreement in my judgments of colour?

430. *Colour-words* are explained like *this*: "That's red" e.g.—Our language-game only works, of course, when a certain agreement prevails, but the concept of agreement does not enter into the language-game. If agreement were universal, we should be quite unacquainted with the concept of it.[15]

Think of "a certain agreement that prevails" as rudimentary agreement, a precondition for human discourse and understanding. By rudimentary I mean a basic initiation into the sociolinguistic networks of a society. Now consider this statement said to a white racist sheriff, "It was wrong to turn the hoses and dogs on the peaceful black protesters." The sheriff can comprehend this assertion. He was trained, with the rest of us, in a form of life that includes such concepts as dogs, hoses, protesters, and wrongdoing. That training, however, and the rudimentary agreement it creates, no more prevents him from disagreeing with the assertion than it prevents an outcry against him. It is true that, on a less basic level, the sheriff probably received an education different from most of ours on some specific moral issues, for example, the respect due to African Americans. His education in this regard is likely to hinder if not to block his ability to accept the judgment "It was wrong." Wittgenstein, however, did not create *that* problem.

Whether I am judging a book's color or a nation's public health care, my judgment, if I am sincere, will be based on what I think is true and not on whether it finds favor with the majority or with any other group.[16] I may lie for gain, I may say what is pleasing for popularity, yet this again is not a problem Wittgenstein created. It is a difficulty humans create for themselves.

Nothing I have said about the possibility of radical social criticism and protest gives us cause for celebration. Society is well equipped to sabotage its critics. There are tremendous pressures to lie or to flatter. There are formal and informal educators who teach or preach the wrong messages. There are bureaucratic and structural problems that seem to defy human intervention. To show that in a Wittgensteinian view there is room for radical protest is also to make plain that there is room for opposition to protesters—often opposition to those we most need to hear. Radicals and reactionaries speak the same basic language. Their messages divide them. To say that we can all understand each other is only to point out that we are standing on the same basic sociolinguistic ground. It does not tell us if we are brandishing swords or worse, or what we are standing for.

Within modern societies, as Durkheim showed us in Chapter 6, there are a variety of social spheres and communities with varying degrees of homogeneity pertaining to different values and commitments. The modern critic, then, is likely to be heard variously, depending on her audience. The specific stances taken by Wittgensteinians have occupied positions across the ideological spectrum. Compare, for example, John Casey or Roger Scruton to P. F. Strawson or Cornel West. My Wittgensteinian defense of internal criticism, then, has not precluded a conservative adaptation of Wittgenstein. Yet my argument is that a Wittgensteinian approach, or an approach that resembles it, such as Durkheim's, does not ineluctably lead to conservatism in social theory or political philosophy. If we can count on any shared features among Wittgensteinians, any family resemblance, they should look something like the mild-mannered pragmatists I described in Chapter 4. They will be antifoundational. They will embrace a host of ad hoc methods and descriptions and explanations. And they will be more comfortable with edifying as opposed to systematic philosophy, to use Rorty's distinction, preferring "hermeneutics" to "epistemology," particular cases to The Theory.

Having argued that within the Wittgenstein camp there can be individuals of many ethical and political stripes, from right to left, I need to explain why I recommend internal over external criticism. Consequently, I now want to contrast internal criticism to its notable alternative, external or suprahistorical criticism. Historically, both have illustrious and infamous records. The will of God, the force of Reason, the text of Nature—these transcendent external beacons have inspired mass death and humane care, radical revolution and reactionary oppression. Likewise, the belief that human thought and action are social (all the way down, as they say) has encouraged both fierce authoritarian rule and liberal utopian scenarios, both complacency in the face of social complexity and social activism armed with the awareness that humans authored the present state of affairs and hence can change it. With respect to democracy, the appeal to universalism has done much to promote tolerance and social justice. But that same appeal has at times stripped societies of many just social traditions that did not conform to the new, more "enlightened" ideals. J. L. Talmon reminds us that repressive measures have been employed in the name of securing a "natural" democratic order. Coercion is frequently deemed justifiable against those who refuse to be free.[17]

Both internal and external critics will have difficulty answering the question I posed earlier: How is the social critic to discriminate between conflicting moral and political norms and arguments? It is no solution for the external critic to claim "I've seen the light" unless we've all seen the same light, and then we don't need the critic. It is no solution for the critic to enforce her vision, because then she has ceased to be a critic and has become a parent, a judge, or a tyrant. External and internal critics alike will have to undergo the hard work of mounting detailed arguments for their cases. I do not mean to underestimate the effectiveness of rhetoric, especially the rhetorical power of invoking the voice of reason or the will of God. Yet that kind of rhetoric is not what we usually have in mind when we think of the activity of social criticism—which is not to say that social critics never employ such rhetoric. Whether internal or external, the critic will have to put together a convincing case, and if the argument is radical, either critic will struggle to gain a hearing. Sanatoriums and prisons admit both internal and external critics.

I endorse internal criticism, first, because I believe that it is epistemologically correct. The historicists are right. "There is nothing 'beneath' socialization or prior to history which is definatory of the human."[18] Much of this book could be read as an argument for that position. Internal criticism may seem unduly limited and provincial when placed beneath the lofty claims of suprahistorical criticism. But the former is honest, and the latter, while not dishonest, is illusory. Societies are not based upon transcendent principles, nor are they evaluated by them. There simply are no such principles. Society is a human, historical arrangement of authorities and institutions, communities and individuals, set in motion by social ideals, traditions, and customs. This is no more an idealist than a materialist statement. It is, for lack of a better term, social realism, as long as "social" is not taken to be in opposition to "natural." I would prefer to avoid these labels. I would prefer simply to call this position Wittgenstein's or Durkheim's alternative to the standard epistemological theories.

If their alternative is correct, becoming aware of the historicity of society and all that it means can assist us in reforming society. Durkheim never tired of reminding us that we cannot change what we do not understand. We need to understand that our commitments and institutions are *ours*. This does not mean that they are arbitrary or easily changed. It does mean, however, that perhaps they should be changed, and if so, that they can be, even if not without great effort. The internal critic's arguments for change are not likely to possess the "crystalline purity" of many Kantian or utilitarian or even Marxist principles, yet the path the social critic needs to travel is rougher than those principles suggest. It is rough, but it is worth taking. "We have got on to slippery ice," Wittgenstein wrote, "where there is no friction and so in a certain sense the conditions are ideal, but also, just because of that, we are unable to walk. We want to walk: so we need *friction*. Back to the rough ground!"[19]

III

Wittgenstein was better than Durkheim at exposing the epistemological problems that arise when we try to get off the rough road, yet Wittgenstein's models for forms of life are usually simple: the exchanges between a builder and a worker ("slab!"), making a joke, solving a problem in practical arithmetic. Durkheim, in contrast, concentrated on the necessarily more complex phenomena of society, its structures and ideals, its authorities and traditions. Durkheim, then, is better than Wittgenstein at teaching us the ways of "rough" internal social criticism. From him we learn to be suspicious of social critics who try to spare us and themselves friction, that is, the messy work of sorting through the varied sociohistorical attributes of society. By looking at Durkheim as a nonfoundational social theorist and critic, we can appreciate the strengths of internal social criticism.

Santayana noted that "those who neglect the study of the past are condemned to repeat it." With this sapient aphorism Durkheim would have agreed. Learning from past mistakes is good counsel, even if it is seldom heeded. (Hegel once complained that "the only thing anyone ever learned from the study of history is that no one ever learned anything from the study of history."[20]) Yet when Durkheim wrote, "if we depart from the present our final aim is to return," he was speaking of returning not only with a list of errors to avoid but with a deepened understanding of those past prejudices and assumptions, institutions, and practices that are currently shaping our present. This was important to Durkheim because he was convinced that "it is necessary to know [the historical constituent components of the

present], in order to change [the present]. . . . One acts effica-
ciously on things only to the degree that one knows their nature."[21] This line of thought goes to the core of internal criticism,
and so I want to flesh it out carefully.

Durkheim once said that "in all forms of human behavior into
which reflection is introduced, we see, to the degree that reflection is so developed, that tradition becomes more malleable and
more amenable to innovations." I suggest we take this as a general principle of internal criticism. Yet it is perhaps too general.
Durkheim had a particular kind of reflection in mind. "Historical investigation of the formation and development of systems,"
he wrote, "reveals that they depend upon religion, political organization, the degree of development of science, the state of
industry, etc. If they are considered apart from all these historic
causes, they become incomprehensible."[22] The necessary reflection, then, entails developing thick genealogies of a variety of
institutions and social forces in which a subject of inquiry is
embedded.

It is easy to imagine how this position may puzzle or annoy
some. They would want to remind us that social critics should
be concerned with the present. History is interesting, of course,
and it may shed some new light on contemporary concerns, but
the disciplines that have made significant advances in the last
century, physics and economics for example, have freed themselves from history, preferring to concentrate on the present.
Should not political philosophy and social theory do the same if
they want practical results? Are not the ideals and reflection of
present-oriented external critics more powerful and effective
than the genealogies and social narratives of historically oriented internal critics? To this Durkheim responded, "How can
the individual pretend to reconstruct, through his own private
reflection, what is not a work of individual thought? He is not
confronted with a *tabula rasa* on which he can write what he
wants, but with existing realities which he cannot create, or destroy, or transform, at will. He can act on them only to the extent
that he has learned to understand them, to know their nature
and the conditions on which they depend."[23] This line of
thought, however, is not self-evident. This is largely because the
sway of history is often not conspicuous. That is why Durkheim
warned, "we don't directly feel the influence of these past selves

[that is, hidden historical influences] precisely because they are so deeply rooted within us."[24] It would be a mistake to neglect what we can't readily see. Our sight requires assistance. And "only history," Durkheim claimed, "can penetrate under the surface" of present institutions and social arrangements.

This is a strong claim, surely an overstatement. Yet it's worth thinking about why Durkheim insisted that "only history" can provide the basis for social criticism. We know that the welfare of the Third Republic commanded Durkheim's attention. It guided his research, whether he was writing on the Australian aborigines or the medieval university. His interest in history, then, was not antiquarian, and it was not commemorative. Unlike MacIntyre, Durkheim had no "glorious age" to celebrate. Moreover, he did not hold the conservative thesis that there is radical continuity between past and present. If this were the case, why look to the past? If the past is but a mirror of the present, why polish the looking glass? Why not gaze at ourselves directly? Durkheim maintained that between present and past there is both continuity and discontinuity, and that studying history can put the one in bold relief against the other. It can display past and present beliefs and institutions in a new light. Social critics want a place to stand to see better. Some try to stand outside history. In Durkheim's view, however, that attempt is futile. We need, rather, to step back. The place to which we can step back is history. It provides us with a broader, less provincial point of view. This I am suggesting was Durkheim's reason for declaring, "only history" can provide the basis for social criticism.

Using history as a place to stand may be a misleading image, because Durkheim recommended that we take a nomadic path—that we move from present to past and back again—not that we occupy a watchtower fixed in past scenes. Note, for example, how he described the process involved in assessing France's educational institutions:

Instead of confining ourselves to our own particular age, we must on the contrary escape from it in order to escape from ourselves, from our narrow-minded points of view, which are both partial and partisan. . . . Step by step, we will follow the series of changes which [education] has undergone, parallel to changes in society itself, until finally we arrive at the contemporary situation. That is where we must end, not where we must begin; and when, by travelling along this road, we arrive at the present-day situation it will appear in a light quite different from that in which we would have seen it had we abandoned ourselves at once and unreservedly to our contemporary passions and prejudices.[25]

This call to escape ourselves, our partisan perspectives, may sound like the entreaty of a universalist, but now we know better. Durkheim wanted to rescue us from provincialism ("our contemporary passions and prejudices"), but not by universalism, a tactic that frequently endorses the current bias as eternal truth. Critical distance, the sagacity and experience of the social critic, is enhanced by travelling in history. In history, critics observe the development and therefore the contingency of present institutions and beliefs. They see that these have been and therefore can still be conceived differently.

We learn, then, two lessons from history, according to Durkheim. Change is constant, so we should not in every case fear it and cling to established ways. But at the same time, change can seldom be willed arbitrarily because it is often linked to complex, sociohistorical conditions. Durkheim stated the lessons like this: by studying history "one acquires immunity from that superstitious respect which traditional . . . practices so easily inspire," yet "one comes to feel at the same time that the necessary innovations cannot be worked out *a priori* simply by our imagination . . . but rather that they must be . . . rigorously related to a totality of conditions which can be objectively specified."[26] He here associated social reformation with the need to generate detailed, empirical descriptions of past and contemporary social life. This makes us aware of the enormity, not the impossibility, of the reformers' task. We discover that although individuals can initiate change, they cannot usually complete it independently. "The lone individual," Durkheim wrote, "reduced to his own resources, is unable to alter the social situation. One can act effectively upon society only by grouping individual efforts in such a way as to counter social forces with social forces."[27] There is no way to go from our present place to a better one except, as the last line of Walzer's *Exodus and Revolution* reads, "by joining together and marching."[28]

Placing front and center the tangled empirical webs of social life is not an invitation to embrace materialism as a theory. In Chapter 5 I contrasted Durkheim's materialism with those Marxist forms that attempt to redescribe all institutions, beliefs, and practices in economic terms. Durkheim recommended the pluralistic approach that I earlier called mild-mannered pragmatism, an approach that entertains a variety of descriptions and explanations, and that puts into doubt the standard materialist/ idealist distinction. At times Durkheim may sound as reductive as some Marxists: what they see as ultimately the result of economics, Durkheim sees as the result of religion. Yet Durkheim's understanding of religion as collective representations that promote moral community was itself pluralistic, for he claimed that "sacred" representations take on many faces and are shaped by a host of influences. His understanding of religion simply did not yield conclusions as reductive as most Marxist, or for that matter, Freudian, comprehensive theories.

An aversion to reductive theories and, more generally, a preference for the concrete to the abstract, does not imply that sweeping pronouncements and general concepts are never useful. In spite of his criticism of Kant's penchant for the abstract, for instance, Durkheim believed that Kant's emphasis on autonomy, the universal, and the impersonal correctly identified significant nascent Western moral traditions. Social ideals, though abstract, were for Durkheim helpful abbreviations of complex and frequently conflicting social realities. We can take Durkheim's work on moral individualism as an investigation of the social ideals of liberal democracies. For Durkheim, then, moral individualism became a useful general concept that identifies significant clusters of meaning and practices embedded in Western societies.

To identify something is not merely to point to what all can plainly see. More often it is to make something plain for all to see. When Durkheim proposed moral individualism as an essential feature of our identity, he constructed a reading of it. This was more than a list of ideals. It specified the nature of various beliefs and practices associated with moral individualism, and it exposed how society fails to embody them adequately or correctly. Durkheim showed, for example, that the practices of laissez-faire liberalism are an aberration of moral individualism, as were the nationalist aspirations of the anti-Dreyfusards. He navigated us between two hazards: methodological individualism, in which social life is supposedly the result of discrete individuals, and national mysticism, in which individuals are supposed to be absorbed into a social mass.

Durkheim, we have seen, supported individual rights and liberties as much as any natural rights theorist, perhaps more so, for in Durkheim's view rights are not immutable, and therefore they can be either progressively extended or, conversely (and alarmingly), defined regressively. Yet his arguments were internal to a set of traditions. They did not fall from above; they spring from within history. Understanding that moral individualism is the result of traditions was not, for Durkheim, simply a matter of making an accurate sociological statement. It was a matter of enhancing liberal democracies. It is not wise to rely on the supposed external warrants of natural rights or the irresistible logic of game theory to promote vigorous democratic societies. We cannot afford merely to hold our truths to be self-evident. It may tempt us to stop reflecting on our traditions and institutions. To realize that liberal democratic practices are the result of traditions, including the critical thought that emerges from these, is to stop counting on ahistorical, universal principles to shore up these practices.

To self-consciously describe liberalism as a set of traditions is not, I have said, to offer a "positivistic" reading. Significant interpretations are not usually that simple. Modern societies are fed by a multitude of traditions, and "liberalism" itself contains positions ranging from libertarianism to totalitarian democracy. Durkheim knew this. Like Rawls and Walzer, occasionally he may have talked as if democratic social traditions are widely acclaimed and shared. Yet he recognized that modern societies have inherited other traditions as well. Recall his lament that moral individualism is "far from having any deep roots in the country. The proof of this is seen in the extreme ease with which we have accepted an authoritarian regime several times in the course of this century."[29] He worried about traditions that threaten liberal democracies, and if at times he wrote as if our shared understandings can resist such threats, it was because he wanted to draw our attention to, and thereby strengthen, a common democratic heritage. The process of inventing something and drawing attention to something are not always that different. Durkheim forged a common inheritance as he pointed us toward it.

I will soon discuss how Rawls and Walzer, like Durkheim, often assume there is a profound overlapping consensus or shared understanding in modern democratic societies. Durkheim, however, more than Rawls or even Walzer, underscored the need to investigate the social dimensions of democratic societies—their traditions and institutions, their values and beliefs—and to cultivate what is good in these. This entails encouraging local and national associations to host debates, formal and informal, on a multitude of social issues. It entails fostering autonomy and community, diversity and social membership, critical thought and respect for moral exemplars. And it involves moral education, having the courage to "socialize" our members, to inculcate virtues such as truth telling and tolerance, integrity and justice. Perhaps contemporary social and political theorists shy away from talk of cultivation because it strikes them as antiliberal and undemocratic. There is, of course, something to this. And perhaps the democratic institutions in Durkheim's France were more precarious, and therefore required more attention, than those in today's North Atlantic democracies. Still, no liberal democracy can afford to become absentminded, forgetful of its social resources. This is to risk complacency or worse.

IV

Could Durkheim say no more than that liberal democratic traditions are praiseworthy because they best express our own moral traditions? We look to our social inheritance for moral resources, but how are we to justify what we find? What kind of normative criteria do we possess for evaluating our shared understandings? Are tradition-bound reasons all we have to draw from? Durkheim's internal social criticism raises the issue of relativism. In Durkheim's view, as we have seen, there is no universal reason, no moral law, residing outside history or inside human nature. The only possible objective evaluation of morality, the only one that allows us to give reasons for our choices, is one that dialectically scrutinizes one portion of our collective life while relying on another portion. Lest this sound viciously circular, I want to examine the actual extent of Durkheim's relativism and the nature of the realist doctrine that he was able to derive from it.

Shortly before his death, Durkheim wrote, "Man is a product of history. If, disregarding his historical context, we attempt to see him as fixed, static, and outside time, we only denature him. . . . The way man situates himself in the world, the way he conceives of his relations with other beings and with his fellow men varies according to conditions of time and place."[30] Viewing human nature as fluid can safeguard against spurning other ways simply because they are not our own, and can make us more receptive to moral innovation within our own land. Again, Durkheim was not only making accurate sociological statements, he was staking out a normative position: a moral vision is enriched by sensitivity to its historical nature. Yet this appreciation of change leads neither to subjectivism nor to majoritarianism. We have seen that morality, by Durkheim's lights, is relative neither to the individual nor to transient social opinion. It is relative to society's best interpretations of its moral traditions, or to what Durkheim sometimes called society's impersonal reason. Not "individual reason but impersonal reason," he claimed, is the ground, the foundation, for our moral judgments. It provides us with "an objective standard with which to compare our evaluations."[31]

Durkheim was relativistic, then, only in that he denied universal, ahistorical moral truth. Yet out of that denial he mounted an interesting argument for moral realism. We discover much about our moral identity as we investigate our moral traditions. We acquire objective, rational viewpoints as we scrutinize and evaluate the very social sources that support our rationality. I portrayed this earlier as a familiar, intricate dialectic. It is not my intent here to supply a full defense of a moral realism based on Durkheim's work. I only want to show that it can be misleading to label him a relativist. His arguments for objective moral judgments disqualify him.[32] Durkheim's approach, then, was relativist only in contrast to Enlightenment foundational approaches. He provided no ahistorical argument to establish the rationality of liberal democracies. When we defend these, especially in specific, not general, ways, he believed, we are bound to draw from social legacies. But these moral resources, though complex and mutable, yield practical objective stances.

Durkheim's position avoided risks associated with both realism and relativism. Unlike many forms of relativism, his ap-

proach escaped capriciousness and the moral *akrasia* (enerva-
tion) that often accompanies it. He described individual rights,
for example, as becoming part of an objective, universal tenet
transcending national and natural borders. Yet unlike many
forms of realism, Durkheim's position anticipated change. It
prepares us to embrace moral innovation even as we guard
against moral decay.

V

Durkheim preserved simultaneously the partiality and objectivity of our moral vision. This balance is characteristic of internal
social criticism. Yet it invites further charges of conservatism. If
our critical judgments are based on our own limited traditions,
are we not blind to systematic or inherent social injustices? By
using our society's standards to appraise our society, are we not
bound to give a good report? Moreover, wouldn't this reduce
moral theory to tallying public opinions, because consensus
building would eclipse truth finding? And if our ethical guides
are but conventions emanating from society, then mustn't society place a premium on a uniform morality, lest anarchy break
out? Along these lines Lewis Coser claims to find in Durkheim's
work an "abiding conservatism": "By conservatism, I mean an
inclination to maintain the existing order of things or to re-
enforce an order which seems threatened. . . . To Durkheim any
type of nonconformity is criminal by definition."[33] Similarly, others have seen in Durkheim's work a nostalgia for traditional religion, for austere authority, and for the bygone days of folk societies knit together by a uniform collective consciousness.[34] I
believe these misgivings about Durkheim are often the result of
a limited understanding of the practices of internal criticism.

   This, however, is not the only explanation for these misgivings. Durkheim's internal social criticism, although a precursor
to much sensible, postmodern thought, is not without its problems. His critics have correctly noted his tendency to identify
moral truths with "society" or with "the collective." When "society" supported practices he found abhorrent, he also found
those practices, almost by definition, abnormal, declaring society to be in a state of transition or crisis. And though Durkheim's
career was that of a freethinker subjecting his society to his own

critical thought, he would frequently assert the vague claim that "it is from society and not from the individual that morality derives."[35] Maintaining there is no way to escape history and discover transcendent moral guides, Durkheim often resisted the conclusion he himself had helped to establish—the conclusion that our social condition is so plural and frequently contradictory that even astute accounts of a society's past and present cannot always clearly guide us through social decisions and impasses, cannot save us from controversy, debate, and doubt.

He wanted a "science of moral facts," a "natural philosophy of social norms." He defined it as "the application of human reason to the moral order, first of all to understand it, and finally to direct its changes."[36] This science (which shortly before his death he called an art) constructs perspicuous descriptions of our collective moral life, its present and past institutions, norms, and ideals, discovering contradiction and harmony, heartless and lovely social practices, obsolete routines and novel paths. It then applies this practical knowledge to specific social circumstances. The second aspect of this science, the practical, normative one, was all-important to Durkheim. He made it clear that "this science, far from preventing us from evaluating reality, gives us the means by which we arrive at *reasoned* evaluations."[37]

At times Durkheim seemed to believe that once this new science matured it could serve as a sure moral compass, directing us toward society's most worthy practices and ideals. This trust illustrates an ambivalence in his thought. He recognized a plurality of collective forces in the face of which argument and power battle as social choices are made. Yet he harbored hope that a science of morals could distill clarity out of social confusion and complexity, as if the "right" ways, with the aid of science, would always win out.

Durkheim, to his credit, never declared that a science of morals had been established. Instead, he wrote, we "do what we can," "taking sides on issues without waiting for our science," relying on the "inspirations of sensibility."[38] He never avoided the hard, controversial work of sorting out which social beliefs and practices were helpful, which required reform, and which should be abandoned. These judgments, it is true, he held to be provisional until a science of morals could be developed. Yet he was wise and honest enough not to claim the authority of "science" for his interpretive judgments. Moreover, increasingly Durkheim came to realize that he had run up against a natural limit to this new science. It was not just that the science was too young. Rather, he came to realize that art—inexact, uncertain in its work—would forever be wed to the study of how we should live together. I suspect that had he lived longer he would have continued to develop the ways of internal social criticism, not the rhetoric of positive science.

As much as I wish that Durkheim had dropped the presumptions of scientism, his adherence to it, jolting though it may be, considering his own mild-mannered pragmatism, reveals an important aspect of his work and of internal social criticism: commitment to the empirical. Within his own historical context, Durkheim saw himself as providing an alternative to the Kantian and utilitarian approaches to ethics and political philosophy. The former grasped the impersonal, universal nature of morality, but was overly speculative and ahistorical; the latter grasped the empirical nature of morality, but denied morality "its specific characteristics and reduced its fundamental ideas to those of economic techniques." [39] Durkheim, as I have shown, attempted to combine the advantages of these two schools while avoiding their liabilities. His faith in science was based on its dedication to observation. Isolated scholars contemplating lofty ideals are too removed from social life to understand that life, he believed. Without reducing the complexities of social life to atomistic facts and calculations, Durkheim and his colleagues undertook major social research programs, investigating such subjects as French industrial plants, Bavarian peasant villages, Australian tribes, and New York slum dwellers.[40] This empirical approach did not endear Durkheim to the humanistic *littérateurs*. They regarded Durkheim and his associates as introducing the techniques of science and history into fields that traditionally employed more intuitive, artistic sensibilities. Durkheim's attachment to science needs to be understood in light of this commitment to concrete, empirical investigation. In opposition to his powerful and aristocratic poetic "colleagues," Durkheim advised social critics to be observant scientists.

I have discussed the problematic aspects of Durkheim's internal social criticism. While recognizing there are no ahistorical moral guides, he believed that society itself possesses the moral resources that, with the help of the "natural philosophy of social norms," allow it to conduct itself through conflict and indecision. It has been assumed that Durkheim's commitment to the absence of a universal vantage point must ineluctably lead him to sanction the status quo, whatever it may be—that he must have been a conservative social theorist and critic. But this assumption is doubtful in view of Durkheim's life work and the critical capabilities of internal criticism. He correctly understood, it seems to me, that our moral lights are informed and sustained by shared beliefs and practices, and that these are continually subject to revision. He realized that, morally speaking, we never start from scratch, but rather we build on the ways, both crooked and straight, that have led up to the present. If he at times spoke as if shared understandings unanimously supported his projects of reform, he did so in the hope of establishing such commonality. This, too, is the work of the social critic, and in any case it does not suggest "an abiding conservatism." Looking back at his life and work, it is evident that Durkheim recognized that modern democracies have inherited clashing and even incommensurate traditions, and that many modern beliefs and practices need to be challenged.

Durkheim repeatedly argued that the status quo requires rational scrutiny, not irrational acceptance. He indeed insisted that when individuals dissent, protesting against existing institutions, they, too, stand in shared forms of life—*la société*—as they pit collective force against collective force, but this theoretical position did not commit him to play the apologist for the status quo. His reputation, in fact, was as its severe critic.[41] In his last written work he argued that the social critic, far from being bound to follow the general opinion, "is at liberty to create something original and break new ground":

Through him all the many currents, which run through society and over which minds are divided, attain awareness and are given conscious expression. It is, in fact, as a direct response to these currents that moral doctrines are engendered. Only those periods which are divided over morality are morally inventive. And when traditional morality goes unchallenged, when there is no apparent need to renew it, moral thought falls into decline.[42]

Compare this to a statement made by Lewis Coser: "Alfred North Whitehead once wrote that periods of transition, although they manifest 'the misery of decay,' also show 'the zest of new life.' Durkheim would have understood only the first part of this statement."[43]

Still, even if I have convinced some that Durkheim did not deplore change, his approach to change may seem disturbing. The issue at stake, I believe, was stated by Durkheim in response to some friendly critics at an address he gave to the Société Française de Philosophie. "A rebellion against the traditional morality you conceive of as a revolt of the individual against the collective, of personal sentiments against collective sentiments. However, what I am opposing to the collective is the collective itself, but more and better aware of itself." Durkheim's view of rebellion might seem unbearably limited, unless one had some sense of the critical leverage available to the internal critic. Then one could appreciate the force of opposing the collective to the collective. Yet did Durkheim think that within society there exists a ready-made, perfect expression of itself? To this question he replied, "I do not know what an ideal and absolute perfection is, and therefore I do not ask you to conceive of society as ideally perfect. I do not even attribute to it, any more than to ourselves, relative perfection. . . . Society has its pettiness and it has its grandeur."[44]

I suggest that once we acquire an adequate grasp of internal criticism Durkheim looks like an interesting and helpful social reformer. It is only within the framework of external criticism that the charge of conservatism makes much sense. The external critic, especially if she has "revolutionary" sensibilities, may claim that modern industrial societies are fraught with false ideologies and contradictions, and that therefore there are no moral resources within these societies, at least none sufficient for the required drastic transformation. Durkheim, however, would want to know how she identifies what changes need to be made. If she appeals to universal moral or economic laws, Durkheim would likely be interested in her specific positions, and would try to show how these, in fact, have emerged from some portion of her society's values and institutions. Her dissent, he would argue, is a sign that she is morally implicated in society. Moreover, if her positions were convincing, Durkheim would describe her as he did Kant: a progressive critical authority often unaware of the relevant sociohistorical warrants supporting his positions. If she appeals to a foreign culture's moral resources, on the other hand, Durkheim would point out that her initial appreciation of these alien ways was grounded in her own social experience.

What if Durkheim were confronted with an anarchist who rejects all established institutions and beliefs? Could an external critic, armed with the authority of universal principles and reason, have a better chance of persuading the anarchist to recognize the value of some existing institutions? Durkheim, once presented with a similar question, answered "No," and suggested, moreover, that the exceptional case is not usually a good test of theories. "Are you now asking how I could convey to an anarchist [the moral understandings of society]? This is just as impossible for me as to communicate the sense of colours to a man blind from birth. But will you [the universalist] be any more successful than I am? Is there a method which can succeed, and succeed for certain in a case like this? . . . Such a state is exceptional."[45] Not being able to convince everyone is not a characteristic peculiar to Durkheim's approach, but to argument in general.

Too often Durkheim is discredited because the ways of internal criticism have not been sufficiently understood. Coser writes that "the problem of order preoccupied Durkheim from his earliest writings to the last pages of the *Introduction à la morale*."[46] Perhaps, but "the problem" was not the preservation of order, but its evaluation and reformation. And if Durkheim investigated the continuity between the present and past, this, too, he did as a reformer exposing enduring constellations of meaning and practice that would otherwise invisibly shape our collective existence. Not preserving the status quo, but working to transform it so that it better realizes and extends liberal democratic institutions and the normative social conditions that sustain them—this describes Durkheim's vocation. If he dived deeply into our social seas, it was so that he could emerge with something new, something edifying.

NINE

Durkheim Among a Company of Critics: Rawls, Walzer, MacIntyre, and Rorty

JUST WHEN MANY thought the universalism of the Kantian project was doomed, Rawls's *A Theory of Justice* appeared and rekindled Enlightenment faith. It enabled us, as Rawls claimed, "to see [our place in society] *sub specie aeternitatis* . . . to regard the human situation not only from all social but also from all temporal points of view."[1] Yet it spared us conversion to German Idealism. This was "deontology with a Humean face," to use Sandel's famous phrase, or as Rawls put it, "a natural procedural rendering of Kant's conception of the kingdom of ends, and of the notions of autonomy and the categorical imperative."[2] It seemed that Rawls had delivered us the best of Kant minus his more cumbersome metaphysical ventures.

It wasn't too long, however, before many argued that Rawls's decision-maker in the original position was flawed. A self, these critics claimed, is constituted by particular loves and goals. Insofar as Rawls's original position requires us to shed our attachments, we lose ourselves, that is, our character. Rawls, in this view, offered us an impoverished and metaphysical picture of the self as the unencumbered decision-maker placing the right over the good.

This description of Rawls and his critics is reminiscent of the "straw men" I presented in the Introduction. It is adequate, however, for my purposes here because I only want to point out that to many it seemed that *A Theory of Justice* claimed to generate what in Chapter 8 I described as external social criticism—

criticism *sub specie aeternitatis*. Rawls's subsequent essays claim to be political, not metaphysical. I will suggest that Rawls's current approach is moving toward Durkheim's, that is, toward an internal social criticism in support of democratic liberalism. I am not concerned whether Rawls's recent essays represent a change of heart, a response to Sandel, a clearer restatement of *A Theory of Justice*, or some combination of these. I will note, however, that Rawls himself claims that *A Theory of Justice* did not emphasize, as do his recent essays, "that the basic ideas of justice as fairness are regarded as implicit or latent in the public culture of a democratic society."[3] This new emphasis, I believe, can be illuminated by our study of Durkheim. In this chapter I show how a Durkheimian perspective contributes novel insight into the work of Rawls, and also of Walzer, MacIntyre, and Rorty.

I

Rawls begins "Justice as Fairness: Political and not Metaphysical" as might any good internal social critic. He disassociates his position from "claims to universal truth, or claims about the essential nature and identity of persons" (p. 223). On what, then, is his theory of justice based, and to whom is it addressed? It is addressed to members of modern liberal democracies, and it is based on their political institutions and traditions. He writes, for example, that justice as fairness is "framed to apply to what I have called the 'basic structure' of a modern constitutional democracy. . . . We look . . . to our public political culture itself, including its main institutions and the historical traditions of their interpretation, as the shared fund of implicitly recognized basic ideas and principles" (pp. 224, 228).

If components of his theory such as the veil of ignorance and the principles of justice still seem Kantian, it must now be because Kant captured or anticipated many of our moral, socially entrenched intuitions. This is what Durkheim claimed: Kant's universal principles are in fact the result of his articulation of and fidelity to our most progressive moral and political sensibilities. Like Durkheim, Rawls suggests that we critically reflect on our institutions and traditions in order to discover who we are and how we can improve our society. If we properly attend to ourselves, that is, to our moral traditions, according to Rawls we will learn that we are Kantian. The original position, then, is a device that helps us in these discoveries.[4]

"The fact of pluralism" as an important feature of the history of modern Western societies figures importantly in Rawls's recent essays. This is what we would expect from a Durkheimian social critic. Rawls's political principles are sensitive to our own "social and historical conditions." He tells us that these conditions have "their origins in the Wars of Religion following the Reformation and the subsequent development of the principle of toleration, and in the growth of constitutional government and the institutions of large industrial market economies."[5] These historical developments have influenced our moral traditions and they need to be considered in our moral and political deliberations. One of the fundamental lessons Rawls draws from such reflection is that a workable conception of political justice "must allow for a diversity of doctrines and the plurality of conflicting, and indeed incommensurable, conceptions of the good affirmed by the members of existing democratic societies."[6] As discussed in Chapter 6, Rawls believes that in spite of the fact of pluralism, and in part because of it, there are widely held beliefs and ideals "embedded in our political institutions" that cut across diverse conceptions of the good. Upon this shared understanding Rawls hopes to find or to build an "overlapping consensus" to support his political conception of justice.

Some scholars have celebrated Rawls's new, or at least revised, approach. Richard Rorty now claims Rawls as one of his own neopragmatists committed to exposing metaphysical phantoms in order to hasten the coming of a genuinely liberal, disenchanted society. He claims that Rawls's new attitude is "thoroughly historicist and anti-universalist. Rawls can wholeheartedly agree with Hegel and Dewey against Kant and can say that the Enlightenment attempt to free oneself from tradition and history, to appeal to 'Nature' or 'Reason,' was self-deceptive. He can see such an appeal as a misguided attempt to make philosophy do what theology failed to do."[7]

I suppose Rawls *can* say such things, but to my knowledge he hasn't.[8] More important, as a political theorist Rawls claims that he can't say such things on principled grounds. His "method of avoidance" prevents him from either asserting or denying "any religious, philosophical or moral views, or their associated philosophical accounts of truth and the status of values."[9] Given the historical and sociological conditions of modern liberal democracies, the fact of pluralism, and the wars that have resulted from it, Rawls insists that a political conception of justice must remain neutral on controversial religious or philosophical claims. Hence Rawls is silent where Rorty is most outspoken, namely, in carrying out the "disenchantment of the world." Rawls, then, is not in a position to share Rorty's philosophical vocation, a vocation that Rorty claims entails constructing models of "the self," "knowledge," "God," and so on. For example, Rawls as a political theorist must remain diffident about Rorty's picture of the self as a "centerless and contingent web."[10] It is not clear to me that Rorty appreciates this stance.

Still, I am impressed with Rorty's essay "The Priority of Democracy to Philosophy." He documents well the social and historical aspects of Rawls's recent essays, and he thereby lends support to my claim that we should read Rawls as an internal social critic. Rorty applauds Rawls for moving toward what I have called a Durkheimian approach. Many, however, are not happy with Rawls's recent move. Some are quite alarmed, and for many of the same reasons that some fear Durkheim's approach and claim that it is inherently conservative.

The general complaint against Rawls goes something like this: Rawls is now more interested in social agreement than in truth. If we follow his lead, political philosophy may lose its nobility. It will require that we trade our traditional vocation of the philosopher seeking truth for that of the politician aspiring to represent. Polling and then reflecting constituents' beliefs, not helping them to reason correctly, will become our new goal. In a phrase, we will lose our normative voice.

An example of this complaint is found in William Galston's contribution to *Ethics'* symposium on Rawls. He writes, "Justice as fairness 'starts from within a certain political tradition' and (we may add) it remains there. The question of truth or falsity is thus irrelevant."[11] Galston supports this criticism with the following statement from Rawls: "Philosophy as the search for truth about an independent metaphysical and moral order cannot, I believe, provide a workable and shared basis for a political conception of justice in a democratic society." Galston comments on this statement that, "as a consequence, the classic distinction between political philosophy and rhetoric collapses." [12]

Galston assumes, along with some of Durkheim's critics, that to start from "a certain political tradition" is "to remain there," that is, to remain strapped to the status quo. Moreover, he assumes that to refuse to be interested in an "independent metaphysical and moral order" is to depart from genuine political philosophy and to enter the relativistic realm of rhetoric. This departure, Galston claims, leads Rawls to replace the central quest of traditional political philosophy with the following questions: "How are 'we'—reflective citizens of a liberal democracy—to understand freedom and equality, the ideals to which we are . . . individually and collectively committed? How are we to resolve the recurrent conflict between these ideals? Which principles of justice are most consistent with them, and how are we to transform these principles into workable institutions?" [13] These are precisely the types of questions we would expect an internal social critic to raise. Galston, however, maintains that they raise three difficulties for Rawls. I hope to show that these are not difficulties specifically for Rawls, and that they arise largely from a lack of understanding on Galston's part of the ways of internal criticism.

The first of the three difficulties is that "it is unlikely (to say the least) that the interpretation of a public culture will be less controversial than the interpretation of a literary creation." [14] This is, of course, a difficulty for Rawls. But for whom is it not a difficulty? What political theorist in a pluralistic society has not encountered opposing points of view? Galston, of course, thinks Rawls's hope for developing an overlapping consensus is particularly susceptible to this difficulty, but I would argue the opposite is the case. Rawls's new emphasis on drawing from and addressing a particular (as opposed to "the Universal") political society is more likely to gain consent than a foundationalist approach. Rawls, of course, won't gain universal consent, and hence I am not arguing that Rawls is exempt from the difficulty. I am, however, arguing that he is not particularly vulnerable to it.

Galston assumes that there can be little agreement on "the interpretation of a literary creation." Why? Some texts are subject to multiple interpretations. Others, however, are easy to interpret. This is true of all human understanding: an action, a treaty, a monument, a right, a gesture—interpreting these can be easy or difficult, depending on the circumstances. Does Galston think agreement between professional philosophers is more likely than agreement between literary critics? Some texts or some bits of culture are not subject to massive debate. This is, in part, what is motivating Rawls's strategy: avoid contestable "texts" such as comprehensive or general conceptions of the good, and focus instead on the "essential convictions and historical traditions" of a particular society. Galston wants us to recognize that these so-called essential convictions or basic social intuitions are in fact subject to dispute. I agree. But I also believe Rawls's (Durkheimian) approach is more likely to produce significant agreement on a moral conception of justice than is Galston's quest for "grounds of transcultural justification."[15]

"The second difficulty with Rawls's account of political philosophy," Galston writes, "is that it leaves no basis for the comparative assessment of regimes. When we are faced with evils like Hitlerism, Stalinism, and apartheid, it is not enough to say that these practices violate our shared understandings. The point is that we insist on the right to apply our principles to communities that reject them. Indeed, these evils challenge the very validity of these principles, which therefore require a defense that transcends interpretation."[16] I remember when Tommy, a twelve-year-old boy from one of the "hollers" of Buckhorn, Kentucky, asked his father why he wouldn't let him "run out the newcomer with all the other boys." "Because that's not the way we do things," replied the father. Not a very liberal response, and one not adequate for many occasions. The father, I can only suppose, had good reasons. But perhaps he knew his son wasn't able to grasp them, or wouldn't accept them. Or perhaps he was tired. In any case, Rawls to my knowledge has never said, "we should treat individuals as free and equal persons because that's the way we do things." In fact, Rawls is well aware that too often that is *not* the way we do things. I have no doubt that Rawls in particular would have many things to say, for example, to the Nazi SS officer persecuting Jews. He could, for instance, elaborate on the reasonable (or fitting or appropriate) conditions that serve as constraints for the principles of justice.[17] But after having exhausted his moral and political reasons for opposing the officer, Rawls, like the boy's father, may be tempted to say, "That's not the way we do things."

Galston, like many critics of Durkheim and Wittgenstein, assumes that internal critics can only appeal to contemporary social opinion and that they have no normative voice. Yet, as I argued in Chapter 8, internal critics are not pollsters, and they are not exempt from the hard work of making compelling arguments and deliberating between competing normative positions. Rawls's arguments against the SS officer would, no doubt, be rooted in specific moral and political traditions. What else could we expect—a leap outside history? Those sharing these traditions obviously are more likely to be persuaded. But this need not imply that, morally speaking, we have nothing to say except, "That's not our way" (even if we are, in the end, driven to this).

Galston's third objection closely follows the previous one.

By asking us to separate general truth-claims from the elucidation of our shared understandings, it distorts the deepest meaning of those understandings. When Americans say that all human beings are created equal and endowed with certain unalienable rights, we intend this not as a description of our local convictions but, rather, as universal truths, valid everywhere and binding on all. . . . If our principles are valid for us only because we (happen to) believe them, then they are not binding even for us. . . . To set aside in advance the quest for truth, to insist as Rawls does that the principle of religious toleration must for political purposes be extended to philosophy itself, is to demand something that no self-respecting individual or public culture can reasonably grant.[18]

The second objection is directed at the validity of cross-cultural judgments; this one at the validity of intracultural judgments. If our judgments cannot be applied to the stranger, then they cannot even be applied to ourselves. I have argued, however, that the judgments of the internal social critic do apply to the stranger; and, moreover, when they are applied to fellow citizens, they do not take the form: believe this because all your friends (or fellow citizens) believe it. Essentially, Galston finds it troubling that our justifications for moral principles are rooted in our own moral and intellectual traditions and institutions. He wants to escape this epistemological circle, and he implies that to be satisfied with it is to be less than self-respecting.

Of course, I disagree, and so does Rawls. But unlike me, Rawls does not want to say that Galston's wish to escape the circle is foolhardy. For Rawls, as a political theorist, that would be disrespectful. Rawls only wants to avoid what Galston asserts, namely, that "to set aside in advance the quest for truth . . . is to demand something that no self-respecting individual or public culture can reasonably grant." Perhaps Rawls, as father, husband, or believer shares Galston's quest for suprahistorical truth. To my knowledge, *pace* Rorty, Rawls hasn't told us whether he thinks or hopes there is an independent moral order. But as a Rawlsian political philosopher he probably would say to Galston: "Fine, you don't want to set aside the quest for transcendent truth. Now tell me, what do you suggest belongs in a political conception of justice?" This is the question that concerns Rawls. He thinks that in spite of peoples' beliefs about God, Reason, or Nature, many of us, perhaps most of us, share similar intuitions—call them reasons—concerning political justice.

He might be wrong. I think that, like Durkheim, he is too sanguine about the possibility of an overlapping consensus. He may not recognize the extent to which individuals' notions of a comprehensive or general good determine their different views of political justice. But I do not believe that his approach warrants Galston's three objections. Indeed, I believe that Galston's objections have more to do with Galston's insufficient acquaintance with the potential normative force of internal social criticism than with any blunders in Rawls's essays. This is not to say that Rawls does not occasionally invite such criticism. I will argue that Rawls himself may not yet have an adequate understanding of the ways of internal criticism. Galston is one of our best theorists, and his objections are not peculiar. Others share them.[19] I suggest that if both Rawls and his critics had a better grasp of a Durkheimian internal social criticism, the present debate on Rawls would not be besieged with the question, Is Rawls after truth or agreement? But before I discuss how Rawls himself has befogged the debate, I want to look at some of his good and sensible remarks that make me think we should consider him an internal social critic who does not shun truth and objectivity per se, but who avoids theories of truth and objectivity.

II

I begin with what literary critics would call a "cento" of Rawls's comments on truth and objectivity, a brief patchwork of quotations that will insure we have a common basis for reading his recent work. First, Rawls denies his constructivist view is concerned with

> a theory of truth. A constructivist view does not require an idealist or a verificationist, as opposed to a realist, account of truth. Whatever the nature of truth in the case of general beliefs about human nature and how society works, a constructivist moral doctrine requires a distinct procedure of construction to identify the first principles of justice.[20]

Rawls's response to the claim that his pursuit of an overlapping consensus may construct a conception of justice that is "known not to be true, as if truth were simply beside the point" is that

> a political conception of justice need be no more indifferent, say, to truth in morals than the principle of toleration, suitably understood, need be indifferent to truth in religion. We simply apply the principle of toleration to philosophy itself. In this way we hope to avoid philosophy's long-standing controversies, among them controversies about the nature of truth and the status of values as expressed by realism and subjectivism.[21]

Rawls states that he prefers the term "reasonable" to "true" because

> given the various contrasts between Kantian constructivism and rational intuitionism, it seems better to say that in constructivism first principles are reasonable (or unreasonable) than that they are true (or false). . . . And here "reasonable" is used instead of "true" not because of some alternative theory of truth, but simply in order to keep to terms that indicate the constructivist standpoint as opposed to rational intuitionism. This usage, however, does not imply that there are no natural uses for the notion of truth in moral reasoning. . . . First principles may be said to be true in the sense that they would be agreed to if the parties in the original position were provided with all the relevant true general beliefs.[22]

I do not intend to provide a full account of the positions articulated in these quotations. I am concerned here only with the claim that Rawls has sacrificed truth for social agreement, objectivity for social unity. To begin, we need to separate two related issues: (1) Rawls's alleged interest in agreement, not truth; and

(2) his method of avoiding unresolvable metaphysical controversies. It seems clear to me that in the first and second quotations Rawls writes nothing that supports the claim that his conception of justice is designed to rest on agreement rather than truth. He wants to exclude *theories* of truth and of value from public deliberation on a political conception of justice. These quotations, then, also address the second issue: Rawls advocates that we avoid controversial metaphysical issues in the context of reflection on a conception of justice for a pluralistic democratic society.

The third quotation pertains to Rawls's alleged abandonment of truth for agreement. Here he prefers the term "reasonable" to "true." Following the method of avoidance, he suggests that we dodge the term "true," lest we lend tacit support to the controversial philosophical position of intuitionism, namely, that there are self-evident truths fixed in an independent moral order. He does not, however, want to avoid the term "true" entirely. There are, he claims, many "uses for the notion of truth in moral reasoning," and, in particular, in our deliberations on first principles: "First principles may be said to be true in the sense that they would be agreed to if the parties in the original position were provided with all the relevant true general beliefs." Rawls, here, has not placed agreement above truth. He has placed true first principles above theories of truth.

If I have only shown that Rawls occasionally uses the word "true," and if "true" for Rawls means only whatever people (happen to) agree on, then I have offered little to console those alarmed over Rawls's new approach. What role does agreement play in the determination of truth? I need to show that truth, in Rawls's view, is not identified with mere agreement.

A condition necessary for the parties in the original position to agree on true first principles is that they be provided with "all the relevant true general beliefs." I take Rawls to be saying that we are most likely to get true first principles of justice when, having freed ourselves reasonably well from external and contingent considerations such as our wealth, class, gender, and power, we have the best information available about our society, its history, institutions, traditions, problems, promise, and so on. Agreement, under these conditions, is a sensible or reasonable way to reach what we may want to call true first principles.

Such judicious agreement, Rawls tells us, does not pertain to an independent moral order, whether this order is based on secular or theological presuppositions.[23] Nor does this agreement result from arbitrary choice, that is, from choice "not based on reasons."[24] If it is not based on a metaphysical moral realism, and it is not the product of a Nietzschean subjectivism, on what does this agreement rest? What is Rawls's middle way between standard notions of realism and subjectivism? I will argue that it is similar to Durkheim's.

Rawls rejects, and not simply avoids, metaphysical realism and subjectivism. Immediately after doing so he writes:

Citizens affirm their public conception of justice because it matches their considered convictions and coheres with the kind of persons they, on due reflection, want to be. . . . One is to imagine that, for the most part, they find on examination that they hold these ideals, that they have taken them in part from the culture of their society. . . . Recall that a Kantian view, in addressing the public culture of a democratic society, hopes to bring to awareness a conception of the person and of social cooperation conjectured to be implicit in that culture, or at least congenial to its deepest tendencies when properly expressed and presented.[25]

Durkheim argued that implicit in France's moral, democratic traditions were ideals and beliefs that sustain moral individualism, and that these ideals bind us to our better selves. Likewise, Rawls seeks to persuade his audience that if under ideal conditions they consult the considered convictions that are implicit in their traditions (at least when those convictions are "properly expressed"), they will find that their traditions support a Kantian political conception of justice that treats persons as free and equal. This approach was not majoritarian for Durkheim, and it is not for Rawls. The thrust of the question is not, What can we come up with that most of us can agree on? Rather, it is, What are the grounds, the means, the reasons available to us for constructing true first principles? Like Durkheim, Rawls believes that these grounds are neither suprahistorical nor subjectively arbitrary. They are objective, but objective in the following sense:

The rational intuitionist notion of objectivity is unnecessary for objectivity. . . . Objectivity is not given by "the point of view of the universe," to use Sidgwick's phrase. Objectivity is to be understood by reference to a suitably constructed social point of view, an example of which is the framework provided by the procedure of the original position. . . . The essential agreement in judgments of justice arises not from the recognition of a prior and independent moral order, but from everyone's affirmation of the same authoritative social perspective.[26]

Objectivity, here, for Rawls as for Durkheim, is the force or pull of a cogent and discriminating articulation of our moral and political traditions, the substance of our normative reasoning powers. It is an "authoritative social perspective." It is authoritative, not authoritarian. If our reasons carry the weight of objectivity, it is not because the rich or the powerful have financed or enforced them, though these forces always pose threats to moral reasoning. Rawls's original position and Durkheim's notion of authoritative social ideals are meant to counter such threats. Spared from such distorting powers, Durkheim and Rawls believe (or hope) that our more virtuous traditions, or our more virtuous interpretations of our traditions, will become manifest. They already know what they think these traditions hold for us. Their goal is to convince us of what we want to be. I'm not sure Rawls, or Durkheim, admits as much. One thing, I hope, is clear: Rawls does not sacrifice truth for agreement. If he thinks we can agree on a political conception of justice, it's because he thinks we can discover a true conception, lodged in the objectivity of our shared moral traditions.

I have shown why and when Rawls does and does not dodge the term "true." I have attributed to Rawls a Durkheimian social epistemology that need not shun "objectivity," "truth," or "reason." To those who want to continue the quest for metaphysical objectivity, truth, and reason, however, I have offered little. Rawls thinks he can woo even these, abiding by his method of avoidance. He's probably wrong. Yet if I have convinced Rawls's critics such as Galston and Hampton that we should take Rawls as an internal social critic and that internal social criticism is defendable, then the present debate over Rawls can move forward a bit. On the defense of internal social criticism I have said all that I want to say. On Rawls as an internal social critic, however, more remains. Perhaps I haven't convinced some that Rawls is an internal critic because Rawls himself hasn't fully embraced internal social criticism. On behalf of textually sensitive critics like Galston and Hampton, I want to show how Rawls himself occasionally fosters the idea that he is after social agreement as opposed to truth. In doing so, however, I am suggesting that Rawls himself may not have a satisfactory grasp of internal social criticism.

Rawls writes, for example, that "the aim of justice as fairness as a political conception is practical, and not metaphysical or epistemological. That is, it presents itself not as a conception of justice that is true, but one that can serve as a basis of informed and willing political agreement between citizens viewed as free and equal persons." [27] Elsewhere he writes, "The idea of approximating moral truth has no place in a constructivist doctrine: the parties in the original position do not recognize any principles of justice as true or correct and so as antecedently given." [28] In these two examples, is Rawls applying the avoidance method to theories of truth or to truth itself? His references to metaphysics and to principles antecedently given suggest he wants to evade only theories of truth. But it's hard to be sure, and that may be because he isn't sure whether he needs to avoid theories of truth or truth per se. Perhaps as good critics such as Galston and Hampton press him on this he will move still more toward internal social criticism. There would be something ironic about that. That he has moved as far as he has is perhaps in part a response to the prodding of "communitarians" like Sandel. Could a "liberal" like Galston push him further? I hope Rawls's next move is to reintroduce unambiguously terms like "truth" and "objectivity" while continuing to make reference to the socially authoritative perspectives of our moral and political traditions. I hope, in other words, he will choose Durkheim's middle way between standard liberalism, with its emphasis on the objectivity of rights, and communitarianism, with its emphasis on sociolinguistic rationalities.

Rawls does describe his own middle way. It is a political liberalism that "steers a course between the Hobbesian strand in liberalism—liberalism as a *modus vivendi* secured by a convergence of self- and group-interests as coordinated and balanced by well-designed constitutional arrangements—and a liberalism founded on a comprehensive moral doctrine." [29] The problem with the Hobbesian approach, according to Rawls and Durkheim, is that it is anomic. In Rawls's words, it "cannot secure an enduring social unity." Moreover, as I argued in Chapter 6, neither Rawls nor Durkheim views justice only as a convenient set of social arrangements designed to check civil war in an age of pluralism. Justice secures, rather, normative ends such as individual rights, and often in spite of sociological consequences. The problem with the comprehensive approach, in the view of both, is that in modern democratic societies it could gain "agreement" only by coercive means. Fatalism, Durkheim tells us, is not appropriate for modern democracies. What, then, is Rawls's middle way? His political philosophy, he writes, "hopes to uncover, and to help to articulate, a shared basis of consensus on a political conception of justice drawing upon citizens' fundamental intuitive ideas about their society and their place in it. . . . Political philosophy assumes the role Kant gave to philosophy generally: the defence of reasonable faith."[30] This reasonable faith, I want to suggest, is similar to what Durkheim called the common faith of modern democracies: the widely shared ideals and values of moral individualism that are embedded in our moral and political traditions.

III

Rawls, like Durkheim, needs to argue for this interpretation of a common faith. Neither can assume that it is there, in some more or less determinate form, waiting to be discovered through introspection of our moral traditions. Rawls's two principles of justice, for example, no doubt emerge from a shared sociolinguistic environment in North Atlantic democracies. By "emerge" I mean that the sociolinguistic environment provides the conceptual resources for Rawls's construction of a conception of justice. But this does not suggest that Rawls's conception will be welcomed by everyone dwelling in this environment, only that they should be able to understand him. Rawls, of course, does not perceive his principles of justice as a majoritarian product or as an accommodation to various interest groups, but he often writes as if a lucid articulation of a democratic society's shared intuitions will inevitably gain an overlapping consensus. Both Durkheim and Rawls must enter into public debate, providing arguments for why we should see ourselves and our traditions along the lines of Durkheim's moral individualism or Rawls's free and equal persons. I have shown that, in fact, Durkheim does this, and of course so does Rawls, but both are slow to admit that much of their work entails convincing us of what they take to be our common or reasonable "faith." As Galston and Gerald Doppelt remind us, there are many conflicting ideals and "basic" conceptions of justice embedded in our moral traditions.[31] Controversy is inescapable. Argument is required. What Rawls claims to be the content of an overlapping consensus cannot avoid dispute, even under the method of avoidance. Internal criticism, remember, neither assumes nor promises social agreement on substantive moral or political issues. It does insist, however, that the way to greater justice is to work self-consciously within the sociohistorical dimensions of our thought and practices. It looks to our sociohistorical condition not to perpetuate it but to shape it. I applaud Rawls's social turn, but it needs to be a starting not an ending point.

At times Rawls seems to acknowledge this, as when he writes, "our society is not well-ordered: the public conception of justice and its understanding of freedom and equality are in dispute." But at other times, as when he speaks of "everyone's affirmation of the same authoritative social perspective," he implies that conflict can be resolved simply by appealing to what we all already believe, as if an overlapping consensus, under the right conditions, will become self-evident.[32] This is to expect too much. It also is what encourages critics like Galston to write, "cultural interpretation is far more likely to recapitulate than (as Rawls supposes) to resolve the deep disputes that now divide our political order."[33] Galston is on the mark if, as Rawls occasionally implies, cultural interpretation is the practice of poll taking. If, however, cultural interpretation is the practice of providing culturally specific arguments in order to move a culture in a particular direction, then I would disagree with Galston's remark. Our possession of shared understandings is a precondition for people like Rawls and Durkheim to convince us, that is, to argue, that we have a distinctive common democratic faith. Appeals to a shared understanding alone will do little work.

All things considered, I think Rawls does much more than merely appeal to a shared understanding or an overlapping consensus. He has presented us with a fairly thick description of a Kantian democratic self and a Kantian political conception of justice. The original position and the principles that Rawls argues would emerge from it offer forceful and controversial challenges to our society. Rawls has helped us recognize how and why we should treat individuals as free and equal persons, and in what ways individuals are presently not treated as such, especially with respect to equal rights and the material conditions necessary to sustain those rights. Rawls's political conception is clearly not all that thin. He enters the truth-game, that is, he offers us reasonable arguments about who we are and who we should want to be as citizens sharing common democratic traditions and institutions.

IV

I have argued for two conclusions. One is that there is conceptual agreement between Durkheim's moral individualism and Rawls's political liberalism. The other and more important conclusion is that, having understood Durkheim as an internal social critic, we are in a better position to appreciate the approach outlined in Rawls's recent essays. In the narrative I have offered, Rawls is moving toward internal social criticism. In other words, to collapse the two conclusions, Rawls, like Durkheim, is an internal social critic defending democratic liberalism. This is not to say that Rawls's theoretical understanding of institutions and traditions is as nuanced as Durkheim's; or that Durkheim's political prowess is as keen as Rawls's. However, it shows that Durkheim can help us make sense of contemporary debates in moral and political philosophy by giving us a point of view from which to interpret the contributions of one of the principal participants, John Rawls. In what follows I want to continue this evaluation of contemporary debates by examining how other principal participants, Walzer, MacIntyre, and Rorty, look from a Durkheimian perspective.

In his little book *Interpretation and Social Criticism*, Walzer delineates three styles or paths in moral philosophy: the way of discovery, the way of invention, and the way of interpretation. The way of discovery entails something similar to what in Chapter 4 I called worldfinding. From the point of view of Western religion, the moral universe, like the physical one, has been set in place by God the Creator. Consequently, moral principles are to be found as part of the God-given order of things. But religious believers are not the only travelers on the path of discovery. Secularists hunt for objective moral principles or natural rights, and this search, Walzer tells us, is usually "internal, mental, a matter of detachment and reflection." In either case, according to this view, morality is part of the objective order of the world, and our job is to find and to follow it. The second path, in contrast, the way of invention, is similar to what I followed Goodman in calling worldmaking. Worldmakers ask, "Why wait for or depend on God or Nature?" They prefer to draw the plans themselves for the moral world that they, and presumably any rational being, would like to inhabit. The third path, Walzer's, is the way of interpretation. "We do not have to discover the moral world," Walzer writes, "because we have always lived there. We do not have to invent it because it has already been invented— though not in accordance with any philosophical method. . . . The experience of moral argument is best understood in the interpretive mode. What we do when we argue is to give an account of the actually existing morality."[34]

Which course was Durkheim's? We know he embraced neither radical discovery nor invention, that he believed we neither discover ahistorical principles nor create something from nothing. Rather, he reworked the paths of discovery and invention, placing them in a dialectical relation. We undoubtedly discover aspects of the natural and social world, but there is no need to posit a transcendent Creator or a natural moral order as the source of what we discover. We certainly invent things, but invention is more like saying new and interesting things in a seasoned language than coming up with a new one. We discover a sociohistorical world, and within that world we make new things, thus adding to its history as we are shaped by it. I take this middle way to be close to Walzer's path of interpretation, except for this: Durkheim traveled closer to the path of discovery.

For some time now Walzer has been characterizing social criticism as a specialized form of common complaint. "Social criticism," he writes, "is less the practical offspring of scientific knowledge than the educated cousin of common complaint." In his recent book, *The Company of Critics*, he claims that "criticism is most powerful . . . when it gives voice to the common complaints of the people or elucidates the values that underlie those complaints."[35] Compare this approach to what I earlier called

Durkheim's hermeneutics of suspicion. Most of the people most of the time, Durkheim believed, are largely unaware of the history and nature of the social webs that surround them. Critics investigate the past and present, often discovering surprising patterns and developments, in order to understand more adequately contemporary social circumstances. Durkheim's model or image for this suspicious investigator is the scientist. There is no opposition between internal criticism and the hermeneutics of suspicion. The methods and conclusions of the leery scientist are meaningful only in the context of common social frameworks.

Walzer, of course, does not disavow social expertise, and Durkheim did not scorn common complaint. But Walzer often speaks as if social meanings are self-evident, even if complex. He shows little sense that "common meanings" can support and conceal structural injustices.[36] Durkheim, in contrast, was wary of popular opinion, of popular movements, and, more generally, of popular agreement on ostensible social meanings. This may sound elitist and antidemocratic, but I do not think it is. Durkheim did not believe that social experts should run the country. His position, in fact, was that they should not become too involved in popular politics. They need to keep their distance. Part of their job is to remain somewhat apart from some contemporary activities and biases so that they can better observe and understand them. Yet the distance ought not to be so great that critics cease to be recognized, or to recognize themselves, as fellow citizens. Epistemological detachment is not the aim. There is no way for the critic to step outside the culture. The goal, rather, is a pragmatic stepping back within the culture and its history that allows critics to see a larger, more contoured social landscape. Or, to change the metaphor, if critics distance themselves from society's contemporary activities and biases, it is to hold a mirror far enough from society to present it with a fuller view of those activities and biases.

I use the mirror metaphor deliberately to link Durkheim closely to Walzer, lest my portrayal of their differences cloud the affinity between them. It has become fashionable to accuse Walzer of "merely" holding a mirror to society, reflecting what it is instead of what it should be. Dworkin, for example, likens Walzer's approach to "only a mirror, uselessly reflecting a community's consensus and division back upon itself." Similarly, Emily Gill claims that "by defending no universal, critical principles of distributive justice, particularists like Walzer leave justice to convention and end by making it our mirror, rather than our critic."[37] This line of attack, we must assume, is aimed not so much at the results of Walzer's approach—his substantive positions—as at the approach itself. My defense of Durkheim's internal criticism challenges this standard line against Walzer's "connected critic," and I see no reason to rehearse those arguments again. I will only note that Walzer, instead of avoiding this metaphor of the mirror, has adopted and developed it. In his new book Walzer borrows a phrase from Breytenbach to describe the role of the social critic: he "holds his words up to us like mirrors." Walzer then asks, "Why is this a critical activity? Because we don't see in the writer's mirror what we want to see. . . . Mirrors presumably don't lie, but people learn how to look in a mirror so as to see only what they want to see. The critic points to the rest."[38]

Walzer, we know, isn't suggesting that critics point to a mirror that reflects a positivistic image of society. His way, remember, is interpretive. He embraces the mirror metaphor, I believe, not to throw it back into the face of his critics but because it illustrates his belief that internal to society are principles and values that, potentially and actually, make claims on how we ought to live. In an exchange with Dworkin, Walzer put it like this: "Social critics . . . don't have to step outside the world they ordinarily inhabit. They appeal to internal principles, already known, comprehensible to, somehow remembered by, the people they hope to convince."[39]

Durkheim never used the image of the mirror, but he employed a similar logic: principles internal to a society can challenge the status quo. In his lectures on pragmatism, for example, he noted that even though truth corresponds to beliefs and institutions internal to society, rather than to suprahistorical, external principles, nonetheless "truth is often painful. . . . The truth is not always attractive and appealing. Very often it resists us, is opposed to our desires and has a certain quality of hardness." Likewise, he argued that socially generated ideals can check immoral social threats, such as those against individual rights and liberties.[40]

Durkheim, then, helps us to see that Walzer's mirror does not cast an uncritical reflection. Still, I have noted a difference between Durkheim and Walzer, and I find it difficult to opt for one position over the other. If you had to select an image to represent the social critic, and your choices were between Walzer's mirror that reflects what we already know but don't want to, and Durkheim's social scientist, you would not exactly confront an enviable choice. Durkheim's social scientist, unlike Walzer's mirror, doesn't just show us what we don't want to see, but what most of us can't see. Although these are caricatures of their thought, they reveal telling characteristics. Perhaps we should scrap both images, the scientist and the mirror. We might want to replace them with an image that avoids their shortcomings, say, with the physician who practices medical care as an art, as well as a science. This physician listens to what her patients have to say, taking seriously their "common complaints." But she also looks for other clues, signs, and symptoms to help her assist them. She is trained to recognize the course—the history—of a disease, even its subtle onset, for example. Her education and skill do not make her infallible, but they do make her medical judgments authoritative. This image captures the strengths of both accounts. The social critic is one of us, as Walzer would have it, but she is qualified to see things that we often fail to see, things we are not trained to see, as Durkheim would have it.

Instead of discarding these other two images I would rather simply add mine to them. There are many good and helpful styles of social criticism. The image of the social scientist fits Marx, the mirror fits Simone Weil. Durkheim and Walzer recognize this pluralism in critical styles. Their work is richer than their favorite images. Walzer's admiration for Gramsci and Foucault suggests he is not opposed to forms of "scientific" social knowledge or to a hermeneutics of suspicion. Durkheim's admiration for those who work for social justice without waiting for science's last word suggests that he recognized that informed protest is not the privileged role of the social scientist. Moreover, even the above caricatures of Durkheim and Walzer contain a common trait: a preference for the concrete, detailed approach of the internal critic over the abstract, speculative flights of the external critic.

V

This preference for the concreteness of internal criticism over external criticism's speculative abstraction places their approach in the same vicinity as MacIntyre's, though they often reach contrary conclusions. In previous chapters I have considered the differences between Durkheim and MacIntyre. It would be a mistake to understate these. Durkheim advanced the same liberal values that MacIntyre spurns. Now, however, I want to make clear their affinities, and also my debt to MacIntyre. Too often MacIntyre is glibly labeled a "conservative," or a "historian" rather than a "philosopher," and his valuable contribution to political philosophy and social theory is not acknowledged. MacIntyre has done much to shape many contemporary debates. He has made us more circumspect about the sociohistorical dimensions of our thought and practices, and also about the status of the common good.

His work on institutions, social goods, and obligations supplies powerful critiques of liberal society. MacIntyre writes, for example, "from the standpoint of [modern] individualism I am what I myself choose to be. I can always, if I wish to, put in question what are taken to be the merely contingent social features of my existence."[41] This form of individualism, we know, Durkheim deplored just as strongly as MacIntyre does. We also know that many liberals for good reason applaud individuals and society when they put aside contingent features of an individual's social existence such as race and gender, status and wealth under circumstances such as elections and hiring, education and medical care. Isn't the elimination of contingent features a merit of Rawls's original position? MacIntyre, however, is not simply indulging in antiliberal rhetoric in his communitarian critique of individualism. His account of inherited identity and social membership generates, for example, a critical perspective on our relation to past generations that many liberal theorists would want to embrace.

[Modern] individualism is expressed by those modern Americans who deny any responsibility for the effects of slavery upon black Americans, saying "I never owned any slaves." It is more subtly the standpoint of those other modern Americans who accept a nicely calculated responsibility for such effects measured precisely by the benefits they themselves as individuals have indirectly received from slavery. In both cases "being an American" is not in itself taken to be part of the moral identity of the individual.[42]

I am not claiming that MacIntyre is a misunderstood liberal, only that the critical import of his communitarian position is often missed due to his antiliberal theoretical assumptions. Jeffrey Stout and Joel Feinberg, who have not missed it, are significant exceptions because neither is a communitarian.[43] If MacIntyre is underappreciated, I suspect one reason is that many are not familiar with the philosophical and critical promise of a sociohistorical approach. There are, of course, good reasons to object to MacIntyre, and Durkheim provides many of these. Yet Durkheim also helps us to understand MacIntyre's historical approach, thus permitting a more nuanced evaluation of MacIntyre. Durkheim's social theory, after all, has much in common with MacIntyre's narrative style. Moreover, Durkheim shared many of MacIntyre's worries about modern individualism, as MacIntyre himself has acknowledged.[44]

Given these similarities, it is striking that their appraisals of liberalism are so divergent. They both provide narratives of the rise of individualism in Western European societies, specifying causes, symptoms, and antidotes. Whereas MacIntyre laments liberalism, however, Durkheim provided a nuanced account that celebrated and promoted its virtues while it identified and combated its dangers. How can we account for such different judgments? One way is to begin with a theoretical assumption shared by both: there are no interesting knockdown arguments. No complex and significant set of facts permits only one conclusion. Yet MacIntyre's almost absolute rejection of liberalism is possible only because he selectively refuses to recognize the history of individualism in the West as a complex set of facts.

In *After Virtue* MacIntyre compared the Aristotelian "tradition" to the liberal "point of view," "stance," "conceptual scheme," or "project"—but never to the liberal "tradition." Only recently has he been willing to describe liberalism itself as a tradition.[45] In *After Virtue* he claimed that a living tradition "is an historically extended, socially embodied argument, and an argument precisely in part about the goods which constitute that tradition."[46] This sounds like an apt description of the development of moral individualism. Why has it taken so long for him to recognize that this description applies to liberalism? Did the term "tradition" seem to MacIntyre to lend too much dignity to liberal "projects"? Surely he wasn't heeding some liberals' desire to see themselves outside all traditions.

Now that he has recognized or admitted that liberalism has all the marks of a tradition, liberalism in *Whose Justice?* appears remarkably consistent and uniform. MacIntyre cannot find a single good thing to say about the liberal tradition because he refuses to recognize its complexity. As Stout notes, "of the four traditions treated in *Whose Justice?* only liberalism is dispensed with in a single chapter. . . . The result is an utterly unsympathetic caricature at the very point where the narrative most urgently requires detailed and fair-minded exposition if it means to test its author's preconceptions rigorously."[47] I suspect that if MacIntyre's account of liberalism were as fair-minded and detailed as his studies of, say, rival Aristotelian traditions, he would discover that "the" liberal project is in fact many projects and traditions, comprising diverse, often conflicting ideals and practices, some grievous, some commendable. Actually, we know from his broad list of liberals, including Reid and Rorty, to name two very different thinkers, that MacIntyre is familiar with the many faces of liberalism. But he distorts these by subjecting them to uniform criticism, portraying a family resemblance stronger than is warranted. If MacIntyre were to modify his narrative, carefully mapping the important and laudable development of human rights, for example, his chronicle of liberalism might not seem as provocative, but it certainly would not be as provoking. A richer account of liberalism would make MacIntyre's scholarship more consistent, more serious, and would permit his critics to appreciate his many insights.

Durkheim started out hating classical liberalism more than he loved anything else. In the end, however, he embraced moral individualism at least as much as he opposed atomistic liberalism. Perhaps MacIntyre will take a few steps along the same path. Rawls, it seems to me, has learned much from communitarians like MacIntyre and Sandel. I hope MacIntyre can learn from his "liberal" colleagues, recognizing that liberalism not only encompasses many traditions, but that many of these have considerable merit. In any case, a Durkheimian approach has helped us to appraise MacIntyre's work, and that assessment has produced a mixed review.

VI

Although in Chapter 4 I stopped short of describing Rorty as a mild-mannered pragmatist, I noted that Rorty and Durkheim hold much in common. Both undermine the idea of suprahistorical entities such as universal reason or "the" natural self. They expose the sociohistorical character of knowledge, deconstruct the Natur-/Geisteswissenschaften distinction, and are committed to supporting liberal society without resorting to metaphysical props. They cherish autonomy and intellectual freedom, and they abhor political and cultural tyranny. Yet the difference between them is as great as that between Durkheim and MacIntyre, if not greater. From a Durkheimian perspective, while MacIntyre neglects the claims of the individual, Rorty slights the needs of the collective.

In *Contingency, Irony, and Solidarity* Rorty claims to make "a firm distinction between the private and the public." This distinction does not follow along metaphysical or epistemological lines, along the border between public reason and private emotion, for example. Even after we have all been converted to historicism, tension persists between the public and the private. While historicists cope with this tension differently, Rorty conveniently divides them into two camps: those dedicated to "self-creation" and "private autonomy," and those dedicated to "a more just and free human community." This is one distinction Rorty is happy to live with. He has no desire to deconstruct or mend this rip, and he wants to give each side "equal weight." His book is committed to maintaining this division between public and private, and it warns against any theoretical attempt to bring them together: "The vocabulary of self-creation is necessarily private, unshared, unsuited to argument. The vocabulary of justice is necessarily public and shared, a medium for argumentative exchange." [48]

Why does Rorty insist that no single vision, vocabulary, or theory can unite these? He wants us to stop our search for a Platonic or any other preordained blueprint promising to relate the private to the public. There is no natural teleology built into the human soul that, if only discerned, can assure a harmonious polis. There is no truth within the breast or above in the heavens to fuse our self-interests and common involvements. The quest for private perfection and for social justice are two different undertakings, and no theory or vocabulary can encompass both. Hence Rorty claims that "the closest we will come to joining these two quests is to see the aim of a just and free society as letting its citizens be as privatistic, 'irrationalist,' and aestheticist as they please so long as they do it on their own time—causing no harm to others and using no resources needed by those less advantaged. There are practical measures to be taken to accomplish this practical goal. But there is no way to bring self-creation together with justice at the level of theory." [49]

This sounds like a standard "liberal" description of the aim of enlightened societies. That's what's remarkable about it. The description brings the two quests, which are supposedly theoretically incommensurable, quite close together by ascribing an individualistic aim to the "just and free society." He does add the familiar liberal postscript, "causing no harm to others," as well as the more radical caveat, "using no resources needed by those less advantaged." Which less advantaged? Brazilians suffering under American markets? Americans suffering under American markets? Either way, this sounds like a rough paraphrase of Rawls's difference principle, and if we were to take it seriously it would pose tremendous demands on many individuals and institutions. Does Rorty mean for us to consider this seriously? Little in *Contingency, Irony, and Solidarity* makes me think so. Most of the time all that Rorty has to say about social justice is that "cruelty is the worst thing we do" and no single theory can help us to reconcile duty to self and duty to others. We are told little about the quest for social justice. This raises some questions. Can Rorty (or anyone else for that matter) make a firm distinction between the public and private? Has Rorty himself attempted to disentangle them by putting the public in service of the private?

Rorty calls "freedom as the recognition of contingency" the "chief virtue of the members of a liberal society." [50] There is something laudable here. Recognizing the contingency of one's beliefs could stymie oppressive dogmatism and prejudice; recognizing the contingency of one's circumstances could foster empathy for those who happen to be less fortunate; and recognizing the contingency of social structures could embolden people to work for a more just, less cruel society. Such things could follow if those possessing this "chief virtue" held all sorts of other beliefs, including the belief that diversity can be a good thing, that chance should not determine the distribution of social goods such as health care and education, and that social structures not only can be but should be changed. Portions of Rorty's book make me think he holds these other beliefs, but barring his celebration of diversity and novelty, these portions of his book are slim indeed. The slimness is not, I take it, a measure of Rorty's good will, but of his sociopolitical competence and awareness. It may not seem fair to judge Rorty on these grounds, yet he claims to give "equal weight" to both private autonomy and social justice.

Before the publication of his new book, Rorty gained a reputation for light-mindedness, to use his own self-description. Until recently, his playfulness had been directed mainly at various philosophical pretensions to "objectivity" and to the mirroring of nature. This playful role, I believe, was helpful, and gave many of us a better sense of what we as philosophers should be doing. In *Contingency, Irony, and Solidarity*, however, Rorty performs more than a metaphysical exorcism. He offers a postmodern view of the relation between the public and private, and, in particular, a defense of liberalism—liberalism without philosophy, or at least without epistemology and metaphysics. His interests have changed, but his light-mindedness has not. He espouses a Romantic liberalism dedicated to allowing individuals to be different, to occupy their own self-made world of unique wishes and feelings without fear of its destruction.

I suppose in a society replete with wealth and justice Rorty's stress on individual differentiation would not appear quixotic. But ours is a time when the wrong kind of differentiation abounds. In the last decade we have seen the distance grow between the rich and the poor, homeowners and the homeless, the well-fed and the hungry, the educated and the illiterate. These distinctions bear on any serious discussion of the public/private distinction. It's not that the aim Rorty has set for a just and free society is without merit; the problem is that our society is not sufficiently just and free, and therefore Rorty's preoccupation with "letting its citizens be as privatistic, 'irrationalist,' and aestheticist as they please" appears frivolous.

I'm not interested here in cheap shots. I just think Rorty is not yet an impressive authority on this new venture of his, the "shift from epistemology to politics."[51] I have discussed similarities between Durkheim and Rorty; now I want to provide a Durkheimian critique. I will argue along two lines. (1) Rorty needs to tell us more about how the private is in fact related to the public. He needs to do more than declare that they can be united in a life but not in a theory. (2) Rorty needs to pay more attention to the material and social conditions of the world found. He needs to take to heart that even if everything is contingent, not everything is easily changed.

"The vocabulary of self-creation," Rorty writes, "is necessarily private, unshared, unsuited to argument." Generosity of interpretation would have us take this not as an epistemological statement, but as something else. Epistemologically, Durkheim and Rorty both reject the private language assumptions found in many Cartesian and empiricist arguments. Both authors also allow for individual creativity and autonomy, but they do so differently. Durkheim described a variety of social spheres, some emphasizing public obligations, others emphasizing private projects. Using this vocabulary, we could call Rorty's self-creating ironists such as Nietzsche and Derrida those who subordinate public spheres to private ones, and Rorty's public philosophers such as Habermas and Marx those who subsume the private under the public. Rorty's liberal ironist, in contrast, keeps the private and the public apart. Both Durkheim and Rorty, then, want to differentiate what others conflate, but they do so differently.

Durkheim, unlike Rorty, was committed to relating, though not to identifying, the private and the public. In this he resembled those so-called benighted theorists like Plato and Marx who hoped, as Rorty puts it, that "the public-private split, the distinction between duty to self and duty to others, could be overcome."[52] The theorists with whom Rorty battles have held that a natural harmony between the public and private can be found, whereas the thinkers Durkheim argued against assumed the opposite, that a natural antagonism makes harmony impossible. Rorty and Durkheim chose to fight different fronts, with the result that Rorty seeks to keep apart what Durkheim wanted to associate. Relating the individual to society, for Durkheim, entails no appeals to Nature or Reason to show the Way. He did not fail to differentiate between more and less public, more and less private spheres, but he tried to show that individual creativity, desires, and rights need to be understood in reference to common social frameworks; that social forces—ideals and institutions, beliefs and practices—often resist the public/private split as defined by classical liberalism because the public and private spheres are interconnected in diverse ways; that it is neither natural nor unnatural for self-interests and common projects to overlap; and that it behooves liberal societies to think about how the public and private should and should not be related, and then work to establish these relations.

Durkheim's work on moral individualism was an example of his efforts to connect the private to the public. He interpreted liberal values such as autonomy and individual rights in the context of public goods. He wanted us to understand liberal benefits as the result of sociohistorical developments not to be taken for granted but actively extended. Self-creation is one good among many; it is not, however, the primary aim of a liberal democracy. Privatism and aestheticism have a place within the spheres of a liberal society, yet the spheres are not dedicated to them alone. Relating self-interests to public goods protects liberal democracies from egoism, and even from fatalism, since disparate individuals are susceptible to blindly collectivist movements. Unlike Rorty, then, Durkheim wanted to situate liberalism in traditions and social practices that feature the individual's involvement in and commitment to public life, lest liberalism be defined in Spencerian terms, and social progress be measured by the elimination of "unnatural" hindrances to individual autonomy such as the active presence of government in the life of the individual.

In the world found, that is, in the actual sociopolitical world individuals encounter, the public and private, for better or worse, already crisscross this way and that. Buying coffee, employing inclusive language, teaching in a private university, choosing a financial portfolio—these so-called private acts are thoroughly intertwined in the public world. Distributing wealth can conflict with individual liberties; so can buying books with tax dollars from the illiterate, or making bombs with money

from pacifists. To talk, as Rorty does, of a firm distinction between the public and the private, or to place the latter over the
former, is to fail to grasp their extensive interrelation. In order
to talk credibly about how they already are related, how they
should and should not be related, and how to achieve that, we
need to produce detailed accounts—thick descriptions—of the
actual circumstances of social life, of the world found. This,
however, is not Rorty's strong suit, and this is where the contrast
between Durkheim and Rorty is greatest.

The moral lessons of Rorty's historicism, I suggested in Chapter 4, often focus on private worldmaking: given the freedom
that accompanies contingency, the individual can make something new. But this emphasis on worldmaking slights the ways
individuals, especially groups of individuals such as African
Americans or women, confront cruel, albeit contingent, social
beliefs and structures deeply embedded in liberal and other societies. As it stands now, Rorty's account of cruelty is often individualistic and aesthetic, the result, perhaps, of Rorty's reading
more novels than sociological studies. He suggests that our
"moral advisers" be literary critics who have read a lot of
books.[53] Given the wide range of moral vocabularies and social
interests that Rorty attributes to literary critics, they probably
would make good counselors. Yet, even assuming this characterization of literary critics is correct, there's little evidence that
they have taught Rorty much about what Cornel West has called
"the complexities of politics and culture."[54] Frequently it seems
as if Rorty believes that enchantment—the spell cast by all sorts
of metaphysical notions—is the greatest obstacle confronting
not just liberal societies but any society. It may seem like this,
but his apparently genuine concern about cruelty and humilia-
tion make me think otherwise. The trick, however, is to discuss
how to alleviate such suffering. To that end, it is not enough to
get the world to recognize the contingency of vocabularies and
institutions.

Durkheim, in contrast to Rorty, highlighted the ways of the
world found: beliefs and institutions, prejudices and biases that
both hinder and assist our capacity for self-creation and social
reformation. He understood that even if the world were purged
of metaphysical guides and sanctifiers, we would still confront
social facts as hard as brick walls. Walls of course can come

down, but it's strenuous work. If Durkheim insisted that we generate detailed accounts of the world found, the objective was to bring down unjust structures and put up more humane ones. He criticized Romantics who exalt the idea of the infinite not because they love possibility, but because they neglect actuality. Rorty, I fear, looks a lot like these Romantics.

Rorty, no doubt, has some sense of large, public problems and the complexities of social life, but this sense is too shallow. For example, note how he describes the "moral purpose behind [his] light-mindedness":

The encouragement of light-mindedness about traditional philosophical topics serves the same purposes as does the encouragement of light-mindedness about traditional theological topics. Like the rise of large market economies, the increase in literacy, the proliferation of artistic genres, and the insouciant pluralism of contemporary culture, such philosophical superficiality and light-mindedness helps along the disenchantment of the world. It helps make the world's inhabitants more pragmatic, more tolerant, more liberal, more receptive to the appeal of instrumental rationality.[55]

It's hard to imagine either heavy-minded or light-minded philosophers having much of an effect on "the world's inhabitants." In any case, ridding the world of its desire for metaphysical comfort is a rather luxurious goal, given all the other comforts that most of the world's inhabitants lack. Rorty, I suppose, sees a connection between receptivity to instrumental reason and the wealth of nations. That is a superficial view of the modern West, neglecting how it became receptive to instrumental rationality and how that receptivity, with the rise of large market economies, has led to exploitation within and outside the United States. There is nothing wrong with instrumental reason per se, but it is easy to forget that discerning what goals to pursue is at least as important as knowing how to reach them. There is nothing wrong with large market economies, but too often we focus on how they benefit some and overlook how they harm others.

I can sum up my critique of Rorty by briefly commenting on his hunch that "Western social and political thought may have had the last *conceptual* revolution it needs. J. S. Mill's suggestion that governments devote themselves to optimizing the balance between leaving people's private lives alone and preventing suffering seems to me pretty much the last word."[56] Optimizing the balance—that's the hard part. This entails the difficult and controversial work of describing how the public and private are already intertwined, and how they should or should not be. It is the characterization and optimization of this balance that I take Durkheim to have written seriously about. Ironically, so did Mill. He developed a "single vocabulary" to assist us in this balancing act, and was willing, if need be, to require sacrificing private pursuits for public ends. I'm not supporting Mill's conclusions, but it seems that, *pace* Rorty, one or more vocabularies devoted to this balance might not be such a bad idea. In any case, Durkheim's descriptions of social spheres with varying degrees of heterogeneity and overlapping memberships, with assorted goals, traditions, and institutions, strike me as a useful way to discuss the interconnections between the public and the private. Moreover, his understanding of "individual freedom as a social commitment," to borrow Sen's phrase,[57] is a more useful approach to the ambiguities, conflicts, and achievements of liberal societies than is Rorty's idea that we make a firm distinction between the public and the private, or see the "aim of a just and free society as letting its citizens be as privatistic, 'irrationalist,' and aestheticist as they please." Rorty, no doubt, could have taught Durkheim much, especially about light-mindedness. Yet Rorty can learn some things from Durkheim, chiefly about being less ironic and more sociological.

Note on the Life of Durkheim: The Moral Imagination of the Social Scientist

I HAVE COMPARED Durkheim to Rawls, Walzer, MacIntyre, and Rorty to elucidate the power of what I have been calling Durkheim's internal criticism, a normative approach that attempts to bring together the social sciences and hermeneutics. Some of the inadequacies usually attributed to Durkheim, I have argued, are often the result of misconceptions about his style as a social critic. Others, I have tried to show, are the result of broader misconceptions. He has been charged with disregarding "the individual" and the role of social innovation; supporting fascism and the sanctified nation; extolling authority and religion because they impose order, deploring modernity and liberalism because they promote lawlessness. These charges will seem difficult to sustain, I hope, in light of my interpretation of Durkheim's theoretical approach. As I have argued before, however, Durkheim himself would insist that we cannot fully evaluate that approach without situating it amid his life, his times, and his commitments to his society.

Durkheim was a Dreyfusard throughout his life. By that I mean he strove to advance the ideals of the French Revolution. Supporting the Third Republic in the late nineteenth century was not tantamount to bolstering the status quo. It was an attempt to reform France's institutions along the lines of its progressive thought. Durkheim, then, was no reactionary. He opposed the restoration of monarchy, the political power of the Roman Catholic Church, and the licensed social advantages of the aristocracy. He championed social and economic reforms, arguing, for example, for the establishment of just occupational groups, the right to employment, and the abolition of inherited wealth.

Durkheim abhorred nationalism. In the strongest terms he condemned nations that engulf their citizens, pursue self-aggrandizement, and ignore "universal" values. Durkheim did put forward a public—even a "sacred"—faith. But this faith articulated the conditions for a rational, pluralistic society committed to extending democratic institutions. He did uphold the value of solidarity and moral authority, but this did not spring from a tacit support of nationalism. He espoused solidarity not to foster collectivism but to challenge laissez-faire capitalism; and he championed not the personal authority of the monarch, but the impersonal moral authority of democratic ideals and institutions. Never did he even indirectly encourage an emotional or blind attachment to "the group" or the nation. We know of his opposition to Action Française and other proto-fascist groups, and of his founding membership in the Ligue pour la Défense des Droits de l'Homme. The Nazis themselves attested to Durkheim's opposition to fascism by destroying his papers during the occupation.[1]

Often I have noted Durkheim's resistance to laissez-faire liberalism. This began early in his life, and in retrospect we see that his career did not suffer because of it. This, however, could not have been plain to the young Durkheim. The third part of his dissertation, *The Division of Labor in Society*, which criticized Spencer and classical liberalism, "so offended influential economists that for a time teaching in Paris was closed to him."[2] Durkheim, in any case, never tolerated conservative liberal impassivity toward social and economic inequalities. Like Rawls and Walzer, he endorsed an active state committed to eradicating those social and material conditions that inhibit citizens from political participation and that severely restrict their social and economic opportunities.

Durkheim's relation to socialism, at the other end of the political spectrum, is a complex subject. Durkheim had many personal and intellectual connections with reformist and radical socialists. He was a good friend to Jaurès and to other leading socialists. These friendships were based in part on Durkheim's admiration for their humane intellectual stances, especially toward empowering workers who, under a Spencerian contract system, were bound to lose every labor dispute. On a more theoretical level, Durkheim's own hermeneutics of suspicion agreed with the Marxist idea that social investigation requires reference to economic, social and historical considerations of which society's members are unaware. Durkheim's collaboration with prominent socialists caused many to identify sociology and socialism. Adding to this confusion, most of Durkheim's contributors to the *Année sociologique* were active socialists. Terry Clark has pointed out that essays appearing in Durkheim's journal were reprinted elsewhere with "fiery introductions" as socialist tracts. Clark also notes that "Durkheim was known to arrive at lectures and to walk out of the Sorbonne conspicuously carrying [the influential socialist paper] *L'Humanité*, a political act in itself."[3]

Yet Durkheim was not a socialist, if by that we mean formal membership in a political party. He was uncomfortable with the emotional appeals often found in their populist writings, and some of their central positions, such as their almost exclusive focus on class relations, he thought lacked intellectual rigor. Moreover, Durkheim disavowed violence for achieving political aims, and, given the continuity of France's history in spite of its many revolutions, he was not impressed with the efficacy of violence. He also worried that the socialist vision often appeared as "materialistic" and as morally shallow as that of classical liberalism. The political community needed to concern itself with more than increased economic production and its fair distribution. Durkheim was not opposed to these goals, but he thought the political community also had other moral obligations, such as extending individual rights and establishing other institutions that promote liberty, equality, and community—democratic education, for example. Still, Durkheim remained close to many of the ideas and advocates of socialism, and we can easily observe this in his work. Raymond Aron goes so far as to claim that Durkheim "conceived sociology as the scientific counterpart of socialism."[4]

In theory and in practice, then, Durkheim had little in common with those we normally call conservatives or reactionaries. This is not to say that there are no elements in his work that could suggest conservatism. These often spring from his faith in the state as a moral agency. In opposition to the predominantly economic roles that both classical liberalism and socialism attribute to the state, Durkheim held something of a "perfectionist" view: the state is to intervene actively to improve its citizens' material *and* moral welfare. This latter role, we have seen, did not involve imposing a moral agenda but helping to articulate society's shared understandings by hosting debate and establishing other democratic institutions. Yet too often Durkheim failed to address the actual and potential corruption of democratic states, especially considering the moral tasks he assigned them.

Related to this limitation is Durkheim's uneven treatment of conflict. Sometimes he analyzed it perceptively, suggesting ways to cope with it, recognizing that from it come both benefits and problems. At other times, however, he failed to address it, often when he most needed to, as in his treatment of the democratic state's role as moral adjudicator. It may be that, in a land of endless revolution, Durkheim was too anxious about how to build agreement. Still, this may have been the best reason to have paid more attention to conflict in modern democratic societies.

These deficiencies, however, are easily exaggerated if they are not placed in the context of Durkheim's overall life and work. That's what I have tried to do. I have claimed that Durkheim's internal approach to social criticism is often misjudged. Let me put this now in other terms. Durkheim was both a modern and a postmodern thinker. As a modern thinker, he was committed to the values of Kantian liberalism and the promises of free inquiry. As a postmodern thinker, he recognized that the aspects of Enlightenment thought that centered on escaping history, tradition, and community were not only illusory but destructive of human happiness.[5] This, we have seen, is not to say that Durkheim endorsed all communities and their traditions. But he did describe progressive, critical thought as rooted in the sociohistorical world, even as it challenges existing institutions and imagines new ones. This alliance of modern and postmodern thought has confused many. I hope it is clear now that if Durkheim paid considerable attention to history, authority, and social order, it was to engage in a radical investigation of the sinews of liberal society. To overlook this is to miss his passion for establishing just social and economic institutions that promote human happiness.

Durkheim was not much of an analytic philosopher, and he shunned speculative philosophy, yet he addressed issues that have concerned moral philosophers: What is the normative relation between the private and public, the individual and society? Are autonomy and authority irreconcilable? What is the nature of knowledge, especially moral knowledge? Consequently we could think of Durkheim as a moral philosopher. Or perhaps Durkheim is better described as a social critic. Without much exaggeration, I could also say his work addressed questions central to modern social criticism: What is distinctive of modern, Western societies? How can happiness and justice be preserved in them? Durkheim's approach to moral issues was historical and, of course, sociological. Was he, then, a historian, or, as they say, "the founder of modern sociology"? Should we call him a historicist moral philosopher?

More important than finding the appropriate professional job description are the questions he devoted his life to and the way he pursued them. For some time now, especially after the religious wars and the eventual decline of European religious states, many have sought to find ways to reconcile individual liberties and associational obligations. Durkheim was not alone in this. Into a similar scheme of issues we could fit, with more or less effort, Hobbes's sovereign, Kant's categorical imperative, Smith's invisible hand, Mill's utilitarianism, and Marx's classless society. I have not claimed that Durkheim's questions were unique, only that his approach to them is valuable and worth pursuing: the construction of a sophisticated theoretical and sociological account of modern social life that seeks to further the moral aims of liberalism and communitarianism.

I have called this project a communitarian defense of liberalism. That description is, of course, somewhat foreign to Durkheim's own language. "Dreyfusard," "republican," "anticlerical," "socialist," "liberty," "equality," "solidarity"—this vocabulary better suits him and his age. Yet I believe I have translated without distortion the core of his thought and vision into a helpful position in the contemporary debates between liberals and communitarians. If these terms—liberal and communitarian—now seem quaint or vague because you are persuaded that rights and virtues, "the individual" and community, autonomy and authority, self-interest and common projects are not necessarily incompatible, then I am pleased. Of course, even if the current debates are needlessly polarized, and I think they are, in them important theoretical issues have been explored and advances have been made. I have proposed what I take to be Durkheim's contribution. It can help along some of our projects, moving us toward the construction of powerful theoretical accounts to address pressing social problems. Durkheim's counsel to us is to begin "setting resolutely to work," reflecting on our common involvements, traditions, and ideals and investigating our institutions, practices, and structural arrangements without waiting for "a plan anticipating everything."[6] He recommends that we join sociohistorical skill to our moral commitment and imagination.

Confronted with today's world, many of us are inclined to think along the lines of Dickens's words, "It was the best of times, it was the worst of times, it was the age of wisdom, it was the age of foolishness." We have seen the Berlin Wall come down while other barriers go up. Debt and poverty here and abroad, sexism and racism, homelessness and illiteracy—these are just a few of the obstacles facing many. If it is assumed that there is a natural antagonism between individual self-interest and social obligation and commitment, a common enough assumption, many will accept that today's dire problems are intractable. As Sen has put it, "if individuals do, in fact, incessantly and uncompromisingly advance only their narrow self-interests, then the pursuit of justice will be hampered at every step by the opposition of everyone who has something to lose from any proposed change."[7] This position, in Sen's view, is not only depressing and dreary, but has little evidence to support it.

Durkheim would agree. He would add, moreover, that modern egoism, insofar as it does exist, springs not from "the" human condition, but from regrettable social practices and traditions. Social conditions can encourage asocial behavior. Not all contemporary beliefs and practices, however, promote narrow self-interest. Durkheim reminds us there are modern traditions and practices that foster commitment to social justice and humane care. He encourages us to attend to these, lest we in fact become egoists, and lose sight of our joy and responsibilities as members of a public, common good. There is, then, much to be done, but no intrinsic reason much can't be done.

Reference Matter

Notes

Introduction

1. Durkheim, "La Science positive," p. 127.
2. Gutmann, "Communitarian Critics of Liberalism," p. 316.
3. MacIntyre, *After Virtue*, p. 2.
4. There are, of course, specimens of ahistorical foundationalism in some whom many would call communitarians—for example, Aristotelian biologism and Thomistic natural law.
5. Some good can come from "ideal types" (in the Weberian sense). Because they are not rich in empirical detail, they can provide unambiguous descriptions of positions in order to highlight otherwise subtle tendencies and dispositions. Durkheim in fact frequently employed this technique, especially when he was trying to find a middle ground between two positions. Of course, sometimes he was just sloppy, as when he ascribed "individualistic" views to all utilitarians.
6. Hampton, "Should Political Philosophy Be Done Without Metaphysics?" p. 811. MacIntyre, *Whose Justice?* p. 346.
7. I take up and elaborate this argument in a work currently in progress, *The Relation Between the Public and the Private in Modern Social Thought*.
8. Patrick Riley interprets Rousseau's general will as a distinctively French product, tracing Rousseau's secularized *volonté générale* to the transformation of Malebranche's theological notion of God's will governing *le bien général*, that is, God's *volonté générale* as opposed to human *volonté particulière*. I have greatly benefited from Riley's excellent work, *The General Will Before Rousseau*.
9. Of Locke, for example, Rousseau complained, "Locke's maxim was to educate children by reasoning with them; and it is that which is now most in vogue. Of all man's faculties, that of reason, which is in fact only a compound of all the rest, unfolds itself the last, and with the

greatest difficulty, yet this is what we make use of to develop the first and easiest of them. The great end of a good education is to form a reasonable man; and we pretend to educate a child by means of reason" (from *Emilius and Sophia*, cited in Fliegelman, *Prodigals and Pilgrims*, p. 30). Rousseau's emphasis on education, one could argue, takes him out of the social contract tradition of Hobbes, for whom not education but reason in the service of self-interest plays the primary role in the individual's voluntary consent.

10. Kant, "Eternal Peace," pp. 452–53.
11. In fact, only Chapters 1–3 and 5 deal exclusively with Durkheim.
12. Lukes, *Emile Durkheim*.
13. Turner, *Dramas, Fields, and Metaphors*, p. 17.

Chapter One

1. Brunetière, "Après le procès," p. 445.
2. Durkheim, "L'Individualisme et les intellectuels." I have frequently relied on M. Traugott's translation, found in Bellah, ed., *Emile Durkheim*. Even when my translation deviates from his, all notes refer to the pagination of Bellah's book.
3. I am grateful to Jeffrey Stout for pointing out to me that the word "ideals" could for good reason give some readers pause. Durkheim used the word variously, but never to designate the concept that Oakeshott rightfully disdains, ideals as universal rules determined by abstract, ahistorical thought. (See Oakeshott, *Rationalism in Politics*, "The Tower of Babel.") Durkheim's notion of ideals usually refers to important social values and norms embodied in institutions and customs. Occasionally ideals refers to an idealized future state, that is, to a time when our highest ideals are more fully realized.
4. There are many fine treatments of the Dreyfus affair; I have profited especially from Kedward, *The Dreyfus Affair*; Lukes, *Emile Durkheim*; and Thomson, *Democracy in France*.
5. Thomson, p. 157; Kedward, p. 55.
6. Thomson, p. 141.
7. P. Miquel, *L'Affaire Dreyfus*, Paris, 1961, p. 51; quoted in Lukes, p. 347.
8. The report of Durkheim's speech comes from his nephew, Henri Durkheim, who was living with Durkheim at the time. See Lukes, p. 347. The letter is quoted in Lukes, p. 348.
9. Durkheim, "L'Élite et la démocratie," pp. 705–6.
10. As reported in a local Bordeaux newspaper. Lukes, p. 348.
11. The Rector's letter is in Durkheim's dossier. Lukes, p. 349.
12. Durkheim, "Individualism and the Intellectuals," p. 44.
13. In "Individualism and the Intellectuals" Durkheim did not provide the necessary arguments to support these claims, largely because he was responding to Brunetière, who would gladly have accepted such anti-utilitarian statements. In the next two chapters I review the development of Durkheim's arguments against utilitarian individualism.

14. Durkheim, "Fouillée, *La Propriété*," p. 450.

15. Durkheim, "Individualism and the Intellectuals," p. 45.

16. Though it does not discuss Durkheim, Hobsbawm and Ranger, eds., *The Invention of Tradition* has helped me understand this aspect of Durkheim's strategy.

17. Durkheim, "Individualism and the Intellectuals," p. 47.

18. Ibid.

19. Ibid., p. 231 n. 4.

20. Durkheim, *Montesquieu and Rousseau*, pp. 83, 131. These lectures on Rousseau were delivered within a year or two of "Individualism and the Intellectuals."

21. Ibid., p. 108.

22. This is Durkheim's summary of Rousseau, ibid., p. 66.

23. Durkheim, "Individualism and the Intellectuals," p. 46.

24. Ibid., p. 51. Durkheim, *The Elementary Forms of the Religious Life*, p. 60. Durkheim's attempt to provide a religious reading of moral individualism strikes me as similar to what Rousseau did in the last chapter of *The Social Contract*. There Rousseau described a civil religion that promotes both social unity and tolerance. Those not accepting the civil religion's dogma, tolerance, are to be banished from the state—not for impiety, but for anti-social behavior.

25. I explore Durkheim's notion of modern, sacred beliefs and practices in Chapter 5.

26. Durkheim, "Individualism and the Intellectuals," pp. 48, 46. This is not to say that individual rights and liberties, given Durkheim's historical understanding of these, are immutable. Because of our high regard for the individual and for the importance of work, employment could become a right. We might want to argue that we cannot be truly free unless employed. In view of this mutability, what, then, would prevent us from becoming an authoritarian state suspending numerous individual rights? Nothing would, absolutely; but we have no strong reason, at this point, to suspect that we will cease to understand ourselves from within our constitutional, republican tradition. That social constraint, Durkheim would say, is fundamental to our freedom.

Our concept of individual liberty is derived from and subject to a host of social contingencies. Understanding as much makes us aware of, among other things, the danger of society's retreat from moral advances. I'm thinking now of the history of civil rights under the Reagan and Bush administrations.

27. Durkheim, "Individualism and the Intellectuals," p. 48. Lest this talk of a "new religion" sound dangerously conservative, I want to point out that Durkheim's notion of moral individualism challenges the status quo by confronting those modern conditions, including racism, classism, and nationalism, which undermine flourishing democratic societies. In the context of the Dreyfus affair, Durkheim opposed those conservative French nationalists who wanted to scapegoat Dreyfus for the sake of "the security of France." Of moral individualism Durkheim wrote, "it springs not from egoism but from sympathy for all that is

human, a broader pity for all sufferings, for all human miseries, a more ardent need to combat them and mitigate them, a greater thirst for justice" (pp. 48–49).

28. Ibid., p. 52.   29. Ibid., p. 53.
30. Ibid., pp. 50, 46–47.   31. Ibid., p. 53.
32. Thomson, p. 159.
33. Durkheim, "Individualism and the Intellectuals," p. 54.
34. Ibid., p. 54.
35. Ibid., p. 54.
36. Many of Durkheim's contemporaries, including Theodore Herzl, assumed that the Dreyfus controversy issued from the inherent racism of the French people. Likewise, H. R. Kedward has claimed that "the Jewishness of Dreyfus was seen to be fundamental: the *sine qua non* of the affair" (*The Dreyfus Affair*, p. 50). Durkheim disagreed. In "Notes sur l'antisémitisme," a short essay published a year after "Individualism and the Intellectuals," Durkheim argued that French anti-Semitism was not a basic and irremediable characteristic of the national identity but "a consequence and superficial symptom of a condition of social malaise." Characteristically, Durkheim sought to locate the anti-Semitic aspects of the affair in a broader social context, a context that held out the possibility of reform. "When society is suffering, it experiences the need to find someone whom it can blame for its sickness, on whom it can avenge its disappointments; and those naturally designated for this role are those who are already linked to unfavorable opinion. These are the pariahs who serve as expiatory victims." The sociological fact that French anti-Semitism was but "one of the many indices by which the grave moral perturbation from which we suffer is revealed," he argued, did not excuse people from the moral duty to combat it. Moral individualism required them to do so.

The means it provided were legal, educational, and "material." "Incitement to hatred" could be made a criminal offense, and although such "repressive measures are not sufficient to convert hearts," they can "recall to the public conscience that lost sentiment: that [racism] is such an odious crime." But the government should also take measures to convert hearts and minds. Having taken a legal stand against racism and the "party of intolerance," the government also could morally educate its citizens [*éclairer les masses*] about this grievous moral offense, bigotry. Education, however, was not a cure-all for Durkheim. He advocated reforms aimed at engendering social and economic justice as well. "Material" changes (for example the establishment of occupational groups) were needed to complement "spiritual" changes (training people to love justice). The two had to go hand in hand to overcome anti-Semitism ("Notes sur l'antisémitisme," pp. 60, 61, 62; my translation).

We can applaud Durkheim's attempt to provide economic, social, and cultural accounts of racism, as well as his insistence that we not be content with "platonic disapprobation" but rather "have the courage to declare [it] aloud . . . and to unite together in order to battle victoriously against this *folie publique*" ("Notes sur l'antisémitisme," p. 63). He clearly viewed racism as contrary to the moral goals of the Third Republic. It is disappointing, however, that he did not deepen his analyses and include in them diverse forms of bigotry, such as those confronting women and blacks. Such disappointment, I believe, is not anachronistic. The rights (and plight) of women and minorities was an issue for many late-nineteenth- and early-twentieth-century thinkers, for example Elizabeth Cady Stanton, John Stuart Mill, and W. E. B. Du Bois. Durkheim's sensitivity to social forces of all kinds, political, cultural, and economic, and his commitment to the ideals of moral individualism, placed him in a good position to identify and combat racial and sexual discrimination. It's a shame he never made full use of that position. Still, he was not silent on these issues, and his moral and sociological approach has enriched, even if indirectly, our ability to address them.

Chapter Two

1. Most commentators on Durkheim ignore his essays prior to *The Division of Labor in Society*. Wallwork and Alexander are two important exceptions from whom I have greatly profited.

2. Durkheim's most severe criticism, however, was reserved for laissez-faire liberalism. The early Durkheim preferred socialism, in spite of its potential authoritarianism, because of its commitment to improving workers' economic conditions. In 1886, glossing A. Coste's *Questions sociales*, Durkheim wrote, "What can the unfortunate worker reduced to his own resources do against the rich and powerful employer? And is it not a downright and cruel irony to liken these two such manifestly unequal forces? When they get into a fight, is it not clear that the second will always and without penalty [*peine*] overwhelm the first? What can be said of such liberty, and what can be said of the satisfied economist who takes no blame and who presents us with words for deeds?" ("Les Études de science sociale," p. 73). The liberties associated with classical liberalism are individualistic. They allow individuals to express themselves in various ways; they ensure legal contracts; they prohibit slavery, thus permitting a worker to quit a job and seek employment elsewhere. In a word, these liberties protect the individual's legal self-determination. Yet Durkheim realized that "self-determination" can be threatened by social, if not legal, injustices. There is, Durkheim noted, a gross inequality between the "rich and powerful" employer's self-determination and the "unfortunate" worker's. The employer is free to establish low wages and poor working conditions, while the most the worker can do is quit—but that requires financial resources often not available to the worker. Durkheim understood that if socialism takes certain liberties away from capitalists, it does so in the name of empowering the relatively powerless.

3. Durkheim, "La Science positive," p. 37.

4. Ibid., pp. 40–41.

5. Ibid., p. 45. See also pp. 125–26 for further support of my interpretation. Here Durkheim, following Wundt, claimed that moral ideas are fashioned by influences of which we are unaware; they are not, then, *pace* Spencer, the result of rational utility.

6. Ibid., p. 40. This should not imply that Durkheim approved of all those things that, sociologically speaking, count as part of the "moral phenomena." There is, in other words, a distinction between what Durkheim descriptively recognized as belonging to a people's moral life and what he normatively considered appropriate for that life. I flesh out this distinction in greater detail in the next chapter.

7. Durkheim, "Les Études de science sociale," pp. 60–69.

8. Ibid., p. 69. In 1887, in a review essay on Guyau's *L'Irréligion de l'avenir, étude de sociologie,* Durkheim referred to religion as a "system of *representations.*" Durkheim complained that both Guyau and Spencer tended to "intellectualize religion," that is, to describe it as a means to understand and explain the mysterious. This, according to Durkheim, is to fail to perceive the practical nature of a *"représentation collective";* he then went on to call religion a *"système de représentations"* (*Revue philosophique* 23 (1887):308). This suggests that the early Durkheim understood religion as a cognitive set of beliefs and not just as collective sentiments such as fear. Steven Lukes claims that "Durkheim started using this concept [collective representations] in about 1897" in *Suicide* (Lukes, p. 6). This is basically correct insofar as Durkheim did not heavily employ the concept until 1897.

9. I do not mean to belittle the more indigenous influence of Renouvier, Comte, Saint-Simon, or Rousseau. These thinkers shaped the very questions Durkheim brought to Germany. But many of Durkheim's early essays were a result of—and inspired by—his German visit. There is no doubt that Durkheim was greatly influenced by the German social economists, the *Kathedersozialisten.* Kant's influence and Wundt's seem to have been as great as theirs.

10. Durkheim, "La Science positive," pp. 127–28.

11. Ibid., p. 128.   12. Ibid., p. 129.

13. Ibid.   14. Ibid., pp. 129–30.

15. Lewis Coser notes that "Wundt's notion of the *Volksseele* (the group soul), which he substituted for the more common Hegelian *Volksgeist,* may have played a part in Durkheim's formulation of the *conscience collective*" (*Masters of Sociological Thought,* pp. 155–56).

16. Taylor, *Hegel and Modern Society,* p. 155.

17. I am here describing Durkheim by borrowing from Taylor. Taylor writes, "If the philosophical attempt to situate freedom is the attempt to gain a conception of man in which free action is the response to what we are—or to a call which comes to us, from nature alone or from a God who is also beyond nature (the debate will never cease)—then it will always recur behind Hegel's conclusions to his strenuous and penetrating reflections on embodied Spirit" (ibid, p. 169). As much as I like Taylor's description of freedom as the response to what we are, I do not think the genealogies behind the notions of situated freedom all lead

back to Hegel. In the French traditions, for example, there is a similar theological notion of freedom developed by Malebranche which is secularized by Rousseau and others, as Riley points out. And of course there are even older notions of situated freedom in authors like Aquinas, the early Augustine, St. Paul, or Aristotle. Durkheim probably came to his understanding of freedom via both the German and French traditions.

18. Durkheim, "La Science positive," pp. 46, 120.

19. Durkheim, "L'Enseignement de la philosophie," p. 337.

20. Durkheim, "Les Études de science sociale," p. 71.

21. Durkheim, "La Science positive," p. 121.

22. Durkheim, *L'Évolution pédagogique en France* 2, p. 209.

23. Spencer, *The Evolution of Society*, pp. 14–15, 58–59, 216.

24. Spencer, *The Man versus the State*, p. 404.

25. Spencer, *Social Statics*, pp. 323–24.

26. Durkheim, *The Division of Labor in Society*, trans. W. D. Halls, pp. 149, 152. All references to *The Division of Labor* refer to this edition; I note when I have modified Halls's translation.

27. Ibid., p. 152. Translation modified.

28. Ibid., p. 308. Translation modified.

29. Ibid., pp. 310, 319 (translations modified); pp. 321, 311.

30. It is distressing that Durkheim could not provide a more detailed account of class-related social injustices. His class analyses do, however, gain sophistication in the later writings, especially in *Professional Ethics and Civic Morals*, which I discuss in Chapter 6.

31. *The Division of Labor*, p. 153. Translation modified. This, of course, is not to imply that social influence assumes only juridical forms.

32. Ibid.   33. Ibid., p. 29.

34. Ibid. Translation modified.   35. Ibid., p. 172.

36. Ibid., p. 173.   37. Ibid.

38. Ibid., pp. 123, 70.

39. Ibid., p. 173. The role of the state is a prominent theme in Durkheim's later writings, and is discussed in Chapter 6.

40. Ibid., p. 158.

41. Ibid., p. 161.

42. See, for example, Alexander, *The Antinomies of Classical Thought* 2, p. 143.

43. Anthony Giddens, however, correctly notes that even material density is a moral notion for Durkheim: "it is clear in his statement of it [population density] in *The Division of Labor*, that the explanation Durkheim offers is a sociological one: physical density is important only in so far as it becomes transformed into moral or dynamic density, and it is the frequency of social contact which is the explanatory factor" (Giddens, *Capitalism and Modern Social Theory*, p. 79).

44. This Kantian tradition is not entirely in line with aspects of Kant's own work, especially with the Kant of "Eternal Peace." There Kant sounds more like the classical economists. He suggested that a person following practical reason would wish for the same political arrange-

ment as would a person motivated by greed and profit: a constitutional republic that supports freedom and equality. Nature has set up things such that if bad people follow their own self-interest, good things can come from this. Kant wrote, "Nature's mechanical course evidently reveals a teleology: to produce harmony from the very disharmony of men even against their will" ("Eternal Peace," p. 448). Nature protects societies from "violence and war" by exploiting "mutual self-interest." Moreover, Kant said, "It is the *spirit of commerce* which cannot coexist with war, and which sooner or later takes hold of every nation" (ibid, p. 455). Kant went further than, say, Montesquieu when he suggested that nature uses passions to promote the public good; it does not simply restrain them.

45. I support this claim in Chapters 6 and 8.

46. Durkheim, *The Division of Labor*, pp. 162, 163.

47. Ibid., p. 163. Translation modified.

48. Ibid., pp. 163, 167.

49. Durkheim, to my knowledge, never appreciated that the classical economists, in their own, limited manner, were committed to individual autonomy as a worthy social ideal. Durkheim discerned in their work only a pathological commitment to individual liberty. This polarized view is unfortunate, though it probably gave at least rhetorical effectiveness to Durkheim's role as a social critic.

50. Durkheim, *The Division of Labor*, pp. 173–74.

51. Ibid., p. 122. Translation modified.

52. Giddens, *Capitalism and Modern Social Theory*, p. 72; Fenton, *Durkheim and Modern Sociology*, p. 19. I take Giddens's and Fenton's books to be among the best Durkheimian scholarship. It is ironic that the very passage that Giddens cites to support his position in fact refutes it. Durkheim wrote: "Doubtless all trace of common consciousness does not vanish because of this [individual mobility]. At the very least there will always subsist that cult of the person. . . . But how insignificant this is if we consider the ever-increasing scope of social life. . . . The division of labor becomes the predominant source of social solidarity, at the same time it becomes the foundation of the moral order" (*The Division of Labor*, p. 333).

53. Durkheim, *The Division of Labor*, p. 122. The translation is slightly modified.

54. Ibid., p. 153.

55. Ibid., p. 174.

56. Ibid., p. 322.

Chapter Three

1. Durkheim, *Suicide*, trans. John A. Spaulding and George Simpson, p. 374. I note when I have modified their translation. All modifications are based on the French edition published by Presses Universitaires de France, 8th edition, 1930.

2. I explore this in Chapter 6.

3. Durkheim, *Suicide*, p. 254.

4. Ibid., p. 255. Translation modified.

5. Ibid., p. 276, n. 25.

6. Ibid., p. 369.

7. Durkheim, *The Elementary Forms of the Religious Life*, p. 475; *Suicide*, p. 369. The full quotation is: "Thus, what the rising flood of voluntary deaths denotes is not the increasing brilliancy of our civilization but a state of crisis and perturbation not to be prolonged with impunity."

8. Durkheim, *Suicide*, p. 365n.

9. Ibid., p. 214.

10. Ibid., pp. 255, 256, 257.

11. Hobbes, *Leviathan*, chapter XI, sec. 44.

12. Durkheim, *Suicide*, p. 389.

13. As I relate Durkheim's arguments to contemporary debates between liberals and communitarians, I will drop the subtle—and some would claim impossible—distinction between egoism and anomie, and between fatalism and altruism. Although I do believe there are situations in which it would prove helpful to maintain the distinctions, for present purposes it would only add an unnecessary complexity. Henceforth, then, "egoism" will encompass "anomie," and "fatalism" will encompass "altruism."

14. It is unfortunate that Durkheim, who wrote much in defense of individual rights, said little about women who were deprived of their rights. In *Suicide*, for example, while arguing that the social differences between men and women need to decrease, he reminded defenders of equal rights for women that "the work of centuries cannot be instantly abolished; that juridical equality cannot be legitimate so long as psychological inequality is so flagrant. Our efforts must be bent to reduce the latter" (p. 386). Durkheim evidently did not see women's rights as a moral test of the Third Republic's integrity. I am not aware, moreover, that Durkheim ever wrote about the rights of blacks in the United States or elsewhere.

15. Durkheim, *Suicide*, p. 234.

16. Ibid., p. 269.

17. Ibid., p. 386. Yet please see note 14 above.

18. I explore this line of thought in Chapter 7.

19. Durkheim, *Suicide*, p. 372.

20. Ibid., p. 374. A few years ago some might have cited countries like the Soviet Union as a counterexample. The recent demands for independent statehood from a variety of ethnic or other segmented populations in the former Soviet Union, however, support Durkheim's belief that identity and a sense of belonging cannot simply be imposed on a population by a state.

21. Durkheim, *Suicide*, p. 375. Translation modified.

22. I think Durkheim was wrong about biblical religion in contemporary society. The rise of both conservative and progressive religion (fundamentalism on the one hand, black and feminist and liberation theology on the other) suggests that, with respect to religion, critical thought

has not unequivocally rejected religion. Ironically, contemporary religiosity vindicates the important social role Durkheim ascribed to religion.

23. I can imagine a wealthy society that loves contemplative activity more than any other activity, and whose members are willing to work together in helpful and productive ways to insure that what they take to be this primary good can be enjoyed by all. Moreover, within a year after the publication of *Suicide*, Durkheim would deem free inquiry a prominent feature of the liberal common good.

24. Durkheim, *Suicide*, pp. 377, 391.

25. Ibid., p. 380.   26. Ibid.

27. Ibid., pp. 382, 379, 384.   28. Ibid., pp. 381, 383.

29. This account is informed by Stout's provocative elaboration of MacIntyre's account of social practices. See Stout, *Ethics After Babel*, pp. 267–76.

30. Ibid., p. 312. See also Chapter 2, note 8. I discuss collective representations in light of Durkheim's later work in greater detail in the next chapter.

31. Ibid., pp. 327, 333.

32. For example, notice how Durkheim, in his seventeenth lecture on pragmatism, contrasted consciousness to habit: "Once it [consciousness] is freed from this task or escapes from it [from having to decide how to act], movements gradually become established in the organism and consciousness itself disappears. This is what occurs in the formation of habit" (*Pragmatism and Sociology*, p. 83).

33. I am grateful to a reader for Stanford Press who pointed this out to me, and detected the same ambiguity in portions of my own work.

34. Durkheim, *Suicide*, p. 378.

35. I take Talcott Parsons's reading of Durkheim to overstate the discontinuity, while Steven Fenton's exaggerates the continuity. See Parsons, *The Structure of Social Action* 1, and Fenton, *Durkheim and Modern Sociology*.

36. I discuss conflicting social ideals and practices in Chapters 6 and 8.

37. Durkheim, *Suicide*, p. 334. Translation modified.

38. Ibid., pp. 333–34. Translation modified.

39. Ferri, *Omicidio-suicidio*, p. 253; Durkheim, *Suicide*, pp. 334, 337.

40. Ibid., pp. 336–37. Translation modified.

41. Durkheim, *The Division of Labor*, p. 122. Translation modified.

42. Durkheim, *Suicide*, p. 336.

43. Ibid., p. 333; see Gadamer, *Truth and Method*, p. 267.

44. Durkheim, *Suicide*, p. 337.

45. I discuss the close political proximity of egoism to fatalism and totalitarianism in Chapter 6.

46. Durkheim, *Suicide*, p. 210. Translation modified.

47. For this contrast between Jonah and Amos, see Walzer, *Interpretation and Social Criticism*, p. 76.

48. This is Rorty's phrase, though Stout pursues the notion further than Rorty. See Rorty, "The Priority of Democracy to Philosophy," p.

272; and Stout, *Ethics After Babel*, Chapter 10, "Liberal Apologetics and Terminal Wistfulness," pp. 220–233.

49. Durkheim, *Suicide*, p. 387.

50. Ibid. Translation modified.

51. Ibid., p. 391.

Chapter Four

1. Stout, *Ethics After Babel*, p. 297.

2. James, *Pragmatism*, p. 13.

3. Ibid., p. 31.

4. Goodman, *Ways of Worldmaking*, pp. 21, 107.

5. Ibid., p. 6.

6. Ibid., p. 119.

7. See James, *Pragmatism*, pp. 32, 43.

8. Goodman, "A Query on Confirmation," p. 383; or *Problems and Projects*, p. 363.

9. Hume, *A Treatise of Human Nature*, part III, sec. ix, p. 111.

10. Goodman, *Fact, Fiction and Forecast*, p. 82.

11. The example of grue emeralds begins on p. 73 of *Fact, Fiction and Forecast*.

12. Goodman, *Fact, Fiction and Forecast*, p. 94.

13. Ibid., p. 96.

14. Ibid., p. 121.

15. I develop this in Chapter 8.

16. Of course, rookies can someday become veterans. When looking under the entry "green," in J. I. Rodale's *Synonym Finder* (Emmaus, Pa.: Rodale Press, 1978), I found "greenish, viridescent, emerald . . . grue." "Grue" was not listed under the heading "blue."

17. Goodman, *Fact, Fiction, and Forecast*, p. 98.

18. "Rookie" here includes a veteran predicate used in a novel way.

19. Durkheim and Mauss, *Primitive Classification*, p. 86; Durkheim, *The Elementary Forms of the Religious Life*, p. 28.

20. Ibid., p. 27.   21. Ibid., pp. 21, 25.

22. Ibid., pp. 28, 490.   23. Ibid., pp. 242–43.

24. Durkheim, *Pragmatism and Sociology*, pp. 12, 85, 37, 24.

25. Ibid., p. 67.

26. Ibid., p. 85.

27. Rorty, *Philosophy and the Mirror of Nature*, p. 344.

28. I thank Henry Levinson for suggesting that philosophical realism itself be considered as an entrenched vocabulary. This strikes me as being true of philosophical notions of relativism as well. And I suspect that both vocabularies are fortified by ordinary discourse. The language of realism is a common feature of everyday speech. We find missing keys, discover distant stars, and stumble over yesterday's laundry. And when the toe bumps against the table leg, no one will ask whether the table was a molecular or an apparent one. No doubt the "impressive biography" of the language of everyday realism is part of the story of

how the philosophical realists' vocabulary became and still remains entrenched. The relativists' vocabulary, too, abounds in our everyday speech. If you smile when you hear that I am the tallest member of my family, and that I am barely five-foot seven, then you know something of relativism without the help of an introductory philosophy course. We are constantly referring to differing "points of view," to the eccentric's "own little world," and to our, as opposed to their, "way of life." I am not arguing that the feud between philosophical realists and relativists is the result of taking ordinary language distinctions too seriously, though that may be part of the story. Mine is a less ambitious point: the present-day dispute can be viewed as the contest between two, somewhat distinct, entrenched vocabularies.

29. Durkheim, *Pragmatism and Sociology*, p. 68.

30. Rorty, *Contingency, Irony, and Solidarity*, p. 7. Durkheim would be more comfortable than I am with the claim that "truth is a property of linguistic entities." As it stands, Rorty here seems to advance a theory of truth that attempts to capture the essence of truth, and hence he is making the very move that he often dismisses. I am inclined to rewrite his statement like this: our sundry justifications for truth, not truth itself, are a property of linguistic entities.

31. Ibid., p. 3.

32. Ibid., pp. 22, 46, 92.

33. See Walzer, *Exodus and Revolution*, pp. 16, 135–41, 144–49.

34. James, *Pragmatism*, p. 35.

35. Ibid., p. 36.

36. Jenny Teichman, *The New York Times Book Review*, 7 (April 23, 1989): 2.

37. See James, *Pragmatism*, pp. 27–28.

38. Teichman, p. 2.

39. Goodman, *Ways of Worldmaking*, p. 102. See also p. 140. Durkheim, "Value Judgments and Judgments of Reality" (1911), found in *Sociology and Philosophy*, p. 95.

40. Durkheim and Mauss, *Primitive Classification*, p. 3.

41. Again, the "pressure of truth" has nothing to do with the correspondence theory or with any other theory of truth, except that it explains in part why some scholars are so very concerned about such theories. The pressure of truth is applied by constraints supported by authority, entrenchment, and tradition, as discussed in this chapter.

Chapter Five

1. Durkheim, "The Determination of Moral Facts," in Durkheim, *Sociology and Philosophy*, p. 59. My emphasis.

2. Durkheim, "The Dualism of Human Nature," in Durkheim, *Emile Durkheim: On Morality and Society*, p. 152.

3. Durkheim, "Individual and Collective Representations," *Sociology and Philosophy*, p. 31. My emphasis.

4. Durkheim, *The Elementary Forms of the Religious Life*, pp. 483, 487, 482, 481, 28 n. 17, 28 n. 18, 483.

5. Ibid., p. 487. Categories, for Durkheim, are fundamental concepts, such as time, space, class, number, personality, cause, substance; they are "preeminent concepts, which have a preponderating part in our knowledge" (ibid., p. 488).

6. Durkheim, "Value Judgments and Judgments of Reality," *Sociology and Philosophy*, pp. 92, 93, 96.

7. Ibid., pp. 93, 94. Durkheim, "The Determination of Moral Facts," p. 59.

8. Durkheim, *The Elementary Forms of the Religious Life*, p. 471.

9. Durkheim occasionally contrasted "sensory reality" to "the framework of our concepts." Specimens of this are found in *The Elementary Forms* and elsewhere, where he suggested that the sacred and the ideal are added to the empirical. See, for example, the opening quotation in this chapter. Yet he always insisted that collective representations—concepts and ideals—are the result of changing traditions, future endeavors, and play.

10. See Durkheim, "Les Études de science sociale," pp. 68–69. I discussed this review article in Chapter 2; Durkheim, *The Division of Labor*, p. 118.

11. Ibid., p. 119.

12. Ibid., pp. 119–20.

13. Durkheim, "De la définition des phénomènes religieux," p. 20.

14. It is to Durkheim's credit that he conceded that "thought and action are closely united to the point of being inseparable" and that "one cannot believe firmly in progress [an example of a secular, sacred belief] without feeling it shape one's way of life." Nevertheless, he maintained that progress, like other secular beliefs, "is a faith with no corresponding ritual" (ibid., p. 22).

15. Durkheim, "Lettres au Directeur de la *Revue néo-scolastique*," pp. 606–7, 612–14; found in Steven Lukes, p. 237.

16. William Robertson Smith, *Lectures on the Religion of the Semites*, pp. 260, 263, 264–65. For an excellent discussion on the relation between Robertson Smith and Durkheim's thought, see Alexander, *Antinomies of Classical Thought* 2, pp. 484–88.

17. Durkheim, *The Elementary Forms of the Religious Life*, p. 62.

18. Durkheim, "The Determination of Moral Facts," pp. 52–53.

19. Durkheim, "Replies to Objections," *Sociology and Philosophy*, p. 72.

20. Durkheim, *Leçons de sociologie*, p. 82. Should fatalism, too, be seen as the result of blind, unthinking forces? Durkheim would not answer the question if it were posed as an ahistorical dilemma. In the context of a modern, democratic society, however, Durkheim described fatalism, understood as the beliefs and practices associated with excessive social conformity, as a social force that could threaten liberal democratic institutions. Fatalism collides with liberal ideals, and therefore, relative to those ideals, it is not a normative social force. It is blind. The Ku Klux Klan, given the roles that it assigns to African Americans and to women, is an example of an association with fatalistic aspirations that is in opposition to liberal democratic institutions. The Amish, on the

other hand, are an example of an innocuous fatalistic community that poses no threat to surrounding democratic institutions. No doubt the Amish live at odds with many aspects of liberalism, yet they do not challenge the liberal democratic institutions of society at large. As sectarians, they are satisfied with relative moral isolation.

The moral threat the Amish pose to themselves, particularly to their children, raises a different set of issues. As citizens of the United States, Amish children are protected from forms of coercion and negligence that hinder their future ability to enjoy the rights and obligations of adult citizenry. This is not the place to assess the extent to which Amish children suffer in their fatalistic communities, as compared with, say, the children of Fundamentalist or Flat Earth communities, or, for that matter, of Suburbia, U.S.A. What if we ignore the fact that the Amish live within a democratic society, however, and then ask whether their fatalism is an example of a blind social force? We can't. Our worries about an Amish child in Pennsylvania nevertheless will spring from our liberal, democratic traditions and institutions, including legal ones. At least this is the description Durkheim would give of such concerns. Our worries are relative to a democratic shared understanding. Those concerns, however, in Durkheim's view, are likely to make little sense, much less carry any moral force, within a fatalistic social framework.

Fatalism, per se, then, is not a thoughtless force. Yet it is blind in the context of liberal, democratic societies. (This raises, at least implicitly, what some would call the specter of relativism. I discuss Durkheim and relativism in Chapter 8.) It is blind in those societies because it is not subject to liberal, democratic social constraints that support, among other values, individual rights and liberties—that is, freedoms. Difficulties emerge, of course, when the rights and liberties of communitarian groups such as the Amish and especially the KKK clash with democratic ideals. Social conflict of this nature is addressed in the following chapters.

21. Durkheim, *The Elementary Forms of the Religious Life*, p. 388.

22. Note that I write, "to speak of," as opposed to "to experience," a door as hard. Durkheim sometimes suggested that sensual experiences are private, and sometimes suggested that they are public. Yet he always insisted that the communication of sensual experiences requires publicly shared concepts. I develop this later in this chapter when I discuss Durkheim's essay, "The Dualism of Human Nature."

23. Durkheim, "The Determination of Moral Facts," p. 59.

24. Ibid., pp. 55–56. Durkheim, *The Elementary Forms of the Religious Life*, p. 388.

25. Durkheim, "The Dualism of Human Nature," pp. 163, 154.

26. I am thinking primarily of Sheldon Wolin's *Politics and Vision* and Jerrold Seigel's excellent yet-unpublished essay, "Objectivity and the Subject in Durkheim." Their arguments for what I am calling the standard reading are among the best. See Seigel, p. 27; Wolin, p. 387.

27. Seigel, pp. 13, 14.

28. Durkheim, "The Determination of Moral Facts," pp. 45–46.

29. Durkheim, "Replies to Objections," p. 70.

30. Seigel, pp. 27, 28.

31. Ibid., p. 29.

32. Durkheim, *The Elementary Forms of the Religious Life*, pp. 485–86.

33. Sabina Lovibond, in *Realism and Imagination in Ethics*, presents many fine arguments against the view that a social epistemology necessarily results in majoritarianism. She writes, "Although (in Wittgenstein's view) it is an agreement, or congruence, in our ways of acting that makes objective discourse materially possible, this agreement does not itself 'enter into' the relevant language-game: when we ask a question about some aspect of reality, we are not asking for a report on the state of public opinion with regard to that question, we are asking to be told the *truth* about it" (p. 148). I explore this line of thought in Chapter 8.

34. Durkheim, "The Dualism of Human Nature," p. 150.

35. Durkheim, *The Elementary Forms of the Religious Life*, pp. 28–29n. 18.

36. Durkheim, "The Dualism of Human Nature," pp. 153, 161.

37. Ibid., p. 156.

38. Ibid., p. 153.

39. Ibid., p. 152.

40. Durkheim, "The Determination of Moral Facts," p. 37.

Chapter Six

1. Emile Durkheim, *Professional Ethics and Civic Morals*, p. 4. The French edition is entitled *Leçons de sociologie: physique des moeurs et du droit*. Subsequent citations in this chapter are given in the text; the first page reference is to the French original, the second to the English translation. I have routinely altered the translation where minor changes emphasize my argument.

2. In the next chapter I note that, in Durkheim's view, moral education usually takes place implicitly in a variety of social settings, as opposed to explicitly in a school hour dedicated to core values.

3. Durkheim, *Suicide*, pp. 254–55.

4. Walzer, *Spheres of Justice*, p. 26.

5. Ibid., p. 19.

6. Durkheim, *Suicide*, p. 381.

7. See Stout, *Ethics after Babel*, Chapter 12, "Social Criticism with Both Eyes Open," especially pp. 267–76.

8. MacIntyre, *After Virtue*, p. 175.

9. Stout, *Ethics after Babel*, p. 269.

10. Ibid., p. 274.

11. MacIntyre, *After Virtue*, p. 178.

12. The charge of fascism and nationalism is what I take Mitchell to be making in "Emile Durkheim and the Philosophy of Nationalism," pp. 87–106; and, to a lesser degree, McGovern, in *From Luther to Hitler*, Chapter 9.

13. Nozick, *Anarchy, State, and Utopia*, p. ix. See also p. 297.

14. Durkheim, *Montesquieu and Rousseau*, p. 109.

15. Durkheim, "L'Etat," pp. 434–35, my translation.

16. I discuss this in greater detail in Chapter 8.

17. Oldenburg, *The Great Good Place*.

18. Buchanan, "Assessing the Communitarian Critique of Liberalism," p. 859.

19. Rawls, "The Priority of Right," p. 272. My understanding of civic humanism is informed by this essay and by Taylor, *Philosophical Papers*, 2: 334–35.

20. See Nozick, *Anarchy, State, and Utopia*, part I; Rorty, *Contingency, Irony, and Solidarity*, p. 92; and Bruce Ackerman, *Social Justice in the Liberal State*, pp. 16–19.

21. Hauerwas, "Freedom of Religion: A Subtle Temptation," p. 317.

22. Ibid., p. 331.

23. This, of course, is not the only Christian assessment of liberal democratic society. For an extreme counterposition arguing that the liberal democratic, capitalistic state is essentially Christian, see George Gilder, "Where Capitalism and Christianity Meet," and Michael Novak, "The Economic System: The Evangelical Basis of a Social Market Economy."

24. On the two occasions I heard Hauerwas, he addressed predominantly "secular" audiences. Speaking at Princeton on nuclearism and at Duke on health care, he convinced many of his material positions—that is, of nontheological conclusions that are based on his theology. Hauerwas's success in doing so puts into doubt his view that there is little overlap between "the church and the world." I might also add that though Hauerwas espouses a moderate sectarianism, he strikes me as an unusually powerful social critic of modern warfare and of U.S. health care. I have little doubt that his distinctive Christian stances have provided him with an insightful "critical distance" from which to view liberal society. I wish, however, he could understand himself not only as an active member of his church community but also of the larger political community.

25. Debate over abortion might appear as a counterexample. In fact, in the United States most religious believers and nonbelievers agree that we should not have laws prohibiting abortions. See *The New York Times*, May 9, 1989, p. A1.

26. MacIntyre, *After Virtue*, pp. 2, 224, 225.

27. See Buchanan, "Assessing the Communitarian Critique of Liberalism," pp. 858–60, and Feinberg, *Harmless Wrongdoing* 4, pp. 97, 108–113, 118, 121.

28. For a discussion on the misleading conclusions drawn from the Socratic interviews in Bellah et al., *Habits of the Heart*, see Stout, *Ethics After Babel*, p. 194, or "Liberal Society and the Languages of Morals," p. 35.

29. MacIntyre, *After Virtue*, p. 213.

30. MacIntyre, *Whose Justice?*, p. 337.

31. Ibid.

32. Ibid. I am not tacitly supporting MacIntyre's belief that individuals should have an overall good supplying an overall unity to life, then adding that in liberal societies there are diverse comprehensive goods and unities from which individuals can choose. I am simply noting that when MacIntyre assumes that a variety of moral spheres precludes an overall good supplying an overall unity, he fails to distinguish between moral pluralism and a plurality of morals.

33. MacIntyre, *After Virtue*, p. 245.

34. Bellah et al., p. 142.

35. Buchanan, "Assessing the Communitarian Critique of Liberalism," p. 855. Buchanan does not apply his distinction to the authors of *Habits of the Heart*.

36. See Bellah et al., p. 143. Throughout his career, Bellah has creatively employed Durkheim, and his Introduction to his edited volume, *Emile Durkheim: On Morality and Society*, is one of the few interpretations of Durkheim that highlights moral individualism.

37. There is another social sphere that, in a limited sense, encompasses the political community. This is the international or universal community. I have said that, according to Durkheim, the political community by definition has no sovereign above it except that of the state. This sovereign, however, is relative. I have shown how it is accountable to the political community; it is also accountable to the international community. See, for example, Durkheim's *L'Allemagne au-dessus de tout*, especially p. 7. In *Elementary Forms of the Religious Life*, Durkheim claimed that: "There is no people and no state which is not a part of another society, more or less unlimited, which embraces all the peoples and all the states with which the first comes in contact, either directly or indirectly; there is no national life that is not dominated by a collective life of an international nature. In proportion as we advance in history, these international groups acquire a greater importance and extent" (p. 474).

Nonetheless, Durkheim held that the international community is too diffuse and general to claim of its members much allegiance and to provide sufficient moral training: "Man is a moral being only because he lives within established societies. There are no morals without discipline and authority, and the sole rational authority is the one that a society is endowed with in relation to its members" (*Professional Ethics and Civic Morals*, p. 73). Thus it is the task "for the individual states, each in their own way," to educate their citizens in international ethics. Still, moral pluralism involves not only a national but an (albeit limited) international political community.

38. Oakeshott, *On Human Conduct*, pp. 201, 203, 284–86.

39. See Covell, *The Redefinition of Conservatism*, pp. 219–22, for an interesting account of how to relate Skinner's *The Foundations of Modern Political Thought* to Oakeshott's "On the Character of a Modern European State" (found in *On Human Conduct*).

40. These essays are collected in Oakeshott, *Rationalism in Politics*.

312   *Notes to Pages 180–87*

41. MacIntyre, *Whose Justice?*, pp. 334, 335, 345.
42. Walzer, *Spheres of Justice*, p. 8.
43. Ibid., pp. 28, 82.
44. Rawls, "Justice as Fairness," p. 225; "The Idea of an Overlapping Consensus," p. 6.
45. Rawls, "Justice as Fairness," p. 247; "The Priority of Right," pp. 274, 269–70.
46. Ibid., pp. 268–69. For Rawls on the role of the virtues, see "Justice as Fairness," p. 247, and "The Priority of Right," p. 63.
47. Rawls, "The Idea of an Overlapping Consensus," p. 19.

Chapter Seven

1. Durkheim, "Fouillée, A., *La Propriété*," p. 449.
2. Durkheim taught courses on education every year from 1887 to 1916, with the exception of the years 1894–98.
3. Durkheim, "Rousseau on Educational Theory," in *Durkheim: Essays on Morals and Education*, p. 162.
4. Ibid., pp. 166–67; or see Rousseau, *Emile*, pp. 5–7.
5. There are exceptions. For example, *The Social Contract* culminates in the chapter on "Civil Religion," which provides a communitarian defense of an important feature of liberalism: tolerance. I call it communitarian because Rousseau wanted to inculcate tolerance as a virtue in the community; he called it a religious dogma. Those not willing to profess the tolerance required by civil faith are to be expelled from the republic. Whereas Locke, for the most part, hoped that the individual would realize the pragmatic value of tolerance, that is, realize that it is in the individual's best interest, Rousseau was less sanguine about the results of enlightened self-interest and therefore required that tolerance be taught and enforced as a civic religious dogma.

Rousseau offered what has appeared to many as a paradoxical vision: he advocated a civil religion that will effectively unite citizens, but a chief feature of this unity will be respect for individual belief, as long as that belief does not threaten the common good. This section of *The Social Contract*, which Durkheim never commented on, represented an early form of moral individualism. In light of Durkheim's work on moral individualism, Rousseau's paradoxical vision now seems more apparent than actual.

Also, in *Emile* Rousseau attempted to reconcile the social and the natural when he contended that the flourishing society is composed of members who have undergone a conversion to what he described as the natural religion of the heart. Individuals need to learn to hear the voice of the heart, that is, the conscience, the source of goodness and moral reasoning. This enables individuals to trade private willfulness and egoism for social cooperation and genuine selfhood. The conversion requires as much social support as it does solitude; one consults the heart as one participates in the general will.

But there is still reason to question whether Rousseau maintained that, even under ideal circumstances, the friction between the natural self and social convention can be entirely effaced. The self's effort at genuine selfhood often conflicts with social demands. Rousseau, in his characteristically unsystematic fashion, depicted aspects of this tension throughout his writing: self-assertion versus social cooperation, private perfection versus social compromise, fidelity to a universal deity versus loyalty to a provincial civil religion, and personal playfulness versus social seriousness. Rousseau recognized these oppositions, yet he refused to surrender either side of them. Instead, he devoted himself to keeping them together, precariously in tension. In the end, his refusal to drop the tension may be one of his greatest contributions to modern social thought, for to be satisfied with such tension is perhaps the hallmark of modern democratic societies. I develop this theme in *The Relation Between the Public and Private in Modern Social Thought*, in progress.

6. Durkheim, *Education and Sociology*, pp. 123, 81; *Moral Education*, p. 64.

7. The "Critical Thought" or neutralist position is dominant in educational theory. The demand for objectivity, that is, never "imposing" a moral view on students, is now commonplace. See for example, Louis Raths et al., *Values and Teaching*. For an alternative view, see David Purple, *Moral and Spiritual Crisis in Education*.

8. T. S. Eliot, "The Hollow Men," p. 77.

9. Durkheim, *The Evolution of Educational Thought*, pp. 336–37.

10. Durkheim, *Moral Education*, p. 125. For an excellent discussion on Hegel's use of *Moralität* and *Sittlichkeit*, see Taylor, *Hegel and Modern Society*, pp. 83–84, 89–90.

11. Durkheim, *Education and Sociology*, p. 91.

12. Oakeshott, *Rationalism in Politics*, pp. 62–63.

13. Durkheim, *Moral Education*, p. 24; *Education and Sociology*, pp. 62–63.

14. Durkheim, *Education and Sociology*, pp. 64, 65.

15. Durkheim, *Moral Education*, p. 25.

16. Rorty, *Contingency, Irony, and Solidarity*, p. xiii.

17. Durkheim, *The Evolution of Educational Thought*, p. 321.

18. Ibid., p. 322.

19. Durkheim, *Moral Education*, p. 3; *Education and Sociology*, p. 65.

20. Durkheim, *Education and Sociology*, p. 66.

21. See Durkheim, *The Evolution of Educational Thought*, pp. 10–11; *Moral Education*, pp. 12–13.

22. Durkheim, *The Evolution of Educational Thought*, p. 66.

23. Ibid., p. 64.

24. Ibid., p. 325.

25. Durkheim, *Moral Education*, pp. 12, 183.

26. Ibid., p. 3.

27. Ibid., p. 9.

28. Durkheim, *Education and Sociology*, p. 68.

---

29. Ibid.

30. Durkheim, *The Evolution of Educational Thought*, p. 320.

31. "Common community" refers primarily to the French, but also to all who share the beliefs and practices associated with modern democracies. Durkheim noted that "if our modern education is no longer narrowly national, it is in the constitution of modern nations that the reason must be sought" (*Education and Sociology*, p. 122). Again, it would be a mistake to say some nations and not others have happily discovered nature's design for humans. Durkheim went on to say, "not only is it society which has raised the human type to the dignity of a model that the educator must attempt to reproduce, but it is society, too, that builds this model." If many nations now share the ideals and practices of moral individualism, this is because traditions can cross state borders—often because traditions are older than state borders.

32. Gutmann, "What's the Use of Going to School?" p. 274.

33. Durkheim, *Moral Education*, pp. 26, 35–36, 50.

34. Ibid., pp. 160, 154, 52–53.

35. Ibid., pp. 45, 53.

36. Ibid., pp. 46, 69. Bloom, *The Anxiety of Influence*, pp. 5–16.

37. Durkheim, *Moral Education*, p. 73. In Durkheim's words, "the moralists refer to them [attachment and discipline] as the good and the necessary. The necessary is morality insofar as it prescribes and proscribes. It is the morality of coercive prescriptions, strict and harsh, the instructions one must obey. The good is morality insofar as it seems to us a desirable thing, a cherished ideal to which we aspire through a spontaneous impulse of the will" (ibid., p. 94).

38. See, for instance, *Moral Education*, p. 66 or p. 221.

39. See the last section of Chapter 6 for qualifications of this claim.

40. Durkheim, *Moral Education*, p. 214.

41. Ibid., p. 59.   42. Ibid., p. 77.

43. Ibid., p. 235.   44. Ibid., pp. 120, 108, 109.

45. Ibid., p. 110; see also p. 113.

46. Ibid., pp. 94, 52; Durkheim, "A Discussion on the Effectiveness of Moral Doctrines," *Durkheim: Essays on Morals and Education*, p. 131.

47. Ibid., p. 132; Durkheim, *Moral Education*, pp. 13, 14.

48. Durkheim, *L'Évolution pédagogique en France* 2, pp. 208–9.

49. Durkheim, *Moral Education*, pp. 276–77.

50. Ibid., p. 275.

51. Durkheim, *The Evolution of Educational Thought*, pp. 332–33.

52. Durkheim, *Moral Education*, p. 262.

53. Ibid.

54. Durkheim, *The Evolution of Educational Thought*, p. 348.

55. Durkheim, *Education and Sociology*, pp. 80–81.

56. Ibid., p. 81.

57. See Amy Gutmann, *Democratic Education*, pp. 22–41.

58. Ibid., p. 28.

59. Mill, *On Liberty*, ch. 5; quoted in Gutmann, *Democratic Education*, p. 33.

60. Durkheim, *Education and Sociology*, p. 80.

61. Ibid., p. 79.

62. Aristotle, *The Politics of Aristotle*, book 8, ch. 1, 1337a; quoted by Gutmann, *Democratic Education*, p. 286.

63. Durkheim, *Education and Sociology*, pp. 81, 79.

64. Ibid., p. 80.

65. Ibid., pp. 81, 80.

66. Gutmann, *Democratic Education*, p. 288.

67. Durkheim, *Education and Sociology*, p. 80.

68. William Bennett, quoted by David Wagner, "Bill Bennett's Dilemma," *National Review*, June 19, 1987, pp. 29, 31.

69. Gutmann, sounding a lot like Durkheim, calls this common culture "a democratic civil religion: a set of secular beliefs, habits, and ways of thinking that support democratic deliberation" (*Democratic Education*, p. 104).

70. Bennett, *History, Geography, and Citizenship*, p. 7.

71. Gutmann, *Democratic Education*, p. 68; *The New York Times*, March 14, 1990, p. A1.

72. Gutmann, *Democratic Education*, p. 70.

73. Bennett, pp. 1–2. It was Karl Popper who said that "Americans are no longer certain that their country and form of government are the best." Bennett fears that he is correct.

74. See Lukes, p. 131; Nisbet, *Emile Durkheim*, p. 23, "Conservatism and Sociology," pp. 165–75; Coser, "Durkheim's Conservatism and its Implications for his Sociological Theory," pp. 211–32; Levitas, *Marxist Perspectives in the Sociology of Education*, p. 31; and Nizan, *Les Chiens de garde*, pp. 191–92.

75. Alexander, *Antinomies of Classical Thought 2*, p. 280.

76. Fenton, *Durkheim and Modern Sociology*, p. 149.

77. Cherkaoui, "Bernstein and Durkheim," pp. 556, 564.

78. Some might claim that Durkheim needed to offer independent arguments for these moral ideals, rather than simply arguing that they represent our moral traditions at their best. My response to this depends on what one takes "independent" to imply. I deal with this issue in the next chapter.

79. Schneewind, "The Divine Corporation and the History of Ethics," p. 176.

80. Clark, *Prophets and Patrons*, p. 172.

81. See Gutmann, *Democratic Education*, pp. 14–15, 256, 287.

82. Gutmann, "What's the Use of Going to School?" p. 277. At least this is what I take Gutmann to imply when she writes, "Liberals can accept Durkheim's claim that the content of education ought to be determined by the social context within which schools operate. . . . But education ought not to serve only to maintain the present state of social and political organization." In the same essay (p. 271) she suggests that Durkheim is unconcerned with equal educational opportunity.

Chapter Eight

1. Given this sense of radical, there could be radical reactionaries, that is, conservatives whose criticism is rich in social and historical detail. Burke comes to mind. In this chapter I mainly set out the theoretical components of what I will call Durkheim's nonconservative internal criticism. Throughout the book and especially in the next chapter I show that Durkheim's criticism can also be understood as radical in the more conventional way, that is, he holds beliefs that reactionaries hate.

2. I am not entirely happy with the term, "internal social criticism." "Internal" may imply the false inference that we can judge and be judged only by fellow participants of our society. "Natural" social criticism might be one alternative. Take natural social criticism as criticism that self-consciously employs the only, and hence, the natural means at our disposal: historically situated, socially produced conventions. Of course the problem with the term "natural" is that it brings to mind the notion of suprahistorical sensibilities built into the human soul.

3. Walzer, *The Company of Critics*, p. ix. Walzer was not referring to Rawls but more generally to a type of social criticism. Walzer's own commitment is "to the cave" (p. x).

4. Gellner, *Words and Things*. Cited in Jones, "Is Wittgenstein a Conservative Philosopher?" p. 274.

5. Marcuse, *One Dimensional Man*, p. 178. Cited in Jones, p. 274.

6. Coser, "Durkheim's Conservatism," pp. 211, 214.

7. Wittgenstein, *Philosophical Investigations*, #23.

8. "The term 'language-game,'" Wittgenstein wrote, "is meant to bring into prominence the fact that the *speaking* of language is part of an activity, or of a form of life." Ibid.

9. My argument here is essentially taken from Stout's *Ethics After Babel*, p. 42.

10. I say the "objectivity" of a statement, and not "the truth of a statement." Durkheim often made the mistake of running objectivity and truth together. I take the truth of a statement to be independent of its entrenchment, even though our justifications for true statements are necessarily more or less socially entrenched. Objectivity, the opposite of subjectivity, refers to an impersonal position, what Durkheim correctly describes as a socially authoritative intellectual position. Truth, in contrast, the opposite of falsity, refers to what is the case, whether we know it or not.

11. Lovibond, *Realism and Imagination in Ethics*, p. 104. My position on Wittgenstein has been greatly enriched by Lovibond's work, and also by conversations with Victor Preller of Princeton University.

12. Wittgenstein, *Philosophical Investigations*, #217, #218.

13. I think Jones's claim about Wittgenstein is wrong when he states that "scientific paradigms are possible because science deals with facts not values; similarly Wittgenstein's 'world-picture' is a persuasive philosophical notion because it too is concerned with our basic concepts not values" (p. 286). This does not agree with the Wittgenstein of the

Philosophical Investigations, the *Zettel*, and *On Certainty*, for whom values as much as facts can belong to a shared "world-picture." To deny this is to keep Wittgenstein to his metaphysical word in the *Tractatus*. Jones goes on to suggest, now on somewhat firmer ground, that the propositions and concepts that constitute a shared "world-picture" are "not ones about which disputes (except among skeptical philosophers) break out." Perhaps Jones, mistakenly I believe, identifies levels of agreement with the fact/value distinction, as if facts alone can command consensus. In any case, Wittgenstein's work directly bears on the nature of values, and, moreover, his work presents normative arguments that challenge Cartesian and empiricist pictures of the world.

14. On moral and political imagination Lovibond writes, "Suppose we do undertake to substitute a different way of life for our familiar one. In this situation, the different way of life envisaged by us may be one which has never actually existed. It may simply be something which we represent to ourselves in thought—a product of our (moral or political) 'imagination.' Yet as long as the extant criteria of moral and political rationality are not so rigid that any innovation in the relevant discursive practices is automatically condemned to be perceived as an *error*, the language in which we express the thought of that different way of life can be the one made available to us by the way of life in which we have been brought up to participate" (p. 195). I soon discuss the various ways the social critic's message may be perceived or heard.

15. Wittgenstein, *Zettel*.

16. Lovibond sums up the situation like this: "Although (in Wittgenstein's view) it is an agreement, or congruence, in our ways of acting that makes discourse materially possible, this agreement does not itself 'enter into' the relevant language-game: when we ask a question about some aspect of reality, we are not asking for a report on the state of public opinion with regard to that question, we are asking to be told the *truth* about it" (p. 148).

17. See Talmon, *The Origins of Totalitarian Democracy*, p. 5.

18. This is how Rorty describes the historicist in *Contingency, Irony, and Solidarity*, p. xiii.

19. Wittgenstein, *Philosophical Investigations*, #107.

20. This quotation is cited by Hayden White, "The Politics of Historical Interpretation," p. 143.

21. Durkheim, *The Evolution of Educational Thought*, p. 14; *Education and Sociology*, pp. 145–46.

22. Durkheim, *Education and Sociology*, pp. 137, 66.

23. Ibid.

24. Durkheim, *The Evolution of Educational Thought*, p. 11.

25. Ibid., pp. 12–13.

26. Ibid., pp. 9–10.

27. Durkheim, *Moral Education*, p. 84.

28. Walzer, *Exodus and Revolution*, p. 149.

29. Durkheim, *Professional Ethics and Civic Morals*, p. 60.

30. Durkheim, "Introduction to Ethics," *Durkheim: Essays on Morals and Education*, p. 86.

31. Durkheim, "Replies to Objections," *Sociology and Philosophy*, p. 65; "The Determination of Moral Facts," *Sociology and Philosophy*, p. 61.

32. The term "relativism" could appropriately describe Durkheim's position on judging foreign (non-Western) and especially past societies. Though he criticized many foreign and past practices as inappropriate for modern Western societies, he maintained that these practices may have been suitable within their indigenous settings.

33. Coser, "Durkheim's Conservatism," pp. 212, 214.

34. See, for example, Nisbet, *The Sociological Tradition*, p. 86.

35. Durkheim, "The Determination of Moral Facts," p. 61.

36. Durkheim, "Introduction to Ethics," p. 92; "Replies to Objections," p. 66. In "Replies" he adds, "I am not concerned with 'the literal meaning of reason.'"

37. Durkheim, "The Determination of Moral Facts," p. 62.

38. Ibid., pp. 61–62.

39. Ibid., p. 62.

40. I have profited from an interesting account of Durkheim and the Durkheimians' involvement in *L'Année sociologique* in Clark, *Prophets and Patrons*, ch. 6.

41. See, for example, Durkheim, *Moral Education*, pp. 122–23. In the next chapter I discuss his particular political stances and affiliations; here I am interested in the theoretical issues surrounding his internal criticism and his alleged conservatism.

42. Durkheim, "Introduction to Ethics," pp. 80–81.

43. Lewis Coser, "Durkheim's Conservatism," p. 214.

44. Durkheim, "Replies to Objections," pp. 66, 74–75.

45. Durkheim, "A Discussion on the Effectiveness of Moral Doctrines," *Durkheim: Essays on Morals and Education*, pp. 137–38.

46. Coser, "Durkheim's Conservatism," p. 213.

Chapter Nine

1. Rawls, *A Theory of Justice*, p. 587.

2. Sandel, *Liberalism and the Limits of Justice*, p. 14; Rawls, *A Theory of Justice*, p. 264.

3. Rawls, "Justice as Fairness," p. 231.

4. See Rawls, ibid., p. 236 n.19.

5. Ibid., p. 225.

6. Rawls, "Justice as Fairness," p. 225. Unfortunately, Rawls's discussion of "the fact of pluralism" waffles between a descriptive and a normative account. Descriptively, it refers to the advent of social pluralism in the wake of early modern Western historical events; normatively, it refers to a human limit: we cannot reason our way to a Divine or natural comprehensive good appropriate for all; and, as a bastion against powers that attempt to go beyond this limit, society requires safeguards pro-

vided by liberal moral ideals and by developments such as individual rights. Such waffling is perhaps endemic to internal social critics who probe history as they furnish normative accounts.

7. Rorty, "The Priority of Democracy to Philosophy," p. 262.

8. Rorty, sensitive to this objection, writes, "notice that although I have frequently said that Rawls *can be content* with a notion of the human self as a centerless web of historically conditioned beliefs and desires, I have not suggested that he *needs* such a theory" (ibid., p. 270).

9. Rawls, "The Idea of an Overlapping Consensus," p. 13.

10. For Rorty's description of the self, see "The Priority of Democracy to Philosophy," p. 270.

11. Galston, "Pluralism and Social Unity," p. 723.

12. Ibid. The Rawls quotation is from "Justice as Fairness," p. 230.

13. Galston, "Pluralism and Social Unity," pp. 723–24.

14. Ibid., p. 724.

15. Ibid., p. 725.

16. Ibid., p. 724.

17. See Rawls, *A Theory of Justice*, pp. 130, 516, 585.

18. Galston, "Pluralism and Social Unity," pp. 725–26.

19. For example, see Hampton, "Should Political Philosophy Be Done Without Metaphysics?" pp. 807–14.

20. Rawls, "Kantian Constructivism in Moral Theory," p. 565.

21. Rawls, "The Idea of an Overlapping Consensus," p. 13.

22. Rawls, "Kantian Constructivism in Moral Theory," p. 569.

23. In a recent public address Rawls said, "speak the truth, but not the whole truth" (I am grateful to Debra Satz of the Stanford Philosophy Department for relaying this to me). As I understand Rawls, the substantive positions of, say, theological ethics can be put forward in public debate on the concept of justice, but theological justifications—for example of individual rights, based on what is it to be made in the image of God—must be avoided. Yet I suspect that severing the theologically or metaphysically based position from its internal justification will often distort the position itself.

24. Rawls, "Kantian Constructivism in Moral Theory," p. 568.

25. Ibid., pp. 568–69.

26. Ibid., pp. 570–71.

27. Rawls, "Justice as Fairness," p. 230.

28. Rawls, "Kantian Constructivism in Moral Theory," p. 564.

29. Rawls, "The Idea of an Overlapping Consensus," p. 23.

30. Ibid., pp. 24–25.

31. See Doppelt, "Rawls's Kantian Ideal and the Viability of Modern Liberalism," p. 437; "Is Rawls's Kantian Liberalism Coherent and Defensible?" p. 842.

32. Rawls, "Kantian Constructivism in Moral Theory," pp. 569, 571.

33. Galston, "Pluralism and Social Unity," p. 724.

34. See Walzer, *Interpretation and Social Criticism*, pp. 3, 5, 20–21.

35. Ibid., p. 65; *The Company of Critics*, p. 16.

36. This is not to deny that Walzer is, in fact, one of our best social critics, and precisely insofar as he reveals structural injustice. His account of his own approach, however, often belies his critical methods and conclusions.

37. Dworkin, "Replies," p. 46; Gill, "Walzer's Complex Equality," p. 36.

38. Walzer, *The Company of Critics*, pp. 230, 232.

39. Walzer, "Spheres of Justice: An Exchange," p. 43.

40. Durkheim, *Pragmatism and Sociology*, p. 74; *Suicide*, p. 337.

41. MacIntyre, *After Virtue*, p. 205.

42. Ibid.

43. Feinberg has noted that while MacIntyre may exaggerate the connection between social roles and one's personal good, "we must concede to MacIntyre that our fixed *inherited* roles do indeed bring with them 'a variety of debts, inheritances, rightful expectations, and obligations.'" He goes on to cite MacIntyre's position on "collective responsibility for past atrocities" (Feinberg, *Harmless Wrongdoing* 4, p. 95).

Stout is both appreciative and critical of MacIntyre. More than anyone, including MacIntyre himself, Stout has explored the importance of MacIntyre's distinction between internal and external goods. For Stout's assessment of MacIntyre, see *Ethics after Babel*, pp. 278–82, and "Homeward Bound: MacIntyre on Liberal Society and the History of Ethics," pp. 220–32.

44. MacIntyre, *Whose Justice?* pp. 368–69.

45. Ibid., p. 345.

46. MacIntyre, *After Virtue*, p. 207.

47. Stout, "Homeward Bound," p. 227.

48. Rorty, *Contingency, Irony, and Solidarity*, pp. 83, xiii–xiv.

49. Ibid., p. xiv.   50. Ibid., p. 46.

51. Ibid., p. 68.   52. Ibid., p. 120.

53. Ibid., pp. 80–81.

54. West, *The American Evasion of Philosophy*, p. 208. In reference to Rorty, West claims that "one cannot embark on a historicist project which demythologizes philosophy without dragging in the complexities of politics and culture." On the next page West writes, "Rorty's limited historicism needs Marx, Durkheim, Weber, Beauvoir, and Du Bois; that is, his narrative needs a more subtle historical and sociological perspective."

55. Rorty, "The Priority of Democracy to Philosophy," pp. 271–72.

56. Rorty, *Contingency, Irony, and Solidarity*, p. 63.

57. Sen, "Individual Freedom as a Social Commitment," p. 49. Sen does not use this phrase in reference to Durkheim but to his own approach. I am, naturally, sympathetic with Sen's commitment to "a view of social ethics that sees individual freedom both (1) as a central value in any appraisal of society, and (2) as an integral product of social arrangements" (p. 49). For a similar effort to relate autonomy to social obligation, see Raz, *The Morality of Freedom*.

Note on the Life of Durkheim

1. Cuvillier, "Preface," p. xii.
2. Richter, "Durkheim's Politics," p. 187.
3. Clark, *Prophets and Patrons*, p. 190. His source is personal communications with George Davy and Armand Cuvillier. I am indebted to Clark's account of Durkheim and socialism, and also to Neyer, "Individualism and Socialism in Durkheim," and to Richter, "Durkheim's Politics and Political Theory."
4. Aron, "Sociologie et socialisme," *Annales de l'Université de Paris*, 30th year (January–March, 1960), p. 33. Cited by Clark, p. 190 n. 82.
5. Postmodern, I recognize, means different things to different people. Here I use it to refer to a recent effort to situate one's tribe or self *critically* within traditions, in opposition to the "modern" attempt to rebuff all things traditional.
6. Durkheim, *Suicide*, last sentence.
7. Sen, "Individual Freedom," p. 54.

Works Cited

Ackerman, Bruce. *Social Justice in the Liberal State*. New Haven: Yale University Press, 1980.

Alexander, Jeffrey C. *The Antinomies of Classical Thought*. Vol. 2, *Marx and Durkheim*. Berkeley: University of California Press, 1982.

Bellah, Robert N., Richard Madsen, William M. Sullivan, Ann Swidler, and Steven M. Tipton. *Habits of the Heart*. Berkeley: University of California Press, 1985.

Bennett, William. *History, Geography, and Citizenship*. Ethics and Public Policy Center, Washington, D.C., April 1986.

Bloom, Harold. *The Anxiety of Influence*. Oxford: Oxford University Press, 1973.

Brunetière, Ferdinand. "Après le procès." *Revue des deux mondes* 146 (Mar. 15, 1898): 428–46.

Buchanan, Allen E. "Assessing the Communitarian Critique of Liberalism." *Ethics* 99 (1989): 852–82.

Cherkaoui, Mohammed. "Bernstein and Durkheim: Two Theories of Change in Educational Systems." *Harvard Educational Review* 47 (1977): 556–64.

Clark, Terry Nicholas. *Prophets and Patrons: The French University and the Emergence of the Social Sciences*. Cambridge, Mass.: Harvard University Press, 1973.

Coser, Lewis A. "Durkheim's Conservatism and its Implications for his Sociological Theory." In Kurt Wolff, ed., *Emile Durkheim*, 211–32. Columbus: Ohio State University Press, 1960.

———. *Masters of Sociological Thought*. New York: Harcourt Brace Jovanovich, 1971.

Covell, Charles. *The Redefinition of Conservatism*. New York: St. Martin's Press, 1986.

Cuvillier, Armand. "Preface" to Durkheim's *Pragmatism and Sociology*, ed. by John B. Allcock, trans. J. C. Whitehouse. Cambridge, Eng.: Cambridge University Press, 1979.

Doppelt, Gerald. "Is Rawls's Kantian Liberalism Coherent and Defensible?" *Ethics* 99 (1989): 815–51.

———. "Rawls's Kantian Ideal and the Viability of Modern Liberalism." *Inquiry* 31 (1988): 413–49.

Durkheim, Emile. *L'Allemagne au-dessus de tout: la mentalité allemande et la guerre.* Paris: Colin, 1915.

———. "De la définition des phénomènes religieux." *L'Année sociologique* 2 (1899): 1–28.

———. *De la division du travail social,* avec une nouvelle préface intitulée, "Quelques remarques sur les groupements professionels." Paris: Alcan, 1902.

———. *The Division of Labor in Society.* Trans. W. D. Halls. New York: Free Press, 1979.

———. *Durkheim: Essays on Morals and Education.* Ed. W. S. F. Pickering, trans. H. L. Sutcliffe. London: Routledge and Kegan Paul, 1979.

———. *Education and Sociology.* Trans. S. D. Fox. Glencoe: Free Press, 1956.

———. *The Elementary Forms of the Religious Life.* Trans. J. W. Swain. New York: Macmillan, 1915.

———. "L'Elite intellectuelle et la démocratie." *Revue bleue,* 5ᵉ série, 1 (1904): 705–6.

———. *Emile Durkheim: On Morality and Society.* Ed. Robert Bellah. Chicago: University of Chicago Press, 1973.

———. "L'Enseignement de la philosophie dans les universités allemandes." *Revue internationale de l'enseignement* 13 (1887): 313–38, 423–40.

———. "L'Etat." *Revue philosophique* 148 (1958): 433–37.

———. "Les Etudes de science sociale." *Revue philosophique* 22 (1886): 61–80.

———. *L'Évolution pédagogique en France.* 2 vols. Paris: Alcan, 1938.

———. *The Evolution of Educational Thought.* Trans. Peter Collins. London: Routledge and Kegan Paul, 1977.

———. "Fouillée, A., *La Propriété sociale et la démocratie.*" *Revue philosophique* 19 (1885): 446–53.

———. "Guyau, M., *L'Irréligion de l'avenir.*" *Revue philosophique* 23 (1887): 299–311.

———. "L'Individualisme et les intellectuels." *Revue bleue,* 4ᵉ série, 10 (1898): 7–13.

———. "Jérusalem, Wilhelm, *Soziologie des Erkennens.*" *L'Année sociologique* 11 (1910): 42–45.

———. *Leçons de sociologie: physique des moeurs et du droit.* Paris: Presses Universitaires de France, 1950.

———. "Lettres au Directeur de la *Revue néo-scolastique.*" *Revue néo-scolastique* 14 (1907): 606–7, 612–14.

———. *Montesquieu and Rousseau: Forerunners of Sociology.* Trans. Ralph Manheim. Ann Arbor: University of Michigan Press, 1960.

———. *Moral Education.* Trans. Everett K. Wilson and Herman Schnurer. Glencoe: Free Press, 1961.

———. "Notes sur l'antisémitisme." In Henri Degan, ed., *Enquête sur l'antisémitisme,* 59–63. Paris: P. V. Stock, 1899.

———. *Pragmatism and Sociology.* Ed. John B. Allcock, trans. J. C. Whitehouse. Cambridge, Eng.: Cambridge University Press, 1979.

———. "Les Principes de 1789 et la sociologie." *Revue internationale de l'enseignement* 19 (1890): 450–56.

———. *Professional Ethics and Civic Morals.* London: Routledge and Kegan Paul, 1957.

———. "La Science positive de la morale en Allemagne." *Revue philosophique* 24 (1887): 33–58, 113–42, 275–84.

———. *Sociology and Philosophy.* Trans. D. F. Pocock. New York: Free Press, 1974.

———. *Le Suicide.* 8th ed. Paris: Presses Universitaires de France, 1930.

———. *Suicide.* Trans. J. A. Spaulding and G. Simpson. Glencoe: Free Press, 1951.

Durkheim, Emile, and Marcel Mauss. *Primitive Classification.* Trans. Rodney Needham. Chicago: University of Chicago Press, 1963.

Dworkin, Ronald. "Replies." *The New York Review of Books* 30 (July 21, 1983): 44–46.

Eliot, T. S. "The Hollow Men." In *Selected Poems.* New York: Harcourt, Brace and World, 1937.

Feinberg, Joel. *Harmless Wrongdoing.* Vol. 4, *The Moral Limits of the Criminal Law.* Oxford: Oxford University Press, 1988.

Fenton, Steven. *Durkheim and Modern Sociology.* Cambridge, Eng.: Cambridge University Press, 1984.

Ferri, Enrique. *Omicidio-suicidio.* 4th ed., Turin, 1895.

Fliegelman, Jay. *Prodigals and Pilgrims.* Cambridge, Eng.: Cambridge University Press, 1982.

Gadamer, Hans-Georg. *Truth and Method.* New York: Crossroad, 1982.

Galston, William A. "Pluralism and Social Unity." *Ethics* 99 (1989): 711–26.

Gellner, Ernest. *Words and Things.* London: Victor Gollancz, 1959.

Giddens, Anthony. *Capitalism and Modern Social Theory.* Cambridge, Eng.: Cambridge University Press, 1971.

Gilder, George. "Where Capitalism and Christianity Meet." *Christianity Today* Feb. 4, 1983.

Gill, Emily R. "Walzer's Complex Equality." *Polity* 20 (1987): 32–51.

Goodman, Nelson. *Fact, Fiction and Forecast.* Cambridge, Mass.: Harvard University Press, 1983.

———. *Problems and Projects.* New York: Hackett, 1972.

———. *Ways of Worldmaking.* New York: Hackett, 1978.

Gutmann, Amy. "Communitarian Critics of Liberalism." *Philosophy and Public Affairs* 14 (1985): 308–22.

———. *Democratic Education.* Princeton: Princeton University Press, 1987.

———. "What's the Use of Going to School?" In Amartya Sen and Bernard Williams, eds., *Utilitarianism and Beyond*, 261–77. Cambridge, Eng.: Cambridge University Press, 1982.

Hampton, Jean. "Should Political Philosophy Be Done Without Metaphysics?" *Ethics* 99 (1989): 791–814.

Hauerwas, Stanley M. "Freedom of Religion: A Subtle Temptation." *Soundings: An Interdisciplinary Journal* 72 (1989): 317–39.

Hobbes, Thomas. *Leviathan*. In D. D. Raphael, ed., *The British Moralists*, Vol. 1, pp. 18–60. Oxford: Oxford University Press, 1969.

Hobsbawm, Eric. "Introduction: Inventing Traditions." In Eric Hobsbawm and Terence Ranger, eds., *The Invention of Tradition*, 1–14. Cambridge, Eng.: Cambridge University Press, 1983.

Hume, David. *A Treatise of Human Nature*. Oxford: Oxford University Press, 1978.

James, William. *Pragmatism* and *The Meaning of Truth*. Cambridge, Mass.: Harvard University Press, 1975.

Jones, K. "Is Wittgenstein a Conservative Philosopher?" *Philosophical Investigations* 9 (1986): 274–87.

Kant, Immanuel. "Eternal Peace." In Carl J. Friedrich, ed., *The Philosophy of Kant*, 430–76. New York: Random House, 1977.

Kedward, Harry R. *The Dreyfus Affair*. London: Longmans, 1965.

Levitas, Maurice. *Marxist Perspectives in the Sociology of Education*. London: Routledge and Kegan Paul, 1974.

Lovibond, Sabina. *Realism and Imagination in Ethics*. Minneapolis: University of Minnesota Press, 1983.

Lukes, Steven. *Emile Durkheim: His Life and Work*. Stanford, Calif.: Stanford University Press, 1985.

McGovern, William M. *From Luther to Hitler*. New York: Houghton Mifflin, 1941.

MacIntyre, Alasdair. *After Virtue*. Notre Dame: University of Notre Dame Press, 1981.

———. *Whose Justice? Which Rationality?* Notre Dame: University of Notre Dame Press, 1988.

Marcuse, Herbert. *One Dimensional Man*. Boston: Beacon Press, 1964.

Mill, John Stuart. *On Liberty*. In Mary Warnock, ed., *On Liberty, Essay on Bentham*, 126–250. New York: New American Library, 1962.

Mitchell, M. M. "Emile Durkheim and the Philosophy of Nationalism." *Political Science Quarterly* 46 (1931): 87–106.

Neyer, Joseph. "Individualism and Socialism in Durkheim." In Kurt Wolff, ed., *Emile Durkheim*, 32–76. Columbus: Ohio State University Press, 1960.

Nisbet, Robert. "Conservatism and Sociology." *American Journal of Sociology* 58 (1952): 165–75.

———. *Emile Durkheim*. Englewood Cliffs, N.J.: Prentice-Hall, 1965.

———. *The Sociological Tradition*. New York: Basic Books, 1966.

Nizan, Paul. *Les Chiens de garde*. Paris: F. Maspero, 1967.

Novak, Michael. "The Economic System: The Evangelical Basis of a Social Market Economy." *The Review of Politics* 43 (1981): 156–74.

Nozick, Robert. *Anarchy, State, and Utopia*. New York: Basic Books, 1974.

Oakeshott, Michael. *On Human Conduct*. Oxford: Oxford University Press, 1975.
——. *Rationalism in Politics*. London: Methuen, 1962.
Okin, Susan Moller. *Justice, Gender, and the Family*. New York: Basic Books, 1989.
——. "Reason and Feeling in Thinking about Justice." *Ethics* 99 (1989): 229–49.
Oldenburg, Ray. *The Great Good Place*. New York: Paragon House, 1989.
Parsons, Talcott. *The Structure of Social Action*. Vol. 1, *Marshall, Pareto, Durkheim*. New York: Free Press, 1949.
Purple, David. *Moral and Spiritual Crisis in Education*. South Hadley, Mass: Bergin and Garvey, 1989.
Raths, Louis Edward, Merrill Harmin, and Sidney B. Simon. *Values and Teaching*. 2nd ed. Columbus, Ohio: Charles E. Merrill, 1978.
Rawls, John. "The Idea of an Overlapping Consensus." *Oxford Journal of Legal Studies* 7 (1987): 1–25.
——. "Justice as Fairness: Political and not Metaphysical." *Philosophy and Public Affairs* 14 (1985): 223–51.
——. "Kantian Constructivism in Moral Theory: The Dewey Lectures 1980." *Journal of Philosophy* 77 (1980): 515–72.
——. "The Priority of Right and Ideas of the Good." *Philosophy and Public Affairs* 17 (1988): 251–76.
——. *A Theory of Justice*. Cambridge, Mass.: Harvard University Press, 1971.
Raz, Joseph. *The Morality of Freedom*. Oxford: Oxford University Press, 1986.
Richter, Melvin. "Durkheim's Politics and Political Theory." In Kurt Wolff, ed., *Emile Durkheim*, pp. 170–210. Columbus: Ohio State University Press, 1960.
Riley, Patrick. *The General Will Before Rousseau*. Princeton: Princeton University Press, 1986.
Rorty, Richard. *Contingency, Irony, and Solidarity*. Cambridge, Eng.: Cambridge University Press, 1989.
——. *Philosophy and the Mirror of Nature*. Princeton: Princeton University Press, 1979.
——. "The Priority of Democracy to Philosophy." In Merrill D. Peterson and Robert C. Vaughan, eds., *The Virginia Statute for Religious Freedom*, pp. 257–82. Cambridge, Eng.: Cambridge University Press, 1988.
Rousseau, Jean-Jacques. *Emile*. Trans. Barbara Foxely. London: Dent, 1974.
——. *The Social Contract*. Trans. G. D. H. Cole. London: Dent, 1973.
Sandel, Michael. *Liberalism and the Limits of Justice*. Cambridge, Eng.: Cambridge University Press, 1982.
Schneewind, J. B. "The Divine Corporation and the History of Ethics." In Richard Rorty, J. B. Schneewind, and Quentin Skinner, eds., *Philosophy in History*, pp. 173–91. Cambridge, Eng.: Cambridge University Press, 1984.

Seigel, Jerrold. "Objectivity and the Subject in Durkheim." Unpublished essay.

Sen, Amartya. "Individual Freedom as a Social Commitment." *The New York Review of Books* 37 (June 14, 1990): 49–54.

Skinner, Quentin. *The Foundations of Modern Political Thought.* Vol. 2, *The Age of Reformation.* Cambridge, Eng.: Cambridge University Press, 1978.

Smith, William Robertson. *Lectures on the Religion of the Semites.* 3rd ed. London: A. and C. Black, 1927.

Spencer, Herbert. *The Evolution of Society.* Chicago: University of Chicago Press, 1967.

———. *The Man versus the State.* New York: D. Appleton, 1897.

———. *Social Statics.* New York: A. M. Kelley, 1969.

Stout, Jeffrey. *Ethics After Babel.* Boston: Beacon Press, 1988.

———. "Homeward Bound: MacIntyre on Liberal Society and the History of Ethics." *The Journal of Religion* 69 (1989): 220–32.

———. "Liberal Society and the Languages of Morals." *Soundings* 69 (1986): 32–59.

Talmon, J. L. *The Origins of Totalitarian Democracy.* Boulder, Colo.: Westview Press, 1985.

Taylor, Charles. *Hegel and Modern Society.* Cambridge, Eng.: Cambridge University Press, 1979.

———. *Philosophical Papers.* Volume 2. Cambridge, Eng.: Cambridge University Press, 1985.

Teichman, Jenny. *The New York Times Book Review* 7 (Apr. 23, 1989): 2.

Thomson, David. *Democracy in France since 1870.* Oxford: Oxford University Press, 1969.

Tönnies, Ferdinand. *Community and Society.* Trans. Charles P. Loomis. New York: Harper Torchbook, 1963.

Turner, Victor. *Dramas, Fields, and Metaphors.* Ithaca: Cornell University Press, 1974.

Wallwork, Ernest. *Durkheim: Morality and Milieu.* Cambridge, Mass.: Harvard University Press, 1972.

Walzer, Michael. *The Company of Critics.* New York: Basic Books, 1988.

———. *Exodus and Revolution.* New York: Basic Books, 1985.

———. *Interpretation and Social Criticism.* Cambridge, Mass.: Harvard University Press, 1987.

———. *Spheres of Justice.* New York: Basic Books, 1983.

———. "Spheres of Justice: An Exchange." *The New York Review of Books* 30 (July 21, 1983): 43–44.

West, Cornel. *The American Evasion of Philosophy.* Madison: University of Wisconsin Press, 1989.

White, Hayden. "The Politics of Historical Interpretation: Discipline and De-Sublimation." In W. J. T. Mitchell, ed., *The Politics of Interpretation,* 119–43. Chicago: University of Chicago Press, 1982.

Wittgenstein, Ludwig. *Philosophical Investigations*. Trans. G. E. M. Anscombe. New York: Macmillan, 1953.
———. *Zettel*. Trans. by G. E. M. Anscombe. Berkeley: University of California Press, 1970.
Wolin, Sheldon. *Politics and Vision*. Boston: Little, Brown, 1960.

Index

In this index "f" after a number indicates a separate reference on the next page, and "ff" indicates separate references on the next two pages. A continuous discussion over two or more pages is indicated by a span of numbers. *Passim* is used for a cluster of references in close but not consecutive sequence.

Library of Congress Cataloging-in-Publication Data

Cladis, Mark Sydney.
   A communitarian defense of liberalism: Emile Durkheim and
contemporary social theory / Mark S. Cladis.
   p. cm. — (Stanford series in philosophy)
Includes bibliographical references and index.
ISBN 0-8047-2042-8 (cloth: acid free paper):
1. Durkheim, Emile, 1858–1917. 2. Liberalism. 3. Social ethics.
4. Sociology—France—History. 5. Sociology—Philosophy.
I. Title. II. Series.
HM22.F8D774   1992
301'.01—dc20
92-10125   CIP

⊗   This book is printed on acid-free paper.